Sustainable Development and Local Economic Empowerment

Ndwakhulu Stephen Tshishonga
https://orcid.org/0000-0002-4918-3552
University of KwaZulu-Natal, South Africa

Hulisani Takalani
University of Venda, South Africa

Eve Diniwe Mafema
https://orcid.org/0009-0006-6716-356X
Ngoma Research Agency, UK

Lucky Ntuthuko Mdletshe
https://orcid.org/0000-0002-4565-5954
University of KwaZulu-Natal, South Africa

IGI Global
Scientific Publishing
Publishing Tomorrow's Research Today

Vice President of Editorial	Melissa Wagner
Director of Acquisitions	Mikaela Felty
Director of Book Development	Jocelynn Hessler
Production Manager	Mike Brehm
Cover Design	Jose Rosado

Published in the United States of America by
IGI Global Scientific Publishing
701 East Chocolate Avenue
Hershey, PA, 17033, USA
Tel: 717-533-8845 | Fax: 717-533-7115
Website: https://www.igi-global.com E-mail: cust@igi-global.com

Library of Congress Cataloging-in-Publication Data

LCCN: 2026035661 (CIP Data Pending)
ISBN13: 979-8-2600-3325-8
Isbn13Softcover: 979-8-2600-3326-5
EISBN13: 979-8-2600-3327-2
British Cataloguing in Publication Data
A Cataloguing in Publication record for this book is available from the British Library.

Table of Contents

Detailed Table of Contents

Climate change, population growth, and uncontrolled urbanization threaten safe drinking water in Kenyan cities, causing shortages in quantity and quality. This study, conducted from October 2023 to July 2024, analyzed water samples from Nyakomisaro-Riana and Nyanchwa-Riana for fecal coliforms using APHA protocols. Data on waterborne diseases were obtained from Kisii Teaching and Referral Hospital, and household water sources were surveyed. Findings showed climate change reduced water availability and quality, with fecal coliforms increasing during rainy seasons. Over 70% of residents relied on alternative water sources. To address this, planned settlements with piped water, protected springs, regulated water testing, and public awareness campaigns are crucial. Water harvesting and community participation are essential for sustainable water management

Kenya's urbanization, particularly in riparian cities, has intensified pollution through unregulated waste dumping, wetland encroachment, and raw effluent discharge, severely contaminating water bodies. This study assessed sustainable waste management in Kisii Municipality, the largest urban center in Kisii County, examining policies, enforcement, and innovations. Rapid urbanization, increased municipal solid waste and unregulated wastewater discharge exacerbate environmental degradation. Empirical surveys and expert analyses identified weak enforcement, low public awareness, and the absence of a dedicated waste policy. While regulations like riparian buffer protection and the plastic bag ban offer partial control, a more integrated approach is needed. The study recommends stronger policy enforcement, community engagement, and advanced waste treatment technologies such as AI-driven monitoring, bio-membrane filtration, and constructed wetlands. Recycling

This chapter explores the challenges of representative participation and proposes direct participation methods as a pathway to sustainable development, with a focus on integrating Broad-Based Economic Empowerment (BBEE) theory for local economic development. A qualitative approach was used to gather data from South African articles that examine participatory development initiatives in marginalized communities. The study included a collection of case studies from successful projects that prioritize Participatory Development in South Africa, purposefully. The Ladder of Participation framework was used to categorize the cases. Most so-called participatory initiatives fall within the "tokenism" category, where community members are engaged in informing, consultation, or placation. However, the selected cases demonstrate that projects with greater community ownership, informed by BBEE principles, are more likely to be sustained over time due to the increased dedication and responsibility that come with this ownership.

This chapter examines the intersection of innovation and community development, emphasizing how sustainable futures can be advanced through local empowerment. It challenges dominant top-down models that marginalize community voices and reframes innovation as a social and contextual process shaped by local knowledge, relationships, leadership, and collective agency. Using an integrative review of literature and selected published cases, the chapter analyzes the role of power, equity, governance, and community participation in shaping meaningful innovation. It illustrates how communities in different contexts develop locally responsive solutions to social, environmental, and economic challenges. The chapter also examines the institutional conditions that support or constrain grassroots innovation, including governance structures, funding arrangements, local leadership, and cross-sector partnerships. It concludes by offering practical directions for inclusive and sustainable innovation that recognize communities as active partners in shaping long-term and resilient development.

Women's empowerment is a crucial element of economic and social development, contributing to gender equality and sustainable growth. This chapter examines the impact of women's cooperatives on economic and social empowerment, focusing on the case of the Burdur Ball Sewing Cooperative in Türkiye. Through qualitative research methods, including in-depth interviews with cooperative members, this study explores how cooperatives contribute to financial independence, expand social networks, and challenge traditional gender roles. The findings indicate that participation in women's cooperatives enhances economic self-sufficiency, strengthens social ties, and promotes gender equality. However, challenges such as financial constraints and social stereotypes persist, necessitating further policy support. The chapter concludes that women's cooperatives serve as an effective tool for social transformation and recommends expanding financial resources, educational programs, and cooperative networks to maximize their impact.

This paper covers the integrated analysis of women's participation in social, political, and religious fields under Islamic law within Central Asia. It takes a step back towards the historical context and newest setbacks and challenges foreseen for women of the region, focusing on the interaction between Islamic law, local customs, and modern legal reforms within this region. It will introduce such study onto how gender roles have changed with the socio-political dynamics since pre-Islamic traditions, Soviet times, and then into the post-Soviet transitions. The attention would be placed on specific areas like family law, political participation, economic empowerment, and religious leadership in respect to a delicate balance between the adherence to traditional values and progressive reforms. Despite impressive steps made in some directions, Central Asian women still face bottlenecks deep down inside patriarchal structures and conservative interpretations of Islamic law.

This chapter examines Local Economic Development Agencies (LEDAs) as a strategy for reducing poverty and unemployment in South Africa, focusing on Enterprise iLembe in KwaZulu-Natal. It argues that LEDAs promote inclusive economic development by integrating previously excluded communities into local economies through support for Small, Medium and Micro Enterprises (SMMEs), investment promotion, and strategic partnerships. A qualitative approach based on stakeholder interviews was used in this chapter. The findings show that LEDA initiatives created more than 18,000 jobs and indirectly benefited over 126,000 people, particularly in agriculture, manufacturing, tourism, and construction. However, the chapter also highlights challenges such as limited funding, resource constraints, and inadequate monitoring and evaluation systems. It concludes that although LEDAs are effective instruments for local economic development, their long-term sustainability depends on improved funding models, stronger institutional support, and comprehensive performance assessment frameworks..

Preface

Sustainable development has evolved beyond an environmental agenda to become a comprehensive framework for advancing economic inclusion, social justice, institutional resilience, and ecological sustainability. Across both developed and developing contexts, communities continue to confront interconnected challenges such as climate change, unemployment, inequality, rapid urbanization, resource degradation, migration, gender disparities, and governance constraints. Addressing these complex realities requires innovative, context-sensitive, and participatory approaches that place local communities at the center of development processes.

This edited volume, Sustainable Development and Local Economic Empowerment, brings together multidisciplinary perspectives from scholars and practitioners across Africa, Asia, Europe, and beyond to examine how sustainable development can be translated into meaningful local action. The contributors explore the opportunities and challenges associated with promoting inclusive economic growth while safeguarding environmental resources, strengthening institutions, and empowering marginalized populations. Although many chapters are grounded in the experiences of developing countries, particularly South Africa and Kenya, the insights offered have broader relevance for policymakers, researchers, practitioners, and development agencies seeking pathways toward sustainable and equitable development.

A defining feature of this volume is its emphasis on local economic empowerment as a catalyst for sustainable development. The chapters demonstrate that lasting development cannot be achieved solely through national policies or economic growth indicators. Rather, sustainable transformation depends on strengthening local institutions, promoting community participation, supporting entrepreneurship, advancing gender equality, protecting natural resources, recognizing indigenous knowledge systems, and fostering innovation that responds to local realities.

CHAPTER OVERVIEW

The volume begins by examining the environmental foundations of sustainable development. Chapter 1 investigates the effects of climate change on urban water provision in Kisii Municipality, Kenya, illustrating how changing climatic conditions threaten both water quality and accessibility while highlighting the importance of integrated water management and community participation. Chapter 2 continues this environmental focus by exploring sustainable waste management practices for ecosystem protection in the same municipality, emphasizing stronger policy implementation, technological innovation, and collaborative governance as essential ingredients for urban environmental sustainability.

Broadening the discussion to demographic and governance dimensions, Chapter 3 examines immigration as both a challenge and an opportunity for sustainable development, demonstrating how inclusive integration strategies can strengthen economic resilience, social cohesion, and innovation. Chapter 4 investigates sustainability assurance within Morocco's southern provinces, showing how sustainable governance practices can promote economic diversification, environmental stewardship, and inclusive regional development.

The volume then shifts toward community participation and local empowerment. Chapter 5 critically examines participatory development through the lens of Broad-Based Black Economic Empowerment (B-BBEE), arguing that genuine community ownership and meaningful participation are fundamental to sustainable local economic development. Complementing this perspective, Chapter 6 explores how innovation driven by local knowledge, community leadership, and inclusive governance can generate resilient and sustainable development outcomes that move beyond conventional top-down approaches.

Culture, language, and identity emerge as important drivers of empowerment in Chapter 7, which demonstrates how indigenous languages can strengthen civic participation, improve governance, enhance education, and stimulate local economic innovation in Kenyan counties. Chapter 8 addresses the structural inequalities affecting rural women's access to land in KwaZulu-Natal, South Africa, emphasizing that equitable land rights remain central to women's economic empowerment and sustainable rural development.

The theme of gender empowerment continues through Chapter 9, which examines women's cooperatives as vehicles for economic independence, social innovation, and community transformation through a case study from Türkiye. Chapter 10 expands the discussion by analyzing women's participation within Islamic legal frameworks in Central Asia, highlighting the complex interaction between religious traditions, legal reforms, and women's evolving roles in social, political, and economic life.

Economic development strategies receive focused attention in the latter part of the volume. Chapter 11 analyzes the impact of foreign direct investment on local supply chains and small business development, offering insights into how stronger linkages between multinational investors and domestic enterprises can contribute to more inclusive economic growth.

Environmental sustainability is reconnected with economic opportunity in Chapter 12, which explores the circular economy as a pathway for green employment creation. The chapter demonstrates how resource efficiency, waste reduction, and industrial innovation can simultaneously address unemployment and environmental degradation. Chapter 13 investigates the contribution of Local Economic Development Agencies (LEDAs) to poverty reduction and employment creation in South Africa, providing empirical evidence of the role that institutional partnerships and strategic local interventions can play in advancing inclusive development.

Collectively, these chapters demonstrate that sustainable development is multidimensional and context-specific. They reveal that environmental sustainability, economic empowerment, social inclusion, institutional effectiveness, gender equality, and participatory governance are mutually reinforcing rather than competing priorities. The volume further illustrates that successful local economic development depends upon collaborative partnerships involving governments, communities, academic institutions, civil society organizations, and the private sector.

As editors, we are grateful to all contributing authors for their scholarly commitment and for sharing diverse perspectives that enrich this collection. We also acknowledge the anonymous reviewers whose constructive feedback strengthened the quality of the chapters, as well as the publisher for supporting this important scholarly endeavor

Chapter 1
Climate Change and Water Provision in Urban Centers:
A Case Study of Kisii Municipality, Kenya

George Mokua Ogendi
http://orcid.org/0000-0003-2279-8423
Kisii University, Kenya

ABSTRACT

Climate change, population growth, and uncontrolled urbanization threaten safe drinking water in Kenyan cities, causing shortages in quantity and quality. This study, conducted from October 2023 to July 2024, analyzed water samples from Nyakomisaro-Riana and Nyanchwa-Riana for fecal coliforms using APHA protocols. Data on waterborne diseases were obtained from Kisii Teaching and Referral Hospital, and household water sources were surveyed. Findings showed climate change reduced water availability and quality, with fecal coliforms increasing during rainy seasons. Over 70% of residents relied on alternative water sources. To address this, planned settlements with piped water, protected springs, regulated water testing, and public awareness campaigns are crucial. Water harvesting and community participation are essential for sustainable water management

INTRODUCTION

Water is an essential natural resource for life and is vital not only for humans but also for plants, animals, and other living organisms (Westall and Brack, 2018;

DOI: 10.4018/979-8-2600-3325-8.ch001

Chaplin, 2001). It provides habitat for aquatic life and is used by both plants and animals for survival (Molden et al., 2010). Water also serves as a medium for transporting various substances, including organic and inorganic chemicals, disease-causing microorganisms, and energy (Chouhan and Flora, 2010; Coppellotti et al., 2012). Therefore, water plays a critical role in supporting human well-being and maintaining environmental health.

Globally, more than 2.1 billion people lack access to safe drinking water, with over 300 million of this population residing in Sub-Saharan Africa (WHO/UNICEF, 2025). Worldwide demand for clean water is projected to exceed supply by over 40%, while in developing nations the deficit is expected to surpass 50% by 2030 (Chellaney, 2013). It is estimated that approximately four billion people experience severe water scarcity for at least one month annually, whereas about 500 million people face acute water shortages throughout the entire year (Bakker, 2012). Furthermore, projections indicate that by 2050, nearly 90% of the additional three billion people expected to join the global population of which mostly in developing countries who will encounter significant challenges in accessing clean water and adequate sanitation services (UN-World Water Assessment Programme, 2009; Hofste et al., 2019). These trends suggest that continued population growth will place increasing pressure on available freshwater resources, leading to a decline in per capita access to clean water (Showers, 2002).

Water covers approximately 75% of the Earth's surface, with 97.5% being saline water and only 2.5% comprising freshwater. Of this meagre 2.5% of freshwater, 2% of it, is locked in the icecaps in permafrost form hence not easily assessable, leaving only 0.5% which is available for use by all organisms. This makes the provision of water in the right quantity and quality in the 21st Century the greatest challenge hence, threatening the existence of humanity, other terrestrial and aquatic life. Water is highly demanded across various sectors, including industry, households, and agriculture, all of which can also contribute to its contamination. Across the world, contaminated water poses a serious threat to the health of all living organisms (Watts et al., 2018). Unsafe water and poor sanitation conditions contribute significantly to the spread of diseases such as cholera, diarrhoea, dysentery, hepatitis A, typhoid, and polio (Gleick, 2002). Postel (1999) identified inadequate and unreliable access to water, in both quantity and quality, as one of the most significant global water challenges.

The intensifying scarcity is likely to continue as water demand for farming, aquaculture, industrial needs, hotel industry, home use, uprising vehicle wash businesses and all other water-using sectors compete for this finite resource. The same free-flowing water is of great necessity in instream uses and support of other environmental services and aquatic organisms' sustenance. In the 20th century, water quantity and quality were thought to be a challenge to rural areas and undeveloped countries (Omarova et al., 2019), but, in recent times, water challenge has encroached into the urban centers. For developed countries and urban centers, piped water was and has been a trusted source for the provision of enough and quality water, a situation which is the reverse in the 21st century.

During the 1980s, the International Drinking Water Supply and Sanitation Decade aimed to ensure universal access to safe water and basic sanitation by 1990 (Najlis & Edwards, 1991). The initiative sought to promote awareness of water cooperation and sustainable water management amid rising human and environmental demands. Despite these efforts, about one-third of the global population still lacks adequate access to clean water, and projections by Deborah (2022) indicate that nearly two-thirds may face unsafe water conditions in the coming years.

In developing nations such as Kenya, common sources of domestic water include freshwater lakes, rivers, dams, ponds, irrigation canals, wells, boreholes, and harvested rainwater. However, these water sources are continually exposed to pollution from both point and non-point sources, including industrial effluents, household waste, sewage discharge, agricultural activities, and leachates originating from landfills and pit latrines (Lukubye and Andama, 2017).

The Constitution of Kenya, under Article 43(1)(d), guarantees every person the right to sufficient, clean, and safe water (GoK, 2010). To realize Vision 2030, the country seeks to enhance access to essential services, including safe water supply. However, in Kisii Municipality, about 70% of residents lack access to piped water and depend on untreated water from both protected and unprotected sources for domestic use (Onjala et al., 2014). Gichaba et al. (2017) report that many households lack awareness of the potential health hazards associated with these water sources, despite evidence showing that they contain elevated concentrations of thermotolerant coliform bacteria.

The population increase in towns due to rural-urban migration has put more pressure to piped water hence its scarcity. The National and County governments are trying primarily to manage this scarcity by either allowing some individuals within the urban centers to sink their own boreholes and water business through unregulated water vendors to augment their unlimited water supplies among others. However, these water sources are not regulated thus compromising water quality - water testing is a tall order. Secondly, the hygiene of these water vendors is equally compromised. Thirdly, the streams from which residents obtain water are located in areas that lack proper sanitation, thus increasing the risk of contamination. These streams and brooks are often located near bus stations, car-wash areas, or bushes frequently used as informal sanitation sites by passersby. Such activities contribute significantly to the deterioration of water quality (Okullo et al., 2017).

Various pollutants such as sediments, varied chemicals, microbiological among others affect water quality (Carr and Neary, 2008). Mostly, chemical contaminants resulting from leached excess nutrients from farms (Ogendi et al., 2022), leaking sewerages, heavy metal contents from garages and laboratories, and sediment loads are the main sources impacting waterbodies. Microbiological contamination may occur due to the presence of bacteria, viruses, and protozoa originating from sewage. Research has shown that most pollutants come from agricultural activities, industrial effluents, sewer leakages, and the improper disposal of waste into water bodies. The expansion of the agricultural sector in Kenya has increased the use of fertilizers and other agrochemicals, which are often washed into rivers, streams, and other water sources, leading to water pollution.

Furthermore, intentional release of partially treated or completely untreated sewerage effluents and sporadic sewer leakages cause biological contamination into our surface water sources. Sometimes, the disposed sewage may contain high levels of toxic substances like Mercury (Hg) and Lead (Pb) among other heavy metals which are key causes of kidney problems and are carcinogenic. Consequently, many residents of urban informal settlements are adversely affected due to limited access to safe and clean water, resulting in disease outbreaks that negatively impact their health and livelihoods.

Unhygienic environmental conditions, together with the impacts of climate change, have made access to clean water increasingly difficult, as climate-related changes continue to exert significant pressure on the environment (IPCC, 2014). These effects include water pollution caused by flooding, increased prevalence of waterborne diseases, rising sea levels, higher temperatures, prolonged droughts, and population movements through migration, all of which disrupt natural ecosystems. Across the globe, humans and other living organisms are experiencing unprecedented climatic impacts, including the drying up of rivers and streams that serve as important sources of water. Moreover, climate change is adversely affecting key social and environmental determinants of health such as clean air, safe drinking water, and adequate nutritious food (WHO, 2015). Water availability has become an even greater concern under changing climatic conditions. Limited water supplies increase the risk of water-borne and food-borne diseases, leading to long-term health challenges (Cissé, 2019) and reduced participation in productive economic activities.

Climate-related hazards are increasingly influencing human mobility and migration as communities search for water and pasture for both themselves and their livestock (Christian Aid, 2007; Biermann & Boas, 2010). Such movements have intensified pressure on available water sources, heightened conflicts over water access, and contributed to cross-border displacement. It is estimated that by 2050, climate-induced migration could affect nearly one billion people worldwide (IOM, 2012). In Kenya, the population has continued to increase at an average annual growth rate of 2.5% since 1948 (KNBS, 2019). The population was projected to reach approximately 53 million by 2022, with a significant proportion settling in urban areas, thereby increasing demand for essential resources and services.

The demand for safe and clean water in urban areas continues to increase each year, while the supply from water treatment facilities is steadily declining. This has led to people seeking and buying unsafe water, from water vendors and entering into violent conflicts when they are unable to access enough and clean water for themselves and their livestock (Omosa, 2005). Limited access to safe freshwater increases the prevalence of waterborne diseases such as cholera, amoebic dysentery, typhoid, and salmonellosis, while also contributing to malnutrition, poverty, and socio-economic and political instability among and within nations (Barry & Victor, 2011). Poor water quality negatively affects the health and well-being of both humans and livestock. Fortunately, knowledge about climate change and its impacts is widely available, and failure to act on this information exposes communities to greater environmental and health risks. For instance, outbreaks of diarrheal diseases have been linked to both periods of heavy rainfall and prolonged drought (Checkley et al., 2000; Effler et al., 2001). This indicates that drought conditions can concentrate enteric pathogens, while rainfall can transport and spread them, thereby contaminating drinking water sources and increasing the risk of human infection.

Waterborne diseases arise from various infections transmitted through contaminated or poor-quality water containing pathogens such as viruses, bacteria, protozoa, and helminths. These microorganisms can lead to a wide range of health problems, including diarrhea, fever, flu-like symptoms, neurological complications, liver damage, and other illnesses. Among these, diarrheal diseases are the most common and account for a significant share of the global disease burden (Troeger et al., 2018). Since the spread of diarrheal diseases is closely linked to inadequate access to safe water, changes in climate conditions have influenced their occurrence and geographical distribution (Urama & Ozor, 2010).

Due to the large burden of diarrheal diseases, even small changes in diarrheal disease risk due to climate change can have profound impacts on population health. Diarrheal diseases choose not urban or rural inhabitants, but strikes both equally and the main sources being contaminated food or water. As a result, diarrheal diseases rank as the second leading cause of death among children under the age of five globally and represent the second largest contributor to mortality and disability in low- and middle-income countries (Liu et al., 2012). The greatest burden of these illnesses is experienced by children living in poor households, where repeated infections can impair physical growth, hinder cognitive development, and contribute to a cycle of poor health and persistent poverty (Bartram & Cairncross, 2010). Although worldwide rates of diarrhea-related illness and death have generally declined in recent years (GBD, 2017), the effects of climate change have slowed this progress, thereby threatening global efforts to reduce the prevalence and consequences of diarrheal diseases, particularly among populations with limited access to safe drinking water. In response to these concerns, the researcher carried out water quality assessments focusing on faecal and total coliform contamination in the Nyakomisaro-Riana and Nyanchwa-Riana rivers, administered questionnaires, and gathered secondary data from Kisii Teaching and Referral Hospital (KTRH). The study aimed to identify major water sources and evaluate the impacts of poor water quality on the health of residents in Kisii Municipality and the surrounding regions.

METHODOLOGY

The study adopted a mixed-methods approach that integrated both quantitative and qualitative data collection techniques. For water quality assessment, purposive transect sampling was employed to collect water samples along the Nyakomisaro-Riana and Nyanchwa-Riana rivers for laboratory analysis. Structured questionnaires were administered to randomly selected residents from various estates to gather information on sources of water and patterns of water use. In addition, secondary data were obtained from records at Kisii Teaching and Referral Hospital regarding patients treated for waterborne diseases. Direct field observations and relevant secondary sources were also utilized to complement and strengthen the findings of the study. The research was conducted within Kisii Municipality, located in Kisii County, Kenya.

Study Area Descriptions

Kisii Municipality is situated at approximately 0°41′ South latitude and 34°46′ East longitude in southwestern Kenya and serves as the administrative headquarters of Kisii County. The area experiences a bimodal rainfall regime, receiving an average annual rainfall of about 1,500 mm, with temperatures ranging between 21°C and 30°C. The municipality functions as a key commercial and urban hub within the Gusii Highlands, serving not only Kisii County but also neighboring counties such as Narok to the south and Homa Bay and Migori to the west. Rapid urbanization has led to the expansion of residential estates and commercial infrastructure, making it one of the fastest-growing towns in the region. Furthermore, the municipality lies within a highly productive agricultural zone and is part of one of the most densely populated regions in Kenya.

According to the 2019 Population and Housing Census, Kisii Municipality had a population of 13,422 residents (Kenya National Bureau of Statistics, 2019). However, the municipality has continued to expand rapidly and, in recent years, has experienced unplanned urban growth. Estimates for 2022 indicate that the town accommodates a daytime population ranging between 200,000 and 500,000 people due to its role as a major commercial and service centre. Kisii Municipality is currently among the most populous urban centres in western Kenya, second only to Kisumu City in the region. The municipality recorded significant population growth following the 2007–2008 post-election violence, as it remained relatively peaceful and free from major conflicts. Consequently, it attracted migrants from different parts of the country, strengthening its position as a multicultural urban centre and a preferred destination for settlement and business activities (Ondieki & Kebaso, 2017).

Kisii Municipality is characterized by a relatively high population density compared to many urban centres in Kenya, largely due to limited land availability within its administrative boundaries. This shortage of land has encouraged the outward expansion of residential settlements into the surrounding rural areas. To accommodate the growing population, development has increasingly extended beyond the municipality's official limits. The municipal authorities have supported this expansion by permitting residential development in adjacent areas, thereby easing pressure on the available urban space and helping to address the challenges associated with rapid population growth. Kisii Municipality is divided into the Central Business District (CBD), Peri-urban which is overwhelmed with unplanned estates like Jogoo, Mwembe, Nyanchwa, Nyamataro, Nyankongo, Gesonso and Menyikwa and mosaics of individual farms. Further, the municipality has a University, National polytechnic, Training institutes, several primary and secondary schools, of which, the majority are not sewer connected. The outskirts of the municipality have demarcated parcels of land which are used for subsistence farming, supporting animal rearing through semi-zero grazing, tea and coffee as cash crops and maize, beans, bananas among others as food crops.

There are a few upcoming industries like banana and avocado processing industries and one slaughterhouse all of which are within the Municipality. A large open-air market at Daraja Mbili which majorly sells agro-based products from within and without surrounding farms of which the remnants are dumped into the two rivers of research. These two rivers (Nyakomisaro-Riana and Nyanchwa-Riana) confluence at Daraja Mbili hence the start of the upper part of Riana River. Running alongside these rivers are sewer lines laid in parallel, which, through occasional leakages and the large amounts of organic waste dumped along them, act as the primary sources of contamination in the river water.

Study Area Map

Figure 1. Map of Kisii Municipality Showing Nyakomisaro-Riana and Nyanchwa – Riana Rivers' Sampling points

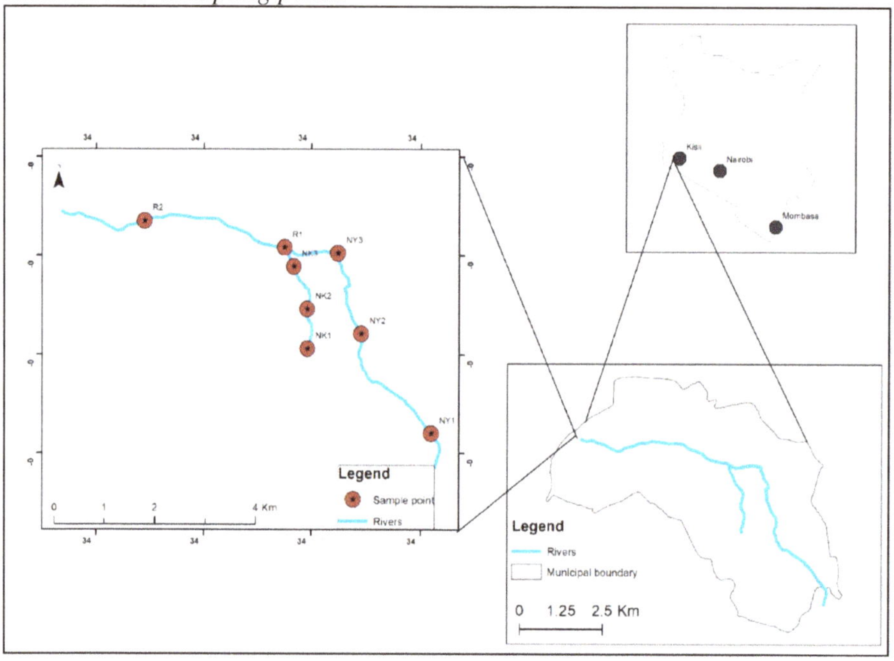

RESULTS AND DISCUSSIONS

Spatial Challenges and Impacts of Water Scarcity in Kenyan Cities and Towns

Water provision and management is a major challenge in Kenyan cities and towns across the decades. However, water scarcity has resulted in inadequate sanitation and hygiene conditions, thereby posing significant health risks, especially in underserved areas, which in turn contributes to the spread of waterborne illnesses and various skin-related diseases. For example, the water analysis of Nyakomisaro-Riana and Nyanchwa-Riana rivers passing through Kisii Municipality indicated the following:

The Feacal (F-Coli) and Total coliforms (T-Coli) analysis showed significant differences in both sampled Rivers. There were significant differences in F-Coli counts between the five sampling sites of Nyanchwa – Riana River ($F_{(4, 145)} = 12.77$;

$p = 0.000$). The mean F-Coli counts in sampling site NY1 were significantly lesser by between 60.3 – 905.8 cfu 100ml^{-1}, 482.5 – 1328.0 cfu 100ml^{-1} and 257.0 – 1102.5 cfu 100ml^{-1} than those at sampling sites NY3, R1 and R2 respectively; but not significantly different from that at sampling site NY2. The mean F-Coli counts at site NY2 was significantly lower by between 400.7 – 1246.3 cfu 100ml^{-1}, and 175.2 – 1020.8 cfu 100ml^{-1} than those at sites R1 and R2 respectively but not significantly different from those at NY3. The mean F-Coli counts at sampling site NY3 was not significantly different from those at site R1 and R2. Finally, the mean F-Coli at site R1 was not significantly different from that at site R2 (Figure 2).

Analysis of T-Coli counts revealed significant differences among the five sampling sites ($F_{(4, 145)} = 15.45$; $p = 0.000$). The mean T-Coli concentration at site NY1 was significantly lower than those recorded at sites NY3, R1, and R2 by margins ranging from 144.4–1285.2 cfu 100 ml^{-1}, 661.4–1802.2 cfu 100 ml^{-1}, and 559.8–1700.5 cfu 100 ml^{-1}, respectively. However, no significant difference was observed between NY1 and NY2.

Similarly, the mean T-Coli count at site NY2 was significantly lower than those at sites NY3, R1, and R2 by 60.9–1201.6 cfu 100 ml^{-1}, 577.9–1718.6 cfu 100 ml^{-1}, and 476.2–1617.0 cfu 100 ml^{-1}, respectively. In contrast, no significant differences were detected between site NY3 and sites R1 and R2. Likewise, the mean T-Coli counts at sites R1 and R2 did not differ significantly from each other (Figure 2).

Figure 2. Average Total and Feacal coliform counts along the Nyanchwa – Riana River during October 2023 - July 2024 sampling period

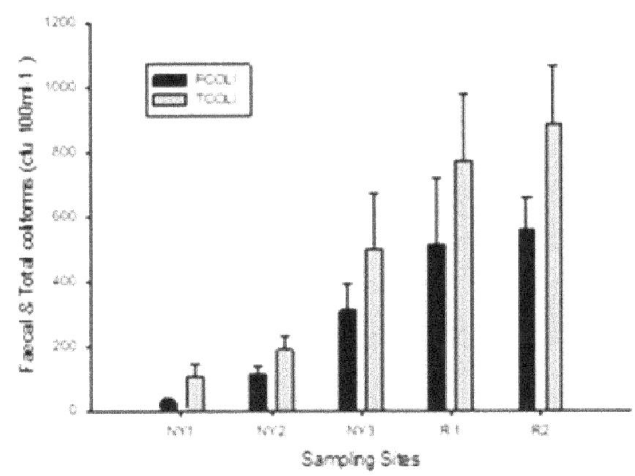

There were significant differences in F-Coli counts between the five sampling sites of Nyakomisaro – Riana River ($F_{(4, 145)} = 9.12$; $p = 0.000$). The mean F-Coli counts in sampling site NK1 were significantly lesser by between 506.3 – 1857.4

cfu 100ml^{-1}, 226.8 – 1577.9 cfu 100ml^{-1} and 1.3 – 1352.4 cfu 100ml^{-1} than those at sampling sites NK3, R1 and R2 respectively; but not significantly different from that at sampling site NK2. The mean F-Coli counts at site NK2 was significantly lower by between 453.8 – 1804.9 cfu 100ml^{-1}, and 174.3 – 1525.4cfu 100ml^{-1} than those at sites NK3 and R1 respectively but not significantly different from those at R2. The mean F-Coli counts at sampling site NK3 was not significantly different from those at site R1 and R2. Finally, the mean F-Coli at site R1 was not significantly different from that at site R2 (Figure 3).

The Total coliforms (T-Coli), also had significant differences between the five sampling sites of Nyakomisaro – Riana River ($F_{(4, 145)} = 12.23$; $p = 0.000$). The mean T-Coli counts in sampling site NK1 were significantly lesser by between 531.0 – 1987.0 cfu 100ml^{-1}, 549.0 – 5005.0 cfu 100ml^{-1} and 447.0 – 1903.0 cfu 100ml^{-1} than those at sites NK3, R1 and R2 respectively; but not significantly different from that at sampling site NK2. The mean T-Coli counts at site NK2 was significantly lower by between 426.0 – 1882.0 cfu 100ml^{-1}, 444.0 – 1899.0 cfu 100ml^{-1}, and 342.0 – 1798.0 cfu 100ml^{-1} than those at sites NK3, R1 and R2 respectively. The mean T-Coli counts at sampling site NK3 was not significantly different from those at site R1 and R2. Finally, the mean T-Coli at site R1 was not significantly different from that at site R2 (Figure 3).

Figure 3. Average Total and Fecal coliform counts in the Nyakomisaro – Riana River Transect during October 2023 - July 2024 sampling period

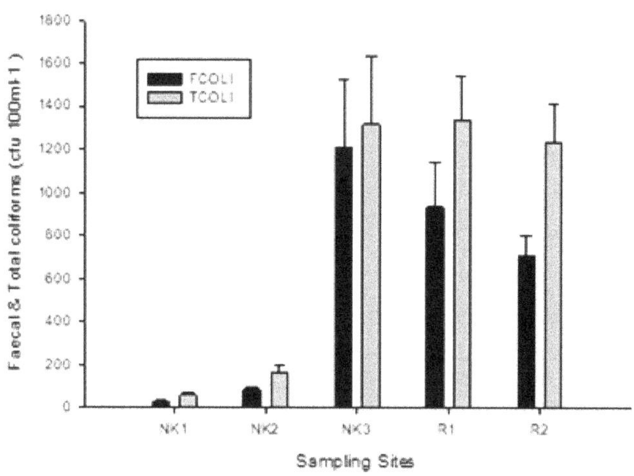

Both rivers showed a monotonic increase of T-Coli and F-Coli. At every sampling site down the rivers, there was an increase of both coliforms. Therefore, it is evident from the research that water from the two Rivers (Nyakomisaro-Riana and Nyanchwa-Riana) is of low quality at all sampling sites along the two rivers (Figure 2 and Figure3). Even at the respective sources of these two rivers (NK1 and NY1), there were presence total and feacal coliforms which is against the WHO Standards of no detectability coliforms in any 100 mL sample, for the water stand counted to be of good quality (WHO, 2008). Presence of feacal coliforms along these rivers can be attributed to the overwhelmed closely constructed sewer lines and mushrooming pit latrines which led to sporadic leakages into the surface waters of River Nyakomisaro-Riana and Nyanchwa-Riana. The overflow of sewer lines, pit latrines and the defeacations in nearby bushes arose from the increase of people in Kisii town (urbanization).

Furthermore, the rising generation of wastewater, coupled with inadequate treatment facilities and insufficient infrastructure, has resulted in both intentional and unintentional discharge of untreated effluent into river systems. These releases have contributed to public health challenges and the degradation of downstream ecosystems, consistent with findings by Wakhungu (2019). For long-term sustainability, residents of Kisii should transition from unsustainable water management practices to more sustainable approaches such as water reuse, as recommended by Jiménez and Asano (2008). In addition, the Kisii County government needs to invest in large-scale water development projects, as suggested by Seckler (1999), to ensure the provision of adequate and safe water for municipal residents. The growing population within the municipality has further intensified the imbalance between water demand and supply, resulting in a persistent water crisis and fostering perceptions that the water provider, KIWASCO, is unable to meet the community's water needs.

Rural-urban migration is increasingly placing pressure on cities and towns such as Kisii to supply adequate and safe water to the growing population, a challenge that the Kisii Water and Sewerage Company (KIWASCO) continues to struggle with. This observation aligns with Engel et al. (2011), who noted that water scarcity is likely to intensify in many developing countries due to rapid population growth, economic development, and urbanization, thereby making it difficult to adequately address water supply and sanitation needs. Similarly, the IPCC (2014) projects that the impacts of climate change in rural areas may accelerate migration to urban centers, further increasing water stress in towns. In many cases, such population movements place additional strain on already limited government capacity, often overwhelming water service delivery systems, particularly in developing countries.

However, the challenges facing the water sector which include; population pressure, water scarcity, climate change, and water quality issues are considerable and should not be underestimated. This situation necessitates the adoption, implementation, and attainment of the 2030 Agenda, with water scarcity being prioritized as a key issue for action (Kibuika and Wanyoike, 2012). Therefore, it is important that detailed plans for the provision of clean and enough water are put in place to mitigate high water demand challenges.

Temporal Challenges and Impacts of Water Scarcity in Kenyan Cities and Towns

Water and climate change are closely interconnected. In recent years, climate change has negatively affected water availability, water quality, and increased water-related hazards such as floods and droughts. Rising global temperatures are altering precipitation patterns and disrupting the hydrological cycle worldwide. In this study, temporal analysis revealed statistically significant differences, with results showing notable variation in mean Fecal Coliform (F-Coli) counts over the 10-month sampling period of the Nyanchwa–Riana River ($F_{(2, 147)} = 6.18; p = 0.003$).

The mean F-Coli counts of the dry season (Jan-Feb 2024) was not significantly different from those of the long rains (March-May 2024) and short rains (Oct-Dec 2023 and Jun-Jul 2024) periods. The mean F-Coli counts of the long rain period (Mar-May 2024) was significantly more by between 117.9 – 704.8 cfu $100ml^{-1}$ than that of the short rains (Oct-Dec 2023 and Jun-July 2024) periods (Figure 4). Similarly, significant variations were observed in the mean T-Coli counts in the 10-month-sampling period of Nyanchwa-Riana River ($F_{(2, 147)} = 4.88; p = 0.009$). The mean T-Coli counts of the dry season (Jan-Feb 2024) was significantly more by between 123.1 – 1062.3 cfu $100ml^{-1}$ than that of the short rains (Oct-Dec 2023 and Jun-Jul 2024) but not significantly different from those of the long rains (March-May 2024). The mean T-Coli counts of the long rain period (Mar-May 2024) was not significantly different from that of the short rains (Oct-Dec 2023 and Jun-Jul 2024) periods (Figure 4).

Figure 4. Total and Fecal coliform counts along the Nyanchwa – Riana River during Oct 2023 – July 2024 sampling period

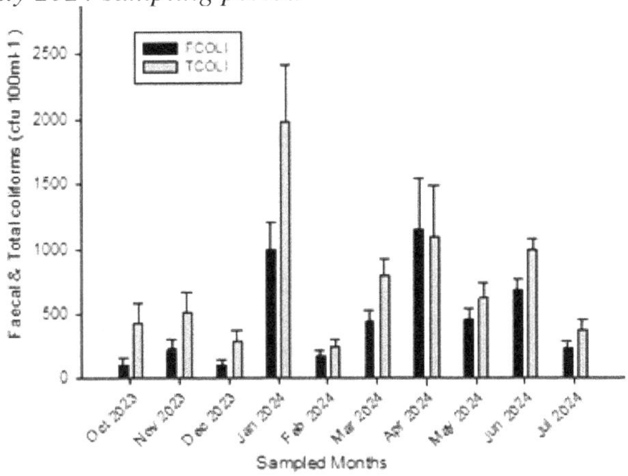

Due to climate changes, water quality varied rapidly and sewer systems became subject to occasional failure. For example, during the long rains period, the rainfall greatly increased the levels of microbial contamination at source and along river, hence a high likelihood of waterborne-disease outbreaks. It is evident from the findings that water from the Nyanchwa-Riana River had significant differences in sampling seasons whereby the long rains period had higher coliforms than the short rains (Figure 4). This concurs with findings of Hill et. al., (2006), who reported that heavy rainfall led to elevated fecal coliform concentrations in the Bayou Dorcheat water body. Similarly, Olds et al. (2018) reported that intense storm events contribute to river pollution through the release of high levels of sewage contamination, often resulting from overloaded or blocked urban sewer systems. This normally is attributed to the flooding which clog sewer lines and pit latrines within the town thus transporting the sewage mix into nearby rivers.

For temporal analyses of both F-Coli and T-Coli in the Nyakomisaro-Riana River, there were no significance differences between the three sampling periods (dry season, short rains and the long rains). This therefore, implied that the polluting sources were loading the river with microbial loads in all seasons. During the dry season, fecal coliform concentrations often accumulate along the river, largely as a result of ongoing discharges from multiple wastewater outfalls. These findings align with those reported by Mitch et al. (2010).

The continuous loading can also be attributed to the leakage of sewer lines which run parallel the river and constant discharge of animal waste from the estates traversed by the Nyakomisaro-Riana River. Furthermore, the persistent introduction of pathogens into the river may be attributed to non-point sources such as nearby human settlements along the riverbanks, as well as the continuous release of animal waste, as reported by Petersen et al. (2005). Indeed, along the Nyakomisaro-Riana River are several possible sources of coliform loadings like the unplanned settlements which are along the river, instream animal watering, instream washing and bathing (Figure 5), constructed pit latrines which are close to the river and car washing along the river.

Figure 5. Instream washing along Nyakomisaro-Riana River

All these possible sources of coliform loading coupled with climate change, contribute to continuous coliform pollution along the transect of Nyakomisaro-Riana River. Many people have moved to urban centers hence an increase of sewage waste which is finding its way to the surrounding waters. This finding is consistent with the IPCC (2014), which projected that the impacts of climate change in rural regions may intensify migration to urban areas, subsequently increasing water stress in towns. As a result, rural–urban migration is exerting pressure on towns such as Kisii to supply adequate and safe water to the growing population. Therefore, the increase of people in Kisii town (urbanization) has put immense pressure on the KIWASCO piped water.

Disease Incidences in Coliform Contaminated Waters

Water contamination has become a major public health concern since it is closely linked to human health outcomes. Globally, microbial contamination of water by coliform bacteria has been associated with deaths caused by gastrointestinal illnesses such as diarrhoea, dysentery, cholera, typhoid, and related diseases. Populations in developing countries are disproportionately affected due to limited access to safe drinking water and inadequate healthcare systems. In response, various international bodies have established water quality standards to safeguard public health. For instance, the United States Environmental Protection Agency (EPA) sets stringent guidelines requiring zero faecal coliforms per 100 mL of water intended for drinking, irrigation of food crops, or commercial processing of raw-consumed produce (EPA, 1992). In Kenya, drinking water standards stipulate that no detectable *Escherichia coli, Shigella, Pseudomonas aeruginosa*, or other coliforms should be present in 250 mL of potable water (WASREB, 2006).

Data obtained from Kisii Teaching and Referral Hospital (KTRH) showed a rise in the number of patients seeking treatment for waterborne diseases during the same period in which water sampling was conducted. It is evident that during the long and short rain seasons, the three diseases (Dysentery, Typhoid and Salmonelosis) increased in comparison to the dry period (Figure 6). Dysentery was higher in comparison to typhoid and salmonellosis. Typhoid and salmonellosis kept exchanging their highs and lows along the 10-month sampling period. When compared with the feacal and total coliforms which were in the rivers in the same period, the three diseases corresponded well weather seasons. In their study, Ondara et al. (2019) reported that during rainy seasons, gastrointestinal protozoan infections were more prevalent among children under five years suffering from diarrhoea in Kisii County.

Figure6. Major Waterborne diseases Reported in Kisii Teaching and Referral Hospital during Oct 2023 – July 2024

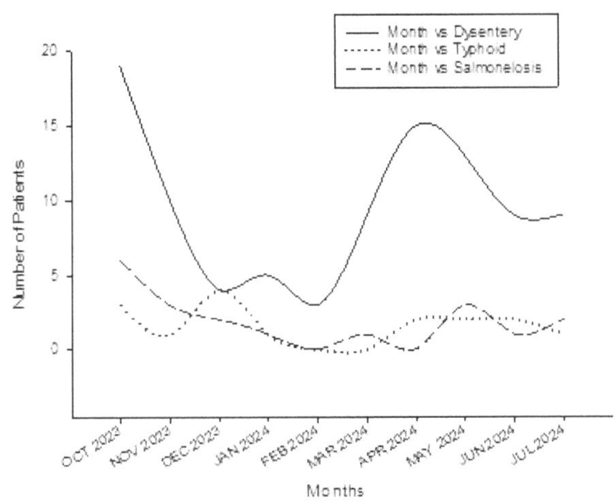

Diarrhoeal diseases remain a leading cause of illness and death among children in developing countries, largely linked to exposure to contaminated water sources (Swierczewski et al., 2013). They account for roughly 20% of child mortality globally, with the majority of deaths occurring in Africa and Asia. In Kenya, approximately 27,400 deaths among children under five are attributed to diarrhoea (Boschi-Pinto et al., 2008). Flooding further increases the risk of waterborne infections such as dysentery by facilitating pathogen spread (Sultana, 2010). Studies in China, the United States, and Germany have similarly shown a strong association between floods and increased diarrhoeal cases (Ni et al., 2014; Wade et al., 2004; Schnitzler et al., 2007). These findings highlight the importance of access to safe water in reducing the burden of waterborne diseases.

Status of Water Sources in Kisii Municipality

The average percentage of sources of water within the Kisii Municipality was as follows; Piped was 30%, Rain water 10%, Vendors 25% Springs 15% Wells 10% and Boreholes 10%. The percentage analysis of the data collected through the 210 questionnaires which were administered to the Nyanchwa, Daraja Mbili, Nyamataro, Mwembe, Jogoo and Nyankongo residents, nearly 70% of the respondents indicated the lack of clean water for their home use. Over 50% of the respondents, further indicated that they spend most of their morning time looking for water or waiting for the cart-delivered water at their gates or door steps. For the working class, the searching for clean water jeopardized their vibarua (Temporary or permanent jobs). The search for water consumes most of their productive time and strains the relationships with their employer to a level of some losing their jobs. This is consistent with findings by Vergunst and Berry (2022), who reported increased stress and anxiety among urban residents regarding the impacts of a warming climate.

Climate change is also aggravating water challenges by increasing the frequency, intensity, and duration of extreme weather events such as droughts, heatwaves, and floods (USGCRP, 2018). Insufficient and contaminated water supplies further contribute to the spread of waterborne diseases, which affect not only household heads but also school-going children through missed learning time (Levy et al., 2018; Ogendi, 2023). Kisii municipality is particularly vulnerable to episodic water shortages and stormwater-related hazards due to hydrological variability. The water sources were independently identified and described as follows:

Wells for Assessing Groundwater for Home use

Most of the wells within Kisii municipality which were sunk to seek for groundwater are not productive year-round and they are sunk haphazardly without considering their closeness to pit latrines. A few of these wells are productive throughout the year while others become dry during the dry spell. Water availability from these wells depend primarily on the type of rock which is not homogeneous. In some estates, the rocks have top permeable layer and the underlying rock are impermeable or semi-permeable hence allowing rainwater to seep through and recharge the aquifer.

Some of the recharged groundwater aquifers allow water to seep through the soil layers through a tortuous process and oozes at nearby lower sprigs where it is collected. Through the seepage process, there is a possibility of water contamination. There are several factors within the municipality that may influence the likelihood of the groundwater becoming contaminated from polluting sources such as several pit latrines which are near or along the water sources within the Municipality. In densely populated settlements, the close proximity between wells and pit latrines reduces the safe separation distance, allowing microorganisms to seep from latrines into nearby water sources. In addition, poor sanitation practices in these overcrowded areas further contribute to the contamination of wells.

The geology has permeable rocks which also have cracks where sewage leakages can pass through more easily into the aquifers. Additional factors include the depth of pit latrines and their vertical separation from the groundwater table. These informal settlements are largely characterized by low-income livelihoods, which contribute to poor hygiene standards and the widespread use of inadequate sanitation facilities (Kimani-Murage and Ngindu, 2007). In many of these areas, shallow wells are commonly located in close proximity to pit latrines (Okotto et al., 2015).

In fact, there are no clearly defined guidelines specifying the appropriate depth of pit latrines or the minimum distance that should separate them from wells. There must be a safe distance from the well to the pit latrine. For instance, pit latrines should be located at least 48 metres away from wells for the water to be deemed safe for human consumption (Kiptum and Ndambuki, 2012). Additionally, where wells are situated on sloping terrain, pit latrines should be positioned downslope from the water source to reduce contamination risks. The use of pit latrines poses a potential threat to groundwater quality (Figure 7). This health risk can be minimized by increasing the distance between latrines and drinking water sources, as a longer separation enhances pathogen travel time through soil and reduces their survival.

Figure 7. Kisii strange disease linked to contaminated water

Kisii strange disease linked to contaminated water, says PS Mary Muthoni

Tuesday, March 04, 2025

Health PS Mary Muthoni in Kisii County.

By Ruth Mbula | Nation Media Group

The strange disease that has hit hundreds of families in Kisii was caused by water contamination, the Health ministry has said. Health Principal Secretary Mary Muthoni on Tuesday said the villagers fell ill after consuming water from community spring contaminated with faecal matter.

Consequently, the government has closed the spring in South Mugirango Constituency after laboratory analysis found the water unfit for human consumption. "We have established that the water from the spring is contaminated and hereby urge the people to stop consuming it, forthwith," Ms Muthoni said at Amarondo village. The PS had visited the area on Tuesday morning on a fact-finding mission after reports that unknown number of residents had fallen ill.

"We ask the people to abstain from drawing water from the spring and instead find alternative sources of supply," she said. She added that more samples were still under examination to ascertain the real cause of the disease. "However, preliminary tests have shown that the water is unsafe," she said. Further, the PS asked residents to observe high levels of hygiene in order to contain the spread of the disease.

Ms Muthoni, who was accompanied by national and county government officers, visited the spring and several homes of the affected villagers. Health PS Mary Muthoni in South Mugirango, Kisii county on a fact-finding mission over the outbreak of a strange disease. Earlier, before receiving the laboratory report, Ms Muthoni had given the spring a clean bill of health, saying that it had existed since time immemorial without posing any health risks to its users. The CS's sentiments appeared to be in tandem with those of the residents who pointed out that they had consumed the water from the spring for many years without any health complications.

Ms Muthoni said that at least 56 people had been treated, adding that an accurate number of those affected would be provided in due course. "Please let's desist from spreading gossip. Wait for us to give accurate information," she said.

rmbula@ke.nationmedia.com

Majority of the wells with the municipality were nearly of the same depth as those of the pit latrines and they were not beyond 30 meters in depth hence drawing rom the same groundwater level. From the observations, majority of the wells were not cased to the requisite minimum height of 60 cm above the surrounding ground level to prevent the entrance of water that run-off the surface of the land, carrying debris, wastes and other pollutants with it as it flows. Equally, most of the wells did not have a concrete cover fitted over the well casing to prevent small animals, dust, insects and any other contaminants from falling in. Their immediate areas were not well fenced to keep animals away and not graded off in order to prevent the flow of storm water run-off into the well. During the oral interviews, it was clear that majority of the wells and their associated structures were not regularly disinfected using aqua-guard (chlorine solution) to eliminate pathogens and ensure the quality of water.

Springs

Majority of the Municipality springs are found at the foot of the surrounding hills and near the banks of both Nyakomisaro-Riana and Nyanchwa-Riana Rivers. Their waters vary in volume and contamination levels all of which is based on the amount of rainfall and sewage discharges. The springs were potential sites to be polluted by direct contamination, especially from run-off seeping through the topsoil since their surrounding land areas are not protected (Figure 8). The animals from the surrounding communities were not excluded from assessing the springs. Also, there were no deep diversion ditches above and around the spring which were constructed so as to collect surface water running towards the spring and divert it away more especially during heavy rainstorms.

Figure 8. One of the springs behind Gudka within Kisii Municipality

Some of the springs within the municipality go dry because they are seasonal in nature, and this really affects water drawers (mostly women and children). Therefore, they have to queue or walk for longer distances to fetch water from the neighboring communities. Some of the springs, the discharge of water reduces, and this causes long queues and conflicts among the community members because everyone wants to fetch water first. During the rainy season, the spring users are able to fetch water comfortably without queueing and fighting at the spring, although the quality of water at this time is questionable. Most of our springs are located at the base of the slopes, and all the rains wash all the dirt down into these springs. This means that the springs without well-placed cut-off drainage are affected, by the dirt will go through the spring, hence hampering the quality of water.

Surface Waters

The Nyakomisaro-Riana and Nyanchwa-Riana rivers are the main surface waterbodies providing water to Kisii municipality. The quality and quantity of surface water along the two rivers varied spatially and over time, influenced by factors such as geology, climate, and surrounding land use. Respondents identified the main sources of pollution in these rivers as the disposal of untreated sewage and the dumping of solid waste. Farming along the rivers was also a major cause of nutrient and sediment contaminations. All these contaminants concurred with the findings in Daily Nation, (2018) and Kerich, and Ndege, (2020).

The variable quality of surface water meant that the water required treatment for it to be safe for domestic consumption. The quantity of water in these rivers varied with seasons. During the dry spell, water was at its lowest level, while, during the long rain periods, the rivers were flooded. These findings corroborated with the results of Mokaya, (2015) who found out that the flows of River Nyakomisaro varied as a result of rainfall changes which ultimately pose a threat to the future water supply in the municipality. In Kisii, increasing pressure on freshwater resources is driven particularly by population growth and rising demand which has led to reduced river flow.

Amazingly, in both seasons, the waters of Nyakomisaro-Riana River had varied levels of coliforms. Therefore, the challenges of maintaining both adequate water quantity and quality are becoming more pronounced with population growth. Existing surface and groundwater sources are increasingly subject to contamination, while the availability of freshwater continues to decline, making concerns over both quality and quantity increasingly urgent (Vigneswaran, 2006). In order to augment the municipality's piped water supply, there is need to construct mini dams in both rivers passing through the municipality so as to create reservoirs from which water can be extracted prior to treatment and used to reduce scarcity during the dry period.

Climate Change and Water Pollution

Climate change poses a significant threat to the availability of safe drinking water not only in arid and semi-arid regions but also in areas traditionally considered water-abundant, such as Kisii. This is because alternating dry and wet conditions can both reduce water availability and increase contamination, thereby undermining drinking water quality and contributing to water shortages. In many cases, water sources are polluted by agricultural runoff, industrial effluents, and inadequate sanitation systems. Additionally, during prolonged rainy seasons, increased river discharge enhances flow energy and erosion potential, leading to the detachment and transport of soil sediments. These processes can alter water quality in receiving water bodies and negatively affect freshwater ecosystems in both rivers and lakes.

Climate variability, combined with water pollution and weak water resource management, has intensified the problem of unsafe drinking water, leading to adverse health outcomes and subsequent negative impacts on economic activities within and beyond Kisii Municipality (Figure 9). These challenges are particularly pronounced in rural areas and urban informal settlements, where access to piped water infrastructure remains limited.

Figure 9. Warnings on Climate change from the Varied Departments

Weatherman warns Kisii Residents of Flash Floods

KNA3 September 16, 2022

Kisii County Director of Weather Services, Mr. Henry Sese has advised the residents to be wary of flash floods which are likely to occur during this short rains season. Speaking to the press at his office in Kisii town, Mr. Sese said there will be occurrences of storms that may cause flash floods despite the below-average rainfall expected during the months of October to December.

"Cases of flooding in few areas, especially low-lying areas or plains as well as landslides in susceptible areas may occur," the Director pointed out. The Weatherman asked the Ministry of Environment and Forestry to encourage residents to plant indigenous trees and embrace soil conservation measures in order to minimize environmental degradation caused by soil erosion.

He noted the possibility of outbreaks of diseases such as malaria, respiratory diseases, and waterborne diseases in some parts of the county and urged the health facilities to equip themselves with the necessary medication to enable them to handle such cases as they arise. Further, the Director told the county government to repair water and sewerage systems to avoid the spilling over of the waste so as to minimize waterborne diseases.Sese asked residents to avoid sheltering under trees or working in quarries while it's raining and urged motorists to drive cautiously on slippery roads in order to steer clear of accidents.

Kisii County Red Cross Director, Wycliff Likhaya said they are forming 'Early Warning, Early Action' Committees which will send flash flood signals and alerts through the Short Message Service (SMS) to residents, especially in low-lying areas. However, Likhaya decried the fact that most people do not take the alerts seriously to act in time to cushion themselves against floods. "My office, the Office of the County Commissioner and all departments concerned shall have these committees to educate our people and we as Red Cross, are ready to support and give information regarding this matter," he noted.

By Vincent Nyambane and Diana Tutu

Water Handling and Increased Demand

The several ways getting and handling water (Vendors, fetching from springs, wells among others) is affecting water quality. From the findings water which was delivered by carts (*Mkokoteni*) was in old, unwashed and open-20-liter plastic jer-ricans. The vendors' attires were of questionable cleanliness (Figure 10), all these compromised the water's quality. Research done by Ondieki et al. (2022) in Kisii Municipality showed a significant relationship between household size and water quality in terms of presence of total coliforms. Further they found out that hygiene and sanitation; source of water; transportation container and covering during transportation had a significant relationship with quality of household drinking water.

As urban populations continue to rise, pressure on water resources is also increasing. According to the 2019 Kenyan Census, the population was estimated at 47.6 million, with an annual growth rate of 2.2%. This growth has heightened water demand, leading to increased extraction from available sources, which may reduce both water quantity and quality. Moreover, rapid population increase, particularly in informal settlements, has contributed to water contamination due to poor sanitation infrastructure, thereby limiting access to safe drinking water. In this regard, urbanization has been accompanied by the expansion of informal settlements where reliable access to clean water remains insufficient.

Figure 10. Water collection and delivery ways by the Vendors in Kisii Municipality

Projections indicate that by 2030, nearly 48% of Kenya's population will reside in urban areas. This growth is expected to significantly increase the demand for safe drinking water. As urban migration continues, pressure on existing water resources and infrastructure is likely to intensify. Consequently, expanding urban populations will require substantial investment in water supply systems to meet the rising demand for safe and reliable drinking water.

FUTURE RESEARCH DIRECTIONS

Regular water quality assessments should be conducted across all water sources, particularly wells, which are susceptible to contamination and may pose health risks to settlement residents. Additionally, further studies are needed to identify effective approaches for addressing the growth of informal urban settlements, especially as the impacts of climate change and global warming continue to intensify and become more complex. Research should also examine the extent to which national and county regulations on pit latrine–well separation distances, as well as climate-related policies and legislation, have been implemented and utilized by local communities to enhance their living conditions and environmental health.

CONCLUSION AND RECOMMENDATIONS

More than half of Kisii Municipality residents have limited access to safe drinking water. The increasing population, coupled with global efforts to improve water access, has resulted in a rising demand for a reliable and adequate supply of clean drinking water. The county government should therefore work towards ensuring universal access to safe water and improving public health by protecting natural springs, promoting and supporting water harvesting and storage, regulating and routinely testing all water sources for quality, and implementing public awareness and education campaigns to encourage community participation in safe water management and conservation.

There is a need for both national and county governments to strengthen urban planning in order to curb the growth of informal settlements, which are often associated with inadequate access to clean water and poor sewerage systems. The county government should also prioritize expanding piped safe drinking water coverage to all residents. In addition, sufficient funding should be allocated to support personnel responsible for enforcing water regulations. The government, in collaboration with relevant stakeholders, should review and update existing water policies to address emerging challenges such as water scarcity, while also integrating climate change adaptation and mitigation strategies. This approach would help ensure that all households in urban areas have reliable access to safe drinking water.

The establishment of an independent and inclusive oversight task force is recommended to guide sustainable settlement across all estates within Kisii Municipality and to coordinate the management of water towers in the county. This body should work in collaboration with key government agencies such as the Kenya Water Towers Agency, Kenya Forest Service, and Community Forest Associations. Such coordination would strengthen the protection and conservation of forest mosaics surrounding the county, which serve as critical catchment areas that sustain the watershed. These conservation efforts require strong political support, particularly in regulating incoming population settlements and preventing illegal developments along riparian zones of water bodies.

There is a need to raise awareness among municipality residents living in various estates on the effects of climate change on water resources, as well as to train them on appropriate coping strategies to minimize negative impacts on their livelihoods. In addition, both short and long-term climate change adaptation and mitigation measures should be developed and implemented within the municipality to address challenges associated with declining water availability. These may include the development and protection of springs, streams, and wells, enhancement of groundwater recharge, rehabilitation of catchment areas, enforcement of watershed management plans, and repair of leaking sewer systems before any discharge into water bodies.

The County should educate and train residents in estates who rely on shallow wells and springs on how to protect and manage their water sources, to ensure a consistent supply of safe water throughout the year for domestic use, particularly drinking and cooking. It is also important to establish designated livestock watering points to minimize contamination from animal waste.

In addition, the County should explore opportunities for developing groundwater resources through the strategic sinking of boreholes within the watershed, while also considering appropriate separation distances between pit latrines and water points. However, it is equally essential to ensure that these facilities remain functional and are not hindered by mismanagement or local political interference among beneficiaries.

ACKNOWLEDGMENT

The author extends sincere appreciation to all stakeholders, particularly Kisii University through its Research Department for providing financial support that facilitated this study, and to the Chief Executive Officer and Records Manager of Kisii Teaching and Referral Hospital (KTRH) for availing data on water-borne disease incidences.

REFERENCES

Bakker, K. (2012). Water Security: Research Challenges and Opportunities. *Science*, *337*(6097), 914–915. DOI: 10.1126/science.1226337 PMID: 22923564

Barry, L., & Victor, S. (2011). Water Rights and Water Fights: Preventing and Resolving Conflicts Before They Boil Over. *American Journal of Public Health*, *101*(5), 778–780. DOI: 10.2105/AJPH.2010.194670 PMID: 21421949

Bartram, J., & Cairncross, S. (2010). Hygiene, sanitation, and water: Forgotten foundations of health. *PLoS Medicine*, *7*(11), e1000367. DOI: 10.1371/journal.pmed.1000367 PMID: 21085694

Biermann, F., & Boas, I. (2010). Preparing for a warmer world: Towards a global governance system to protect climate refugees. *Global Environmental Politics*, *10*(1), 60–88. DOI: 10.1162/glep.2010.10.1.60

Boschi-Pinto, C., Velebit, L., & Shibuya, K. (2008). Estimating child mortality due to diarrhoea in developing countries. *Bulletin of the World Health Organization*, *86*(9), 710–717. DOI: 10.2471/BLT.07.050054 PMID: 18797647

Carr, G. M., & Neary, J. P. (2008). *Water Quality for Ecosystem and Human Health*. UNEP/Earthprint.

Checkley, W., Epstein, L. D., Gilman, R. H., Figueroa, D., Cama, R. I., Patz, J., & Black, R. E. (2000). Effects of El Nino and ambient temperature on hospital admissions for diarrhoeal diseases in Peruvian children. *Lancet*, *355*(9197), 442–450. DOI: 10.1016/S0140-6736(99)06215-7 PMID: 10841124

Chellaney, B. (2013). *Water, Peace, and War: Confronting the Global Water Crisis*. Rowman & Littlefield.

Christian Aid. (2007). Human tide: The real migration crisis. *Christian Aid Report*.

Cissé, G. (2019). Food-borne and water-borne diseases under climate change in low- and middle-income countries: Further efforts needed for reducing environmental health exposure risks. *Acta Tropica, 194*, 181–188. DOI: 10.1016/j.actatropica.2019.03.012 PMID: 30946811

Daily Nation, (2018). Outraged residents demand solution for filthy, stinking Kisii Town.

Deborah, B. (2022). *How Does Population Growth Affect Water Scarcity?* Healing Water International.

Effler, E., Isaacson, M., Arntzen, L., Heenan, R., Canter, P., Barrett, T., Lee, L. C., Mambo, C., Levine, W., Zaidi, A., & Griffin, P. M. (2001). Factors contributing to the emergence of Escherichia coli O157 in Africa. *Emerging Infectious Diseases, 7*(5), 812–819. DOI: 10.3201/eid0705.017507 PMID: 11747693

Engel, K., Jokiel, D., Kraljevic, A., Geiger, M., & Smith, K. (2011). Big Cities, Big Water, Big Challenges: Water in an Urbanizing World. World Wildlife Fund, Koberich.

EPA. (1992). Guidelines for Water Reuse. Washington, DC, Environmental Protection Agency. *Technical Report no.* EPA/625/R-92/004).

FAO. (2017). The Future of Food and Agriculture – Trends and Challenges. https://www.fao.org/3/a-i6583e.pdf

Gichaba, M. A., Ogendi, G., Peletz, R., Khush, R., & Kumpel, E. (2017). Can sanitary surveys replace water quality testing? Evidence from Kisii, Kenya. *International Journal of Environmental Research and Public Health, 14*(2). PMID: 28178226

GOK, (2010). Laws of Kenya National Council for Law Reporting.

Hill, D. D., Owens, W. E., & Tchounwou, P. B. (2006). The impact of rainfall on fecal coliform bacteria in Bayou Dorcheat (North Louisiana). *International Journal of Environmental Research and Public Health, 3*(1), 114–117. DOI: 10.3390/ijerph2006030013 PMID: 16823083

Hofste, W., Reig, R., & Schleifer, L. (2019). 17 countries, home to one-quarter of the world's population, face extremely high-water stress. World Resources Institute. https://www.wri.org/blog/2019/08/17-countries-home-one-quarter-world - population-face-extremely-high-water-stress

IOM. (2012). *International dialogue on migration 18: climate change, environmental degradation and migration*. IOM.

IPCC. (2014). Climate change 2014: synthesis report. In Pachauri, R. K., & Meyer, L. A. (Eds.), *Contribution of working groups I, II and III to the fifth assessment report of the intergovernmental panel on climate change* (pp. 1–168). Academic Press.

Jiménez, B., & Asano, T. (2008). *Water Reuse: An International Survey of Current Practice, Issues and Needs*. IWA., DOI: 10.2166/9781780401881

Kenya National Bureau of Statistics. (2019). Kenya Population and Housing Census Volume II: Distribution of Population by Administrative Units. p. 252.

Kerich, E., & Ndege, F. (2020). Sources of Water Pollution and Selected Physico-chemical Parameters of the Nyakomisaro River in Kisii County, Kenya. *American Journal of Biological and Environmental Statistics*, *6*(2), 17–23. DOI: 10.11648/j.ajbes.20200602.11

Kibuika, F. M., & Wanyoike, D. (2012). Assessment of Factors Affecting Sustainability of Rural Water Supply Schemes in Nyandarua County, Kenya: A Case of Kangui Water Scheme. [IJSR]. *International Journal of Science and Research*, *3*, 578–584.

Kimani-Murage, E. W., & Ngindu, A. M. (2007). Quality of water the slum dwellers use: The case of a Kenyan slum. *Journal of Urban Health : Bulletin of the New York Academy of Medicine*, *84*(6), 829–838. DOI: 10.1007/s11524-007-9199-x PMID: 17551841

Kiptum, C. K., & Ndambuki, J. M. (2012). Well water contamination by pit latrines: A case study of Langas. *Int. J. Water Res. Environ. Eng.*, *4*(2), 35–43.

KNBS. (2019). Kenya Population and Housing Census, Volume II: Distribution of Population by Administrative Units. KNBS, Nairobi.

Levy, K., Smith, S. M., & Carlton, E. J. (2018). Climate Change Impacts on Water-borne Diseases: Moving Toward Designing Interventions. *Current Environmental Health Reports*, *5*(2), 272–282. DOI: 10.1007/s40572-018-0199-7 PMID: 29721700

Liu, L., Johnson, H. L., Cousens, S., Perin, J., Scott, S., Lawn, J. E., Rudan, I., Campbell, H., Cibulskis, R., Li, M., Mathers, C., & Black, R. E. (2012). Global, regional, and national causes of child mortality: An updated systematic analysis for 2010 with time trends since 2000. *Lancet*, *379*(9832), 2151–2161. DOI: 10.1016/S0140-6736(12)60560-1 PMID: 22579125

Mitch, A. A., Gasner, K. C., & Mitch, W. A. (2010). Feacal coliform accumulation within a river subject to seasonally-disinfected wastewater discharges. *Water Research*, *44*(16), 4776–4782. DOI: 10.1016/j.watres.2010.05.060 PMID: 20580053

Najlis, P., & Edwards, A. (1991). The international drinking water supply and sanitation decade in retrospect and implications for the future. *Natural Resources Forum, 15*(2), 110–117. DOI: 10.1111/j.1477-8947.1991.tb00121.x

Ni, W., Ding, G., Li, Y., Li, H., Liu, Q., & Jiang, B. (2014). Effects of the floods on dysentery in north central region of Henan Province, China from 2004 to 2009. *The Journal of Infection, 69*(5), 430–439. DOI: 10.1016/j.jinf.2014.05.016 PMID: 24955987

Ogendi, G. M. (2022). Effects of nutrients on the water quality and the algal community of River Nyakomisaro-Riana, Kisii, Kenya. *International Journal of Fisheries and Aquatic Studies, 10*(5), 111–118. DOI: 10.22271/fish.2022.v10.i5b.2734

Ogendi, G. M. (2023). Climate Change and Its Implications on School Education in Kenya. In Keengwe, J., & Nyatuka, B. O. (Eds.), *Climate Change Education for Sustainable Development* (pp. 144–167). IGI Global., DOI: 10.4018/978-1-6684-9099-0.ch007

Okotto-Okotto, J., Okotto, L., Price, H., Pedley, S., & Wright, J. (2015). A longitudinal study of long-term change in contamination hazards and shallow well quality in two neighbourhoods of Kisumu, Kenya. *International Journal of Environmental Research and Public Health, 12*(4), 4275–4291. DOI: 10.3390/ijerph120404275 PMID: 25898406

Okullo, J. O., Moturi, W. N., & Ogendi, G. M. (2017). Open Defeacation and Its Effects on the Bacteriological Quality of Drinking Water Sources in Isiolo County, Kenya. *Environmental Health Insights, 11*, 1–8. DOI: 10.1177/1178630217735539 PMID: 29051705

Olds, H. T., Corsi, S. R., Dila, D. K., Halmo, K. M., Bootsma, M. J., & McLellan, S. L. (2018). High levels of sewage contamination released from urban areas after storm events: A quantitative survey with sewage specific bacterial indicators. *PLoS Medicine, 15*(7), e1002614. DOI: 10.1371/journal.pmed.1002614 PMID: 30040843

Omarova, A., Tussupova, K., Hjorth, P., Kalishev, M., & Dosmagambetova, R. (2019). Water Supply Challenges in Rural Areas: A Case Study from Central Kazakhstan. *International Journal of Environmental Research and Public Health, 16*(5), 688. DOI: 10.3390/ijerph16050688 PMID: 30813591

Omosa, E. K. (2005). *The Impact of Water Conflicts on Pastoral Livelihoods The Case of Wajir District in Kenya. International Institute for Sustainable Development.* IISD.

Ondara, C. O., Nyachong'i, B. O., & Orucho, V. O. (2019). Prevalence and predisposing factors associated to gastro intestinal protozoan infections among diarrheal children under 5 years in Kisii county, Kenya. *Research Square*, pp 1-11. DOI: 10.21203/rs.2.13014/v1

Ondieki, C., & Kebaso, B. (2017). Water Supply Challenges and Storm Water Management in Kisii Municipality, Nyakomisaro Sub Catchment, Kenya. *OAlib*, *4*(9), 1–12. DOI: 10.4236/oalib.1103769

Ondieki, J. K., Akunga, D. N., Warutere, P. N., & Omanga, K. (2022). Socio-demographic and water handling practices affecting quality of household drinking water in Kisii Town, Kisii County, Kenya. *Heliyon*, *8*(5), e09419. DOI: 10.1016/j.heliyon.2022.e09419 PMID: 35600434

Onjala, J., Ndiritu, S. W., & Stage, J. (2014). Risk perception, choice of drinking water and water treatment: Evidence from Kenyan towns. *Journal of Water, Sanitation, and Hygiene for Development : a Journal of the International Water Association*, *4*(2), 268–280. DOI: 10.2166/washdev.2014.131

Petersen, T. M., Rifai, H. S., Suarez, M. P., & Stein, A. R. (2005). Bacteria loads from point and nonpoint sources in an urban watershed. *Journal of Environmental Engineering*, *131*(10), 1414–1425. DOI: 10.1061/(ASCE)0733-9372(2005)131:10(1414)

Schnitzler, J., Benzler, J., Altmann, D., Mucke, I., & Krause, G. (2007). Survey on the population's needs and the public health response during floods in Germany 2002. *Journal of Public Health Management and Practice*, *13*(5), 461–464. DOI: 10.1097/01.PHH.0000285197.23932.3e PMID: 17762689

Seckler, D., Barker, R., & Amarasinghe, U. (1999). Water Scarcity in the Twenty-First Century. *International Journal of Water Resources Development*, *15*(1-2), 29–42. DOI: 10.1080/07900629948916

Showers, K. B. (2002). Water Scarcity and Urban Africa: An Overview of Urban-Rural Water Linkages. *World Development*, *30*(4), 621–648. DOI: 10.1016/S0305-750X(01)00132-2

Sultana, F. (2010). Living in hazardous waterscapes: Gendered vulnerabilities and experiences of floods and disasters. *Environmental Hazards*, *1*(1), 43–53. DOI: 10.3763/ehaz.2010.SI02

Swierczewski, B. E., Odundo, E. A., Koech, M. C., Ndonye, J. N., Kirera, R. K., Odhiambo, C. P., Cheruiyot, E. K., Shaffer, D. N., Ombogo, A. N., & Oaks, E. V. (2013). Enteric pathogen surveillance in a case-control study of acute diarrhoea in the town of Kisii, Kenya. *Journal of Medical Microbiology*, *62*(Pt 11), 1774–1776. DOI: 10.1099/jmm.0.059139-0 PMID: 23842139

Troeger, C., Colombara, D. V., Rao, P. C., Khalil, I. A., Brown, A., Brewer, T. G., Guerrant, R. L., Houpt, E. R., Kotloff, K. L., Misra, K., Petri, W. A.Jr, Platts-Mills, J., Riddle, M. S., Swartz, S. J., Forouzanfar, M. H., Reiner, R. C.Jr, Hay, S. I., & Mokdad, A. H. (2018). Jr, Platts-Mills, J., Riddle, M.S., Swartz, S.J., Forouzanfar, M.H., Reiner, R.C. Jr., Hay, S.I., & Mokdad, A.H. (2018). Global disability-adjusted life-year estimates of long-term health burden and undernutrition attributable to diarrhoeal diseases in children younger than 5 years. *The Lancet. Global Health*, *6*(3), 255–269. DOI: 10.1016/S2214-109X(18)30045-7

Troeger, C., Forouzanfar, M., Rao, P. C., Khalil, I., Brown, A., Reiner, R. C.Jr, Fullman, N., Thompson, R. L., Abajobir, A., Ahmed, M., Alemayohu, M. A., Alvis-Guzman, N., Amare, A. T., Antonio, C. A., Asayesh, H., Avokpaho, E., Awasthi, A., Bacha, U., Barac, A., & Mokdad, A. H.GBD. (2017). Diarrhoeal Diseases Collaborators. Estimates of global, regional, and national morbidity, mortality, and aetiologies of diarrhoeal diseases: A systematic analysis for the Global Burden of Disease Study 2015. *The Lancet. Infectious Diseases*, *17*(9), 909–948. DOI: 10.1016/S1473-3099(17)30276-1 PMID: 28579426

UN-World Water Assessment Programme. (2009). *Water in a Changing World*. Earthscan.

Urama, K. C., & Ozor, N. (2010). Impacts of climate change on water resources in Africa: the role of adaptation. https://www.researchgate.net/publication/267218899_Impacts_of_climate_change_on_water_resources_in_Africa_the_role_of_adaptation#fullTextFileContent

USGCRP. (2018). Impacts, Risks, and Adaptation in the United States: Fourth National Climate Assessment, Volume II [Reidmiller, D.R., C.W. Avery, D.R. Easterling, K.E. Kunkel, K.L.M. Lewis, T.K. Maycock, and B.C. Stewart (eds.)]. U.S. Global Change Research Program, Washington, DC.

Vergunst, F., & Berry, H. L. (2022). Climate Change and Children's Mental Health: A Developmental Perspective. *Clinical Psychological Science*, *10*(4), 767–785. DOI: 10.1177/21677026211040787 PMID: 35846172

Vigneswaran, S. (2006). *Quantity and Quality of Drinking Water Supplies*. University of Technology.

Wade, T. J., Sandhu, S. K., Levy, D., Lee, S., LeChevallier, M. W., Katz, L., & Colford, J. J. (2004). Did a severe flood in the Midwest cause an increase in the incidence of gastrointestinal symptoms? *American Journal of Epidemiology, 159*(4), 398–405. DOI: 10.1093/aje/kwh050 PMID: 14769644

Wakhungu, M. J. (2019). An Ethnography of Policy: Water Reuse Policy in Kenya. *Water Policy, 21*(2), 436–448. DOI: 10.2166/wp.2019.160

WASREB. (2006). *Drinking Water Quality and Effluent Monitoring Guidelines.* Water Service Regulatory Board.

WHO. (2008). Guidelines for Drinking-Water Quality, 3rd edition: Volume 1 - Recommendations incorporating the first and second addenda.

WHO. (2015). Effects of Climate Change on the Social & Environmental Determinants of Health in Africa: What can communities do to strengthen their climate resilience? COP 21/CMP 11 - Paris, France Technical Paper for WHO/UNEP Side Event. Pages 1 – 17.

WHO/UNICEF. (2025). Progress on Household Drinking Water, Sanitation and Hygiene 2000–2024: Special Focus on Inequalities

ADDITIONAL READING

IPCC Climate Change. (2021). *The Physical Science Basis. Contribution of Working Group I to the Sixth Assessment Report of the Intergovernmental Panel on Climate Change.* Cambridge University Press.

IPCC Climate Change. (2022). *Impacts, Adaptation, and Vulnerability. Contribution of Working Group II to the Sixth Assessment Report of the Intergovernmental Panel on Climate Change.* Cambridge University Press. Key Terms and Definitions **Climate Change:** Long-term, significant shifts in global or regional temperatures and weather patterns. **Fecal coliform**: these are the group of the total coliforms that are considered to be present specifically in the gut and feces of warm-blooded animals **Disaster:** Sudden calamitous event that disrupts the functioning of a community or society and that exceeds its ability to cop using its own resources. **Impact:** Something having a strong effect on someone or something.

Total coliforms: these are the bacteria that are found in the soil, in water that has been influenced by surface water, and in human or animal waste.

Waterborne Diseases: Illnesses caused by microscopic organisms, like viruses and bacteria, that are ingested through contaminated water. refers to

Chapter 2
Sustainable Waste Management for Ecosystem Protection in Kisii Municipality, Kenya

Merceline Bosibori Angima
http://orcid.org/0000-0002-9562-5841
Kisii University, Kenya

Job Ombiro Omweno
County Government of Kisii, Kenya

George Mokua Ogendi
http://orcid.org/0000-0003-2279-8423
Kisii University, Kenya

ABSTRACT

Kenya's urbanization, particularly in riparian cities, has intensified pollution through unregulated waste dumping, wetland encroachment, and raw effluent discharge, severely contaminating water bodies. This study assessed sustainable waste management in Kisii Municipality, the largest urban center in Kisii County, examining policies, enforcement, and innovations. Rapid urbanization, increased municipal solid waste and unregulated wastewater discharge exacerbate environmental degradation. Empirical surveys and expert analyses identified weak enforcement, low public awareness, and the absence of a dedicated waste policy. While regulations like riparian buffer protection and the plastic bag ban offer partial control, a more integrated approach is needed. The study recommends stronger policy enforcement, community engagement, and advanced waste treatment technologies such as AI-

DOI: 10.4018/979-8-2600-3325-8.ch002

driven monitoring, bio-membrane filtration, and constructed wetlands. Recycling and multi-stakeholder collaboration are vital for sustainable waste management and ecosystem protection

INTRODUCTION

Municipal Solid Waste (MSW), urban effluents, and industrial waste have become major environmental concerns globally, with their production expected to rise from 2.3 billion tonnes in 2023 to 3.8 billion tonnes by 2050 due to rapid urbanisation, industrialisation, and climate change (Kaza et al., 2018). Urban populations are projected to constitute nearly 70% of the global population by 2050, further exacerbating waste management challenges (Kurniawan et al., 2022). However, financial and behavioural constraints, along with inadequate disposal strategies, continue to hinder effective municipal waste management. Between 2004 and 2019, per capita urban effluent and MSW production rose significantly, a trend that, if sustained, could result in severe environmental consequences by 2050 (Zhao et al., 2020; Maalouf & Mavropoulos, 2023). Many regions continue to operate below acceptable waste management standards, leading to unregulated dumping in poorly sited landfills and dumpsites.

Figure 1. Human Impacts on Urban Ecosystems (2010 - 2025)

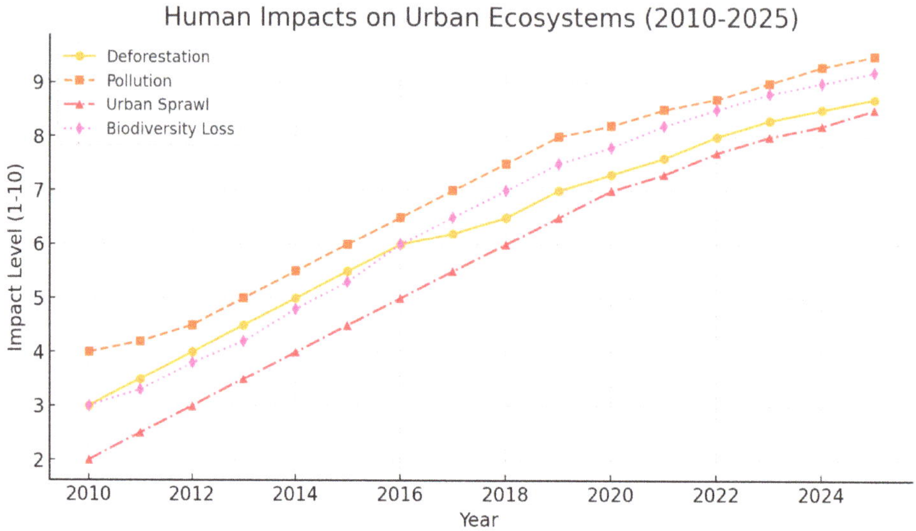

Figure 1: illustrates four key human-induced impacts on urban ecosystems—deforestation, pollution, urban sprawl, and biodiversity loss—between 2010 and 2025, aligning with global reports on urban environmental changes and providing a detailed analysis of each trend (UN-Habitat, 2024; UN-Habitat, 2024; Ritchie & Roser, 2021; UNEP, 2021)

As a result, rivers and streams have become repositories for both organic and non-biodegradable pollutants, including plastics, heavy metals, and pesticides, which persist in the environment and disrupt aquatic ecosystems (Mor & Ravindra, 2023). The ongoing increase in waste generated by human activities poses significant challenges to waste reduction efforts, necessitating the development of comprehensive, sustainable waste management frameworks in major Kenyan cities and globally. To address these challenges, global efforts have promoted concepts such as the circular economy, sustainable development, and low-carbon industries (Maalouf & Mavropoulos, 2023). In Kenya, both national and county governments have enacted policies to improve waste management; however, serious challenges persist in their implementation and enforcement. Kisii Municipality, for example, faces increasing pollution risks due to the absence of context-specific, sustainable waste management solutions. Addressing these challenges requires a coordinated effort among stakeholders to invest in infrastructure, promote public education and develop cost-effective waste management strategies (World Bank, 2019; Mutua & Wambua, 2024). Public-private partnerships and community engagement initiatives have been leveraged to address these persistent waste management challenges (Mwangi & Otieno, 2023).

As urban areas struggle to mitigate the negative impacts of solid waste and untreated effluents, there is increasing emphasis on adopting sustainable waste management practices and integrating digital technologies to enhance waste monitoring and collection efficiency (Otiso, 1993). The rapid urbanisation occurring in many developing nations, particularly in Africa, necessitates the adoption of waste management solutions that align with sustainability principles and digital advancements. Addressing current development trends and ensuring resource availability are critical for the long-term progress of developing countries and ecosystem stability. Without effective interventions, urbanisation, industrialisation, and poor waste management will continue to degrade aquatic ecosystems, threatening biodiversity and livelihoods (Ogechi, 2023). The deterioration of water quality adversely affects fisheries, agriculture, and other economic activities reliant on unpolluted water resources (Mironga, 2006). Therefore, implementing a holistic and sustainable waste management strategy is essential for environmental conservation and economic stability.

Aquatic ecosystems play a crucial role in maintaining planetary health by providing essential services such as water purification, biodiversity conservation, and resources for human use (Millennium Ecosystem Assessment, 2005; Smith & Brown, 2023). However, these ecosystems face increasing threats from pollution, urban waste, and unsustainable land use, necessitating the adoption of innovative management strategies (UNEP, 2021; Johnson & Lee, 2022). In Kenya, urban effluents and solid waste significantly impact water bodies, requiring urgent intervention (KMFRI, 2022; Ochieng & Mutiso, 2023). The ecological and economic stability of Kisii Municipality and surrounding communities depends on well-managed aquatic ecosystems that provide essential services for agriculture, fisheries, and domestic water supply (Omweno et al., 2021). Integrated waste management approaches, including bio-remediation, AI-driven monitoring, and community education programs, are critical for reducing urban waste and water contamination, consequently ensuring sustainable development (Kuppan et al., 2024). Successful initiatives, such as Lake Victoria's bio-remediation projects, offer valuable insights into effective waste management strategies that Kisii Municipality could adopt.

Despite these growing challenges, minimal research has been conducted on appropriate waste management strategies for Kisii Municipality. The region's current waste management efforts are scattered across multiple programs, often hindered by inadequate funding and weak regulatory enforcement. Limited community participation and awareness further exacerbate the situation, accelerating environmental degradation. Addressing these challenges requires innovative strategies for managing stormwater and urban waste discharges. Solutions such as urban forests and waste-sequestration lagoons can help mitigate greenhouse gas emissions by absorbing waste, shading, transpiring, and cooling (Nowak et al., 2018). However, further research is needed to optimise their ecosystem service provisions, including carbon sequestration and stormwater regulation, under different climatic conditions (Pataki et al., 2011). Developing spatial and statistical models will aid in identifying optimal urban forest configurations to maximise environmental benefits (Livesley et al., 2016).

Integrating water resource management laws with urban planning policies is crucial for protecting aquatic ecosystems. Establishing legally protected riparian buffer zones has been effective in maintaining ecosystem health and preventing land-use practices from compromising water bodies (Wambui et al., 2019). Kenya's Vision 2030 framework supports environmental sustainability by promoting green technologies and sustainable waste management practices, such as Black Soldier Fly farming, Azolla cultivation and microalgae production for organic waste recycling (Mutua et al., 2020). Addressing these environmental challenges requires interdisciplinary collaboration in urban waste management, emphasising the importance of coordinated efforts among multiple stakeholders (Wachira, 2023).

STUDY DESIGN

Study area description

Kisii Municipality houses the County headquarters of Kisii, which is located at 0° 41′ 0″ South, 34° 46′ 0″ East and is the biggest among all towns of Kisii County. It is a fast-growing town with many upcoming residential and commercial buildings. The residential estates are unequally distributed from the Central Business District (CBD) and include: Jogoo, Nyanchwa, Nyankongo, Nyamage, Nyamataro, Gesonso, and Mwembe (Figure 2).

Figure 2. Map of Kisii Municipality with its Estates

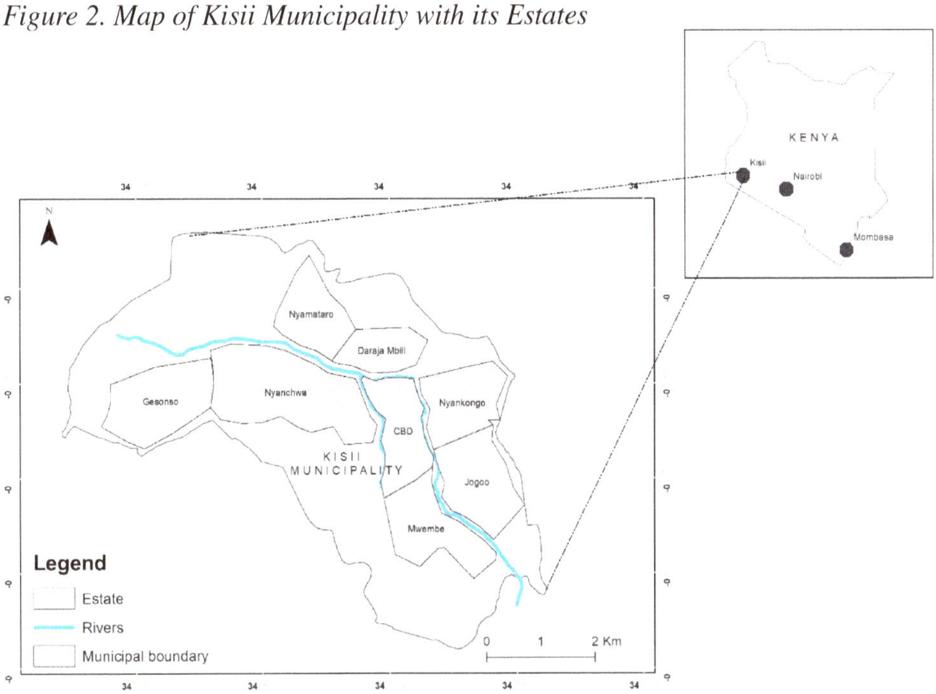

These estates have no planned waste collection stations. Therefore, the municipality faces the challenge of waste management, as there are no properly designated dumping sites. Access to the deeper parts of these estates also poses challenges, as most connecting roads are impassable and blocked by unplanned structures (Figure 3).

Figure 3. Interactions between human systems, waste management and ecological systems in Kisii Municipality.

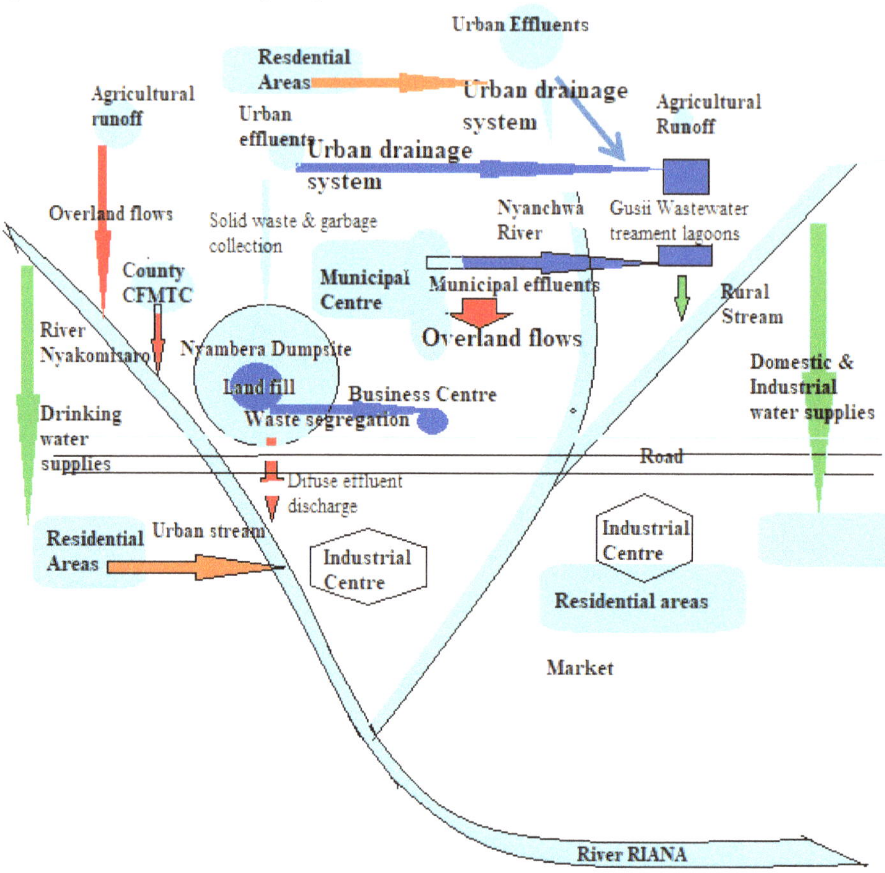

The red arrows indicate pollution flows, blue arrows indicate waste management strategies, and green arrows indicate ecological processes.

The Municipality has seen a tremendous increase in its human population, resulting in significant solid waste production. It faces severe environmental challenges due to rapid urbanisation, industrial growth and inadequate waste management infrastructure, which contribute to declining water quality and biodiversity loss (Rayori et al., 2023). Channels draining the municipality are clogged with solid waste, obstructing drainage systems, disrupting transportation, and posing safety risks in residential areas. Additionally, the encroachment of riparian buffer zones, originally meant to regulate stream flows, has weakened the area's resilience to flooding and water pollution.

DATA COLLECTION

This study employed a mixed-methods approach, combining empirical site surveys, expert interviews and policy content analysis to assess waste management challenges in Kisii Municipality. Field observations documented waste generation patterns, disposal practices and pollution hotspots, while interviews with policy-makers, environmental officers and community representatives provided insights into regulatory enforcement and potential solutions. A review of existing policies identified gaps in waste management regulations and enforcement. Quantitative data were analysed using descriptive statistics, while qualitative data underwent thematic analysis.

FINDINGS AND DISCUSSIONS

Status of Waste and Effluents Management in Kisii Municipality

Kisii Municipality has experienced a significant increase in solid waste generation, primarily driven by rapid urbanisation and population growth. The types of waste generated in urban, municipal, industrial and agricultural settings vary widely, each contributing differently to environmental degradation. Urban and municipal waste primarily consists of plastics, organic matter, paper, glass, metals and electronic waste, while industrial waste includes hazardous chemicals, heavy metals and non-biodegradable byproducts (Figure 4).

Figure 4. Trends in Assorted solid wastes generated in Kisii Municipality (Source: County Government of Kisii).

In addition, agricultural waste, such as pesticide residues, fertilisers, and livestock manure, contributes to nutrient pollution, leading to eutrophication in water bodies. This surge in waste production has posed critical challenges to urban waste management, particularly in safeguarding aquatic and terrestrial ecosystems. Without proper management strategies, these waste materials contaminate both terrestrial and aquatic environments, harming biodiversity and human health. Municipal solid waste management in Kisii involves the collection, sorting and disposal of various waste materials. Upon collection by municipal vehicles, casual labourers sort and weigh the waste before disposal (Figure 5).

Figure 5. Identified solid wastes in landfills observed during empirical surveys

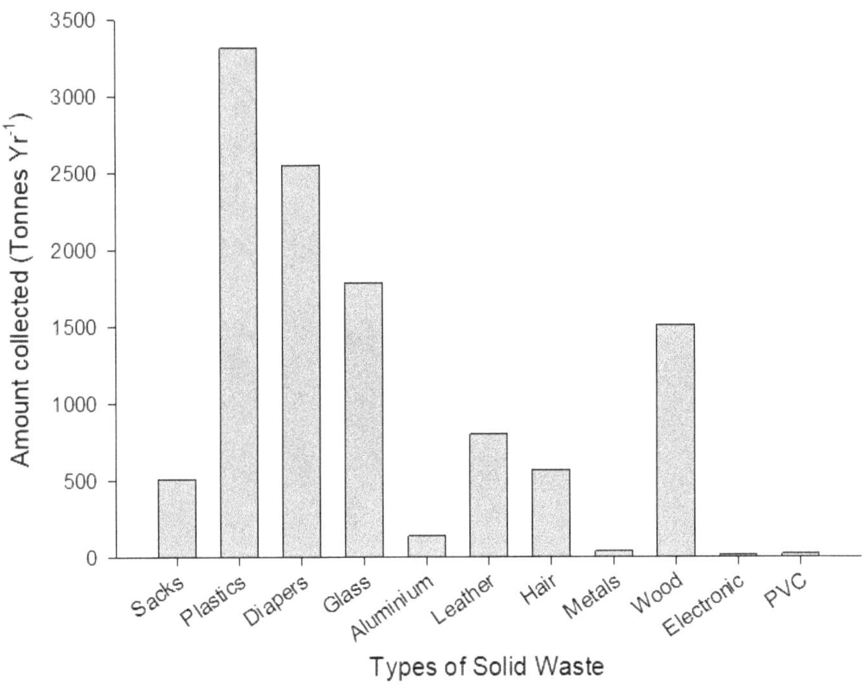

Plastics constitute the largest portion (3,318 tons), followed by diapers (2,556 tons), while electronic waste accounts for the smallest fraction (23 tons). Some plastic waste is collected for recycling by private companies, while diapers are incinerated on-site. Organic waste is left for open-air decomposition, and metals are in high demand, often scavenged from dumpsites and sold at KSh 16 per kilogram. The high value of scrap metal has led to informal waste recovery efforts, with street children actively collecting metals for resale. However, improper disposal of organic waste and non-recyclable materials contributes to severe pollution, affecting both land and water systems.

Figure 6. Plastic waste dumped into the Nyakomisaro-Riana River at Makutano Junction

The study found that wastewater from households and industries is often discharged directly into rivers, exacerbating pollution in Kisii's aquatic ecosystems (Figure 6). The existing drainage infrastructure is inadequate, leading to frequent overflows and leakages from municipal sewage systems. Studies indicate that untreated domestic and industrial wastewater significantly contributes to water pollution in urban areas (Ochieng & Mutiso, 2023). This results in the accumulation of organic pollutants, heavy metals and pathogenic microorganisms in rivers and streams, severely affecting water quality. Pollution of key aquatic systems, such as the Nyakomisaro-Riana River, impacts local water-dependent activities, including fishing, recreation, and domestic water supply (Mogaka, 2022). Sustainable waste management approaches, such as bio-retention systems, can help capture and treat contaminated water, reducing pollutant loads and improving water quality (Davis et al., 2009).

Poor waste and wastewater management in Kisii Municipality poses serious environmental and public health risks. Contaminated water sources contribute to the spread of gastrointestinal diseases and skin infections, particularly affecting vulnerable populations with limited access to clean water (Nyamache, 2021). Pollutants such as high nutrient loads, microplastics, heavy metals and pesticides disrupt the functioning of terrestrial and aquatic ecosystems, leading to loss of aquatic biodiversity (Ondemo et al., 2022). Agricultural activities also suffer as polluted water affects soil fertility and crop productivity. The integration of preventive and corrective waste management strategies is essential to mitigate these risks, emphasising waste reduction, resource recovery, and the use of innovative treatment technologies (Naftal et al., 2023).

Despite the severity of waste management challenges, the study found that most estate residents in Kisii are not involved in municipal waste management processes. Over 80% of respondents indicated that they would participate in waste sorting at their doorsteps if given proper support and incentives. Organic waste could be redirected to kitchen gardens or large-scale farms for composting, reducing landfill waste and promoting sustainable agriculture. Engaging local communities through waste management committees and clean-up initiatives can help address illegal dumping in urban and peri-urban areas. Stakeholder involvement, combining efforts from local governments, private waste management firms and community-based organisations, is crucial for effective waste management (Mwangi & Otieno, 2023). Financial incentives and environmental subsidies for waste segregation and collection could further encourage community participation in sustainable waste practices (Hettiarachchi et. al., 2018).

Integrated Waste Management Approaches

Uncontrolled waste disposal and untreated effluent discharge pose severe threats to aquatic ecosystems by deteriorating water quality, destroying habitats and reducing species diversity. Addressing these challenges requires a multifaceted approach that integrates policy initiatives, public awareness, technological advancements and environmental restoration programs (Hanna, 2010). Implementing proper waste management systems is essential to minimising disruptions to natural ecosystems while ensuring biodiversity conservation. Urban areas like Kisii must prioritise strategies that not only reduce pollution but also enhance ecosystem resilience.

Kisii Municipality in particular, faces significant environmental challenges due to the accumulation of urban wastewater and solid waste, leading to water contamination and biodiversity loss. Rapid urbanisation, industrial expansion and insufficient municipal infrastructure exacerbate these issues with untreated sewage and industrial discharge introducing organic pollutants, heavy metals and pathogenic microorganisms into local water bodies (Rayori, 2023; Rayori et al., 2024). To mitigate these concerns, adopting integrated waste management strategies is crucial. These approaches require collaboration among governments, industries and communities to ensure effective waste management and environmental sustainability (Mwangi & Otieno, 2023; Mutua & Wambua, 2024).

Constructed wetlands

In Kenya, constructed wetlands have demonstrated success in improving water quality and biodiversity in urban areas, such as Nairobi City (Kimani & Wanjiku, 2023). Kisii Municipality, with its growing population and increasing wastewater challenges, can greatly benefit from cost-effective, low-maintenance systems that integrate wastewater treatment with habitat restoration (Nyamache, 2021; Ogechi, 2023; Oseko, 2023). Constructed wetlands are engineered systems designed to mimic the purification processes of natural wetlands and are used to treat urban runoff and improve water quality through natural filtration (Vymazal, 2011). Constructed wetlands have proven effective in removing heavy metals and pesticides through bioaccumulation, bioconcentration, and biomagnification. In Kisii municipality. The rapid rise in carwash businesses within the municipality needs to be re-examined and regulated, lest they continue to add more waste and pollute the environment (Figure 7).

Figure 7. Wastewater effluents discharged from the car wash site along the Nyakomisaro-Riana River

There is a need to replicate the constructed wetlands at carwash points. For instance, the Gusii wastewater treatment plant, located within the Kisii municipality, is a successful example of using constructed wetlands to treat wastewater and provide habitat for aquatic organisms. It has been reported to be effective in removing pollutants, such as pesticides, nutrients and heavy metals from wastewater. To implement this strategy, site selection, design, and construction technical expertise must be considered. Wetland plants must also be carefully selected for planting, and a scheduled program for regular monitoring of pollutant levels at the influent and effluent must be established. However, the use of constructed wetlands (CWs) is currently facing sustainability issues, especially in densely populated areas, due to the large land area required for initial setup and the potential for mosquito breeding, which can pose a health risk to residents of Kisii municipality. In addition, regular maintenance needs make it labour-intensive, may entail high operational costs, and complicate its expansion due to land acquisition, high initial costs, and ongoing maintenance. These systems rely on vegetation, soil and microbial activity to remove contaminants while simultaneously creating habitats for wildlife (Thakur et al., 2023).

Technological Solutions and Integration

Kisii Municipality can significantly enhance its waste management efficiency by adopting innovative solutions such as bioremediation, artificial intelligence (AI)-driven monitoring systems, and constructed wetlands. Technological advancements are essential for balancing waste management with ecosystem protection. Modern wastewater treatment facilities equipped with advanced filtration systems significantly reduce the amount of harmful pollutants entering water bodies. Kisii Municipality is currently exploring decentralised wastewater treatment systems and waste-to-energy technologies as potential solutions to its growing waste management challenges while simultaneously creating economic value (Nyamache, 2018). Additionally, recycling programs and composting initiatives help minimise solid waste volumes and their environmental impact (Bolong et al., 2009). Beyond traditional waste treatment methods, technological integration enhances efficiency in waste management operations. Tools such as Geographic Information Systems (GIS) and mobile applications enable real-time waste tracking, optimise collection routes, and detect illegal dumping (Neene, 2017). By leveraging smart technology, Kisii's municipal authorities can swiftly identify waste-related issues, improve response times and enhance accountability among stakeholders. Digital platforms further support data-driven policymaking by monitoring waste distribution trends, allowing for more effective long-term waste management strategies (Mohamed et al., 2024). Integrating these technological solutions into Kisii's waste management framework will not only improve operational efficiency but also contribute to environmental sustainability. By combining modern treatment systems, smart monitoring tools and innovative waste-to-resource strategies, the municipality can move toward a cleaner, more resilient urban environment.

Use of Artificial Intelligence (AI) in Waste Management

AI-driven monitoring systems have proven effective in detecting and addressing pollution sources, as observed in the Nairobi River, where they enhance pollution detection and mitigation efforts (Mwangi et al., 2020; Kamau & Njoroge, 2024). Similarly, bioremediation projects in the Lake Victoria basin have improved water quality and fish health, while waste-sequestration techniques, such as urban forests and lagoons, have shown potential for managing municipal, industrial, and agricultural waste (Nowak et al., 2018). A multidisciplinary approach that integrates remote sensing, computational modeling and field monitoring is crucial for evaluating the effectiveness of these methods in reducing pollution and enhancing urban sustainability (Livesley et al., 2016). AI significantly enhances waste management by enabling real-time monitoring and predictive analytics. Integrated with sensors and data analytics, AI-driven systems detect pollution sources, predict contamination events and optimise waste treatment processes, leading to greater accuracy and efficiency in pollution control (Mwangi et al., 2020; Wang & Zhang, 2024). These technologies provide real-time environmental intelligence, allowing professionals to conduct timely interventions that minimise ecological damage (Andeobu et. al., 2022). The success of AI-based monitoring in the Nairobi River underscores its potential in waste management as it has helped identify pollution patterns and effectively control their sources (Kamau & Njoroge, 2024).

Integrating AI into Kisii Municipality's waste management programs could address challenges such as illegal waste disposal, untreated wastewater discharge and inefficient waste collection. AI-powered systems can enhance public awareness by providing real-time water quality updates and localised pollution data, fostering environmental conservation efforts among residents (Fang et al., 2023). Additionally, AI-driven mobile applications could enable citizens to report waste-related concerns, creating an interconnected system that promotes cleaner aquatic environments (Munir et al., 2023; Ameh, 2024). The successful implementation of AI in waste management requires a data-driven approach that actively engages municipal authorities, local communities, and private-sector stakeholders (Kristian et al., 2024). Effective coordination among government agencies, researchers and businesses is essential for developing sustainable solutions (Ahmed & Ali, 2006). To ensure long-term success, Kisii Municipality must prioritise organisational development and public training programs that educate residents about their environmental responsibilities. Such initiatives will help reduce waste generation while preserving aquatic ecosystems and supporting sustainable urban development.

Advanced filtration systems

Modern filtration technologies, such as membrane bioreactors and nanofiltration, offer efficient ways to remove contaminants from water and serve as the core component of managing urban and municipal effluents. These include membrane bioreactors, ultrafiltration systems, and nanofiltration units, which now offer highly skilled techniques for effectively eliminating pollutants (Gkotsis et al., 2014). Research has shown that advanced filtration systems can achieve high removal efficiencies for a wide range of pollutants, small microscopic wastes in the aquatic ecosystems, such as microplastics and pathogens, making them suitable for both municipal and industrial wastewater treatment, ensuring adequate clean and safe water for use (Johnson & Lee, 2022).

Furthermore, the filtration system's advanced technology also removes dissolved chemical pollutants, allowing water to achieve sufficient quality for both safe environmental release and potential reuse (Kamali et al., 2019). In Nairobi City, for instance, advanced filtration systems have been implemented to treat wastewater, resulting in significant improvements in water quality, thus establishing baseline standards for Kenyan urban wastewater management (Kamau & Njoroge, 2024). The deployment of advanced filtration systems in Kisii Municipality can help manage growing water system stress resulting from the rapid pace of urban development. Nevertheless, these systems require significant installation costs as well as ongoing maintenance. Private sector partnerships with government subsidies will reduce capital expenditures for advanced filtration systems while promoting their sustainable implementation across Kisii Municipality (Mungai, 2022). Initiatives to deploy decentralised water filtration systems across diverse communities in Kisii Municipality would evenly spread pollution-control benefits and stabilise water conditions throughout the region (Nyamache, 2021).

Bioremediation

Bio-remediation is a natural and cost-effective technique that uses microorganisms to degrade and remove pollutants from water. This method can be tailored to target specific contaminants, making it a viable solution for urban wastewater management. Studies on Lake Victoria have demonstrated its effectiveness in mitigating aquatic pollution, highlighting its potential for broader application in urban areas (Odada et al., 2004; Smith & Brown, 2023). In Kenya, bioremediation projects have shown significant success in reducing pollution and improving water quality (Ochieng & Mutiso, 2023). Microorganisms such as bacteria, fungi, and algae play a crucial role in this process by metabolising hazardous substances and converting them into less toxic end products (Altowayti et al., 2022; Kuppan et al.,

2024). For example, certain bacteria can break down oil spills from garages while others can remove heavy metals from industrial wastewater. Research has confirmed that bioremediation can significantly lower heavy metal concentrations and organic waste contaminants, ultimately enhancing water quality (Smith & Brown, 2023; Ochieng and Mutiso, 2023).

Additionally, urban forests and waste sequestration lagoons serve as natural filtration systems, improving water quality while mitigating greenhouse gas emissions (Nowak et al., 2018). Implementing bio-remediation solutions in Kisii Municipality's rivers and streams can help combat pollution, ensuring cleaner water for both ecological and human use. The success of Lake Victoria's bio-remediation efforts depended on continued community engagement, capacity development, and sustained monitoring.

For effective implementation in Kisii Municipality, native microorganisms with demonstrated pollution resistance should be integrated to develop customised, sustainable solutions for local environmental challenges (Kitaka et al., 2024). Moreover, combining bio-remediation with advanced filtration systems and AI-driven monitoring can create functional frameworks for sustainable urban waste management, ensuring long-term environmental resilience.

Riparian buffer zones: Protection

Protecting riparian buffer zones is vital for maintaining the health of aquatic ecosystems, especially in urban areas like Kisii Municipality, where rapid population growth, increased waste generation, and unregulated development along riparian zones pose significant environmental challenges. These zones act as natural filtration systems, helping to reduce pollution from urban runoff while simultaneously providing habitats for aquatic and terrestrial wildlife (Odhiambo & Achieng, 2024). However, ongoing construction along these sensitive areas threatens the ecological balance and must be halted to prevent further degradation of water bodies (Ogendi, 2022). In Kenya, the establishment of riparian buffer zones has been linked to improved water quality and ecosystem health (Kimani & Wanjiku, 2023). Riparian buffer zones are critical in mitigating the impacts of urban pollution on aquatic ecosystems. Research shows that well-maintained buffer zones filter contaminants before they reach water bodies, slow stormwater runoff, and prevent pollutants from entering rivers and lakes (Kimani and Wanjiku, 2023).

Additionally, these zones stabilise riverbanks, reducing soil erosion and preventing sedimentation that can suffocate aquatic life. The combined benefits of buffer zones not only protect water quality but also enhance biodiversity by creating natural habitats (Angima, 2021). Legally protecting riparian buffer zones and strictly enforcing environmental regulations are essential steps in safeguarding Kisii's water bodies (Wambui et al., 2019). Collaboration among local authorities, environmental organisations, and community stakeholders is necessary for the implementation and maintenance of these buffer zones. Effective partnerships can ensure regular monitoring, promote community awareness and enhance the overall effectiveness of buffer zones in preserving aquatic ecosystems (Ebregt & Greve, 2000). Establishing and enforcing buffer zone regulations will be crucial to balancing urban development with environmental sustainability.

METHODS OF WASTE REUSE AND RECYCLING

Recycling of Organic Waste

Recent advancements in waste treatment and recycling technologies offer promising solutions for sustainable waste management. Kisii Municipality has adopted waste-sorting practices to minimise solid waste accumulation in dumpsites, thereby helping prevent water, soil, and air pollution. Major Kenyan cities are currently exploring integrated waste management strategies to enhance waste control, aiming to promote a circular economy by emphasising waste reduction through reuse and recycling of domestic, urban and industrial waste (Mutua & Wambua, 2024). These integrated approaches divert materials from landfills and water bodies, reducing pollution and conserving natural resources (Lieder & Rashid, 2016). Additionally, community sensitisation programs that educate the public about recycling foster behavioural change and enhance understanding of proper waste-disposal practices (Kebaso, 2015).

Organic waste, which often decomposes in open spaces, can be repurposed through controlled decomposition processes such as composting, anaerobic digestion and pyrolysis. Anaerobic digestion involves the breakdown of organic materials in an oxygen-free environment, producing biogas for energy and nutrient-rich digestate for use as fertiliser. Similarly, pyrolysis decomposes organic waste at high temperatures under low-oxygen conditions, generating biochar, bio-oil, and syngas, which serve as renewable fuel sources (Nyamache, 2018; UNEP, 2021; Ndegwa & Karanja, 2023). These technologies not only enhance waste management but also contribute to the circular economy by converting waste into valuable products. In Kenya, anaerobic digestion and pyrolysis have been successfully applied in urban areas, reducing waste volumes and increasing resource recovery (Mutua & Wambua, 2024).

The adoption of anaerobic digestion and pyrolysis in Kisii Municipality presents a transformative opportunity for waste recycling. Biogas production from anaerobic digestion provides an alternative energy source while reducing environmental pollution. Likewise, pyrolysis generates biochar, which improves soil fertility and bio-oil, which serves as a sustainable fuel substitute. These technologies align with circular economy principles by repurposing organic waste rather than discarding it, thereby minimising its environmental impact (Nyamache, 2021). Studies have demonstrated that implementing anaerobic digestion and pyrolysis in Kenya enhances municipal waste management. For example, anaerobic digestion plants in Nairobi and Mombasa have successfully provided sustainable energy and pollution-reduction benefits, while pyrolysis trials have converted plastic and organic waste into fuel and biochar, reducing reliance on landfilling and incineration (Dharmaraj et al., 2021; Mutua & Wambua, 2024).

Kisii Municipality, which faces increasing population pressure and rising waste production, stands to benefit significantly from these advanced waste treatment methods (Otiso, 1993). Integrating anaerobic digestion into urban wastewater treatment can help manage effluent discharge from households, businesses and industries, thus protecting aquatic ecosystems from contamination. Additionally, pyrolysis offers an effective solution for processing plastics and agricultural residues, reducing solid waste accumulation (Huang et al., 2020). However, beyond adopting technology, the success of these methods depends on stakeholder engagement, supportive policies and community awareness. Waste segregation education programs and incentives for proper disposal practices are crucial in ensuring the effectiveness of anaerobic digestion and pyrolysis systems. Public-private partnerships can facilitate funding and scale up these solutions to achieve long-term sustainability (Meissner, 2019).

Innovative and durable waste management solutions are necessary to address solid waste challenges. Composting offers homeowners a practical way to manage organic waste while producing nutrient-rich soil for gardening. Given that a significant portion of Kisii's municipal solid waste consists of organic materials, composting initiatives can generate economic benefits for residents while reducing landfill waste. Community awareness campaigns play a vital role in promoting composting, fostering environmental responsibility and encouraging participation in waste management programs (Mongkolnchaiarunya, 2005; Rahman et al., 2022; Etim, 2024).

Despite these waste management efforts, some uncollected waste from inaccessible areas in Kisii Municipality, particularly along the Nyakomisaro-Riana and Nyanchwa-Riana Rivers, is either intentionally dumped into water bodies or carried away by floods. The combination of urban solid waste and sewage is a major source of pollution in aquatic systems, introducing excessive nutrients, heavy metals, toxins and pathogens. These pollutants contribute to eutrophication, hypoxia and outbreaks of waterborne diseases (Mironga, 2006). Additionally, leachate from open dumpsites contains heavy metals that contaminate aquatic environments, disrupting biodiversity and food chains. Plastic waste further exacerbates the issue by obstructing water flow, suffocating aquatic organisms and releasing toxic chemicals into ecosystems

(Mosoti et al., 2024). Addressing these challenges requires a multi-faceted approach, including improved waste collection systems, stricter regulations and enhanced community participation in waste management.

Recycling of inorganic wastes

Kisii Municipality has experienced the growth of businesses dedicated to waste management solutions. Addressing the growing challenges of organic and inorganic waste requires both recycling and upcycling initiatives. For instance, Gasia Poa Waste Management Services handles solid waste collection and pit emptying, while Gusii Water & Sanitation Company (GWSC) provides essential water and sanitation services. Integrated Solid Waste Management (ISCoD Kenya) focuses on waste segregation and recycling, whereas Best Care Services specialises in exhauster and sludge disposal. Through collaboration with relevant stakeholders such as the County Government of Kisii, these enterprises have played a crucial role in mitigating urban waste challenges and advancing environmental sustainability by embracing technological advancements and implementing sustainable waste management strategies. These initiatives have established dedicated recycling centres for plastics, glass, and metals, helping minimise waste accumulation in water systems. Public-private sector partnerships facilitate the development of value chains from recovered materials, promoting circular economy principles. Upcycling transforms plastics into construction materials while glass and metal undergo industrial processing for reintegration into supply chains. These initiatives contribute to both environmental conservation and economic development (Thakur et al., 2023). Such initiatives have enabled Kisii Municipality to thrive in sustainability and improve the ecosystem health of its aquatic and terrestrial ecosystems, creating a cleaner, more resilient urban environment for future generations (World Health Organisation, 2016; Gesimba, 2020; Momanyi, 2021).

Decentralised wastewater treatment systems (DEWATS) offer an effective, environmentally friendly solution for urban wastewater management. These systems rely on biological wastewater treatment processes and operate without centralised sewer networks, making them suitable for peri-urban areas in Kisii (Singh et al., 2019). DEWATS can be customised to treat wastewater at household, institutional and small-scale industrial levels, ensuring efficient performance. The treated water can be repurposed for irrigation, thereby conserving water resources. Widespread implementation of DEWATS in Kisii Municipality would significantly reduce the discharge of untreated effluent into aquatic ecosystems, thereby enhancing environmental protection (Kumar et al., 2022). To protect waterbodies from the destructive impacts of waste and maintain environmental health, there is a need to embrace sustainable waste management approaches (Oseko, 2023).

Policy and Community-Based Approaches

Effective waste management in Kisii requires coordinated efforts among all stakeholders to invest in infrastructure, enhance public education and implement cost-effective strategies (World Bank, 2019; Mutua & Wambua, 2024). In Kenya, initiatives such as public-private partnerships and community engagement programs are being leveraged to tackle these challenges and promote long-term environmental sustainability (Mwangi & Otieno, 2023). Due to the realisation that sustainable waste management extends beyond infrastructure, it also depends on public participation and education, the management of Kisii Municipality has continued to promote community engagement programs to sensitise the urban community on proper waste segregation at the source and discourage indiscriminate disposal (Otiso, 1993).

Raising awareness about the negative impacts of waste on aquatic environments fosters responsible behaviour and encourages eco-conscious lifestyle choices. This, combined with local awareness of waste management strategies, ensures that these strategies will align and effectively address community needs and challenges (Kung'u, 2023). For instance, raising awareness, encouraging household-level waste segregation and involving local residents in cleanup initiatives can foster a culture of environmental responsibility. Stakeholder collaboration, bringing together local governments, private waste management firms and community-based organisations, will be instrumental in developing sustainable waste management systems (Mwangi & Otieno, 2023).

For sustainable waste management policy interventions, there is a need to create essential conditions alongside technical solutions. The Kisii Municipality should establish compulsory regulations for responsible waste management systems and must punish those responsible for unauthorised disposals (Nyamache, 2021). Community-based waste management systems, when integrated, empower residents to independently preserve their local environment. Non-governmental organisations, along with academic institutions, should team up to deliver capacity-building training which uses their technical expertise to enhance waste management capabilities (Agamuthu & Hansen, 2007).

Currently, in Kisii municipality, there is no stand-alone county-based policy to regulate solid waste disposal and effluent discharges. However, Kenya's Environmental Management and Coordination Act (EMCA) serves as a cornerstone for environmental protection. Studies have highlighted the importance of enhancing enforcement mechanisms. For example, Aboelnour and Abuelela (2019) emphasise the need for increased monitoring and compliance capacity to ensure adherence to waste management standards. The National Environment Management Authority (NEMA) has been pivotal in this regard, working to bolster its enforcement capabilities. Customising policies to specific urban challenges has proven effective in

Kenyan cities like Nairobi and Kisumu. A case study by Otieno and Omondi (2022) demonstrates how localised waste segregation mandates and stricter discharge limits for industries near aquatic ecosystems have led to improved environmental outcomes.

Greenpeace Africa (2023) also supports this approach, advocating for context-specific solutions that address unique urban challenges. The Water Act 2016 provides a legal framework for water resource management in Kenya. It emphasises the protection of water catchment areas and the sustainable use of water resources. A study by Kariuki and Ngugi (2018) discusses the impact of this act on improving water quality and availability. These examples illustrate how Kenya has domesticated global initiatives and policy frameworks to address the unique challenges of urban effluent and solid waste management in aquatic ecosystems. By strengthening existing policies, implementing localised regulations and adopting integrated legal approaches, Kenya will make significant strides towards sustainable waste management.

The NSWMS aims to provide a comprehensive framework for managing solid waste in Kenya. It emphasises waste reduction, recycling and safe disposal practices. A study by Njenga et al. (2021) highlights the success of this strategy in promoting sustainable waste management practices. The implementation of the Polluter Pays Principle has been instrumental in deterring environmental degradation. According to a study by Karanja et al. (2020), financial penalties for entities discharging untreated effluents have significantly reduced pollution levels. Revenues from these penalties are used to fund waste management infrastructure and ecosystem restoration projects, as highlighted by the United Nations Environment Programme (UNEP, 2023). Maladministration of resources leads to a wide range of detrimental effects. Water pollution poses health risks to residents by causing them to contract diseases like cholera and typhoid from contaminated drinking water.

Solid waste management requires proper implementation of laws and regulations to create a robust framework for sustaining compliance. The Kisii Municipality requires heightened enforcement of current laws governing waste disposal and pollution control to discourage harmful practices (Mogaka, 2022). Correct waste disposal behaviour requires consistent application of both regulatory penalties and incentives through proper waste disposal procedures. Local regulations that meet national and international sustainability requirements will enable Kisii to support a wide range of environmental initiatives (Oseko, 2023). Policies and regulations should support sustainable practices, while public awareness campaigns can encourage community participation in waste reduction efforts.

CHALLENGES AND SOLUTIONS

Despite global advancements in waste management technologies, Kisii Municipality continues to face significant challenges in this sector. These challenges include high initial costs of advanced systems, inadequate infrastructure and limited public awareness. Consequently, solid waste management in Kisii falls short of acceptable standards, with open, unregulated dumping a common practice. This mismanagement leads to the accumulation of plastics, metals and other non-biodegradable materials in rivers and streams, causing blockages, altered aquatic conditions and severe flooding during heavy rainfall events (Mosago, 2010).

Pollution of water sources poses serious health risks to residents, increasing the prevalence of waterborne diseases such as cholera and typhoid. Additionally, pollutants disrupt aquatic ecosystems, reducing biodiversity and harming the ecological balance. The degradation of water quality further affects key economic activities, including fishing and agriculture, which depend on clean water resources (Mosago, 2010). Several factors contribute to the waste management challenges in Kisii Municipality:

1. Weak Policy Enforcement: The absence of a dedicated waste management policy and inadequate enforcement of existing regulations have led to widespread improper disposal of solid waste and effluent. This has resulted in increased pollution levels, causing severe damage to aquatic ecosystems and public health risks (Mosago, 2010).
2. Inadequate Public Awareness: Limited community involvement and awareness hinder sustainable waste management solutions. The lack of education on proper waste disposal practices contributes to the persistence of unregulated dumping (Mosago, 2010).
3. Rapid Urban Expansion: The swift urban growth has overwhelmed existing waste management systems, leading to improper disposal practices and increased pollution (Mosago, 2010).

Current waste management efforts in Kisii are fragmented, with multiple scattered programs suffering from insufficient funding and weak regulatory enforcement. While national and county governments have introduced new regulations to improve waste management, enforcement remains inconsistent, allowing pollution levels to rise in Kisii's aquatic systems (UN-Habitat, 2023).

To address these challenges, research is needed to identify key sources of contamination and evaluate existing waste management systems. Advanced waste management approaches, such as AI-driven monitoring for efficient waste tracking, bio-membrane filtration and constructed wetlands for improved wastewater treatment, offer promising solutions. Integrating eco-friendly waste management practices can enhance ecosystem integrity while ensuring long-term sustainability (Garg et al., 2024).

CONCLUSION AND RECOMMENDATIONS

Conclusion

Kisii Municipality's escalating waste crisis necessitates urgent intervention through integrated waste management approaches. Strengthening waste management infrastructure, enforcing environmental laws, promoting stakeholder engagement and adopting modern waste treatment technologies are essential steps toward improving efficiency and protecting both terrestrial and aquatic ecosystems. Without proactive measures, the adverse effects of poor waste management, including public health risks, loss of biodiversity and economic setbacks, will continue to intensify. This study has critically examined urban effluent in Kisii Municipality and its effects on the aquatic environment. However, notable limitations include the study's geographic focus and the lack of a detailed water-quality analysis, which may not fully capture the broader impacts of urban solid waste on aquatic ecosystems. Despite these limitations, this research provides valuable insights into waste management practices and their implications for environmental health. Analysing the relationship between waste management strategies and water quality offers practical guidance for policymakers, environmentalists and the community.

Furthermore, this study aligns with both global and national sustainability goals by investigating urban waste management in relation to environmental protection and public health. The findings offer practical solutions for Kisii Municipality and demonstrate their potential application to other cities facing similar waste management challenges. Kenya's Vision 2030 emphasises sustainable waste management technologies such as Black Soldier Fly farming, Azolla cultivation and microalgae production, which can be integrated into Kisii's waste management strategies to enhance resource recovery (Mutua et al., 2020). Additionally, digital monitoring systems can improve waste management by tracking pollution levels and ensuring compliance with environmental regulations.

This research underscores the need for practical, affordable and community-driven waste management solutions to enhance sustainability in Kisii Municipality. The study's findings provide a valuable resource for policymakers, environmental stakeholders, and residents, helping municipal authorities identify effective waste-disposal strategies to improve water quality. By comparing existing waste management systems, this study highlights best practices tailored to Kisii's specific needs.

Ultimately, sustainable waste management is crucial for protecting Kisii's aquatic ecosystems, which are vital for environmental conservation and economic activities such as agriculture and fishing. Without immediate corrective measures, continued environmental degradation will lead to severe economic, social and ecological consequences. Therefore, protecting Kisii Municipality's water resources and ecosystem services is critical not only for sustainability and public health but also for the region's long-term economic well-being. Ultimately, urgent efforts to implement sustainable waste management solutions will ensure a cleaner, healthier and more resilient urban environment for both present and future generations.

Recommendations

To effectively address Kisii Municipality's waste management challenges, a multifaceted approach is necessary.

i. Strengthening policy enforcement and regulatory frameworks is critical. Enhanced enforcement of environmental laws, regular inspections and improved coordination between national and county governments will ensure compliance and streamline waste management systems.
ii. Increasing public awareness and community engagement will foster a culture of environmental responsibility. Public education campaigns, school-based programs, and community-driven waste initiatives will encourage sustainable waste-disposal practices and enhance local participation.
iii. Investing in modern waste treatment technologies will improve efficiency and reduce pollution. The adoption of bio-membrane filtration, constructed wetlands, and AI-driven waste monitoring will enhance solid waste and effluent management. Additionally, waste-to-resource strategies such as composting, waste-to-energy technologies, and organic waste recycling (e.g., Black Soldier Fly farming, *Azolla* cultivation and microalgae production) will contribute to environmental sustainability and economic growth (Mutua et al., 2020).
iv. Fostering public-private partnerships (PPPs) will facilitate cost-effective and innovative waste management solutions. Collaborating with private waste management companies, environmental organisations, and municipal authorities can enhance service delivery. Furthermore, incentivising businesses and supporting local waste entrepreneurs through microfinance initiatives will promote sustainability and job creation.
v. Implementing digital monitoring and data-driven waste management solutions will improve oversight and compliance. AI-driven waste tracking and real-time water quality monitoring will optimise waste collection, ensure regulatory adherence and enable swift responses to pollution threats.

Finally, continuous research and assessment are essential for sustainable waste management. Further studies on the impact of urban waste on aquatic ecosystems will provide data-driven recommendations, while long-term monitoring will assess the effectiveness of waste management interventions. Collaborating with academic institutions and research organisations will foster innovation and generate locally adaptable solutions.

REFERENCES

Aboelnour, A., & Abuelela, M. H. (2019). Increase adherence to waste management policy at healthcare facility in Egypt. *Bulletin of the National Research Center, 43*(29), 1–11. DOI: 10.1186/s42269-019-0065-2

Agamuthu, P., & Hansen, J. A. (2007). Universities in capacity building in sustainable development: Focus on solid waste management and technology. *Waste Management & Research, 25*(3), 241–246. DOI: 10.1177/0734242X07079155 PMID: 17612324

Ahmed, S. A., & Ali, S. M. (2006). People as partners: Facilitating people's participation in public–private partnerships for solid waste management. *Habitat International, 30*(4), 781–796. DOI: 10.1016/j.habitatint.2005.09.004

Altowayti, W. A. H., Shahir, S., Othman, N., Eisa, T. A. E., Yafooz, W. M., Al-Dhaqm, A., Soon, C. Y., Yahya, I. B., Che Rahim, N. A. N., Abaker, M., & Ali, A. (2022). The role of conventional methods and artificial intelligence in the wastewater treatment: A comprehensive review. *Processes (Basel, Switzerland), 10*(9), 1832. DOI: 10.3390/pr10091832

Ameh, B. (2024). Digital tools and AI: Using technology to monitor carbon emissions and waste at each stage of the supply chain, enabling real-time adjustments for sustainability improvements. *Int J Sci Res Arch, 13*(1), 2741–2754. DOI: 10.30574/ijsra.2024.13.1.1995

Andeobu, L., Wibowo, S., & Grandhi, S. (2022). Artificial intelligence applications for sustainable solid waste management practices in Australia: A systematic review. *The Science of the Total Environment, 834*, 155389. DOI: 10.1016/j.scitotenv.2022.155389 PMID: 35460765

Angima, B. M. (2021). Effects of Anthropogenic Activities on the Diversity of Macrophytes and Water Quality in Sironga and Kapkatet Wetlands, Kenya (Master's dissertation, KISII UNIVERSITY).

Bolong, N., Ismail, A. F., Salim, M. R., & Matsuura, T. (2009). A review of the effects of emerging contaminants in wastewater and options for their removal. *Desalination, 239*(1-3), 229–246. DOI: 10.1016/j.desal.2008.03.020

Davis, A. P., Hunt, W. F., Traver, R. G., & Clar, M. (2009). Bioretention technology: Overview of current practice and future needs. *Journal of Environmental Engineering, 135*(3), 109–117. DOI: 10.1061/(ASCE)0733-9372(2009)135:3(109)

Dharmaraj, S., Ashokkumar, V., Pandiyan, R., Munawaroh, H. S. H., Chew, K. W., Chen, W. H., & Ngamcharussrivichai, C. (2021). Pyrolysis: An effective technique for the degradation of COVID-19 medical wastes. *Chemosphere, 275*, 130092. DOI: 10.1016/j.chemosphere.2021.130092 PMID: 33984908

Ebregt, A., & Greve, P. D. (2000). Buffer zones and their management. Policy and best practices for terrestrial ecosystems in developing countries. Theme Studies Series, 5.

Etim, E. (2024). Leveraging public awareness and behavioural change for entrepreneurial waste management. *Heliyon, 10*(21), e40063. DOI: 10.1016/j.heliyon.2024.e40063 PMID: 39553649

Fang, B., Yu, J., Chen, Z., Osman, A. I., Farghali, M., Ihara, I., Hamza, E. H., Rooney, D. W., & Yap, P. S. (2023). Artificial intelligence for waste management in smart cities: A review. *Environmental Chemistry Letters, 21*(4), 1959–1989. DOI: 10.1007/s10311-023-01604-3 PMID: 37362015

Garg, M. C., Kumari, S., & Agarwal, S. (2024). The integration of artificial intelligence in advanced wastewater treatment systems. In The AI Cleanse: Transforming Wastewater Treatment Through Artificial Intelligence (pp. 1–27). Springer. DOI: 10.1007/978-3-031-67237-8_1

Gesimba, L. (2020). A Critical Analysis of the Cooperative Frameworks on Shared Natural Resources in the East African Community: a Case Study of Lake Victoria (Doctoral dissertation, University of Nairobi).

Gkotsis, P. K., Banti, D. C., Peleka, E. N., Zouboulis, A. I., & Samaras, P. E. (2014). Fouling issues in membrane bioreactors (MBRs) for wastewater treatment: Major mechanisms, prevention and control strategies. *Processes (Basel, Switzerland), 2*(4), 795–866. DOI: 10.3390/pr2040795

Greenpeace Africa. (2023). *Kenya's poisoned waters*. Retrieved from https://www.greenpeace.org/africa/en/

Hanna, N. K. (2010). Transforming government and building the information society: Challenges and opportunities for the developing world.

Hettiarachchi, H., Meegoda, J. N., & Ryu, S. (2018). Organic waste buyback as a viable method to enhance sustainable municipal solid waste management in developing countries. *International Journal of Environmental Research and Public Health, 15*(11), 2483. DOI: 10.3390/ijerph15112483 PMID: 30405058

Huang, B. C., He, C. S., Fan, N. S., Jin, R. C., & Yu, H. Q. (2020). Envisaging wastewater-to-energy practices for sustainable urban water pollution control: Current achievements and future prospects. *Renewable & Sustainable Energy Reviews*, *134*, 110134. DOI: 10.1016/j.rser.2020.110134

Johnson, M., & Lee, K. (2022). Advanced Filtration Technologies for Water Treatment. *Water Research*, *78*(4), 456–467.

Kamali, M., Suhas, D. P., Costa, M. E., Capela, I., & Aminabhavi, T. M. (2019). Sustainability considerations in membrane-based technologies for industrial effluents treatment. *Chemical Engineering Journal*, *368*, 474–494. DOI: 10.1016/j.cej.2019.02.075

Kamau, J., & Njoroge, W. (2024). AI-Driven Pollution Monitoring in Nairobi River. *Kenya Environmental Review*, *15*(1), 34–50.

Karanja, M., Wambui, N., & Njenga, M. (2020). The impact of the polluter pays principle on waste management in Kenya. *Environmental Economics and Policy Studies*, *22*(4), 789–805. DOI: 10.1007/s10018-020-00267-3

Kariuki, P., & Ngugi, J. (2018). The Water Act 2016: Implications for water resource management in Kenya. *Water Policy Journal*, *20*(2), 215–230. DOI: 10.2166/wp.2018.001

Kaza, S., Yao, L., Bhada-Tata, P., & Van Woerden, F. (2018). *What a Waste 2.0: A Global Snapshot of Solid Waste Management to 2050*. World Bank Publications. DOI: 10.1596/978-1-4648-1329-0

Kebaso, B. M. (2015). The effects of hydrological characteristics of the river Nyakomisaro on the water supply of Kisii municipality, Kenya (Doctoral dissertation, Kenyatta University).

Kenya Marine and Fisheries Research Institute. (2022). *Annual report 2022*. KMFRI.

Kimani, J., & Wanjiku, M. (2023). Biodegradable Materials and Their Impact on Aquatic Environments. *Journal of Environmental Protection*, *14*(2), 112–128.

Kimani, J., & Wanjiku, M. (2023). Biodegradable Materials and Their Impact on Aquatic Environments. *Journal of Environmental Protection*, *14*(2), 112–128.

Kitaka, N., Omondi, L. A., Mureithi, P. W., Bauer, A., Melcher, A., & Ssanyu, G. A. (2024). A critical review of biomonitoring in East African rivers: Fostering community-based collaboration for environmental change observation. *Frontiers in Water*, *6*, 1360941. DOI: 10.3389/frwa.2024.1360941

Kristian, A., Goh, T. S., Ramadan, A., Erica, A., & Sihotang, S. V. (2024). Application of ai in optimizing energy and resource management: Effectiveness of deep learning models. *International Transactions on Artificial Intelligence*, *2*(2), 99–105. DOI: 10.33050/italic.v2i2.530

Kumar, S., Pratap, B., Dubey, D., & Dutta, V. (2022). Integration of Constructed Wetland Technology as a Decentralised Wastewater Treatment Facility and Water Reuse in Agriculture. In *Environmental Studies and Climate Change* (pp. 565–582). CRC Press. DOI: 10.1201/9781003220824-39

Kung'u, M. N. (2023). Challenges and Possible Solutions for Effective Solid Waste Management in Githunguri Town, Kiambu County (Doctoral dissertation, University of Nairobi).

Kuppan, N., Padman, M., Mahadeva, M., Srinivasan, S., & Devarajan, R. (2024). *A comprehensive review of sustainable bioremediation techniques: Eco-friendly solutions for waste and pollution management.* Waste Management Bulletin.

Kurniawan, T. A., Maiurova, A., Kustikova, M., Bykovskaia, E., Othman, M., & Goh, H. H. (2022). Accelerating sustainability transition in St. Petersburg (Russia) through digitalisation-based circular economy in waste recycling industry: A strategy to promote carbon neutrality in the era of Industry 4.0. *Journal of Cleaner Production*, *363*, 132452. DOI: 10.1016/j.jclepro.2022.132452

Lieder, M., & Rashid, A. (2016). Towards circular economy implementation: A comprehensive review in the context of the manufacturing industry. *Journal of Cleaner Production*, *115*, 36–51. DOI: 10.1016/j.jclepro.2015.12.042

Livesley, S. J., McPherson, G. M., & Calfapietra, C. (2016). The urban forest and ecosystem services: Impacts on urban water, heat, and pollution cycles at the tree, street, and city scale. *Journal of Environmental Quality*, *45*(1), 119–124. DOI: 10.2134/jeq2015.11.0567 PMID: 26828167

Maalouf, A., & Mavropoulos, A. (2023). Re-assessing global municipal solid waste generation. *Waste Management & Research*, *41*(4), 936–947. DOI: 10.1177/0734242X221074116 PMID: 35075952

Meissner, D. (2019). Public-private partnership models for science, technology, and innovation cooperation. *Journal of the Knowledge Economy*, *10*(4), 1341–1361. DOI: 10.1007/s13132-015-0310-3

Millennium Ecosystem Assessment. (2005). *Ecosystems and human well-being: Synthesis*. Island Press.

Mironga, J. M. (2006). Degradation of wetland ecosystems: A case study of Kisii District, western Kenya. *Biodiversity (Nepean), 7*(3-4), 3–16. DOI: 10.1080/14888386.2006.9712806

Mogaka, E. (2022). Project Planning on Implementation of Solid Waste Management Practices in Kisii Central Sub-County, Kisii County, Kenya (Doctoral dissertation, University of Nairobi).

Mohamed, A. M. O., Mohamed, D., Fayad, A., & Al Nahyan, M. T. (2024). Enhancing decision making and decarbonation in environmental management: A review on the role of digital technologies. *Sustainability (Basel), 16*(16), 7156. DOI: 10.3390/su16167156

Momanyi, M. D. (2021). Land-use Transformation and Changes in Peri-urban Livelihoods in Kisii Municipality, Kisii County, Kenya (Doctoral dissertation, University of Nairobi).

Mongkolnchaiarunya, J. (2005). Promoting a community-based solid-waste management initiative in local government: Yala municipality, Thailand. *Habitat International, 29*(1), 27–40. DOI: 10.1016/S0197-3975(03)00060-2

Mor, S., & Ravindra, K. (2023). Municipal solid waste landfills in lower- and middle-income countries: Environmental impacts, challenges and sustainable management practices. *Process Safety and Environmental Protection, 174*, 510–530. DOI: 10.1016/j.psep.2023.04.014

Mosago, F. A. (2010). *Factors influencing solid waste management in Kisii Municipal Council.* University of Nairobi., https://erepository.uonbi.ac.ke/handle/11295/4938

Mosoti, R. D., Obed, N., Albert, G., Reuben, O., Paul, O., & Argwings, O. (2024). *Phytoplankton Diversity and Heavy Metal Accumulation: A Case of Suneka Wastewater Treatment Plant.*

Mungai, E. (2022). An Evaluation of the Effectiveness of Alternative Water Supply: A Case Study of Nairobi Water Central Region, Zone 1 (Doctoral dissertation, University of Nairobi).

Munir, M. T., Li, B., & Naqvi, M. (2023). Revolutionising municipal solid waste management (MSWM) with machine learning as a clean resource: Opportunities, challenges and solutions. *Fuel, 348*, 128548. DOI: 10.1016/j.fuel.2023.128548

Mutua, E., & Wambua, J. (2024). Overcoming Challenges in Waste Management: A Kenyan Perspective. *Journal of Environmental Policy, 17*(1), 45–60.

Mutua, E., & Wambua, J. (2024). Overcoming Challenges in Waste Management: A Kenyan Perspective. *Journal of Environmental Policy*, *17*(1), 45–60.

Mutua, J., Kariuki, P., & Ngugi, J. (2020). Kenya Vision 2030 and environmental sustainability. *Sustainable Development Review*, *28*(3), 345–359. DOI: 10.1002/sd.2045

Mwangi, A., & Otieno, D. (2023). Integrated Waste Management Strategies in Kenya. *Journal of Sustainable Development*, *11*(2), 78–92.

Mwangi, H., Otieno, P., & Omondi, R. (2020). Application of AI in monitoring urban river pollution in Nairobi. *Environmental Monitoring and Assessment*, *192*(5), 1–12. DOI: 10.1007/s10661-020-08311-5

Naftal, M. O., Mutua, B. K., & Moronge, J. M. (2023). Existing Governance Structures for Sustainable Solid Waste Management in Kisii Town, Kenya. *Water Technology*, *11*(2), 102–111.

National Environment Management Authority (NEMA). (2023). *Environmental best practices in waste management*. Retrieved from https://www.nema.go.ke

Ndegwa, S., & Karanja, T. (2023). Anaerobic Digestion and Pyrolysis: Waste to Energy Solutions. *Renewable Energy Journal*, *22*(4), 299–315.

Neene, V. (2017). Mobile GIS for enhanced property tax collection: a case of Lusaka province local authorities (Doctoral dissertation, The University of Zambia).

Njenga, M., Mutua, J., & Kariuki, P. (2021). National solid waste management strategy: Achievements and challenges. *Waste Management Journal*, *34*(1), 67–79. DOI: 10.1016/j.wasman.2021.01.012

Nowak, D. J., Hirabayashi, S., Bodine, A., & Greenfield, E. (2018). Tree and forest effects on air quality and human health in the United States. *Environmental Pollution*, *193*, 119–129. DOI: 10.1016/j.envpol.2014.05.028 PMID: 25016465

Nyamache, C. M. (2021). Challenges in the Use and Conservation of Urban Green Spaces: a Case of Kisii Municipality, Kisii County, Kenya (Doctoral dissertation, University of Nairobi).

Nyamache, T. J. (2018). The Effects of Solid Waste Dumping on Infrastructures and Human Health: Dandora Dump Site, Nairobi County (Doctoral dissertation, University of Nairobi).

Ochieng, P., & Mutiso, S. (2023). Bioremediation in Lake Victoria: Successes and Challenges. *African Journal of Environmental Science*, *12*(3), 210–225.

Odada, E. O., Olago, D. O., Kulindwa, K., Ntiba, M., & Wandiga, S. (2004). Mitigation of pollution in Lake Victoria, East Africa: Causal chain and policy options analyses. *Ambio, 33*(1-2), 13–23. DOI: 10.1579/0044-7447-33.1.13 PMID: 15083646

Odada, E. O., Olago, D. O., Kulindwa, K., Ntiba, M., & Wandiga, S. (2004). Mitigation of pollution in Lake Victoria, East Africa: Causal chain and policy options analyses. *Ambio, 33*(1-2), 13–23. DOI: 10.1579/0044-7447-33.1.13 PMID: 15083646

Odhiambo, L., & Achieng, M. (2024). Buffer Zones and Their Role in Pollution Control. *Environment Conservation Journal, 19*(1), 56–70.

Ogechi, B. O. I. (2023). *Influence of anthropogenic activities on Nyangongo wetland in Nyaribari Chache sub-county*. Kisii County.

Ogendi, G. M. (2022). Effects of Anthropogenic Activities on the Water Quality of River Nyakomisaro-Riana, Kisii, Kenya. *European Journal of Applied Sciences, 10*(5), 171–190.

Omweno, J., Opiyo, S., Omondi, A., & Zablon, W. (2021). Natural and anthropogenic changes threatening the ecological and limnological integrity of Lake Baringo, Kenya: A Review. Pan Africa Science Journal.

Ondemo, F., Getabu, M. A., Gichana, Z., & Omweno, J. O. (2022). Length-weight relationships (LWRs) and condition factor of seven fish species in River Nyangweta Tributary, Kenya. *Journal of Engineering Research and Sciences, 1*(3), 193–199. DOI: 10.55708/js0103020

Ondemo, F. M., Getabu, A., Gichana, Z., & Omweno, J. O. (2022). Length-weight relationships (LWRs) and condition factor of seven fish species in River Nyangweta Tributary, Kenya. *Journal of Engineering Research and Sciences, 1*(3), 193–199. DOI: 10.55708/js0103020

Oseko, M. B. (2023). Assessing Land Use Suitability in Relation to Ecologically Sensitive Areas-a Case of Kisii Central Ward in Kisii County (Doctoral dissertation, University of Nairobi).

Otieno, P., & Omondi, R. (2022). Localised waste management strategies in Nairobi and Kisumu. *Urban Environmental Studies, 15*(3), 45–60. DOI: 10.1007/s11252-022-01134-5

Otiso, K. M. (1993). Urban environmental problems: the case of solid waste pollution and management in Kisii Town, Kenya (Master's thesis, Ohio University).

Pataki, D. E., Carreiro, M. M., Cherrier, J., Grulke, N. E., Jennings, V., Pincetl, S., & Zipperer, W. C. (2011). Coupling biogeochemical cycles in urban environments: Ecosystem services, green solutions, and misconceptions. *Frontiers in Ecology and the Environment, 9*(1), 27–36. DOI: 10.1890/090220

Rahman, A., Ai Ping, T., Mubeen, S. K., Mahmud, I., & Abbasi, G. A. (2022). What influences home gardeners' food waste composting intention in high-rise buildings in DHAKA MEGACITY, BANGLADESH? An integrated model of TPB and DMP. *Sustainability (Basel), 14*(15), 9400. DOI: 10.3390/su14159400

Rahman, M. A., Moser, A., Gold, A., Rötzer, T., & Pauleit, S. (2015). Vertical air temperature gradients under the shade of two contrasting urban tree species during different types of summer days. *The Science of the Total Environment, 633*, 100–111. DOI: 10.1016/j.scitotenv.2018.03.168 PMID: 29573677

Rayori, D. M. (2023). Assessment of Efficiency of Wastewater Treatment Based on Physico-Chemical and Biological Parameters of Kisii Town Wastewater Treatment Plant, Kenya (Doctoral dissertation, Kisii University).

Ritchie, H., & Roser, M. (2021). Deforestation and forest loss. Our World in Data. https://ourworldindata.org/deforestation

Singh, A., Sawant, M., Kamble, S. J., Herlekar, M., Starkl, M., Aymerich, E., & Kazmi, A. (2019). Performance evaluation of a decentralised wastewater treatment system in India. *Environmental Science and Pollution Research International, 26*(21), 21172–21188. DOI: 10.1007/s11356-019-05444-z PMID: 31119547

Smith, J., & Brown, L. (2023). Bioremediation of Oil Spills: A Review. *Environmental Science Journal, 45*(2), 123–135.

Souch, C. A., & Souch, C. (1993). The effect of trees on summertime below canopy urban climates: A case study, Bloomington, Indiana. *Arboriculture & Urban Forestry, 19*(5), 303–312. DOI: 10.48044/jauf.1993.049

Thakur, T. K., Barya, M. P., Dutta, J., Mukherjee, P., Thakur, A., Swamy, S. L., & Anderson, J. T. (2023). Integrated phytobial remediation of dissolved pollutants from domestic wastewater through constructed wetlands: An interactive macrophyte-microbe-based green and low-cost decontamination technology with prospective resource recovery. *Water (Basel), 15*(22), 3877. DOI: 10.3390/w15223877

UN-Habitat. (2023). Kenya's Kisii Town validates draft solid waste management strategy. UN-Habitat. https://unhabitat.org/kenyas-kisii-town-validates-draft-solid-waste-management-strategy

United Nations Environment Programme. (2021). *Global Environment Outlook 6: Healthy Planet, Healthy People*. UNEP.

United Nations Environment Programme (UNEP). (2021). The sixth Global Environment Outlook (GEO) for Cities report. UN-Habitat. https://unhabitat.org/the-sixth-global-environment-outlook-geo-for-cities-report

United Nations Environment Programme (UNEP). (2023). *Harnessing data, awareness, and investment to tackle Africa's wastewater woes*. Retrieved from https://www.unep.org

United Nations Human Settlements Programme (UN-Habitat). (2022). World Cities Report 2022: Envisaging the Future of Cities. UN-Habitat. https://unhabitat.org/sites/default/files/2022/06/wcr_2022.pdf

United Nations Human Settlements Programme (UN-Habitat). (2024). World Cities Report 2024: Cities and Climate Action. UN-Habitat. https://unhabitat.org/world-cities-report-2024-cities-and-climate-action

Vymazal, J. (2011). Constructed wetlands for wastewater treatment: Five decades of experience. *Environmental Science & Technology*, *45*(1), 61–69. DOI: 10.1021/es101403q PMID: 20795704

Wachira, J. M. (2023). Molecular characterisation of denitrifying Bacteria and their potential in the reduction of nitrogenous Compounds In Lake Victoria, Kenya (Doctoral dissertation, UoEm).

Wambui, N., Kariuki, P., & Ngugi, J. (2019). Integrated legal approaches to water resource management in Kenya. *Journal of Environmental Law*, *31*(2), 123–140. DOI: 10.1093/jel/eqz011

Wang, X., & Zhang, Y. (2024). AI in Environmental Monitoring: Applications and Challenges. *Journal of Environmental Management*, *90*(1), 89–102.

Wang, X., & Zhang, Y. (2024). AI in Environmental Monitoring: Applications and Challenges. Journal of Environmental Management, 90(1), 89–102. *Waste Management & Research*, *41*, 936–947.

World Bank. (2019). *Innovative waste management practices in developing countries*. World Bank Publications.

World Health Organisation. (2016). Health as the pulse of the new urban agenda: United Nations conference on housing and sustainable urban development, Quito, October 2016.

Chapter 3
The Immigrant Phenomenon Sustainable Development:
Strategies, Challenges, and Opportunities

Murat Şengöz
http://orcid.org/0000-0001-6597-0161
Independent Researcher, Turkey

ABSTRACT

This paper explores sustainable development with a particular focus on the immigration and integration phenomena, emphasizing the integration of immigrants as a key component of growth strategies. In the face of increasing urbanization and demographic shifts, incorporating immigrants into development plans is essential for fostering economic vitality and social cohesion. The study examines the multifaceted contributions of immigrants to development, including their impact on labor markets, cultural diversity, and economic innovation. By analyzing successful case studies and current policies, the paper identifies best practices and strategies for integrating immigrant populations into sustainable development frameworks. Additionally, it highlights challenges such as socio-economic barriers and discrimination, offering recommendations to improve integration efforts. Ultimately, this research advocates for a holistic development approach that leverages the diverse skills and perspectives of immigrants to enhance resilience and sustainability.

DOI: 10.4018/979-8-2600-3325-8.ch003

INTRODUCTION

The main objective of this research is to examine how integrating immigrants into growth strategies can promote sustainable development. As regions experience increasing urbanisation and significant demographic shifts, effectively incorporating immigrants into development frameworks has become essential for achieving balanced, robust growth. This study investigates the multifaceted contributions of immigrants to development, such as their impact on labour markets, cultural diversity, and economic innovation. By analysing the topic effectively, the research aims to identify effective practices and propose strategies to maximise immigrants' potential in the context of sustainable development.

To meet these goals, the study employs philosophical methods and a comprehensive literature review, including academic articles and policy documents, to assess the effectiveness of national and local policies in supporting immigrant integration and fostering economic growth. In this context, the concept of immigration derives from the Latin word "immigrare," meaning "to move into." Beyond its etymology, immigration represents not only physical relocation but also the transmission of identities, skills, and cultural heritages into a new social and spatial context. Philosophically, immigration raises critical questions about the permeability of borders, the ethics of inclusion, and the human right to mobility, challenging traditional notions of sovereignty and belonging (Kymlicka, 2018).

In this respect, to ensure clarity, key terms are defined. Sustainable development refers to a holistic approach to growth that balances economic, social, and environmental objectives, ensuring long-term resilience and adaptability. Immigrants are individuals who relocate for reasons such as work, education, or family reunification, contributing to the labour market and enriching cultural diversity. The term "integration" stems from the Latin "integrare," meaning "to make whole." Conceptually, integration encompasses not only the acceptance of immigrants but also their active participation in the host community's economic, social, and cultural systems. Focusing on reciprocity and interaction, integration carries profound ethical implications. It underscores the importance of mutual recognition and the dismantling of structural barriers, aligning with principles of justice and equity (Laurence, 2020).

Growth strategies are policies and plans designed to drive economic development, enhance living standards, and manage spatial planning in specific areas. Sustainable development, a cornerstone of this research, gained prominence with the 1987 Brundtland Report, defining it as meeting "the needs of the present without compromising the ability of future generations to meet their own needs." Philosophically, it emphasises intergenerational justice and the ethical imperative to harmonise economic growth with ecological and social responsibility (World Commission on Environment and Development, 1987).

In this respect, this research is significant for providing insights to guide policies and practices for integrating immigrants into development, as effective immigrant integration can play a pivotal role in advancing sustainable growth. By showcasing rationale approaches and identifying obstacles, this study offers valuable recommendations for policymakers, urban planners, and community organisations working toward inclusive and resilient development.

The paper is structured to provide a comprehensive overview of sustainable development, discussing its definition, objectives, and the interplay of economic, social, and environmental factors. It highlights the role of immigrants in economic growth and emphasises the benefits of their integration. The study explores successful integration strategies, including policies, programs, and initiatives that facilitate immigrant involvement in development, while also addressing barriers such as discrimination and limited access to resources. Existing policies and frameworks are evaluated to identify best practices and international examples, supported by case studies and success stories from diverse regions. The paper concludes by summarising key findings and offering practical recommendations to improve immigrant integration and promote sustainable growth, with references to the sources used throughout. By systematically addressing these areas, the research not only contributes to understanding immigrant integration but also reaffirms the ethical and practical imperatives of sustainable development in a rapidly evolving global landscape.

SUSTAINABLE DEVELOPMENT: CONCEPTS AND OBJECTIVES

Sustainable development represents a holistic strategy aimed at achieving balanced, long-term growth by harmonising economic, social, and environmental objectives. The United Nations (2015) defines sustainable development as a framework that aligns economic progress with social equity and environmental preservation, fostering conditions for communities to thrive while safeguarding resources for future generations. This framework integrates the three pillars—economic, social, and environmental sustainability—into a single cohesive approach, ensuring that no dimension is prioritised at the expense of the others.

From a doctrinal perspective, sustainable development is often framed in terms of "weak" versus "strong" sustainability. Weak sustainability assumes that human capital can substitute for natural capital, while strong sustainability asserts that certain environmental resources are non-substitutable and must be preserved in their own right. For example, strong sustainability principles are applied in the protection of biodiversity, where the loss of species cannot be offset by technological innovation or economic growth, a concept that is central to international agreements like the Convention on Biological Diversity.

Economic Sustainability emphasises the promotion of inclusive and resilient economic growth. This entails diversifying economic activities, fostering innovation, and ensuring equitable distribution of economic benefits (World Bank, 2020). An example of economic sustainability is the "circular economy" model, which encourages the reuse of materials and resources, reducing waste and reliance on finite resources. Countries like the Netherlands have pioneered circular economy practices, where industries such as construction and agriculture actively minimise waste and maximise resource efficiency (European Commission, 2015). Strengthening economic resilience can involve supporting small and medium-sized enterprises (SMEs) and investing in local infrastructure, both of which help regions adapt to economic fluctuations and global shifts (Porter, 1998). For instance, in regions affected by economic shocks, the development of resilient supply chains and diversified local economies—supported by SMEs—can provide buffers against global market volatility, thus ensuring long-term economic sustainability (UNDP, 2020).

Environmental Sustainability centres on conserving natural resources and minimising the environmental footprint of human activities. Strategies include mitigating climate change, reducing pollution, and protecting biodiversity (MEA, 2005). For example, the "green economy" concept, as outlined by the United Nations Environment Programme (UNEP), promotes sustainable practices across industries, emphasising energy efficiency, waste reduction, and the transition to renewable energy sources (UNEP, 2011). Integrating sustainability into land-use planning, resource management, and urban development is vital to effective environmental stewardship (Pretty, 2003). The "smart cities" approach represents an innovative model for urban sustainability, utilising technology and data analytics to optimise resource use, improve energy efficiency, and reduce pollution, as seen in cities like Barcelona and Singapore (Geertman, 2020).

Social Sustainability prioritises equity and social cohesion by addressing inequalities and improving the overall quality of life. This includes providing access to essential services such as education, healthcare, and housing while fostering community engagement (Dempsey, Bramley, Power, & Brown, 2011). A concept aligned with social sustainability is "just sustainability," which emphasises integrating social justice into environmental and economic decision-making. For example, in South Africa, the government's focus on equitable land distribution and access to resources for historically disadvantaged communities exemplifies this approach (Sachs, 2015). Building inclusive communities where individuals from all backgrounds have equal opportunities to participate and succeed is a critical aspect of enhancing social sustainability (Haughton & Hunter, 1994). One clear doctrinal example is the concept of "inclusive growth," which seeks to ensure that the benefits of economic growth are widely distributed, particularly among marginalised groups such as low-income communities and immigrants (OECD, 2018).

A key element of sustainable development is spatial planning, which involves managing and organising land use to meet diverse needs while balancing competing priorities. This concept draws heavily on the theory of "spatial justice," which explores how equitable distribution of resources across space can reduce socio-economic inequalities (Soja, 2010). Spatial planning helps ensure efficient land use, supports sustainable growth, and safeguards natural and cultural heritage (Faludi, 2000). Effective spatial planning requires collaborative efforts involving government agencies, private stakeholders, and local communities to design and implement strategies that align with development goals (Healey, 2006). For instance, in urban planning, participatory approaches have been shown to enhance the legitimacy and effectiveness of development projects, as seen in the "Participatory Budgeting" model, which gives communities a say in how public funds are allocated for local development (Wampler, 2012).

The principles of sustainable development are increasingly pertinent due to challenges such as rapid urbanisation, demographic changes, and environmental pressures. For example, the rise of megacities, defined as urban areas with populations exceeding 10 million, poses significant challenges for sustainability due to the strain on infrastructure and natural resources. Urban sustainability initiatives, such as those implemented in Tokyo and Mexico City, focus on managing urban sprawl, reducing emissions, and enhancing public transport to reduce environmental impact (UN-Habitat, 2019). Integrating immigrants into development strategies is pivotal in addressing these challenges. Immigrants bring valuable contributions to growth through their diverse skills, cultural insights, and entrepreneurial initiatives (OECD, 2018). In countries like Canada and Germany, immigrants have significantly contributed to economic growth through entrepreneurship, with immigrant-founded businesses accounting for 30% of all new businesses in Canada (Statistics Canada, 2020). Designing and executing strategies to integrate immigrants effectively can strengthen the capacity to achieve sustainable development while meeting the diverse needs of the population. Furthermore, focusing on immigrant integration helps to combat demographic challenges such as ageing populations in developed countries, ensuring that regions have the workforce needed for long-term growth and sustainability (OECD, 2024).

THE ROLE OF IMMIGRANTS IN SUSTAINABLE DEVELOPMENT

Immigrants play a key role in advancing sustainable territorial development by driving economic growth, enhancing cultural diversity, and fostering social cohesion. Their involvement in development strategies is crucial for addressing shifting demographic and economic landscapes. Recognising their contributions and effectively incorporating them into development plans can significantly bolster efforts to achieve sustainable growth.

Economically, immigrants contribute in various impactful ways. For example, in the European Union, immigrants represent approximately 5.4% of the total workforce, yet they account for 10% of the self-employed population (Eurostat, 2020). They address labour shortages in sectors such as healthcare, construction, and technology, particularly in areas with pronounced skill gaps (OECD, 2017). In the U.S., immigrants make up 17% of the healthcare workforce, including essential roles in nursing, medical technology, and eldercare, sectors crucial for ageing populations. Many immigrants also engage in entrepreneurial activities, founding businesses that generate employment and stimulate local economies (Wauters & Lambrecht, 2008). A study by the National Bureau of Economic Research (2019) shows that immigrant-owned businesses in the U.S. alone create over 1.5 million jobs annually, contributing significantly to local job growth. Research indicates that immigrant entrepreneurs often introduce innovative goods and services, boosting competitiveness and economic vitality (Portes & Rumbaut, 2014). In Canada, immigrant entrepreneurs are responsible for starting 30% of all new businesses, despite making up only 21% of the population (Statistics Canada, 2020). Beyond creating jobs, immigrants strengthen economic resilience in the long term by diversifying the labour force and increasing consumer demand (Perkins, 2017). For instance, immigrants' economic contributions in the U.S. led to a 9% increase in GDP between 2010 and 2020, due to their role in expanding the workforce and stimulating consumer spending (OECD, 2021).

Culturally, immigrants bring new perspectives, traditions, and practices, enriching the communities they join (Vertovec, 2007). A study by the McKinsey Global Institute (2017) found that cultural diversity led to a 7-10% increase in innovation output across firms in Europe and North America, particularly in industries such as technology and the creative arts. This cultural diversity encourages intercultural dialogue and mutual understanding, contributing to greater social cohesion. Immigrants enhance the cultural vibrancy of urban areas, improving the quality of life and making regions more appealing to tourists and potential new residents (Clemens & Hunt, 2017). In cities like New York and London, cultural tourism—often fueled by immigrant communities—accounts for over $50 billion in annual revenue, further demonstrating the economic value of cultural diversity (UNWTO, 2019). Demographically, immigrants help address challenges such as population ageing by contributing to a younger and more dynamic workforce (Dustmann & Frattini, 2014). In Japan, where the population is ageing rapidly, immigrant workers in their

20s and 30s make up 15% of the total workforce, significantly alleviating pressures on social security systems (Japan Ministry of Health, 2020).

However, immigrants often face obstacles that limit their full participation in development. Language barriers, discrimination, and restricted access to education and training can hinder their integration into the labour market and broader community life (Chiswick & Miller, 2015). According to the OECD, immigrants with limited language proficiency earn, on average, 20% less than native-born workers, illustrating the economic disadvantage caused by language barriers (OECD, 2018). Various strategies have been implemented to address these challenges, such as language and vocational training programs, anti-discrimination measures, and social inclusion initiatives (Bendel, 2020). For instance, Germany's integration courses, which include language instruction and job market orientation, have helped over 500,000 immigrants annually gain full-time employment since their introduction in 2005 (German Federal Office for Migration and Refugees, 2020). Successful integration requires a coordinated effort among government agencies, local communities, and private-sector partners (Haas, 2018).

Case studies illustrate effective approaches to immigrant integration. For instance, "Integration through Education" programs seek to improve educational outcomes for immigrant children and enhance their career opportunities (Pfeiffer & Nentwig, 2019). In Sweden, over 90% of immigrant students who participated in such programs graduated from high school, compared to only 60% of non-participating immigrant students (Swedish Ministry of Education, 2018). Similarly, initiatives that support immigrant entrepreneurship have had positive effects on local economic growth and job creation (Alesina & La Ferrara, 2005). For example, immigrant-run startups in California generate an estimated $4 billion in annual revenue, directly impacting local economies and creating thousands of new jobs (California State Government Report, 2020).

In conclusion, immigrants are a valuable resource for sustainable territorial development. Their contributions to the economy, cultural enrichment, and their potential to alleviate demographic challenges make them indispensable to achieving balanced, resilient growth. According to a 2020 report by the International Migration Organisation (IMO), if immigrant integration strategies are enhanced, global GDP could increase by 2-3% by 2030, underscoring the economic importance of inclusive policies. By continuing to develop and enhance integration strategies, their positive impacts on territorial development objectives can be further amplified.

SUCCESSFUL INTEGRATION STRATEGIES AND POLICIES

Effectively integrating immigrants is essential for maximising their contributions to development while fostering social cohesion. Numerous successful strategies and policies have been implemented to integrate immigrants into society and the economy. This section evaluates these approaches, highlighting their impact and effectiveness in promoting immigrant integration.

Education is a primary focus in integration efforts, as it plays a critical role in fostering long-term success for immigrant children and youth. For instance, programs such as "Integration through Education" offer specialised support, including language instruction, mentoring, and academic assistance, tailored to immigrant students (Pfeiffer & Nentwig, 2019). These initiatives aim to close educational gaps, improve academic performance, and enhance future employment opportunities for immigrant children (Bendel, 2020).

Facilitating access to employment and vocational training is another cornerstone of integration policies. "Competence Centres for Integration" provide immigrants with vocational training and job placement services, helping them develop the skills needed for success in the local labour market (Schmidt & Bader, 2018). Additionally, "Integration Funds" support programs that aid in the recognition of foreign qualifications, enhancing the employability of immigrants (Bendel, 2020).

Addressing discrimination is vital for achieving successful integration. Several anti-discrimination measures, such as "Equal Treatment Acts," ban discrimination based on nationality, ethnicity, and religion while offering legal protections for affected individuals (OECD, 2018). Public awareness campaigns promoting diversity and inclusion have also been instrumental in reducing prejudice and fostering a more inclusive society (Haas, 2018).

Community engagement and social inclusion are crucial for building strong ties between immigrants and local residents. Initiatives that encourage intercultural dialogue and community interaction are supported. Programs like "Integration through Sport" and "Cultural Exchange Projects" can create opportunities for meaningful interactions, promoting mutual understanding and collaboration. These efforts help immigrants feel a sense of belonging and strengthen community relationships.

Several case studies showcase successful integration models. For example, integration models facilitating collaboration among local authorities, businesses, and non-governmental organisations to support immigrant entrepreneurs have positively impacted local economic growth and job creation (Alesina & La Ferrara, 2005). Similarly, "Language Academies" offering intensive language training and cultural orientation equip immigrants with the tools needed for successful integration (Clemens & Hunt, 2017).

In summary, integration policies and strategies have significantly improved immigrants' inclusion in society and the economy. By prioritising education, employment, anti-discrimination measures, and community engagement, these initiatives have strengthened integration outcomes. Continued investment and refinement of these strategies are vital to supporting sustainable development and promoting social cohesion.

CHALLENGES AND BARRIERS TO IMMIGRANT INTEGRATION

Although significant progress has been made in integrating immigrants, various challenges and obstacles remain that can hinder their successful inclusion into society. Identifying and understanding these barriers is crucial for crafting effective strategies to overcome them and enhance integration outcomes.

Language proficiency is a key factor in successful integration. Many immigrants face difficulties in mastering the language, which can obstruct their access to education, employment, and social services (Wächter, 2021). Language barriers often restrict job prospects and complicate communication with public institutions and the wider community (Chiswick & Miller, 2015). Providing comprehensive language training programs and support services is essential to mitigate these challenges and facilitate integration (OECD, 2017).

In the labour market, immigrants frequently encounter obstacles such as difficulty securing employment and underemployment relative to their skills and qualifications. Problems with the recognition of foreign credentials and prior work experience often result in a mismatch between immigrants' abilities and available job opportunities (Bendel, 2020). Furthermore, discriminatory hiring practices can exacerbate employment issues (Schmidt & Bader, 2018). Policies that improve the recognition of foreign qualifications and offer targeted support for job seekers are necessary to address these problems (Perkins, 2017).

Discrimination and social exclusion are notable barriers to integration. Immigrants often experience prejudice and xenophobia, leading to social isolation and limited access to resources and opportunities. This exclusion can negatively impact mental health and restrict their ability to engage fully in community life (Vertovec, 2007). Combating discrimination through anti-discrimination legislation, public awareness initiatives, and community engagement programs is vital for fostering social inclusion (Haas, 2018).

Access to essential services, such as healthcare, education, and social welfare, poses another critical challenge. Immigrants may struggle with navigating the complex public service system, particularly if they lack adequate language skills or are unfamiliar with bureaucratic processes (Chiswick & Miller, 2015). Additionally, disparities in the quality of services available to immigrants compared to those available to native-born residents may persist (Dustmann & Frattini, 2014). Ensuring equitable access to services and offering tailored support for immigrants can help address these inequities (Bendel, 2020).

Cultural differences and social norms can also complicate integration. Adapting to new cultural practices and societal expectations may be challenging for immigrants, affecting their ability to integrate and develop a sense of belonging (Wauters & Lambrecht, 2008). Initiatives that promote intercultural dialogue and understanding, alongside programs encouraging community participation, can help bridge cultural divides and enhance social cohesion.

In conclusion, despite substantial progress in integrating immigrants, addressing the persistent challenges and barriers is essential to achieving comprehensive, lasting integration. By focusing on language development, expanding employment opportunities, combating discrimination, improving service access, and fostering cultural integration, efforts to support immigrant communities and build a more inclusive society can be strengthened.

RECOMMENDATIONS FOR ENHANCING IMMIGRANT INTEGRATION

To enhance immigrant integration and maximise its benefits for both immigrants and the host society, a range of strategies and policies can be adopted. These recommendations aim to address the challenges and barriers highlighted earlier and ensure more effective integration outcomes.

A key factor in successful integration is language proficiency. Expanding and improving language training programs can greatly enhance immigrants' ability to engage in the labour market and participate in community life. These programs should be widely accessible and tailored to different proficiency levels and age groups (OECD, 2017). Integrating language instruction with practical skills training—such as job-specific vocabulary and communication skills—can further boost their effectiveness (Wächter, 2021).

Tackling employment challenges requires a comprehensive approach. Efforts should continue to support measures that facilitate the recognition of foreign qualifications and prior work experience. Streamlining pathways for credential recognition and providing targeted job placement services can help immigrants capitalise on their skills and expertise in the local job market (Bendel, 2020). Mentorship programs and networking opportunities for immigrant professionals should also be developed to connect them with potential employers and support their integration into their respective fields (Perkins, 2017).

Addressing discrimination is vital for building a more inclusive society. Strengthening anti-discrimination laws and enforcement mechanisms, alongside public awareness campaigns, can help combat prejudice and bias. Educational initiatives that promote diversity and inclusion are equally important for changing public attitudes and reducing social exclusion (Haas, 2018). Furthermore, readily available support services, such as legal assistance and counselling for victims of discrimination, are essential (OECD, 2018).

Ensuring equitable access to essential services is another critical aspect of integration. The focus should be on reducing barriers to healthcare, education, and social welfare for immigrants. Simplifying administrative procedures, providing multilingual support, and offering customised services can help immigrants navigate public systems more effectively (Dustmann & Frattini, 2014). Community-based organisations can play a pivotal role in delivering these services and advocating for immigrants' needs (Schmidt & Bader, 2018).

Promoting community connections and social integration is crucial for fostering a sense of belonging among immigrants. Investments in programs that encourage intercultural dialogue and collaboration, such as community events, cultural exchange initiatives, and joint projects between immigrant and native populations, can help bridge cultural divides. Additionally, involving immigrants in local decision-making and community development efforts can enhance their engagement and integration (Wauters & Lambrecht, 2008).

Learning from successful integration models can offer valuable guidance for improving practices. For instance, adopting insights from the "Salzburg Integration Model" and other effective initiatives can refine integration strategies (Alesina & La Ferrara, 2005). Evaluating and adapting successful approaches from other regions or countries can yield more innovative and effective solutions to integration challenges.

In summary, implementing these recommendations can lead to a stronger approach to integrating immigrants. Focusing on language acquisition, improving employment opportunities, combatting discrimination, expanding access to services, fostering community engagement, and drawing from successful models are all essential steps toward creating a more inclusive and sustainable integration process.

EVALUATION OF INTEGRATION POLICIES: MEASURING SUCCESS AND IMPACT

Evaluating the effectiveness of integration policies is crucial to ensure they achieve their goals and contribute to sustainable development. This section examines the methods and criteria used to assess the success and impact of integration policies, focusing on the evaluation processes, performance metrics, and outcomes.

The evaluation of integration policies considers various criteria, including economic, social, and educational outcomes. Economic success is often measured by analysing employment rates, income levels, and entrepreneurial activity among immigrants (Dustmann & Frattini, 2014). Social outcomes are assessed using indicators such as social cohesion, community involvement, and experiences with discrimination. Educational outcomes are evaluated through metrics such as academic performance, language skills, and school attendance rates among immigrant students (OECD, 2017).

Several methods and tools are used to assess the effectiveness of integration policies. Quantitative methods, such as surveys and statistical analysis, are commonly used to measure economic and social indicators (Bendel, 2020). For example, national surveys and labour market data provide insights into employment trends and income levels among immigrants (Schmidt & Bader, 2018). Qualitative methods, such as interviews and focus groups, offer a deeper understanding of the personal experiences and challenges immigrants face (Vertovec, 2007). A combination of both quantitative and qualitative approaches can offer a more comprehensive evaluation of policy outcomes (Haas, 2018).

Key performance indicators for evaluating integration policies include employment rates, educational achievement, and levels of social inclusion. Employment metrics may involve analysing job placement rates, wage increases, and the occupational status of immigrants (Perkins, 2017). Educational indicators assess improvements in language proficiency, school performance, and graduation rates among immigrant students (Pfeiffer & Nentwig, 2019). Social inclusion metrics evaluate participation in community activities, social integration experiences, and perceptions of discrimination (Chiswick & Miller, 2015).

Examining case studies of successful integration programs can provide valuable insights into effective evaluation practices. For instance, the "Vienna Language Academy" has been assessed based on its impact on language skills and educational outcomes for immigrant students (Clemens & Hunt, 2017). Similarly, the "Salzburg Integration Model" has been evaluated for its effectiveness in supporting immigrant entrepreneurs and promoting local economic development (Alesina & La Ferrara, 2005). These case studies underscore the importance of using both quantitative and qualitative data to evaluate the success of integration policies.

Challenges in policy evaluation can arise due to various factors. One challenge is the availability and accuracy of data, as data collection methods may not fully capture all aspects of integration outcomes (Dustmann & Frattini, 2014). Furthermore, attributing specific outcomes directly to integration policies can be difficult due to complex interactions among various factors (OECD, 2017). Addressing these challenges requires ongoing improvements in data collection techniques and evaluation frameworks.

Effective evaluation of integration policies is vital for understanding their impact and guiding future improvements. By combining quantitative and qualitative methods and focusing on key performance metrics, a more robust assessment of integration efforts' success can be achieved, enabling informed decisions to enhance policy effectiveness. Continuous evaluation and adaptation of policies will contribute to more successful and sustainable immigrant integration.

FUTURE DIRECTIONS AND POLICY IMPLICATIONS

As the approach to immigrant integration continues to evolve, it is essential to consider future directions and the broader implications for policy development. This section explores potential areas for growth, identifies emerging trends, and provides recommendations to enhance integration strategies to address current and future challenges.

The landscape of immigration is continually changing, influenced by global dynamics and shifting demographics. Future trends include increased migration flows from regions affected by conflict and climate change, as well as the rising prominence of skilled migration (Haas, 2018). It is crucial to anticipate these trends and adapt integration policies to accommodate the diverse needs of new immigrant populations. Emphasising flexibility and adaptability in policy frameworks will be crucial for effectively managing these changes (OECD, 2017).

Technology and innovation offer new opportunities to improve integration processes. Digital platforms can facilitate language learning, job matching, and access to essential services for immigrants (Dustmann & Frattini, 2014). For instance, online language courses and mobile applications can provide flexible learning options, while data-driven tools can enhance job placement and skills matching (Chiswick & Miller, 2015). Integrating technology into integration efforts can help address logistical challenges and improve overall efficiency.

Immigration is a global issue that requires multilateral cooperation. Countries can benefit from increased collaboration with other nations and international organisations to share best practices, coordinate policies, and address cross-border challenges (Schmidt & Bader, 2018). Participating in international forums and networks focused on migration can provide valuable insights and strengthen integration strategies through collaborative efforts and knowledge exchange (OECD, 2018).

Inclusive policy development involves engaging various stakeholders, including immigrants, local communities, and policymakers, in the design and implementation of integration strategies. Ensuring that policies reflect the diverse perspectives and needs of all stakeholders can enhance their effectiveness and acceptance (Vertovec, 2007). Regular consultations and feedback mechanisms can help identify gaps and opportunities for improvement, fostering a more inclusive and participatory approach to policy-making (Wächter, 2021).

Anticipating and preparing for future challenges is essential for maintaining effective integration policies. This includes addressing potential economic impacts, social cohesion issues, and evolving demographic patterns. Developing robust contingency plans and conducting regular policy evaluations can help ensure that integration strategies remain relevant and effective amid changing conditions (Haas, 2018). Additionally, investing in research and data collection will provide the necessary evidence base for informed decision-making and policy adjustments.

Looking ahead, innovation, international collaboration, and prioritising inclusivity in integration policies will be essential. By focusing on emerging trends, leveraging technology, and addressing future challenges, countries can enhance their integration efforts and contribute to a more cohesive and sustainable society. Proactive and adaptive policy approaches will be key to successfully managing immigration and ensuring positive outcomes for both immigrants and the host community.

COMPARATIVE ANALYSIS: INTEGRATION POLICIES IN HUNGARY, CANADA, THE UNITED KINGDOM, FRANCE, BELGIUM, AND GERMANY

The integration of immigrants reflects broader philosophical debates over belonging, identity, and justice, with countries such as Hungary, Canada, the United Kingdom (UK), France, Belgium, and Germany offering diverse approaches. These policies are not merely technical solutions but manifestations of national histories, ideologies, and priorities, revealing how each society conceptualises membership within its borders. To facilitate a clearer comparison, integration policies are categorised under three main dimensions: language acquisition, economic inclusion, and social cohesion. This structure helps highlight both the practical measures and underlying ideologies shaping each country's approach.

Hungary's approach emphasises cultural homogeneity, reflecting its nationalistic framework. While language acquisition is prioritised in theory, programs are underfunded and poorly institutionalised. Employment support, particularly in recognising foreign qualifications, is limited, relegating immigrants to precarious labour market positions. Social inclusion measures are minimal, revealing a policy logic that prioritises restriction over engagement. This raises philosophical questions about the ethics of exclusion and the permeability of borders in modern nation-states. Hungary's restrictive model also has significant economic implications, as it fails to fully harness immigrants' potential to address labour shortages. Hungary's restrictive model underscores the challenges of reconciling national identity with the realities of global migration.

In contrast, Canada's integration policies embrace multiculturalism, reflecting its self-conception as a nation of immigrants. Programs like the "Settlement Program" provide tailored support for language learning, employment, and social integration (IRCC, 2020). Beyond practical measures, Canada's ethos of pluralism recognises diversity as a societal asset (Kymlicka, 2018). However, tensions persist between multiculturalism and pressures for assimilation, especially regarding shared values and national identity. Critics argue that while Canada promotes diversity, immigrant communities sometimes face pressure to conform to mainstream values, which can undermine the principle of multiculturalism. Canada's approach illustrates the potential of inclusivity but also highlights the enduring challenge of balancing unity and diversity.

The UK balances multicultural principles with pragmatic integration measures. Language acquisition is facilitated through English for Speakers of Other Languages (ESOL) programs, and employment policies aim to address immigrant barriers, although structural inequalities persist (OECD, 2020). Social inclusion efforts focus on community engagement but fail to address systemic exclusion fully (Modood, 2019). While ESOL programs have expanded, their effectiveness remains contingent on local resources and the ability to overcome regional disparities. The UK's integration policies reflect an ongoing negotiation between liberal ideals of pluralism and structural realities of inequality.

France adopts an assimilationist model, rooted in the republican ideal of universalism. Programs like the "Contrat d'Intégration Républicaine" mandate language and civic education courses to align immigrants with national values (OECD, 2017). However, this emphasis on uniformity often clashes with the realities of diversity, leading to critiques of systemic exclusion (Laurence, 2020). The French model's focus on assimilation has been criticised for overlooking immigrants' cultural and religious identities, leading to tensions between national unity and cultural diversity. France's model raises fundamental questions about the tension between equality as sameness and equality as recognition of difference.

Belgium's decentralised approach highlights the interplay between regional autonomy and national cohesion. Language programs like "Inburgering" and employment support initiatives vary across regions, enabling tailored approaches to local contexts (OECD, 2017). Social inclusion emphasises community engagement and fosters grassroots integration (Witte, 2019). This decentralisation allows for flexibility but also leads to inconsistencies across regions, particularly in terms of the availability and quality of integration services. However, the fragmented approach risks uneven outcomes, raising questions about the balance between centralisation and adaptability. Belgium's policies underline the advantages and challenges of aligning localised flexibility with national goals.

Germany's integration model is marked by its comprehensiveness. Programs like the "Integrationsgesetz" (Integration Act) and "Integrationskurse" (integration courses) combine language acquisition with cultural orientation, offering a holistic framework (Schmidt & Bader, 2018). Employment support includes systematic recognition of foreign qualifications, while robust social inclusion measures, such as anti-discrimination campaigns, foster cohesion (Dustmann & Frattini, 2014; OECD, 2018). Germany's emphasis on comprehensive integration programs not only addresses the immediate needs of immigrants but also promotes long-term social cohesion by focusing on shared values and anti-discrimination efforts. Germany's approach demonstrates the importance of combining practical support with measures to promote mutual accommodation and cohesion.

Across these countries, integration policies can be understood as negotiations between three conceptual poles: language acquisition as a gateway to participation, economic inclusion as a foundation for autonomy, and social cohesion as the fabric of belonging. Each country's policy emphasis reflects its underlying ideological stance—whether it be assimilationist, multicultural, or something in between. While all countries address these dimensions, their emphases reveal distinct ideological and structural tendencies. Language acquisition reflects the dual role of language as a practical necessity and a symbolic marker of belonging. Employment policies highlight the tension between recognising immigrants' skills and integrating them into local labour markets, with Germany and Canada offering structured frameworks in contrast to Hungary's neglect. Social inclusion efforts vary significantly, with Canada and Germany prioritising anti-discrimination and dialogue, while Hungary lags in fostering community integration.

This comparative analysis invites reflection on integration as a political and moral project, confronting the paradox of difference and unity: how to accommodate plural identities within a shared societal framework. As global migration continues to reshape societies, the evolution of integration policies will be crucial in determining the future of social cohesion and economic growth. The divergent approaches reflect not only practical constraints but also deeply held beliefs about justice, identity, and community. These policies are not static but evolving processes, shaping and being shaped by broader societal transformations.

CULTURAL INTEGRATION: UNDERSTANDING KEY CONCEPTS AND THEIR APPLICATION

Understanding the concepts of cultural integration and acculturation is crucial for evaluating the success of immigration policies. This section delves into these concepts, highlighting their differences and the implications they have for integration strategies.

Cultural Integration refers to the process in which immigrants join the host society while preserving their cultural identity. It involves adjustments from both the immigrants and the host society to ensure harmonious coexistence. The focus of integration is on mutual adaptation, enabling immigrants to maintain their cultural heritage while fully participating in societal structures. This approach fosters coexistence without requiring immigrants to relinquish their cultural backgrounds (Berry, 1997).

In contrast, cultural acculturation involves the interaction between individuals from different cultural backgrounds, leading to mutual adaptation and influence. Unlike assimilation, which typically entails the full adoption of the host culture, acculturation allows for a two-way exchange where both immigrants and the host society shape each other's cultural values and practices (Berry, 1997). Acculturation emphasises the process of adjustment while still preserving aspects of one's original culture.

Language acquisition plays a key role in both integration and acculturation strategies. Programs such as language courses help immigrants communicate effectively and fully engage with the host society. This aligns with acculturation by facilitating immigrants' adaptation while enabling them to retain their cultural identities. Multicultural education and language support services further reflect an integration strategy, promoting language proficiency while supporting cultural diversity (Haas, 2018).

Employment support policies aim to integrate immigrants into the labour market by recognising foreign qualifications and offering vocational training. These measures not only support the economic integration of immigrants but also respect their cultural backgrounds. By helping immigrants adjust to new economic settings, these policies align with acculturation goals, allowing them to become part of the economic system without abandoning their cultural identities (Dustmann & Frattini, 2014).

Social inclusion policies focus on promoting intercultural dialogue and reducing discrimination, reflecting an integrationist perspective. These policies encourage both immigrants and the host society to adapt to one another, fostering immigrants' active participation in community life while respecting cultural differences (Haas, 2018). This approach contrasts with a more assimilationist stance by promoting the preservation of minority cultures and advancing a more inclusive societal framework.

A significant challenge for host countries is finding the right balance between integration and acculturation objectives. While language skills and economic participation are vital, policies must also focus on cultural preservation and mutual respect. Failing to consider cultural preservation when emphasising integration can lead to tensions and challenges in maintaining cultural identities. Conversely, prioritising acculturation ensures that immigrants can preserve their heritage while fully participating in society (Berry, 1997).

As societies become increasingly diverse, the need for policies that support both integration and acculturation becomes more urgent. Developing adaptable integration strategies that respect various cultural backgrounds and foster genuine inclusivity is essential to addressing potential conflicts and creating a more cohesive society.

Understanding the concepts of cultural integration and acculturation provides valuable insights into immigration policies. While integration stresses mutual adaptation and full participation in societal structures, acculturation focuses on the exchange of cultural practices while preserving cultural identities. The goal is to balance language acquisition, economic participation, and cultural preservation to foster societal harmony and inclusivity. Moving forward, policies should continue to meet the needs of an increasingly diverse population while nurturing a harmonious and inclusive society.

SUSPENDED PERSPECTIVES: BETWEEN ORIENTALISM AND OCCIDENTALISM IN INTERCULTURAL UNDERSTANDING

While cultural integration often focuses on tangible factors such as language proficiency, economic participation, and social inclusion, these structural measures do not fully capture the lived experience of immigrants who inhabit what can be described as a "suspended space" between cultures. Such individuals are neither fully anchored in their place of origin nor entirely assimilated into the host society. This intermediate state, although potentially fertile for creativity and hybridity (Bhabha, 1994), can also lead to incomplete understanding, fractured identity, and superficial cultural interpretation.

Observations made by immigrants about their host societies often remain "in suspension"—articulated, shared, and generalised, yet lacking a firm grounding. This stems from the reality that the observers themselves exist in a suspended state, belonging fully to neither the society they left nor the one they have entered. Consequently, their sense of belonging is fragmented, their understanding partial, and their commentary inconclusive.

A primary cause of this suspension is limited mastery of the host society's language. Language is not merely a communication tool but a carrier of culture

(Whorf, 1956). Without linguistic fluency, one cannot dream, laugh, or grieve in that language—nor can one genuinely access the emotional and symbolic layers of the culture. As a result, interactions remain superficial, and the deeper meanings embedded in social life often go unnoticed.

Yet language alone is not sufficient. Even among those fluent in the host language, a lack of conceptual and critical frameworks can hinder understanding. Cultural contact without analytical tools—such as Geertz's (1973) "thick description"—produces observations that are descriptive but not interpretive. Critical thinking, contextual knowledge, and philosophical awareness are necessary to move beyond surface impressions toward deeper cultural insight.

True understanding of a society emerges from engagement with its unfiltered, everyday moments: the exuberance of weddings, the solemnity of funerals, the reflexive gestures in moments of crisis, or the subtle etiquette in public spaces. Cultural meaning is often embedded in these unscripted interactions, which reveal a society's "habitus" (Bourdieu, 1990)—its ingrained patterns of perception and behaviour.

The absence of such immersive and interpretive engagement leaves room for reductive frameworks such as Orientalism (Said, 1978) or Occidentalism (Buruma & Margalit, 2004). In these cases, immigrants may idealise the host society as a model of civilisation, positioning their own culture as inferior, or conversely, dismiss the host society as morally or culturally deficient while elevating their own heritage. Both positions obscure the complexities of cultural life and perpetuate hierarchical worldviews.

Stuart Hall's (1997) conception of identity as historically produced and dynamically reconstructed underscores the instability of observations made from a suspended position. Similarly, Sen's (2006) notion of "multiple identities" offers a way forward—viewing individuals not solely through ethnic or national categories but through overlapping roles (e.g., worker, parent, neighbour, citizen). Nussbaum's (1997) idea of cosmopolitan citizenship extends this perspective, urging individuals to approach cultural interpretation with a universalist ethical framework.

In contemporary contexts, the tendency toward superficial and context-free judgments is not unique to immigrants. Social media has amplified rapid, decontextualised commentary, contributing to a broader epistemic shallowness in public discourse. This "aerial view" of culture—lacking sustained engagement—mirrors the pitfalls of both Orientalist and Occidentalist thinking.

For the integration policy, the implications are clear: fostering language proficiency is necessary but insufficient. Programs must also cultivate critical cultural literacy, encouraging immigrants to engage deeply with the host society's everyday life and to reflect on their own interpretive frameworks. Cultural orientation should go beyond functional adaptation to include training in cross-cultural analysis, reflexivity, and the avoidance of reductive stereotypes.

By recognising the suspended position not as a fixed deficit but as a transitional stage with transformative potential, integration strategies can help individuals move toward a dual perspective that enables them to view the host culture both from within and without. This, in turn, enriches intercultural understanding, strengthens social cohesion, and mitigates the risks of distorted perception that hinder genuine mutual recognition.

ECONOMIC IMPACTS OF CULTURAL ACCULTURATION AND INTEGRATION

The economic impacts of cultural acculturation and integration are substantial and multifaceted. So it is very important to recognise how these processes affect economic outcomes, including labour market participation, economic growth, and social welfare systems, and provide recommendations for optimising the economic benefits of integration policies.

Immigrants play a vital role in the labour market, contributing across sectors by filling both low- and high-skilled jobs and addressing labour shortages in crucial industries (Dustmann & Frattini, 2014). The processes of acculturation, such as language learning and cultural adaptation, enhance immigrants' ability to engage effectively in the labour market. Integration policies that support these processes can lead to improved productivity and long-term economic growth (Ager & Strang, 2008).

Immigrants are also significant contributors to entrepreneurship. Many immigrants start their own businesses, creating new job opportunities and stimulating economic growth. For example, immigrant-owned businesses drive innovation and market diversity (Bendel, 2020). Policies that promote entrepreneurial activities, such as providing access to financing and business training, can further strengthen their economic contributions.

Cultural diversity resulting from acculturation and integration can spur economic growth and innovation. Diverse teams offer a wide range of perspectives and ideas, fostering creativity and problem-solving abilities. The varied backgrounds and experiences of immigrants can open up new market opportunities, enhancing the global competitiveness of businesses (Haas, 2018).

Despite these contributions, there are fiscal challenges related to immigrant integration. The costs associated with social services, language courses, and job placement programs can be considerable. However, these costs should be weighed against the long-term economic benefits of successfully integrating immigrants, such as increased tax revenue and reduced dependency on welfare programs (OECD, 2017). Targeted policies that effectively manage these costs can help maximise the economic advantages of integration.

The integration of immigrants can also influence social welfare systems. In the early stages, immigrants may rely more heavily on social services as they adjust to their new surroundings. Over time, however, successful integration leads to greater economic independence and reduced reliance on welfare (Dustmann & Frattini, 2014). Policies that support immigrants during the initial adjustment phase while promoting long-term self-sufficiency are essential for balancing these effects.

Addressing skill gaps is another important aspect of integrating immigrants into the labour market. Many immigrants face challenges related to credential recognition, language barriers, and unfamiliarity with local job markets. Targeted training and support to address these gaps can improve their employability and increase their economic contributions (Ager & Strang, 2008). Ensuring that immigrants have the necessary skills to meet labour market demands is critical to maximising their economic potential.

Investing in language and vocational training programs is crucial for enhancing immigrants' labour market outcomes. These programs should be designed to meet both immediate needs and long-term career development, improving immigrants' ability to contribute to the economy (Bendel, 2020).

Support for immigrant entrepreneurs, such as access to financing, mentorship, and business development services, can further stimulate economic growth and innovation. Policies that encourage entrepreneurial activity can help immigrants establish businesses and generate job opportunities (Haas, 2018).

It is also important to develop policies that balance the immediate costs of integration with the long-term economic benefits. This includes ensuring that social welfare systems are equipped to support immigrants during their early adjustment period and to create pathways to greater economic self-sufficiency (OECD, 2017).

Cultural acculturation and integration have profound economic impacts, affecting labour market participation, entrepreneurial activities, and overall economic growth. By investing in targeted policies that promote language acquisition, vocational training, and entrepreneurship, countries can optimise the economic benefits of integration while addressing associated challenges. Successfully balancing short-term costs with long-term economic gains will be crucial to fostering a sustainable and successful integration

NATIONAL SECURITY AND POPULATION PLANNING: THE ROLE OF CULTURAL ACCULTURATION AND INTEGRATION

Cultural acculturation and integration have significant implications for national security and population planning. This section explores how these processes intersect with national security concerns and population management strategies, and provides recommendations to ensure that integration policies effectively support both security and demographic goals.

The successful integration of immigrants can enhance national security by reducing social tensions and fostering community cohesion. Integration policies that promote mutual understanding and respect help mitigate potential sources of conflict and radicalisation (Massey et al., 1993). However, inadequate integration can lead to social isolation and marginalisation, creating environments where extremist ideologies may take root, posing security risks (Cesari, 2019).

Addressing these risks through community outreach programs and counter-radicalisation initiatives, aimed at engaging immigrant communities and preventing the rise of extremist groups, is essential. By focusing on language training, social inclusion, and economic opportunities, integration policies can reduce the likelihood of radicalisation, thereby contributing to overall security (Hoffmann, 2020).

Cultural acculturation and integration also play a key role in managing population growth and demographic changes. Integrating immigrants into the workforce and broader society helps address labour shortages, which in turn supports economic growth. Furthermore, successful integration can contribute to demographic stability by encouraging family formation, thereby countering the challenges posed by population decline (Lanzieri, 2014).

Population planning must consider the long-term impacts of immigration and integration on demographic trends. Supporting immigrants' economic participation, social inclusion, and cultural cohesion can help balance the challenges and opportunities posed by demographics. Well-integrated immigrants can enhance population stability, foster economic development, and strengthen the social fabric over time (Bendel, 2020).

To achieve both national security and population planning objectives, countries should enhance their integration programs. This includes expanding language and vocational training, promoting social inclusion, and supporting community engagement initiatives. Such measures will help reduce security risks, address demographic challenges, and contribute to long-term stability (OECD, 2017).

Comprehensive population strategies must be developed that account for both immediate and long-term demographic needs. Immigration policies should align with economic and social goals to ensure immigrants positively contribute to population stability and economic growth. Moreover, policies should consider the impacts of demographic changes on social services, infrastructure, and community cohesion (Lanzieri, 2014).

Collaboration between policymakers, researchers, and community organisations is crucial for creating effective integration and population planning strategies. Continuous research and dialogue can identify emerging challenges and opportunities, ensuring policies remain responsive to evolving demographic and security needs (Cesari, 2019).

In conclusion, cultural acculturation and integration are integral to national security and population planning. By implementing comprehensive integration programs and developing effective population strategies, societies can mitigate security risks, address demographic challenges, and foster societal stability. Aligning integration efforts with national security and demographic objectives is key to ensuring a secure and prosperous society.

THE FUTURE OF CULTURAL ACCULTURATION, INTEGRATION, AND ECONOMIC AND SECURITY IMPLICATIONS

Over the next decade, increased cultural diversity is expected due to ongoing immigration and refugee movements. The focus on cultural acculturation will continue, emphasizing language acquisition, social inclusion, and community engagement. Integration strategies will evolve to respond to demographic changes, fostering intercultural understanding and cooperation. These policies will aim to support social cohesion and mitigate potential conflicts, with educational and community programs playing a key role in shaping a harmonious multicultural society.

Economically, the short-term impact of integration will depend on how well immigrants are incorporated into the labour market. Effective policies will enhance workforce participation, entrepreneurial activities, and overall economic growth. However, challenges such as skill gaps, access to opportunities, and the recognition of foreign qualifications will persist. Over the next two decades, immigrants' contributions to economic growth and demographic stability will become increasingly evident, enhancing productivity and competitiveness. Long-term economic planning should focus on sustaining these benefits while addressing any disparities and ensuring equitable access to economic opportunities.

National security will also be influenced by ongoing integration efforts. Effective policies that promote inclusion and address potential radicalisation will be crucial for maintaining security. Proactive measures, including community engagement and counter-radicalisation programs, will remain pivotal. Over time, the integration of diverse populations is expected to foster greater social stability and security, though vigilance will remain important against emerging security threats and evolving demographic trends.

To meet these future challenges, integration frameworks should be strengthened, focusing on long-term language and vocational training, promoting social cohesion, and supporting immigrant entrepreneurship. These measures will help reduce security risks, address demographic challenges, and contribute to societal stability. By aligning integration strategies with economic and social goals, it will be possible to ensure that immigrants positively contribute to population stability, economic growth, and national security. Adaptable policies and collaboration among policy-makers, researchers, and community organisations will be essential to effectively manage a diverse and evolving society.

EMBRACING PLURALISM: A PATHWAY TO SOCIAL HARMONY, ECONOMIC GROWTH, AND NATIONAL SECURITY

In an increasingly interconnected world, pluralism has emerged as a powerful force for fostering social harmony and driving progress. It encourages the coexistence of diverse cultures, identities, and values within a society, grounded in mutual respect and understanding. Embracing pluralism is not just about enriching societies—it becomes a catalyst for global change, particularly in the context of migration and integration. Effectively integrating immigrants is key to promoting social cohesion, boosting economic participation, and enhancing national security.

Pluralism goes beyond merely accepting diversity—it involves actively engaging with it. By recognising and valuing differences among people, societies foster dialogue and collaboration, enabling diverse groups to contribute to collective progress. This dynamic interaction strengthens societal cohesion and spurs innovation across various sectors, including technology, economics, and social policies. By embracing pluralism, societies can create an inclusive environment that promotes belonging, reduces inequalities, and nurtures shared progress.

While pluralism offers substantial benefits, it also presents challenges such as prejudice, discrimination, and cultural misunderstandings. These challenges can be addressed through education, open dialogue, and inclusive policies that prioritise respect for all cultures. Pluralism fosters vibrant, dynamic communities where people from different backgrounds contribute to a richer cultural landscape, driving economic growth and strengthening democratic values. It also plays a key role in shaping migration and integration policies, enhancing international relationships, and promoting global cooperation.

In the context of migration, pluralism allows host societies to incorporate new cultural elements while maintaining their own identity. Striking a balance between integration and cultural preservation is essential to fostering mutual respect and understanding. A pluralistic approach encourages the coexistence of diverse identities within a unified societal framework. Integration processes must involve mutual adjustment, with both immigrant and host communities engaging actively to foster understanding and reduce xenophobia. Language training, vocational programs, and social inclusion initiatives are critical for enhancing immigrants' participation in the labour market and their social contributions, while combating discrimination and ensuring equal opportunities.

Economically, immigrants contribute significantly to growth through their involvement in the labour market, entrepreneurial activities, and innovation. However, disparities in labour market outcomes must be addressed by supporting skill development, credential recognition, and entrepreneurial efforts. These measures not only enhance economic contributions but also drive innovation and job creation. Although short-term integration costs, such as those associated with social services and training programs, may arise, effective management can ensure long-term sustainable benefits.

Culturally, integration also plays a critical role in national security. Effective integration reduces social tensions and strengthens societal stability, whereas poor integration can lead to marginalisation and potentially foster radicalisation. Preventive measures like community engagement and counter-radicalisation programs are essential for maintaining security and fostering social cohesion. Adapting policies to address emerging demographic shifts and new security threats is crucial, requiring collaboration between governments, community organisations, and researchers to develop strategies that promote stability and inclusivity.

Furthermore, population planning must align with integration and economic policies to manage demographic changes effectively. Immigrants play a pivotal role in addressing population decline and supporting economic growth, especially in ageing societies. Long-term planning is essential to balance the needs of both immigrant and native populations, ensuring equitable access to resources and services.

In conclusion, pluralism and integration policies are fundamental for promoting social cohesion, economic prosperity, and national security. Comprehensive strategies—such as language training, vocational education, and anti-discrimination efforts—are crucial for facilitating immigrants' participation in both economic and societal activities. While integration may present short-term challenges, its long-term benefits, including economic dynamism and societal resilience, far outweigh the costs.

By embracing pluralism, societies can strengthen themselves and foster a more just, harmonious world. Through active engagement with diversity and adaptable integration policies, societies can navigate the complexities of cultural integration, economic impact, and demographic changes. This requires ongoing research, strategic planning, and collaboration among policymakers, researchers, and community stakeholders. As the saying goes, "In diversity lies strength"; by championing pluralism, societies can build a prosperous, inclusive, and stable future.

CONCLUSION

This study has provided a comprehensive analysis of the acculturation and integration processes, examining their implications for economic development, national security, population, workforce and capacity planning. It is very clear that effective integration strategies foster social cohesion, enhance economic participation, and ensure national security. As Aristotle once said, "The whole is greater than the sum of its parts," which encapsulates the essence of integration—the harmonious blending of diverse elements to create a stronger, more resilient society.

Successful cultural acculturation is essential for constructing a harmonious and inclusive society. Effective integration policies that facilitate language acquisition, social inclusion, and mutual understanding between immigrant and host communities contribute to reduced social tensions and enhanced community resilience (Ager & Strang, 2008). This echoes the wisdom of John Stuart Mill, who argued that "the worth of a state, in the long run, is the worth of the individuals composing it." Continuous adaptation of these policies is required to address evolving demographic and cultural dynamics, ensuring that society's fabric remains strong and inclusive.

Economic integration of immigrants benefits addressing labour shortages, stimulating entrepreneurship, and contributing to overall economic growth. While there are short-term costs associated with integration, such as providing social services and training, the long-term economic benefits are substantial. Ensuring that immigrants are effectively integrated into the labour market and have access to equal opportunities is crucial for maximising these benefits (Dustmann & Frattini, 2014; Bendel, 2020). As Adam Smith famously noted, "The real wealth of a nation consists of the skills of its people," highlighting the importance of human capital in driving economic prosperity.

Cultural integration has significant implications for national security. Effective integration policies can reduce the risk of radicalisation and enhance social stability. Conversely, inadequate integration may lead to marginalisation and potential security risks (Cesari, 2019). Implementing preventive measures, such as community engagement and counter-radicalisation programs, is essential for maintaining security while promoting social cohesion (Hoffmann, 2020). This aligns with the philosophy of Immanuel Kant, who posited that "the highest end of a civil constitution is the preservation of the rights of man as a citizen."

Integrating immigrants effectively supports demographic stability by mitigating population decline and addressing labour market needs. Long-term population planning must consider the impacts of immigration on social services, infrastructure, and community cohesion. Policies that promote equitable access to resources and services for both immigrants and native populations are crucial for balanced demographic development (Lanzieri, 2014; OECD, 2017). In the words of John F.

Kennedy, "Immigration policy should be generous; it should be fair; it should be flexible. With such a policy, we can turn the dynamic force of millions of immigrants into an indispensable force for economic growth."

Countries should continue to invest in and enhance their integration frameworks to address both immediate and long-term needs. This includes expanding language and vocational training programs, promoting social inclusion, and supporting community engagement initiatives. Ensuring that integration policies are adaptable and responsive to changing demographics will be key to achieving long-term success (OECD, 2017). As Confucius wisely advised, "The strength of a nation derives from the integrity of the home," underscoring the foundational role of cohesive, inclusive communities.

Economic strategies should align with integration goals to harness the full potential of a diverse and skilled workforce. Supporting immigrant entrepreneurship, addressing skill gaps, and ensuring fair access to economic opportunities are essential for sustaining economic growth and innovation (Bendel, 2020). This perspective resonates with the insight of Joseph Schumpeter, who emphasised that "the process of creative destruction is the essential fact about capitalism," underscoring the transformative potential of integrating diverse talents and ideas.

Future security policies should focus on enhancing community relations and addressing emerging threats. Developing strategies that promote social cohesion, prevent radicalisation, and align with national security objectives is crucial for maintaining stability. Collaboration with community organisations and ongoing research will support effective security measures (Hoffmann, 2020). The philosophy of Sun Tzu, who stated, "The greatest victory is that which requires no battle," underscores the importance of proactive, preventive approaches to maintaining societal harmony.

Future research should explore the effectiveness of integration policies and their impact on economic, security, and demographic outcomes. Investigating the long-term effects of cultural acculturation and integration on various aspects of society will provide valuable insights for policy development. Collaborative efforts among researchers, policymakers, and community stakeholders will be essential to address future challenges and opportunities (OECD, 2017). As Albert Einstein famously remarked, "In the middle of difficulty lies opportunity," highlighting the potential for innovative solutions to arise from complex challenges.

The integration of immigrants into society presents both challenges and opportunities. By implementing comprehensive and adaptable policies, countries can enhance social cohesion, economic growth, and national security. Addressing the complexities of cultural acculturation and integration through strategic planning and research will ensure a prosperous and stable future. In the spirit of Martin Luther King Jr., who believed that "we may have all come on different ships, but we're in the same boat now," societies can navigate the waters of change towards a more inclusive and vibrant society.

REFERENCES

Ager, A., & Strang, A. (2008). Understanding integration: A conceptual framework. *Journal of Refugee Studies, 21*(2), 166–191. DOI: 10.1093/jrs/fen016

Alesina, A., & La Ferrara, E. (2005). Ethnic diversity and economic performance. *Journal of Economic Literature, 43*(3), 762–800. DOI: 10.1257/002205105774431243

Bendel, P. (2020). *Integration policies and practices in Austria: A comprehensive review*. Springer.

Berry, J. W. (1997). Immigration, acculturation, and adaptation. *Applied Psychology = Psychologie Appliquée, 46*(1), 5–34. DOI: 10.1111/j.1464-0597.1997.tb01087

Bhabha, H. K. (1994). *The Location of Culture*. Routledge.

Bourdieu, P. (1990). *The Logic of Practice*. Stanford University Press. DOI: 10.1515/9781503621749

Buruma, I., & Margalit, A. (2004). *Occidentalism: The West in the Eyes of Its Enemies*. Penguin.

California State Government Report. (2020). *Immigrant Investment Program.* State of California. Search CA.gov | CA.gov

Cesari, J. (2019). *Islam, secularism, and liberal democracy: Toward a democratic theory for Muslim societies*. Oxford University Press.

Chiswick, B. R., & Miller, P. W. (2015). The economics of immigration. In J. C. M. (Ed.), International Encyclopedia of the Social & Behavioral Sciences (2nd ed., pp. 153-160). Elsevier. https://doi.org/DOI: 10.1016/B978-0-08-097086-8.81026-6

Clemens, M. A., & Hunt, J. (2017). The labor market effects of refugee waves: Reconciling conflict and evidence. *The Review of Economic Studies, 84*(2), 1533–1558. DOI: 10.1093/restud/rdx021

Dempsey, N., Bramley, G., Power, S., & Brown, C. (2011). The social dimension of sustainable development: Defining urban social sustainability. *Sustainable Development (Bradford), 19*(5), 289–300. DOI: 10.1002/sd.417

Dustmann, C., & Frattini, T. (2014). The fiscal impact of immigration to the UK. *Economic Journal (London), 124*(580), F293–F343. DOI: 10.1111/ecoj.12181

European Commission. (2015). *Circular Economy Action Plan*. https://ec.europa.eu

Eurostat. (2020). *Immigrant workforce in the European Union*. https://ec.europa.eu/eurostat

Faludi, A. (2000). *The performance of spatial planning*. Routledge. DOI: 10.1080/713691907

Geertman, S. (2020). *Smart Cities and Urban Sustainability: Opportunities and Challenges*. Springer.

Geertz, C. (1973). *The Interpretation of Cultures*. Basic Books.

German Federal Office for Migration and Refugees. (2020). *Germany's integration course statistics*. Federal Office for Migration and Refugees. https://www.bamf.de

Haas, H. (2018). *Successful integration policies: Lessons from Austria*. Routledge.

Hall, S. (1997). Representation: Cultural Representations and Signifying Practices. *Sage (Atlanta, Ga.)*.

Haughton, G., & Hunter, C. (1994). *Sustainable cities*. Jessica Kingsley Publishers.

Healey, P. (2006). *Collaborative planning: Shaping places in fragmented societies* (2nd ed.). Macmillan. DOI: 10.1007/978-1-137-08600-6

Hoffmann, C. (2020). *Counter-radicalization and integration policies in Europe: A comparative analysis*. Routledge.

Immigration, Refugees and Citizenship Canada. (2020). *Settlement program report*. Retrieved from https://www.canada.ca/en/immigration-refugees-citizenship.html

International Migration Organization. (2020). *Global GDP and immigration integration*. International Migration Organization. https://www.iom.int

Japan Ministry of Health. (2020). *The role of immigrant workers in Japan's economy*. Ministry of Health, Labour and Welfare. https://www.mhlw.go.jp

Kymlicka, W. (2018). Multiculturalism and immigrant integration in Canada. In Triandafyllidou, A. (Ed.), *Handbook of migration and globalization* (pp. 97–112). Edward Elgar Publishing.

Lanzieri, G. (2014). *The demographic impact of migration in Europe*. Eurostat.

Laurence, J. (2020). Discrimination and integration in France. In Kaufmann, E., & Goodwin, P. (Eds.), *The integration of migrants: Challenges and policies* (pp. 67–88). Routledge.

Massey, D. S., Arango, J., Hugo, G., Kouaouci, A., Pellegrino, A., & Taylor, E. J. (1993). Theories of international migration: A review and appraisal. *Population and Development Review*, *19*(3), 431–466. DOI: 10.2307/2938462

McKinsey Global Institute. (2017). *The economic value of cultural diversity in firms*. McKinsey & Company. https://www.mckinsey.com

MEA. (2005). *Millennium Ecosystem Assessment: Ecosystems and human well-being: Synthesis*. Island Press.

Modood, T. (2019). Multiculturalism and integration in the UK. *Journal of Ethnic and Migration Studies*, *45*(8), 1315–1331.

National Bureau of Economic Research. (2019). *Immigrant entrepreneurs and job creation*. https://www.nber.org

Nussbaum, M. C. (1997). *Cultivating Humanity: A Classical Defense of Reform in Liberal Education*. Harvard University Press.

OECD. (2017). Making integration work: Refugees and others in need of protection. OECD Publishing. Making Integration Work | OECD

OECD. (2018). *Skills proficiency and the labour market outcomes of migrants*. OECD Publishing. Skills proficiency and the labour market outcomes of migrants | OECD

OECD. (2021). *The economic impact of immigration*. OECD Publishing. Economic impact of migration | OECD

OECD. (2024). *Climate change, demography and migration*. OECD Publishing. Climate change, demography and migration | OECD

Perkins, R. (2017). *Migration and the economy: Economic impacts of migration on the UK economy*. Palgrave Macmillan.

Pfeiffer, C., & Nentwig, T. (2019). *Integration through education: Evidence from Austria*. Cambridge University Press.

Porter, M. E. (1998). *On competition*. Harvard Business Review Press.

Portes, A., & Rumbaut, R. G. (2014). *Immigrant America: A portrait*. University of California Press.

Pretty, J. (2003). Social capital and the collective management of resources. *Science*, *302*(5652), 1912–1914. DOI: 10.1126/science.1090847 PMID: 14671287

Sachs, J. (2015). *The Age of Sustainable Development*. Columbia University Press. DOI: 10.7312/sach17314

Said, E. W. (1978). *Orientalism*. Pantheon Books.

Schmidt, E., & Bader, M. (2018). *Vocational training and employment support for immigrants in Austria*. Palgrave Macmillan.

Sen, A. (2006). *Identity and Violence: The Illusion of Destiny*. Norton.

Soja, E. (2010). *Seeking Spatial Justice*. University of Minnesota Press. DOI: 10.5749/minnesota/9780816666676.001.0001

Statistics Canada. (2020). *Immigrant entrepreneurs in Canada: Economic impact*. Statistics Canada. https://www.statcan.gc.ca

Swedish Ministry of Education. (2018). *Educational outcomes for immigrant students*. Ministry of Education and Research. https://www.regeringen.se

UN. (2015). *Transforming our world: The 2030 agenda for sustainable development*. United Nations.

UN-Habitat. (2019). *The Future of Sustainable Cities: Urbanization and Development*. United Nations Human Settlements Programme.

UNEP. (2011). *Towards a Green Economy: Pathways to Sustainable Development and Poverty Eradication*. United Nations Environment Programme.

UNWTO. (2019). *The economic impact of cultural tourism*. World Tourism Organization. Economic contribution of Tourism and beyond: Data on the economic contribution of Tourism

Vertovec, S. (2007). Super-diversity and its implications. Centre on Migration, Policy and Society.

Wächter, T. (2021). *Language barriers in immigrant integration: A comparative analysis*. Routledge.

Wampler, B. (2012). Participatory Budgeting in Latin America: A New Challenge for Sustainable Development. *Journal of Latin American Studies*, *44*(1), 71–97.

Wauters, B., & Lambrecht, J. (2008). The role of immigrant entrepreneurs in the local economy: The case of Flanders. *Entrepreneurship and Regional Development*, *20*(4), 331–355. DOI: 10.1080/08985620802002590

Whorf, B. L. (1956). *Language, Thought, and Reality: Selected Writings of Benjamin Lee Whorf*. MIT Press.

Witte, N. (2019). *Regional integration strategies in Belgium: A comparative analysis*. Routledge.

World Bank. (2020). *World development report 2020: Trading for development in the age of global value chains*. World Bank Group.

World Commission on Environment and Development. (1987). *Our common future*. Oxford University Press.

KEY TERMS AND DEFINITIONS

Term 1 (Sustainable Development): A development approach that balances economic growth, social equity, and environmental protection to meet present needs without compromising future generations. It emphasizes long-term resilience, justice, and adaptability.

Term 2 (Immigrant Integration): The process through which immigrants become active participants in the host society's economic, cultural, and social systems. Integration requires both the host society and immigrants to adapt, aiming for mutual inclusion and cohesion.

Term 3 (Cultural Acculturation): A two-way process where immigrants and the host society influence each other's cultural practices. Unlike assimilation, acculturation preserves immigrants' cultural identity while promoting mutual adaptation.

Term 4 (Pluralism): A philosophical and policy-based commitment to embracing cultural, ethnic, and social diversity. Pluralism fosters social harmony by encouraging inclusive dialogue, cooperation, and mutual respect within diverse societies.

Term 5 (Social Cohesion): The strength of relationships and the sense of solidarity among members of a society. In the context of immigration, it refers to the ability of diverse groups to coexist peacefully, equitably, and cooperatively.

Term 6 (Economic Inclusion): Ensuring immigrants have equitable access to labor markets, entrepreneurship, and financial resources. It includes recognizing foreign qualifications, removing employment barriers, and supporting immigrant business initiatives.

Term 7 (Integration Policy Frameworks): Structured plans and strategies implemented by governments to support the social, economic, and cultural inclusion of immigrants. These include language programs, anti-discrimination laws, and community-based initiatives.

Term 8 (Demographic Change): Shifts in the population structure, such as aging or declining birth rates, that influence workforce needs. Immigration is often used as a strategy to address demographic challenges and maintain economic stability.

Chapter 4
The Impact of Sustainability Assurance on Development in the Southern Provinces

El Karmaoui Fatima Zahra
http://orcid.org/0009-0009-1023-7267
Université Ibn Zohr, Morocco

El Ouali El Balaidi
http://orcid.org/0000-0002-6410-906X
Université Ibn Zohr, Morocco

ABSTRACT

This research explores the impact of sustainability assurance on the development of Morocco's southern provinces through a qualitative analysis. The research integrated various stakeholders to obtain a global vision of sustainable development issues. Due to limited responses to solicitations, thee researchers opted for semi-structured interviews with local stakeholders and experts in various fields, in order to gather data on the economic, environmental and social dimensions of sustainability. The interviews focused on five areas: local economic growth, poverty reduction, quality of life, environmental preservation and economic resilience. The results show that integrating sustainable practices boots the economy through green agriculture, sustainable tourism and renewable energies, while reducing the ecological footprint. Overall, ensuring sustainability is proving to be an essential socio-economic development lever for these regions, fostering an inclusive and resilient growth model.

DOI: 10.4018/979-8-2600-3325-8.ch004

INTRODUCTION

In Morocco, sustainability has become a national priority, integrated into various public policies aimed at ensuring balanced, environmentally-friendly development. This movement is part of a long-term vision, supported by strategic initiatives such as the National Sustainable Development Policy (PNDD) adopted in 2017. This ambitious framework seeks to promote the protection of natural resources, combat climate change, and include local populations in decision-making processes for more equitable development (Ministry of the Environment, 2017).

In particular, the southern provinces, rich in natural and cultural resources, are at the heart of these sustainability efforts. These regions are characterised by their high potential for renewable energies, particularly solar and wind power, making them ideal locations for large-scale projects such as the Noor solar complex in Ouarzazate. This project, supported by international partnerships, is an example of Morocco's determination to reduce its dependence on fossil fuels and develop a green economy (IRENA, 2018; World Bank, 2021).

In this context, sustainability assurance represents an essential lever for the development of the southern provinces. This concept is based on integrating environmental, social, and governance (ESG) criteria into economic activities to ensure a long-term, positive impact. By contributing to the creation of green jobs and promoting inclusive socio-economic development, sustainability assurance offers a solution to the specific challenges of these regions, where economic opportunities are limited, and ecosystems are fragile (OECD, 2022).

Initiatives such as Vision 2020 for sustainable development, which aims to promote environmentally-friendly tourism, illustrate Moroccan efforts to support sustainability in the southern provinces. This program encourages tourism development that enhances local resources and respects ecosystems, while ensuring socio-economic benefits for local communities (Regional Environmental Action Plan, 2019). Thus, ensuring sustainability is a means of accompanying Morocco in its transition to an inclusive, sustainable development model while preserving the natural and cultural assets of its southern regions.

1. DEFINING SUSTAINABILITY ASSURANCE AND ITS ROLE IN REGIONAL DEVELOPMENT

Sustainability assurance, a relatively recent concept, aims to ensure that economic projects and activities take into account long-term environmental, social, and governance (ESG) impacts. It is manifested in practices that ensure balanced, environmentally-friendly development, minimising the negative effects of human activities on natural resources and local communities. As part of sustainability assurance, targets are set to guide organisations and companies towards practices aligned with the Sustainable Development Goals (SDGs), reinforcing measurable criteria such as ecological footprint, resource management, and social well-being (UN Global Compact, 2017).

In developing regions, such as Morocco's southern provinces, this type of insurance plays a central role in contributing to balanced socio-economic development. By integrating ESG dimensions into regional activities, sustainability insurance helps create green jobs, support the local economy, and protect vulnerable ecosystems. In Morocco's southern provinces, renewable energy and sustainable tourism projects illustrate this approach, contributing to economic resilience and the preservation of local culture (Ministry of the Environment, 2017).

2. LITERATURE REVIEW: IMPACT OF SUSTAINABILITY PRACTICES IN COMPARABLE REGIONS

a) Sustainable tourism:

Sustainable tourism is a key sector for sustainability in developing regions, including Morocco. Research indicates that sustainable tourism, when well structured, can stimulate the local economy while preserving cultural and natural resources. A study by Lane (1994) of rural areas in Europe points out that sustainable tourism can increase the income of local communities by creating direct employment in hotels and leisure activities, while promoting balanced economic development (Lane, 1994). In Morocco, Vision 2020 promotes environmentally-friendly and culturally enriching tourism in the southern provinces. The focus is on training local stakeholders and managing natural resources to avoid harmful impacts on local ecosystems (Ministry of Tourism, 2018).

However, the sustainable tourism sector has been widely studied in recent years as an engine of economic development while protecting natural resources. A recent study by Sharpley and Telfer (2021) points out that sustainable tourism helps preserve environmental resources while stimulating local economies, particularly in remote regions with high cultural potential. In their analysis, the authors showed that in regions such as Southeast Asia, local communities benefit directly from tourism-generated income when it is structured to incorporate sustainable practices.

Further research by Gössling and Peeters (2022) examines the impact of sustainable tourism in Mediterranean countries and reveals that sustainability is crucial to avoid damage to coastal ecosystems and to promote a resilient local economy. Their study highlights the importance of limiting tourism's carbon footprint and diversifying tourism offerings to include eco-friendly activities. This model may inspire Morocco in its Vision 2020 project, which aims to develop environmentally-friendly tourism in the southern provinces.

b) Sustainable agriculture:

Sustainable agriculture is another key sector for regional development, particularly in arid and semi-arid zones. Indeed, in regions with high agricultural potential, ensuring sustainability in this sector is important. This includes agricultural practices aimed at preserving soil quality, minimising the use of chemical inputs and promoting biodiversity (Tilman et al., 2002). Sustainable agriculture contributes to food security and the resilience of rural areas by protecting them from fluctuations in agricultural prices and yields. In Morocco, micro-irrigation projects and agricultural techniques adapted to arid climates have been implemented in the southern provinces to improve water-use efficiency and guarantee the sustainability of agricultural production (FAO, 2019). In addition, studies show that promoting locally adapted crops contributes to poverty reduction and the empowerment of local communities (World Bank, 2018).

However, in 2020, Lybbert and Sumner conducted a study of climate-resilient agricultural practices in North African countries. Their research revealed that micro-irrigation systems and drought-resistant crops are essential for maintaining agricultural productivity and preserving water resources. These findings are particularly relevant to Morocco's southern provinces, where water resources are limited.

Other researchers, such as Rockström and Falkenmark (2021), emphasise the importance of integrated water resource management for sustainable agriculture. Their study analyses agricultural practices implemented in countries such as Egypt and Morocco, which aim to optimise water use and minimise environmental impacts. The researchers emphasise adapting farming practices to specific climatic conditions, a strategy that could promote sustainable agriculture in Morocco's southern regions.

c) Renewable energies:

Renewable energies are a fundamental pillar of sustainable development, particularly in the arid regions of southern Morocco. By reducing dependence on fossil fuels and capitalising on abundant resources such as sun and wind, these energies support a transition to greener practices. The Noor project in Ouarzazate is one of the world's largest solar projects, and a model for other developing arid regions. This project demonstrates how ensuring sustainability in renewable energy can generate economic benefits, such as job creation, while minimising the ecological footprint (IRENA, 2018). Research by Byrne et al. (2016) shows that a transition to renewable energy is essential for developing countries seeking to meet their climate goals while fostering local economic growth.

More recently, a 2022 report by the International Renewable Energy Agency (IRENA) analyses the impacts of major solar and wind projects in North Africa, of which Morocco is a part, and shows that these energies help reduce CO_2 emissions while creating local jobs. IRENA's study (2022) focuses on the Noor project in Ouarzazate, which has become a model for solar energy in desert environments. It concludes that such projects can generate significant economic development and social benefits, particularly in terms of training and employment.

According to a study by Sovacool and Griffiths (2021), renewable energy projects in rural sub-Saharan Africa demonstrate how the transition to clean energy can stimulate local development while improving access to electricity in historically underserved areas. The researchers point out that investment in renewable energy infrastructure promotes economic resilience and energy independence, both of which are crucial for Morocco's southern provinces, where energy needs are growing.

In conclusion, sustainability practices in sectors such as tourism, agriculture and renewable energies have shown encouraging results in internationally comparable regions. Comparative studies indicate that sustainability initiatives, such as those observed in Latin America or Asia, can generate local economic growth while preserving the integrity of natural resources and improving the well-being of local populations (OECD, 2020). For Morocco, sustainability assurance can play a transformative role in the southern provinces, steering these regions towards a long-term development model that is both environmentally friendly and socially inclusive. Indeed, the integration of these practices would not only boost the local economy but also ensure the preservation of its natural resources. However, by strengthening green infrastructure and supporting local initiatives, Morocco could foster sustainable development in the southern provinces while aligning itself with the Sustainable Development Goals (SDGs).

3. EMPIRICAL STUDY

The aim of this research is to analyse the impact of sustainability assurance on the development of Morocco's southern provinces. This formulation paves the way for an in-depth analysis of the mechanisms and impacts of integrating sustainability assurance into sustainable development processes, while keeping a specific eye on Morocco's economic, cultural, and social realities.

We conducted qualitative research, collecting data from semi-structured interviews with a range of stakeholders from diverse perspectives and knowledge to understand the impact of sustainability assurance on the development of Morocco's southern zone provinces.

3.1 Data and Methods

In this empirical part, we enter the phase of confrontation between theory and practice. The literature review focused on the scientific literature related to the two central themes of our research. Sustainability assurance and the development of Morocco's Southern Zone provinces. We presented the data in a structured manner to facilitate our field analysis and to establish a comprehensive interview guide that covers all aspects of sustainability assurance data and development.

3.1.1 Sampling:

Our research question explores how sustainability assurance contributes to the development of Morocco's southern zone provinces. We explored the concrete steps that stakeholders can take to integrate sustainability assurance practices that promote the development of Morocco's southern zone provinces.

In order to respond as comprehensively as possible to our problem, our sample is diverse, consisting of local and regional government officials, sustainability and economic development experts, private sector players, local communities and leaders, professionals from key sectors and training and research organizations will provide diverse perspectives and enable us to obtain an overview of the issues and challenges of sustainable development in the southern provinces, covering both the economic, environmental and social aspects of ensuring sustainability. The table below provides an overview of the various interviews.

Table N°1: Summary of interviews conducted during the exploratory phase (source: our survey):

Table 1. Summary of Interviews Conducted in the Exploratory Phase.

Companies	Position	Duration
Local and regional authorities	- Local officials: Regional directors a government representative involved in sustainable development. - Local elected representatives: Regional councilors and members of municipal councils who play a role in strategic decision-making for the region	
Sustainability and economic development experts	- Sustainable development policy specialists: Researchers, academics and consultants in sustainable development and regional economics. - Renewable energy and water management engineers and technicians in the solar, wind and sustainable irrigation sectors.	
Private sector players	- Local entrepreneurs: Leaders of small and medium-sized entreprises (SMEs) in the tourism, agriculture and renewable energy sectors, who can provide insights into the opportunities and challenges of sustainability. - Investors and lenders: Representatives of financial institutions involved in green financing and sustainability projects in the southern provinces.	
Communities and local leaders	- Community representatives: community leaders, members of local tribes, and representatives of resident's associations, to understand local people's expectations and perceptions of sustainability. - NGOs and local associations: civil society organizations working for social development and environmental protection.	
Professionals in key sectors	- Farmers and agricultural cooperatives: these are at the heart of the adoption of sustainable agricultural practices adapted to arid conditions. - Sustainable tourism professionals: Owners of tourist accommodations, local guides, and travel agencies who integrate eco-responsible practices into their tourism offerings	
Training and research organizations	- Education and training establishments: Representatives of technical institutes and schools that train the local workforce in renewable energies and natural resource management. - Researchers and research institutes: Specialists in sustainable development and climate adaptation from regional or national research centres.	

3.1.2 Data collection method:

To carry out our research, we opted for a qualitative analysis. In fact, the subject concerns the analysis of the effect of sustainability assurance on the development of the southern provinces of Morocco.

From January (2024). I set out to find stakeholders who would provide diverse perspectives and help me obtain an overview of the issues and challenges of sustainable development in the southern provinces through the internet, social networks, networks of sustainability and economic development experts and consultancies, and direct contact with certain officials through our relational network. I sent out requests to a dozen or so people, received a good number of no replies, and had a few people who agreed to answer my questions. This was one of the difficulties I encountered in my search.

For our scientific research, we will first draft an interview guide to help us conduct our individual semi-structured interviews (El Hammoumi, A. et al., 2024). However, the semi-directive interview is the main source of data for our practical investigation. To demonstrate the importance of this data source, Royer, C. et ali (2009) state that "the semi-directive or semi-directed interview is certainly the most widely used in social research. It is semi-directive in the sense that it is neither entirely open-ended nor channelled by a large number of precise questions. Generally, the researcher has a series of relatively open-ended guiding questions, about which it is imperative that he receives information from the interviewer. But he doesn't necessarily ask all the questions in the order in which he has written them down, and in the form in which he intends to ask them. As far as possible, he will "let the interviewee come", so that the latter can speak openly, in the words he wishes and in the order that suits him. The researcher will simply endeavour to refocus the interview on the objectives whenever he deviates from them, and to ask the questions to which the interviewee does not come for himself, at the most appropriate moment and in as natural a manner as possible" MOULAI, S., & BOUKRIF, M. (2018).

A series of meetings with groups will provide diverse perspectives and enable us to obtain an overview of the issues and challenges of sustainable development in the southern provinces, covering both the economic, environmental, and social aspects of ensuring sustainability, which will form the core of our empirical base. In this first exploratory phase, we conducted semi-structured interviews with local and regional government officials, sustainable development policy specialists, engineers and technicians in renewable energy and water management, local entrepreneurs, community representatives, professionals in key sectors and researchers and research institutes operating in Morocco's southern provinces, with varying perspectives and knowledge of sustainability assurance and local development. However, semi-structured interviews are a qualitative research method used to study social relations and organisational processes. They involve the use of a set of predefined open-ended questions posed to participants, which also allow a freer exploration of participants' ideas and experiences (Wollesen, B. et al., 2020).

When it comes to understanding the link between sustainability assurance and local development, semi-structured interviews can be particularly useful, as they enable researchers to gather detailed information on participants' perceptions and experiences of these areas. Semi-structured questions can be adapted to explore different facets of sustainability assurance, such as sustainability investment based on green infrastructure, renewable energy, and sustainable agricultural practices; sustainability policy implementation; local stakeholder engagement; green innovation and technology; and access to green finance.

Using this research method, researchers can obtain rich, contextualized qualitative data that can be analyzed to identify emerging themes and patterns, as well as to understand the nuances and complexities of sustainability assurance.

3.2 Interview Results

The results of the interviews have been collated in a table. We have listed the categories of questions we discussed with our interviewees. The aim is to compare their answers and highlight similarities.

As our research question was to understand how sustainability assurance impacts the development of Morocco's southern provinces, it seemed obvious to us that my questions would revolve around five axes: local economic growth, poverty reduction and improved quality of life, environmental preservation and natural resource management, social and cultural development, and economic and ecological resilience.

We began the interview with the interviewee's introduction. We then explored various topics, starting with sustainability assurance and local development. We then moved on to current initiatives and practices, socio-economic impacts and community commitments. We also discussed future prospects and recommendations, as well as the company's performance in corporate social responsibility (CSR) and environmental sustainability.

3.3 Use of Interview

Based on the data collected, we will first look for any similarities between the different responses according to the various themes:

3.3.1 Understanding Sustainability Assurance and Local Development

During the interviews, it was clear that all interviewees understood the relationship between sustainability assurance and local development. However, sustainability assurance involves several key elements that ensure that the practices and initiatives put in place contribute to sustainable development. Indeed, these key dimensions are: environmental impact assessment, regulatory compliance, stakeholder engagement, sustainability strategies, education and awareness, and innovation and continuous improvement. Sustainability assurance is essential to ensure that today's efforts do not compromise future generations' ability to meet their own needs. It aims to create a balance between economic growth, environmental protection and social well-being. Ensuring sustainability is seen as an important lever for socio-economic development in the southern provinces. Sustainability projects help to create jobs, reduce poverty and improve quality of life, while strengthening economic resilience in the face of climate change and market fluctuations.

In summary, we can conclude that ensuring sustainability in Morocco's southern provinces is an essential vector for economic and social development. An integrated approach, involving support for sustainable infrastructure and the active participation of local populations, is needed to overcome climatic and socio-economic challenges. Thanks to sustainability strategies and the private sector's commitment, these provinces have the potential to become a model of sustainable development for other developing regions.

3.3.2 Local Economic Growth

To assess the impact of sustainability assurance and measure economic growth in Morocco's southern provinces, it is important to measure changes in regional GDP and average per capita income, as well as job creation in sustainable sectors.

Change in regional GDP and average per capita income

The integration of sustainability practices in Morocco's southern provinces has had a significant impact on local economic growth, as measured by variations in regional Gross Domestic Product (GDP) and average per capita income. According to data from the High Commission for Planning (HCP), these provinces have experienced moderate economic growth in recent years, with notable fluctuations due to the adoption of sustainability policies.

Initiatives such as the development of sustainable agriculture, promoted by government programs like Plan Morocco Vert, have not only increased agricultural production but also improved product quality. This has led to higher farmers' incomes, thereby positively influencing average per capita income. For example, the development of organic crops and sustainable irrigation techniques has improved yields while preserving water resources, a crucial factor in these semi-arid regions.

Job creation in sustainable sectors

The transition to sustainable practices has also spurred job creation in key sectors such as agriculture, tourism, and renewable energy.

Sustainable agriculture: The implementation of environmentally-friendly farming techniques has created new jobs, not only for farmers, but also for specialists in agronomy and natural resource management. For example, organic farming and food crop projects have increased the number of farmers while supporting local economies.

- Sustainable tourism:

Initiatives to promote sustainable tourism have also generated employment in the southern provinces. Programs to develop eco-lodges and tourist circuits based on local culture and environmental preservation have not only attracted tourists but have also required the training and hiring of local staff, thus stimulating the regional economy. By 2023, the tourism sector had recovered, with a significant increase in visitor numbers in areas such as Agadir and the Souss-Massa National Park, where efforts have been made to preserve biodiversity while offering unique tourist experiences.

- Renewable energies:

The region has also seen growing investment in renewable energies, particularly solar and wind power. Projects such as the Tarfaya wind farm and the Noor Ouarzazate solar complex have created thousands of jobs during construction and continue to do so in maintenance and operations. These initiatives not only diversify the local economy but also reduce dependence on fossil fuels, contributing to a more sustainable future.

The impact of sustainability practices on economic growth in Morocco's southern provinces is undeniable. The positive variation in regional GDP and average per capita income, coupled with job creation in sustainable sectors, underlines the importance of integrating sustainability into economic development. These efforts contribute not only to a more resilient and diversified local economy but also to improved living conditions for local populations, reinforcing the link between sustainability and economic growth.

3.3.3 Reducing poverty and improving quality of life:

Reducing the poverty rate

The implementation of sustainability practices has played a key role in reducing poverty levels in Morocco's southern provinces. According to data from the High Commission for Planning (HCP), these regions have seen a gradual decline in poverty levels thanks to various development programs focused on sustainability. These initiatives aim to strengthen local communities' capacities by providing training and resources to improve their living conditions.

For example, sustainable agriculture, promoted by programs such as the Plan Morocco Vert, has not only improved productivity but also enabled farmers to diversify their sources of income. By investing in high-value-added crops, such as organic produce and aromatic herbs, farmers have increased their incomes, helping reduce poverty in rural areas. In addition, microcredit initiatives and support for cooperatives have given communities the means to develop their economic activities, reducing dependence on traditional, often less lucrative agriculture.

Improved access to basic services

Access to basic services, such as drinking water and green electricity, is a key factor in improving the quality of life for local populations. In the southern provinces, several projects have been set up to ensure that these essential services are accessible to all.

- Drinking water:

The Moroccan government, in collaboration with non-governmental organisations, has invested in infrastructure to improve access to drinking water. Water resource management projects, such as irrigation systems and water treatment plants, have been developed to meet the population's needs. These efforts have not only ensured a constant supply of drinking water but have also reduced the public health risks associated with water insecurity.

- Green electricity:

The transition to renewable energy sources has also improved access to electricity in these regions. Projects such as the "Renewable Energy for All" program aim to bring green energy solutions, including solar and wind power, to rural communities. These initiatives have connected many households to electricity, improving the quality of life by facilitating access to modern services such as education and healthcare. Green electricity also contributes to environmental sustainability, reducing dependence on fossil fuels.

It can be concluded that poverty reduction and improved quality of life in Morocco's southern provinces are closely linked to the adoption of sustainable practices. The reduction in poverty rates, coupled with improved access to basic services such as drinking water and green electricity, underlines the positive impact of sustainability initiatives on the well-being of local populations. These efforts are essential not only to improve living conditions for local residents but also to promote inclusive, long-term, sustainable economic development.

3.3.4 Environmental Protection and Natural Resource Management

Environmental preservation and natural resource management are at the heart of sustainability initiatives in Morocco's southern provinces. Reducing the ecological footprint is reflected particularly in efforts to cut CO_2 emissions in sectors such as renewable energy and industry. Solar and wind power projects, which are well established in the region, contribute to this objective by replacing fossil fuels with clean alternatives. In addition, water conservation, essential in this arid zone, is reinforced by efficient irrigation programs and sustainable farming techniques. At the same time, biodiversity and local ecosystems are protected through the establishment of nature reserves and strict regulations that safeguard the region's endemic species and sensitive habitats.

3.3.5 Social and Cultural Development

Social and cultural development in Morocco's southern provinces focuses on strengthening local communities and preserving cultural identity by involving local people in sustainable tourism initiatives. These initiatives highlight local cultural riches, artisanal traditions, ancestral customs and know-how, offering visitors an immersive and respectful experience, while generating income for local residents.

In addition, educating local populations and raising their awareness of sustainability practices are key pillars of this strategy. Educational programs and awareness-raising campaigns are set up to explain the importance of protecting the environment and natural resources, thus fostering collective awareness of the impact of individual and community actions on sustainable development that will benefit future generations.

3.3.6 Economic and Ecological Resilience

Economic and ecological resilience in Morocco's southern provinces is based on sustainable practices that strengthen the region's ability to cope with environmental and economic crises. Thanks to the development of renewable energies (solar and wind power) and agricultural practices adapted to arid conditions, the region is better equipped to manage economic fluctuations and climatic challenges, such as prolonged droughts.

Indicators of resilience include the stability of local incomes, supported by activities such as sustainable tourism and handicrafts, which diversify the economy by minimising dependence on non-renewable natural resources. Adaptation to harsh climatic conditions is also reflected in investments in sustainable infrastructure and efficient irrigation technologies, enabling communities to maintain their productivity and quality of life, even in hostile environments.

DIRECTIONS FOR FUTURE RESEARCH

Future research should place greater emphasis on the lived experiences of the communities residing in Morocco's southern provinces. While this study highlights the positive contribution of sustainability assurance to economic growth, environmental preservation, and social development, further research is needed to understand how these benefits are perceived and experienced by local populations over time. Future studies could adopt a longitudinal approach to examine whether sustainability initiatives continue to generate lasting improvements in employment opportunities, income stability, education, health services, and overall well-being. Such research would provide valuable insights into the long-term social impacts of sustainability assurance and its ability to create resilient communities.

Particular attention should also be given to the voices of groups that are often underrepresented in development research, including women, youth, small-scale farmers, artisans, and rural populations. Exploring how these groups participate in and benefit from sustainability projects would contribute to a more inclusive understanding of sustainable development in the southern provinces. In addition, future research could investigate the effectiveness of community participation mechanisms in the planning, implementation, and monitoring of sustainability initiatives. Understanding the extent to which local stakeholders influence decision-making processes would help identify strategies to strengthen local ownership and ensure that development projects respond to community needs and aspirations. Comparative studies between Morocco's southern provinces and other arid or semi-arid regions in Africa and the Middle East could further enrich the literature by identifying best practices and transferable lessons in renewable energy, sustainable agriculture, and eco-tourism development. Such comparisons would help policymakers and practitioners design more context-sensitive sustainability strategies.

Finally, future research may benefit from adopting mixed-methods approaches that combine qualitative insights with quantitative indicators of economic, environmental, and social performance. This would enable a more comprehensive assessment of sustainability assurance and provide stronger evidence regarding its contribution to inclusive and sustainable regional development. By focusing on people, community empowerment, and long-term outcomes, future research can contribute to a deeper understanding of how sustainability assurance not only supports economic development but also improves the everyday lives of individuals and communities across Morocco's southern provinces

CONCLUSION

This study examined the impact of sustainability assurance on the development of Morocco's southern provinces through a qualitative analysis of stakeholder perspectives. The findings indicate that sustainability assurance is a key driver of sustainable development, contributing to economic growth, environmental protection, and social well-being. The results show that initiatives in renewable energy, sustainable tourism, and climate-resilient agriculture have created employment opportunities, diversified local economies, and improved living conditions. At the same time, sustainable practices have supported the preservation of natural resources, enhanced water management, and strengthened environmental resilience in a region particularly vulnerable to climate change.

The study also highlights the positive social impacts of sustainability assurance, including poverty reduction, improved access to basic services, greater community participation, and the promotion of local cultural heritage. These outcomes demonstrate that sustainable development can be achieved when economic, social, and environmental objectives are integrated into regional development strategies. Despite these achievements, challenges remain in financing, infrastructure, technical expertise, and stakeholder coordination. Addressing these constraints will require continued commitment from public authorities, private sector actors, local communities, and development partners.

Overall, the research concludes that sustainability assurance represents an important lever for inclusive and resilient development in Morocco's southern provinces. By strengthening sustainable practices and stakeholder collaboration, these regions have the potential to become a model of sustainable regional development that balances economic progress, environmental preservation, and social inclusion.

REFERENCES

Byrne, J.. (2016). Renewable energy and climate change mitigation in developing countries. [Volume, issue, and page numbers required]. *Climate Policy*.

El Hammoumi, A., Seghyar, N., Gouiouez, M., Amane, M., & Berdi, A. (2024). The adoption of a qualitative approach in management science: An exploratory survey on the effects of big data on the performance of companies. In *Applying qualitative research methods to management science* (pp. 283–309). IGI Global. DOI: 10.4018/979-8-3693-5543-5.ch011

Food and Agriculture Organization. (2019). *Water-efficient agriculture in arid regions*. FAO.

Gössling, S., & Peeters, P. (2022). Tourism and environmental sustainability. *Journal of Sustainable Tourism*, *30*(4), 789–804.

International Renewable Energy Agency. (2018). *Renewable energy outlook*. IRENA.

International Renewable Energy Agency. (2022). *Renewable energy in Africa: Challenges and opportunities*. IRENA Publications.

Lane, B. (1994). Sustainable rural tourism strategies. *Journal of Sustainable Tourism*, *2*(1-2), 102–112. DOI: 10.1080/09669589409510687

Lybbert, T. J., & Sumner, D. A. (2020). Agriculture in North Africa: Adaptive strategies for climate change. *Agricultural Economics*, *51*(2), 207–219.

Ministry of the Environment. Morocco. (2017). *Politique nationale de développement durable*. Government of Morocco.

Moulai, S., & Boukrif, M. (2018). The choice of successor in family SMEs. *Revue Africaine de Management*, *1*(3).

Organisation for Economic Co-operation and Development. (2020). *Sustainable development goals in emerging economies*. OECD Publishing.

Rockström, J., & Falkenmark, M. (2021). Water resilience for agriculture in semi-arid regions. *Science*, *374*(6566), 375–380.

Royer, C., Baribeau, C., & Duchesne, A. (2009). Individual interviews in social science research in Quebec: Where do we stand? Un panorama des usages. *Recherches Qualitatives*, *7*, 64–79.

Sharpley, R., & Telfer, D. J. (2021). *Tourism and development in the developing world* (2nd ed.). Routledge.

Sovacool, B. K., & Griffiths, S. (2021). Renewable energy in Sub-Saharan Africa: Emerging lessons for sustainable development. *Renewable & Sustainable Energy Reviews*, *137*, 110600.

Tilman, D., Cassman, K. G., Matson, P. A., Naylor, R., & Polasky, S. (2002). Agricultural sustainability and intensive production practices. *Nature*, *418*(6898), 671–677. DOI: 10.1038/nature01014 PMID: 12167873

United Nations Global Compact. (2017). *Achieving SDGs through sustainable business practices*. United Nations Global Compact.

Wollesen, B., Wildbredt, A., van Schooten, K. S., Lim, M. L., & Delbaere, K. (2020). The effects of cognitive-motor training interventions on executive functions in older people: A systematic review and meta-analysis. *European Review of Aging and Physical Activity : Official Journal of the European Group for Research into Elderly and Physical Activity*, *17*(1), 1–22. DOI: 10.1186/s11556-020-00240-y PMID: 32636957

Chapter 5
Integrating Broad-Based Economic Empowerment for Local Economic Development:
Using Participatory Development, Representivity, and "Other" to Achieve Sustainable Development

Lindani Sthembele Maphumulo
http://orcid.org/0000-0002-8362-2133
University of Western Cape, South Africa

Nombuso Zakwe
University of Westen Cape, South Africa

Rolda Kafaar
University of Westen Cape, South Africa

ABSTRACT

This chapter explores the challenges of representative participation and proposes direct participation methods as a pathway to sustainable development, with a focus on integrating Broad-Based Economic Empowerment (BBEE) theory for local economic development. A qualitative approach was used to gather data from South African articles that examine participatory development initiatives in marginalized communities. The study included a collection of case studies from successful projects that prioritize Participatory Development in South Africa, purposefully. The Ladder

DOI: 10.4018/979-8-2600-3325-8.ch005

of Participation framework was used to categorize the cases. Most so-called participatory initiatives fall within the "tokenism" category, where community members are engaged in informing, consultation, or placation. However, the selected cases demonstrate that projects with greater community ownership, informed by BBEE principles, are more likely to be sustained over time due to the increased dedication and responsibility that come with this ownership.

INTRODUCTION

Local economic development (LED) has undergone a major transformation globally and within South Africa, shifting from traditional top-down models toward participatory, community-driven, and empowerment-focused approaches. These shifts reflect international recognition that sustainable development depends on how power operates within communities, who participates in decision-making, and whose interests shape development agendas. In development contexts, power refers to the ability of individuals, communities, or organisations to influence decisions, allocate resources, and set priorities (Kapilashrami, Quinn, and Das, 2025).

Marginalisation occurs when certain communities are systemically excluded. Marginalization refers to the social, economic, and political exclusion of specific groups within society. This exclusion is often based on characteristics such as race, class, gender, ethnicity, religion, and geographic location (Makwana, and Elizabeth, 2022). Marginalized groups are systematically denied opportunities, resources, and rights, making them disproportionately vulnerable and disadvantaged in development processes (Saaida and Saaidah, 2023). In many cases, these marginalized groups are excluded from decision-making, have limited access to development resources, and experience the negative consequences of development policies and interventions.

A glaring example of the relationship between power dynamics and marginalization in South Africa is the persistence of spatial inequality, which divides communities based on race and economic status. During the apartheid era, policies such as the Group Areas Act forcibly relocated non-white communities to designated townships on the outskirts of urban centers (Ntsebeza and Hall, 2007). The legacy of these policies continues today, as affluent suburbs have access to superior infrastructure, services, and economic opportunities, while townships and informal settlements suffer from inadequate housing, sanitation, and transportation (Turok, 2011). This spatial segregation and economic marginalization leave residents of townships with limited access to jobs, education, healthcare, and other essential services (Turok, Visagie, and Scheba, 2021). Thus, the geographical location of a community plays a significant role in determining its level of access to resources, opportunities, and overall development outcomes.

The connection between power dynamics and marginalization is also evident in the formulation of development policies and strategies, where decision-making processes are often dominated by powerful actors such as government officials, international organizations, and multinational corporations. These entities frequently set agendas that are disconnected from the needs and priorities of local communities (Novovic, 2022). For instance, Western-led development programs often focus on economic growth and efficiency, sometimes at the expense of social, cultural, and environmental concerns that are integral to local communities. This top-down approach to development planning can overlook local knowledge, desires, and goals, thereby further marginalizing communities whose voices are not included in decision-making processes (Ahmad and Islam, 2024; Sebunya and Gichuki, 2024).

In South Africa, this power imbalance is particularly evident in the ongoing challenge of achieving inclusive development. While the country has made strides in addressing some of the socio-economic disparities left by apartheid, challenges remain in ensuring that all communities, particularly marginalized groups such as rural populations, women, and informal sector workers, have meaningful participation in development processes. Power dynamics in South Africa, shaped by both historical legacies and contemporary economic structures, continue to shape the experiences of marginalized communities, limiting their opportunities for empowerment and inclusion. The legacy of apartheid spatial planning, where the Group Areas Act relegated Black communities to peripheral townships, continues to reinforce deeply unequal access to services, economic opportunities, and development resources (Ntsebeza and Hall, 2007; Turok, 2011; Turok et al., 2021). These inherited spatial and economic inequalities make the relationship between power, community inclusion, and LED particularly urgent. This chapter argues that integrating Broad-Based Black Economic Empowerment (BBEE) principles into participatory LED frameworks provides a strategic pathway for addressing these historical injustices. It also situates the South African experience within global debates on whether LED is genuinely transformative or merely replicates old inequalities under new policy labels.

Although LED policy frameworks emphasise participation, the lived reality in many South African communities remains one of tokenism, limited influence, and constrained access to development benefits. Decision-making processes are still dominated by government elites, external experts, and donor organisations whose agendas often diverge from the priorities of local communities (Novovic, 2022; Escobar, 1995). As a result, many LED initiatives remain at the lower rungs of Arnstein's Ladder of Participation, focusing on informing or consulting rather than enabling citizen power, control, or genuine co-creation (Willness et al, 2023). Through analysing how power, community representation, and marginalisation shape LED outcomes, this chapter offers two major contributions: first, an analytical critique of the gaps between participatory rhetoric and practice; and second, a framework for advancing more inclusive, community-empowered LED by merging participatory development with BBEE. Ultimately, the chapter argues that sustainable LED in South Africa requires reimagining not only policy design but also the power relations and community dynamics that define who participates, who decides, and who benefits from development.

This chapter will explore how power dynamics influence development initiatives, particularly in the context of Western influence in development programs and its implications for marginalized communities, or the "Other." The discussion will critically examine the tension between homogenization and the recognition of diverse community realities, focusing on the challenges of representative participation in development processes in South Africa. Drawing on case studies of successful participatory development initiatives in South Africa, the chapter will analyze these projects using the Ladder of Participation framework, highlighting how community involvement and direct participation contribute to sustainable development. Finally, the chapter will emphasize the importance of inclusivity and diversity in development practices, arguing that these principles are essential for fostering more equitable, effective, and long-lasting development outcomes.

Problem Statement

Participatory development has gained widespread acceptance as a development practice and is utilized by diverse organizations such as the World Bank Development (Wampler et al., 2021; Williams, 2006). Once the global leading institutions, such World Bank, used the participatory development approach, the rest of the world followed (Sondarjee, 2021). Perhaps it is a universal truth in international development that underdeveloped countries are compelled to implement new buzzwords whenever the major international development agencies do. According to Williams (2006), participation was then increasingly incorporated into governments' social development programs, both as a means of delivery and as a desired result in and of itself. However, it can also be observed that whenever the progressive bottom-up development agencies adopt an idea, scholars and practitioners who identify as top-down capitalist, post-colonial, and anti-development groups outside the mainstream usually try their utmost to keep a distance from it.

Participatory development is often positioned as an alternative to the usual "top-down" development approaches, although there is some ambiguity regarding its precise definition due to conflicting perspectives. Makwana and Elizabeth (2022) argue that participatory development is not beneficial for vulnerable populations, as it often includes marginalized groups in major organizations initiatives, leading to unaccountability and questioning the power and nature of communities. Makwana and Elizabeth (2022) mention that despite this, participation can potentially help those previously included in development projects, serving as tools for manipulation by organizations.

Aim of the Chapter

This chapter aims to explore the challenges of representative participation and propose direct participation methods to achieve sustainable development.

Chapter Objectives

- To unpack the role of power dynamics in participatory development initiatives.
- To explore sustainable participatory development cases in marginalized communities.
- To understand the impact of the other in the development processes.

APPROACH - QUALITATIVE DESIGN

The human science is concerned with the lived experiences of people. Singh (2007) maintains that social research plays a huge role in the development process and social change. Mikkelsen (2005) insists that qualitative research methods dominate in development studies. In social sciences, applied research and qualitative methods are commonly employed in studies that seek to understand the lived experiences of people to influence change. According to Guest et al (2013: 02), applied research normally used in qualitative studies "strive to improve our understanding of a problem, with the intent of contributing to the solution of that problem". It touches on the real-life experiences of the people. Therefore, to understand the experiences of the homeless "other" concerning development issues and processes, there is a need for a research method that seeks to explore their lived experiences at hand, through case studies, observation, and mutual learning.

This chapter interpretatively explores marginalized communities' subjective experiences from development practitioners and beneficiaries. The interpretative perspective according to Guest et al (2016: 05), "starts from the position that our understanding of reality, including the domain of human action, is a social construction by human factors and that this applies equally to researchers." Qualitative research is concerned with the real life of the people; it allows for the interpretation of events as described by people to minimize assumptions. For the purpose of this research, the interactive paradigm is adopted to allocate the researcher in the context and realities of marginalized communities the "Other" through the interpretation of documented case studies and observation.

Sampling Strategy- Purposive Sampling and Random

The purpose of sampling is to identify the units or the segments in the from a larger population. Guest et al (2013) maintain that it identifies the relevant group or community as well as individuals to participants in the research on the basis of their ability to provide rich information to represent the entire population. The unit of analysis, according to Guest et al (2013: 26), "is the level of abstraction at which you look for variability.

Sampling defines the relevant cases for the chapter from the larger population, informed by objectives and the aim of the chapter. Guest et al (2013: 26) continue to state that the "analysis of qualitative data can be carried out at higher levels of abstraction." This chapter used purposive sampling guarded by the above definition of the unit of analysis. The advantage of sampling and unit analysis is that the validity of the chapter depends on the sampling methods employed in selecting who shall participate in the chapter to give rich information (Guest et al, 2013). These strategies were used to identify the case studies and research participatory development initiatives from the internet and documented projects.

Method of data analysis- Thematic analysis

This collected data in written words by researching participatory development projects through the internet and documenting projects available in public domains. There were many connections and disconnections between what participatory development is and experiences within the development contexts. Therefore, there was a need for a tool that would help show such disconnections and connections. Thematic analysis was the relevant data analysis method for this chapter, as it helped to draw together different themes. The thematic process, according to Guest et al (2013: 13) "consists of reading through textual data, identifying themes in the data, coding those themes, and then interpreting the structure and content of the themes." Because qualitative research and data are dependent on the information that is given freely, there was a need for an analysis method that is inductive in nature to indicate the connections or themes from the data.

LITERATURE DISCUSSION ON UNDERSTANDING HOW THE 'OTHER' IS OFTEN MARGINALIZED IN DEVELOPMENT INITIATIVES

In the context of development, "marginalization" describes the deliberate and systemic exclusion of particular social and economic groups from the advantages of advancement. Ethnic minorities, Indigenous populations, women, people with disabilities, and the impoverished living in rural areas are examples of these marginalized groups. According to Makwana, and Elizabeth, (2022, marginalized groups as include those who are denied equal opportunities and capabilities to participate in and benefit from the development process. Hossain, (2024) asserts to the way that development projects frequently exclude the "Other." People, cultures, and countries who do not belong to the dominant Western civilization are referred to as the "Other" and are frequently seen as inferior or in need of assistance and development.

The power dynamics at play are a major factor in the marginalization of the 'Other' in development projects. Western nations and organizations, with their own objectives and priorities, frequently spearhead development programs (Onyango, 2025). Consequently, the 'Other' is shown as passive recipients of assistance and growth instead of active contributors to their own development (Hossain, 2024). Furthermore, the varied and intricate realities of these communities are frequently ignored when the "Other" is homogenized and reduced to a single story. As a result, their culture, needs, and goals are represented in a skewed and reduced way. Their agency and voices are thus suppressed, and they are unable to oppose or influence the development projects that have an impact on them.

The idea of the "development expert" also plays a role in the marginalization of the "Other." These are frequently Westerners who are viewed as the experts on development and who are bestowed with the ability to decide what to do and how to do it in the "Other" communities (Zhou, 2021). This serves to maintain the existing power disparity and the notion that the "Other" must be "developed" or preserved by the West. Furthermore, the marginalization of the "Other" is frequently reinforced by the rhetoric used in development discourse (Hossain, 2024). These communities are characterized by terms like underdeveloped, traditional, backward, and poor, which foster a sense of inferiority and dependence. The 'Other' is portrayed as lacking agency and in need of outside intervention, which serves to further the power dynamic.

The marginalization of the 'Other' in development endeavours is also clarified by Spivak's (1988) idea of the 'subaltern'. The downtrodden and disenfranchised communities whose opinions are not heard in mainstream society are referred to as subaltern. 'Other' communities that are not included in development projects or decision-making processes are considered to be part of the 'subaltern' in the development context (Hossain, 2025; Akbar, 2025). Power disparities, homogenization, and the terminology employed in development discourse led to the marginalization of the 'Other' in development attempts. Their voices and agency are suppressed as a result, and their cultures and needs are portrayed in an inaccurate way. The 'Other' must be given a meaningful and equal role in directing their own development in order to address this problem, and more inclusive, participatory, and self-reflexive development initiatives are required.

As previously mentioned, information draws attention to a crucial part of power dynamics and representation in the debate on development (Zhou, 2021). It highlights how language can change to become more politically correct and sensitive, substituting more neutral or positive phrases like "beneficiaries," "partners," or "clients" for derogatory ones like "poor," "underdeveloped," or "disadvantaged." But the fundamental dynamics of power frequently do not change. The "Other" typically marginalized or impoverished communities in the Global South tend to be defined and represented by people with wealth, knowledge, and power during development processes, sometimes without taking into account their needs, agency, or viewpoints (Moosa, 2023). This has the potential to maintain a paternalistic approach in which development interventions are imposed instead of planned and conducted cooperatively. Terms like "beneficiaries," "target groups," or "partners" may not seem judgmental or stigmatizing, but they do not always address the core problem of power dynamics in the definition of development objectives and tactics. The passage implies that language does not change the "us/them" relationship.

Western Influence in Development Programs: Implications for the 'Other' in South Africa

Western influences in the development of natives have had a deep and diverse impact on marginalized communities in South Africa, also known as the 'Other' (Onyango 2025). Since the end of apartheid. South Africa has received significant international aid and development support, most of which is influenced by Western donor objectives and agendas. While these interventions seek to promote growth and prosperity, their impact on marginalized communities. Exposes important considerations regarding power dynamics, culture, hegemony, and dependency (Onyango 2025).

One implication of Western influence in development initiatives is the persistence of power disparities and marginalize local voices and perspectives. Western funders and institutions frequently dominate decision making process, undermining marginalized group's ability to shape and design the implementation of development efforts. This exclusion undermines the democratic and participatory government norms inherent in South Africa's Constitution, reinforcing patterns of inequality and exclusion (Ntsebeza and Hall, 2007)

A further impact of Western dominance is cultural hegemony which promotes Western governance, education, and development models as global norms. Indigenous knowledge systems are frequently overlooked in favor of Western techniques, hindering efforts to promote cultural diversity and social cohesion in South Africa (Mawere, 2024; Olaopa and Ayodele, 2022). The imposition of cultural hegemony reinforces the marginalization of the 'Others' by subordinating their identities and perspectives to Western ideals.

Furthermore, Western-funded development projects have the potential to create a cycle of dependency among South Africa's vulnerable groups. While aid and support might provide immediate comfort, they can also weaken local autonomy and self-determination over time. This dependency syndrome impedes efforts to promote sustainable development and empower communities to address their own issues (Turok 2011)

Western involvement in development initiatives has far-reaching consequences for the 'Other' in South Africa, sustaining power disparities, cultural hegemony, and resilience. Addressing these implications necessitates a critical reevaluation of the Western development paradigm. As well as a commitment to promoting more inclusive, equitable, and locally developed techniques that allow marginalized groups to define their own future (Olaopa and Ayodele, 2022).

CONCEPTUAL FRAMEWORK - LADDER OF PARTICIPATION FRAMEWORK

The application of the Ladder of Participation framework offers a structured lens through which to evaluate the level of community empowerment and involvement in participatory development initiatives. This framework, which dates back to the work of Arnstein in 1969, consists of eight rungs that signify different degrees of participation, from token involvement to true citizen control (Willness et al, 2023; Arnstein, 2025). Through the application of this framework, scholars and professionals can ascertain the degree to which communities are genuinely involved in decision-making procedures and possess agency in molding the consequences of development endeavors. This section examines the value of utilizing the Ladder of Participation framework to analyze participatory development and provides insights into the subtleties of community empowerment and engagement in promoting sustainable development outcomes.

The ladder of participation perfectly explains the types of participation and non-participation. As stated by Willness et al. (2023), the eight types are arranged in a ladder pattern for illustrative purposes, with each rung corresponding to the degree of the ability of citizens to influence the final product. According to Willness et al. (2023), the first and second rungs of the ladder are manipulation and therapy, respectively. These two rungs represent artificially created "nonparticipation" levels by some to take the place of sincere involvement. Their true goal is to give those in positions of authority the ability to "educate" or "cure" participants rather than to allow people to take part in program planning or execution (Willness et al, 2023).

According to Varwell (2022), rungs three and four advance to "tokenism" levels that give the voiceless a chance to be heard: (3) Disseminating and (4) Consulting. When they are put forth by those in positions of authority as the utmost level of involvement, allowing citizens to be heard. However, in these circumstances, they are unable to guarantee that the influential will take their opinions into consideration (Arnstein, 2025). There is no "muscle" or follow-through when participation is limited to these levels, so there is no guarantee that the status quo will be changed (Arnstein, 2025).

It is mentioned by Arnstein (2025) that since the ground rules permit those who lack resources to offer advice while preserving the ultimate decision-making authority of the powerholder, rung (5) placation is merely a higher degree of tokenism. According to Arnstein (2025), there are progressively higher tiers of citizen power that confer greater degrees of influence over decision-making. To negotiate and make trade-offs with those who hold traditional power, citizens can form a (6) Partnership (Varwell, 2022). The highest rungs, (7) Delegated Power and (8) Citizen Control, according to Varwell (2022), are where non-citizens get most seats in decision-making bodies or total managerial authority.

In the context of participatory development, the explanation of the Ladder of Participation is essential because it offers a framework for comprehending the various levels of community empowerment and involvement in development projects. The framework illustrates the range of power dynamics at work in decision-making processes by classifying participation into eight rungs, ranging from manipulation and therapy to citizen control (Willness et al, 2023; Arnstein, 2025). Practitioners and legislators engaged in participatory development initiatives must comprehend these participation levels. They can evaluate the degree to which communities are truly empowered to have an impact on project planning, execution, and decision-making thanks to it.

By identifying potential tokenistic or limited participation areas, this knowledge enables changes to be made to foster more meaningful engagement and collaboration with local stakeholders. Participatory development initiatives can promote true empowerment and ownership in communities by aiming for the higher rungs of the ladder: partnership, delegated power, and citizen control (Varwell, 2022). Because local opinions are respected and decisions are made cooperatively in response to community needs and priorities, this produces more equitable and sustainable results. All things considered, practitioners looking to advance inclusive and successful participatory development practices can benefit greatly from the advice provided by this framework.

CHAPTER MAIN THEMES

Theme 1: Homogenization vs Recognition of Diverse Communities' Realities in South Africa

Homogenization refers to the tendency to ignore the different realities and nuances within communities in favor of using uniform or standardized techniques to address complicated challenges (Amin, 2024). This approach is often motivated by the desire for efficiency and scalability in development interventions, with policymakers and practitioners preferring simplified solutions that can be easily repeated across diverse contexts (Cornwall and Brock, 2005). The implications of this approach are particularly critical when considering Broad-Based Economic Empowerment (BBEE) policies, which are sometimes implemented as top-down solutions that fail to address the unique socio-economic needs of local communities. Patel and Graham (2012) argue that BBEE, despite its broad intentions, often falls short of achieving genuine empowerment due to its tendency to apply uniform strategies without sufficient consideration of local contexts. This leads to a situation where marginalized communities are left as passive recipients rather than active agents in their own development.

Recognizing varied community realities, on the other hand, highlights the significance of acknowledging and valuing societal heterogeneity and plurality of experiences. This method entails actively integrating communities in the development process while respecting local knowledge, practices, and perspectives (Ahmad and Islam, 2024; Sebunya and Gichuki, 2024). By recognizing the diversity within communities, development initiatives can be tailored to the specific needs and aspirations of different groups, facilitating more effective and contextually relevant interventions. As Turok (2011) suggests, such participatory approaches lead to the creation of development strategies that better reflect local conditions, improving the sustainability and inclusivity of these initiatives. Furthermore, integrating broad-based economic empowerment (BBEE) theory into participatory development practices can encourage deeper engagement from local communities, fostering ownership and responsibility for development projects. This is crucial for ensuring that interventions result in lasting change rather than perpetuating the cycles of inequality that often arise from homogenized approaches (Horwitz and Jain, 2011).

The tension between homogeneity and awareness of varied community realities is a critical topic in development practice, influencing the design, execution, and effects of interventions aimed at reducing socioeconomic gaps and fostering long-term development. While homogenization may result in the imposition of standardized solutions that fail to take into account local contexts and preferences, recognizing diverse community realities can lead to more participatory and inclusive approaches.

By empowering communities to shape their own development paths, as noted by Pike et al. (2018), development projects become more likely to succeed because of the heightened sense of ownership and accountability fostered by such engagement. This participatory process aligns with the ideals of BBEE, which seeks to create broad-based participation in the economy, not just among the elite but across entire communities.

In South Africa, homogeneity can be evident in the implementation of top-down development policies and programs that do not consider the country's unique socio-cultural terrain. For example, projects focused on poverty alleviation or infrastructure development often overlook the specific needs of marginalized populations, such as indigenous communities or rural women, resulting in limited impact and reinforcing cycles of inequality (Ntsebeza and Hall, 2007). This is where recognizing varied community realities becomes pivotal—development interventions must move beyond one-size-fits-all models to genuinely engage with the cultural, economic, and social needs of underrepresented groups.

Recognizing varied community realities is especially crucial in South Africa, a country with a history of deep divisions and inequality. By engaging with local communities, acknowledging their diverse needs, and integrating their knowledge into development processes, the country can ensure more sustainable, inclusive development outcomes. Sebunya and Gichuki (2024) emphasize the importance of community participation in development processes, arguing that when communities are recognized as active participants, development interventions not only address local challenges more effectively but also foster a sense of collective ownership and empowerment. In this context, BBEE can play a critical role in facilitating the economic empowerment of marginalized groups, particularly when it is integrated with participatory development principles that prioritize the voices and needs of local communities.

The tension between homogeneity and acceptance of varied community experiences is a significant issue in development discourse, particularly in diverse countries like South Africa. By critically engaging with these approaches and adopting the ideals of recognition and inclusion, policymakers and practitioners can move toward more equitable and long-term development outcomes that better represent the social fabric of the country (Minkov, 2021; Amin, 2024). Incorporating BBEE within this framework not only strengthens the participation of disadvantaged groups but also ensures that development strategies are genuinely inclusive, fostering more resilient and sustainable communities.

Theme 2. Successful Case Studies of Participatory Development Projects in South Africa

In this section, we examine effective case studies of participatory development in South Africa, focusing on programs that exemplify the transformative power of community-driven development strategies. These case studies provide compelling narratives of resilience, collaboration, and empowerment within marginalized communities in South Africa. By highlighting initiatives that enable local people to directly influence development priorities and be heard, we uncover important lessons on addressing historical injustices and fostering long-term change. These examples illustrate how participatory development can unlock the untapped potential of communities, leading to significant progress and social transformation through genuine engagement and inclusive decision-making processes.

Madzivhandila and Maloka (2014) argue that the shift in the planning of service delivery from a centralized (national) to a more localized (municipal) sphere of government marks a pivotal transformation in South Africa's development trajectory. This transition underscores the significance of decentralized governance, where communities are no longer passive recipients but active participants in the decision-making process. They emphasize that this shift has moved planning from a top-down approach to a more inclusive, bottom-up model, recognizing communities as key stakeholders in shaping their own futures. This approach ensures that services and development initiatives are tailored to the unique needs and priorities of local communities, thus enhancing the relevance and impact of these interventions. By actively involving community members in the decision-making process, development projects are more likely to achieve sustainable and lasting outcomes.

Madzivhandila and Maloka (2014) further highlight that the legislative and policy framework supporting participatory development has played a crucial role in empowering communities. For instance, the White Paper on Local Government (1998) defines developmental local government as a government committed to working in partnership with local communities to find sustainable ways of meeting economic, political, social, and material needs, while improving the overall quality of life. This document emphasizes the importance of participatory development, where the government fosters cooperation between the public and government to address community needs. The shift toward participatory governance models promotes inclusive decision-making, transparency, accountability, and empowerment, resulting in more adaptable and efficient local governance structures that are better equipped to address local challenges.

The integration of Broad-Based Black Economic Empowerment (BBBEE) principles with participatory development is also illustrated in several case studies of successful projects in South Africa. According to Horwitz and Jain (2011), while

BBBEE policies have made strides in promoting economic equity, they have often faced challenges in reaching beyond the elite to include broader community participation. However, successful cases of participatory development demonstrate how BBBEE principles can be better implemented when local communities are actively involved in the decision-making process. These initiatives reflect a more holistic approach to empowerment, where economic, social, and political empowerment are intertwined. For example, participatory projects that prioritize local economic development often use BBBEE policies as a tool to increase access to resources and opportunities for marginalized groups, including women, youth, and rural populations.

The success of participatory development in South Africa is also evident in the emphasis on community-led planning and governance. Participatory development programs that integrate BBEE not only encourage local ownership of development projects but also ensure that the economic benefits of these projects are more widely distributed among community members. According to Pike et al. (2018), when BBEE initiatives are combined with participatory development practices, communities are able to exercise greater control over economic resources, leading to more sustainable and inclusive economic growth. This approach fosters a sense of accountability and ownership, which is crucial for the long-term success of development programs.

Case studies of community-driven projects such as local cooperatives, small business support initiatives, and community-based infrastructure development highlight the effectiveness of participatory development in promoting local economic empowerment. By ensuring that community members are involved in every step of the development process from planning and decision-making to implementation and evaluation these projects provide tangible evidence of how participatory development can lead to more equitable and sustainable outcomes. Madzivhandila and Maloka's (2014) observation that the devolution of power to local governments has resulted in more effective service delivery is particularly relevant here. When local governments are empowered to work directly with communities, they can tailor interventions to address specific challenges and needs, ensuring that development efforts are both relevant and impactful.

Ultimately, the success of participatory development projects in South Africa lies in the commitment to community engagement and empowerment. By actively involving local communities in the development process and integrating BBEE policies into these efforts, South Africa can continue to build on its successes in local economic development. The examples discussed in this section demonstrate that when development programs are driven by the active participation of local communities, they are more likely to result in transformative, long-lasting change that benefits marginalized populations and reduces social and economic inequality.

Case Study 1 - One successful case study of a participatory development project is the Masisebensizane crèche in Gugulethu, Cape Town, Western Cape (Lyons et al., 2001). As stated by Lyons et al. (2001), the project was launched to give a permanent home to a crèche to run successfully in a garage. This project was extremely successful since it provided approximately 15 jobs, it frees mothers to work, the building was well maintained and further funding applications have already been made (Lyons et al., 2001). Active committee members and planning participants acquire political skills, offering opportunities for apprenticeship in projects and these individuals bring political experience from various spheres and have special interests in the project (Lyons et al., 2001). According to Lyons et al. (2001) a clear example of the previous made statement could be seen at the Masisebensizane Educare, where the head teacher had a good understanding of the township politics and was clever to involve members of her committee in compromises for permission to use a specific site effectively.

The Masisebensizane crèche project is a prime example of the value of participatory development, demonstrating the ability of local involvement to produce long-lasting and significant results. In addition to addressing the urgent need for childcare facilities, the project empowered women to enter the workforce, created employment opportunities, and promoted a sense of community pride by actively involving community members in the planning and decision-making processes. Furthermore, the ability of the project to negotiate complicated political dynamics and secure additional funding shows how successful participatory approaches can be in overcoming obstacles and optimizing resources for the good of the community (Zondo, 2022; Ngubane and Makua, 2021). All things considered, the Masisebensizane crèche project is a powerful illustration of how participatory development can result in comprehensive and long-lasting enhancements to local livelihoods and well-being.

Case Study 2 - Another successful project is the Ulwasi Youth Centre. According to Lyons et al. (2014), was situated in Langa, which is an older formal township on the outskirts of Cape Town, there are good transport links to the centre, and it is strongly linked with the Municipality. Lyons et al. mention that the following have been involved in the community structure of this project, all CBO representatives, local political parties, business and institutions, good participation, and broad leadership. The Ulwasi Youth Centre project serves as an excellent example of the value of participatory development since it uses a multi-stakeholder strategy that promotes sustainability and community ownership. Through the involvement of multiple actors, including businesses, institutions, political parties, and community-based organizations, the project guarantees diverse perspectives and wide representation in decision-making processes.

This inclusive strategy not only improves community cohesion but also successfully addresses complex challenges by utilizing resources and expertise from various sectors (Dushkova and Ivlieva, 2024). Furthermore, by providing access to resources and support for long-term viability, the project's close ties to the municipality show the possibility of government and grassroots initiatives working together. All things considered, the Ulwasi Youth Center project is a prime example of participatory development, emphasizing community involvement, collaboration, and group efforts in order to produce significant and long-lasting effects on youth empowerment and community development.

Theme 3. Fostering Sustainable Development through Community Involvement

The pursuit of sustainable development places a strong emphasis on community involvement as a central pillar in achieving meaningful and enduring results. Initiatives that prioritize community engagement unlock the potential for inclusive and holistic development because they recognize the deep interconnections that exist between local communities, their environment, economy, and social systems (Dushkova and Ivlieva, 2024). By actively involving community members in decision-making, resource management, and project implementation, these initiatives foster a sense of ownership and responsibility among participants, while leveraging the local knowledge and expertise that these communities hold. Sustainable development is often described as development that meets the needs of the present without compromising the ability of future generations to meet their own needs (Behera and Erasmus, 1999, as cited in Fourie, 2003). This definition highlights the importance of sustainable approaches that consider both the current demands and the preservation of resources for future generations.

Community involvement in sustainable development becomes especially significant in the South African context, where historical inequities and the effects of apartheid have shaped the socio-economic landscape (Dushkova and Ivlieva, 2024). Williams (2006) acknowledges that community involvement is far from a simple process, as it often involves navigating complex power dynamics and addressing contestatory relationships. Despite these challenges, Williams (2006) argues that community involvement is essential for ensuring that all people, particularly those marginalized historically, can participate in and benefit from the development process.

Broad-Based Black Economic Empowerment (B-BBEE) has been an essential part of the South African development framework, aiming to redress the imbalances created by apartheid and foster inclusive economic participation. Patel and Graham (2012) discuss how B-BBEE has been pivotal in promoting economic empowerment, though they note that its impact is often debated, as it sometimes focuses on elite empowerment rather than broad-based community upliftment. Horwitz and Jain (2011) similarly explore the complexity of employment equity and B-BBEE developments, noting that while there have been advancements, the effectiveness of these initiatives in achieving true empowerment for marginalized communities remains limited. These critiques underscore the need for community-driven development that goes beyond tokenistic inclusion to ensure long-term, sustainable change.

The key to sustainable development in South Africa lies in embracing participatory strategies that incorporate the diverse needs and perspectives of local communities. Madzivhandila and Maloka (2014) highlight that the shift in service delivery planning from a centralized to a more localized municipal sphere of government has allowed communities to directly influence decisions that affect their lives. This localized approach helps ensure that services are tailored to meet the specific needs of different communities, fostering more sustainable and effective development outcomes.

Pike et al. (2018) and Mkhize (2017) also discuss the role of small and medium enterprises (SMEs) within the B-BBEE framework, noting that these businesses can serve as key drivers of local economic development when supported adequately. By integrating SMEs into broader economic empowerment strategies, community members can take an active role in their own development, contributing to both economic and social sustainability. Furthermore, the involvement of SMEs helps to diversify the economy and create more resilient local economies (Mkhize, 2017).

An important aspect of participatory development that contributes to sustainability is its ability to utilize local knowledge and expertise. Communities often possess valuable insights into environmental management and resource utilization that can contribute to more sustainable development practices. Local knowledge can thus complement technical expertise, creating more contextually appropriate and sustainable solutions (Sebunya and Gichuki, 2024). Moreover, participatory processes that allow marginalized communities to shape their own development strategies help to ensure that development is more inclusive, equitable, and sustainable.

Moreover, sustainable development strategies should address the systemic issues of inequality that continue to affect marginalized communities, including women, rural populations, and low-income groups. As noted by Arya and Bassi (2011), corporate social responsibility (CSR) and policies like B-BBEE have increasingly become tools to address these inequalities, though their implementation often faces challenges. The inclusion of marginalized groups in decision-making processes not only contributes to social cohesion but also fosters a stronger sense of collective ownership, which is essential for long-term development.

Fleermuys et al. (2007) provide an example from Namibia, where broad-based empowerment initiatives have similarly sought to address the economic imbalances of the past, showing how local communities can be empowered through inclusive strategies. Similarly, Luiz and Van Der Linde (2006) examine the challenges in measuring the success of broad-based empowerment initiatives, emphasizing the importance of monitoring and evaluating these programs to ensure they achieve their intended outcomes. These insights are particularly relevant for South Africa, where the experience of previous policies and initiatives can offer valuable lessons for the future.

Theme 4. Prioritising Inclusivity and Diversity in Development Practices

When it comes to development practices, putting inclusivity and diversity first becomes essential to promoting fair and long-lasting results (Maphumulo, 2025). Acknowledging the intrinsic worth of varied viewpoints, experiences, and voices, inclusive initiatives aim to guarantee that every person, irrespective of their background or situation, is given a seat at the table. These initiatives, which aggressively encourage participation from underrepresented and marginalized groups, address systemic injustices and advance social justice in addition to improving the relevance and efficacy of development interventions.

Inclusive development practices in South Africa should concentrate on addressing historical injustices and systemic barriers that prevent underrepresented groups from having equitable access to education and economic opportunities (Ndebele, 2013). In addition to affirmative action or token policies, the author highlights the necessity of transformative policies. The Employment Equity Act of 1998 is one such initiative that requires employers to implement affirmative action plans to address historical discrimination and advance equal employment opportunities (Department of Labour, 2021). Because of this law, historically underrepresented groups are now more prevalent in a variety of fields, such as work and education.

Another illustration is the 2012 launch of the National Development Plan (NDP), which places a strong emphasis on inclusive growth in an effort to combat poverty and inequality (National Development Plan (NDP), 2012). There is a significance of rectifying historical inequalities by means of focused interventions like social grants, skill development initiatives, and infrastructure development. Additionally, community-based participatory approaches have become more and more popular in South Africa as a way to guarantee that local perspectives are taken into account during the development planning stages (Mkhize et al., 2017). With the help of these strategies, marginalized communities can interact with decision-makers and participate in the creation and execution of initiatives that have a direct impact on their lives.

Putting a conscious emphasis on making sure that people from all backgrounds and situations are actively included and empowered to participate in decision-making processes and benefit from development initiatives is what it means to prioritize inclusivity and diversity in development practices. This strategy is essential for addressing systemic barriers and historical injustices that have sustained disparities among various demographic groups in South Africa. Ndebele (2013) emphasizes the need for revolutionary policies to address historical discrimination in the workplace and in education. These laws, such as the Employment Equity Act of 1998, mandate that employers create affirmative action plans to advance equal opportunities.

Through encouraging diversity and representation in a range of domains, such as education and the workforce, these policies aid in dismantling obstacles and paving the way for historically marginalized groups to avail opportunities that have previously eluded them. Moreover, initiatives such as the National Development Plan (NDP) emphasize the importance of inclusive growth to combat poverty and inequality. By prioritizing inclusive development strategies, the NDP seeks to rectify historical inequalities through targeted interventions such as social grants, skills development programs, and infrastructure development. These efforts aim to create an enabling environment where all individuals, regardless of their background, can actively participate in and benefit from the development agenda of the country.

According to Mkhize et al. (2017), community-based participatory approaches are essential for making sure that local viewpoints are considered during the development planning process. Through the facilitation of communication and cooperation between communities and decision-makers, these strategies enable marginalized groups to influence the creation and execution of programs that have a direct impact on their lives. Overall, fostering justice, equity, and long-term sustainability requires giving inclusivity and diversity top priority in development processes. Development initiatives can address systemic injustices, advance social justice, and build a more inclusive society where everyone has the chance to thrive by embracing diverse perspectives, experiences, and voices.

CONCLUSIONS AND RECOMMENDATIONS

The chapter shows how important it is that inclusiveness and diversity be given top priority in sustainable development programs as a means of addressing the systemic power dynamics and marginalization that are common in development initiatives, especially in the context of South Africa. Analyzing power relations and marginalization reveals systemic injustices that sustain the marginalization and disempowerment of particular groups in communities, frequently on the basis of geography, gender, race, and class. Moreover, these issues are made worse by the impact of Western agendas on development initiatives, which upholds cultural hegemony, power disparities, and dependency among marginalized people. Thus, diversity and inclusivity must be given top priority in sustainable development initiatives, encouraging participatory methods that highlight underrepresented viewpoints, give voice to the voiceless, and support local autonomy and self-determination. Development programs can lessen the marginalization of the "Other" and promote fair, resilient, and sustainable outcomes for all societal members by adopting inclusive practices.

The critical importance of community involvement, inclusivity, and equity in fostering sustainable development outcomes is highlighted by the examination of homogenization versus recognition of diverse community realities, successful case studies of participatory development projects, analysis using the Ladder of Participation framework, BBEE, and the imperative of prioritizing inclusivity and diversity in development practices. To overcome participation challenges, inclusiveness and diversity must be given top priority in sustainable development programs. This will ensure that marginalized voices are heard, diverse perspectives are valued, and development interventions are customized to meet the specific needs of communities. Development initiatives have the potential to create more equitable, resilient, and sustainable outcomes that address historical injustices and promote social justice by embracing inclusive practices and empowering marginalized groups.

In conclusion, fostering sustainable development through community involvement is essential for creating long-term, inclusive, and resilient outcomes. By empowering communities to play an active role in shaping their own development, these initiatives can address historical imbalances and ensure that development efforts are grounded in local realities. While challenges such as power imbalances and resource constraints persist, the integration of community knowledge, participation, and empowerment within development policies, such as those related to B-BBEE, is critical for achieving more sustainable and equitable development..

REFERENCES.

Ahmad, I., & Islam, M. R. (2024). Empowerment and participation: Key strategies for inclusive development. In *Building strong communities: Ethical approaches to inclusive development* (pp. 47–68). Emerald Publishing Limited. DOI: 10.1108/978-1-83549-174-420241003

Akbar, T. (2025). Power and resistance: exploring the conceptions and experiences of gender and career aspirations of young people in Bangladesh (Doctoral dissertation, University of Glasgow)

Amin, T. (2024). Globalization and cultural homogenization: A critical examination. *Kashf Journal of Multidisciplinary Research, 1*(03), 10–20.

Arnstein, S. (2025). A Ladder of Citizen Participation. Journal of the American Institute of Planners (1969). In *The City Reader* (pp. 306–321). Routledge. DOI: 10.4324/9781003519508-36

Arya, B., & Bassi, B. (2011). Corporate social responsibility and broad-based black economic empowerment legislation in South Africa: Codes of good practice. *Business & Society, 50*(4), 674–695. DOI: 10.1177/0007650309332261

Cornwall, A., & Brock, K. (2005). What do buzzwords do for development policy? A critical look at 'participation', 'empowerment' and 'poverty reduction'. *Third World Quarterly, 26*(7), 1043–1060. DOI: 10.1080/01436590500235603

Dushkova, D., & Ivlieva, O. (2024). Empowering communities to act for a change: A review of the community empowerment programs towards sustainability and resilience. *Sustainability (Basel), 16*(19), 8700. DOI: 10.3390/su16198700

Escobar, A. (1995). *Encountering development: The making and unmaking of the Third World.* Princeton University Press.

Fleermuys, F., Nakusera, F., Shangula, F., & Steytler, J. (2007). Overview of Broad-Based Economic Empowerment in Namibia. In *Bank of Namibia 9th Annual Symposium Publication* (pp. 13-63).

Fourie, M. (2003). Beyond the ivory tower: service learning for sustainable community development.

Government of South Africa. (2012). National Development Plan: Vision for South Africa's Future - Unlocking Our Potential: Creating Work Opportunities for All [online]. Available at: https://www.ndp.gov.za/ [Accessed: 3 March 2023]

Guest, G., Namely, E. E., and Mitchell, M. L. (2013). Collecting Qualitative Data: A Field Manual for Applied Research. Sage Publications. United State of America

Horwitz, F. M., & Jain, H. (2011). An assessment of employment equity and broad based black economic empowerment developments in South Africa. *Equality, Diversity and Inclusion*, *30*(4), 297–317. DOI: 10.1108/02610151111135750

Hossain, M. I. (2024). Creation of 'other'in their own country, politicized identity-based division, and the rise of hostility toward 'out-group'in a multi-ethnic, poly-cultural world: A study on genocide prevention, human security, and peacebuilding. *Social Identities*, *30*(2), 88–109. DOI: 10.1080/13504630.2024.2342613

Hossain, M. I. (2025). Gender Inequality, Deprivation and Seclusion of Indian Muslim Women: Reflections on the 'Intersectionality'of Marginalization. *Hawwa*, *23*(1), 94–116. DOI: 10.1163/15692086-12341433

Kapilashrami, A., Quinn, N., & Das, A. (2025). 'Communities', power, and participation: unpacking concepts from praxis. In *Advancing Health Rights and Tackling Inequalities* (pp. 44–66). Policy Press. DOI: 10.1332/policypress/9781447361398.003.0003

Luiz, S., & Van Der Linde, K. (2006). Broad-based Economic Empowerment: Some Challenges in Measuring Ownership of Companies. *S. Afr. Mercantile LJ*, *18*, 473.

Lyons, M., Smuts, C., & Stephens, A. (2001). Participation, empowerment and sustainability:(How) do the links work? *Urban Studies (Edinburgh, Scotland)*, *38*(8), 1233–1251. DOI: 10.1080/00420980125039

Madzivhandila, T., Maloka, C. (2014). Community Participation in Local Government Planning Processes: A Paramount Step Towards a Successful Service Delivery.

Makwana, G., & Elizabeth, H. (2022). The Concept of the Indian Marginalized Communities. *Madhya Bharti Manviki Evam Samaj Vigyan Shodh Patrika*, *82*(2), 166–174.

Maphumulo, L. S. (2025). Empowering Traditional Leadership for Effective Community Development. African Journal of Religion. *Philosophy and Culture*, *6*(3), 213.

Mawere, M. (2024). *Mawere: Culture, Indigenous Knowledge and Develo*. African Books Collective.

Mikkelsen, B. (2005). *Methods for Development Work and Research: A New Guide for Practitioners*. Sage Publications. DOI: 10.4135/9788132108566

Minkov, M., Kaasa, A., & Welzel, C. (2021). Economic development and modernization in Africa homogenize national cultures. *Journal of Cross-Cultural Psychology*, *52*(8-9), 801–821. DOI: 10.1177/00220221211035495

Mkhize, M. L. (2017). The role of sense of community in promoting community based entrepreneurship in rural KwaZulu-Natal, South Africa: an exploratory study of agricultural co-operatives (Doctoral dissertation, University of KwaZulu-Natal, Howard College).

Mkhize, S., Mlatsheni-Mathebula, T., & Mashaba-Nkosi, L. (Eds.). (2017). Community Based Participatory Research: A Guide for Practitioners [online]. Available at: https://www.researchgate.net/publication/334644677_Community_Based_Participatory_Research_A_Guide_for_Practitioners [Accessed: 3 March 2023]

Moosa, I. A. (2023). *The West Versus the Rest and The Myth of Western Exceptionalism*. Palgrave Macmillan. DOI: 10.1007/978-3-031-26560-0

Ndebele, N. (2013). Decolonising the University: The Wits Experience [online]. Available at: https://www.witsuniversitypressscholarshiponline.com/view/titlepage/witsup-978-1-77614-468-5 [Accessed: 3 March 2023]

Ngubane, N., & Makua, M. (2021). Ubuntu pedagogy–transforming educational practices in South Africa through an African philosophy: From theory to practice. *Inkanyiso*, *13*(1), 1–12. DOI: 10.4102/ink.v13i1.9

Novovic, G. (2022). Can Agenda 2030 bring about "localization"? Policy limitations of Agenda 2030 in the broader global governance system. *Development Policy Review*, *40*(4), e12587. DOI: 10.1111/dpr.12587

Ntsebeza, L., & Hall, R. (2007). *The land question in South Africa: The challenge of transformation and redistribution*. HSRC Press.

Olaopa, O. R., & Ayodele, O. A. (2022). Building on the strengths of African indigenous knowledge and innovation (AIKandI) for sustainable development in Africa. *African Journal of Science, Technology, Innovation and Development*, *14*(5), 1313–1326. DOI: 10.1080/20421338.2021.1950111

Onyango Ouma, S. (2025). Rethinking of Development in the Twenty-First-Century Africa: Development Strategies, Governance, and Foreign Aid. In *Indigenous Systems, Colonialism, Colonial Legacies, and Africa's Economic Challenges: Why is Africa Failing?* (pp. 139–163). Springer Nature Switzerland. DOI: 10.1007/978-3-032-00317-1_6

Patel, L., & Graham, L. (2012). How broad-based is broad-based black economic empowerment? *Development Southern Africa*, *29*(2), 193–207. DOI: 10.1080/0376835X.2012.675692

Pike, A., Puchert, J., & Chinyamurindi, W. T. (2018). Analysing the future of Broad-Based Black Economic Empowerment through the lens of small and medium enterprises. *Acta Commercii*, *18*(1), 1–10. DOI: 10.4102/ac.v18i1.566

Saaida, M., and Saaidah, I. (2023). Understanding the Dynamics of Failure Development in Marginalized Areas: A Comprehensive Analysis.

Sebunya, J., & Gichuki, A. (2024). The impact of participatory planning on sustainable development: A literature review. *Journal of Strategy and Management*, *4*(4), 1–9.

Singh, K. (2007). *Quantitative Social Research Methods*. Sage Publications. DOI: 10.4135/9789351507741

Sondarjee, M. (2021). Collective learning at the boundaries of communities of practice: Inclusive policymaking at the World Bank. *Global Society*, *35*(3), 307–326. DOI: 10.1080/13600826.2020.1835833

Spivak, G. C. (1988). Can the subaltern speak? In Nelson, C., & Grossberg, L. (Eds.), *Marxism and the Interpretation of Culture* (pp. 271–313). University of Illinois Press.

Turok, I. (2011). Cities and economic development: A polarisation view. In Parnell, S., & Pieterse, E. (Eds.), *Africa's urban revolution: Policy press scholarship online* (pp. 119–134). University of Cape Town Press.

Turok, I., Visagie, J., & Scheba, A. (2021). Social inequality and spatial segregation in Cape Town. In *Urban socio-economic segregation and income inequality: A global perspective* (pp. 71–90). Springer International Publishing. DOI: 10.1007/978-3-030-64569-4_4

Varwell, S. (2022). A Literature Review of Arnstein's Ladder of Citizen Participation: Lessons for contemporary student engagement. Exchanges. *The Interdisciplinary Research Journal*, *10*(1), 108–144. DOI: 10.31273/eirj.v10i1.1156

Wampler, B., McNulty, S., McNulty, S. L., & Touchton, M. (2021). *Participatory budgeting in global perspective*. Oxford University Press. DOI: 10.1093/oso/9780192897756.001.0001

White Paper on Local Government. (1998). South African Government Publications.

Williams, J. J. (2006). Community participation: Lessons from post-apartheid South Africa. *Policy Studies*, *27*(3), 197–217. DOI: 10.1080/01442870600885982

Willness, C. R., Boakye-Danquah, J., & Nichols, D. R. (2023). How Arnstein's ladder of citizen participation can enhance community-engaged teaching and learning. *Academy of Management Learning & Education*, *22*(1), 112–131. DOI: 10.5465/amle.2020.0284

Zhou, S. (2021). The Chinese path of integration and development among all ethnic groups from a comparative perspective between China and the west. *International Journal of Anthropology and Ethnology*, *5*(1), 17. DOI: 10.1186/s41257-021-00058-1

Zondo, R. W. D. (2022). Participatory approach and good governance: The alpha and omega of sustainable local development in South Africa. *International Journal of Special Education*.

Chapter 6
Innovation and Community Development:
Building Sustainable Futures Through Local Empowerment

Jaysi Tanguilan Corpuz
http://orcid.org/0000-0003-3505-0377
Cavite State University, Philippines

ABSTRACT

This chapter examines the intersection of innovation and community development, emphasizing how sustainable futures can be advanced through local empowerment. It challenges dominant top-down models that marginalize community voices and reframes innovation as a social and contextual process shaped by local knowledge, relationships, leadership, and collective agency. Using an integrative review of literature and selected published cases, the chapter analyzes the role of power, equity, governance, and community participation in shaping meaningful innovation. It illustrates how communities in different contexts develop locally responsive solutions to social, environmental, and economic challenges. The chapter also examines the institutional conditions that support or constrain grassroots innovation, including governance structures, funding arrangements, local leadership, and cross-sector partnerships. It concludes by offering practical directions for inclusive and sustainable innovation that recognize communities as active partners in shaping long-term and resilient development.

DOI: 10.4018/979-8-2600-3325-8.ch006

1. INTRODUCTION AND BACKGROUND OF THE CHAPTER

Innovation and community development are increasingly recognised as complementary forces in achieving inclusive and sustainable futures. Traditionally, innovation has been defined through the lens of technological advancement, institutional research, and market competitiveness. However, these conventional views often overlook the social dimensions of innovation, particularly the role of local communities as key agents of change. This chapter proposes a reframing of innovation as a community-embedded process driven by empowerment, collective agency, and contextual knowledge. Many development initiatives continue to rely on top-down approaches that centralise decision-making power in institutions or donor agencies. These frameworks often marginalise the lived experiences of local populations and fail to engage them meaningfully in the design, implementation, and evaluation of development efforts. Avelino (2021) challenges this model by emphasising that transformative social change requires shifts in power structures that enable community actors to become co-creators of innovation rather than passive recipients.

Community development, as a field and practice, is rooted in participatory engagement and collective problem-solving. It prioritises empowering local people to assess their needs, harness their resources, and shape their environments. When innovation is integrated into this process, it extends beyond technological solutions to include social, cultural, and political transformation. In this broader view, innovation is not a product or outcome alone; it is an ongoing practice of adaptation, resilience-building, and agency enhancement within communities. Empowerment plays a critical role in this context. Empowerment is more than community involvement; it involves control over decisions, access to resources, and the capacity to influence outcomes. Innovation that is truly empowering must enable communities to define their own development agendas. This means recognising and valuing local knowledge systems, cultural traditions, and social networks as foundational to the innovation process.

Contemporary global challenges, including climate change, inequality, displacement, and governance crises, underscore the need for locally driven responses. While large-scale innovation policies often focus on replicability and scale, the most effective community initiatives tend to be deeply context-specific. They are embedded in local realities, responsive to local priorities, and adaptive to shifting conditions. This calls for a more pluralistic understanding of innovation, one that supports diverse pathways to development based on the principle of self-determination. Adelle, Pereira, and Pereira (2019) argue that sustainability governance must be contextual, inclusive, and attentive to the values of those it aims to serve. Their work highlights how top-down sustainability interventions frequently lack legitimacy and impact because they exclude local perspectives. In contrast, community-driven innovation, when grounded in empowerment, offers a more durable and just approach to sustainability. It enables communities to act not only as implementers but also as designers and evaluators of change.

This chapter's foundation is on the premise that innovation should be democratised and localised. It challenges the prevailing assumption that innovation must originate with institutions or experts and instead advocates a model in which communities are seen as knowledge holders and innovators in their own right. The focus is not merely on creating new tools or services, but on transforming power dynamics and relationships within the development ecosystem.

The chapter's structure reflects this mission. Section 2 will define key concepts of innovation, empowerment, and sustainability as they relate to community development. Section 3 presents a literature review that synthesises trends and identifies gaps in current research. Section 4 discusses the theoretical frameworks underpinning the chapter's analysis, particularly those related to systems thinking and participatory governance. Section 5 outlines the methodological approach, followed by Section 6, which provides a contextual analysis of real-world examples and thematic findings. Section 7 identifies future research directions, and Section 8 concludes with practical insights and policy recommendations.

Furthermore, this chapter argues that innovation, to be truly transformative, must be rooted in empowerment. Communities must be empowered to define, implement, and sustain their own development processes. Only by centering local agency and shifting institutional mindsets toward partnership can innovation serve as a tool for building resilient and equitable futures.

2. CONCEPTUAL/DEFINITIONAL ISSUES

This chapter centers on three interrelated and foundational concepts: innovation, community development, and empowerment. These terms, while often used interchangeably in development discourse, carry distinct meanings that shape how interventions are designed, implemented, and evaluated. Clarifying these definitions is essential to understanding how innovation grounded in local empowerment can lead to more sustainable and equitable outcomes.

2.1 Innovation as a Social Process

Innovation is commonly associated with technological advancement, institutional research, and economic competitiveness. However, this interpretation narrows the scope of innovation and often excludes community-led practices that do not fit within high-tech or market-driven paradigms. In this chapter, innovation is understood more broadly as a social and relational process that emerges within specific cultural and community contexts. It includes adapting traditional practices, developing new systems collectively, and creating creative responses to local challenges.

Rather than being viewed as something imposed from above, innovation is re-framed as something communities generate from within through their relationships, experiences, and problem-solving strategies. This inclusive understanding creates space for everyday innovations, which are often unrecognised by conventional development indicators but hold deep significance for community resilience. Avelino (2021) highlights the importance of recognising the power dynamics that underpin innovation. She argues that innovation must be viewed not only in terms of new outputs but also in terms of who controls the process, who benefits, and whose knowledge is considered valid. This recognition transforms innovation into a political act, one that can either reinforce or disrupt existing hierarchies.

2.2 Community Development as Collective Agency

Community development is a process in which local groups come together to identify shared goals, mobilise resources, and improve their environment. It is rooted in the values of participation, equity, and collaboration, emphasising the development of local capacities over the delivery of external solutions.

This chapter views community development not just as a technical activity but as a form of collective agency. Communities are not passive recipients of innovation or development; they are agents capable of defining their own priorities, designing interventions, and assessing outcomes. As such, community development serves as the platform for local innovation to flourish.

Community development and innovation intersect when the development process becomes a space for creativity, experimentation, and systems thinking. When communities are trusted to innovate, they often generate solutions that are contextually appropriate, cost-effective, and aligned with their values.

2.3 Empowerment as Transformation

Empowerment is both a goal and a process. It refers to the expansion of individuals' and groups' ability to make meaningful decisions, access necessary resources, and influence the systems that shape their lives. Empowerment is central to both innovation and community development because it redistributes power, enabling people to become leaders of their own development pathways.

In this chapter, empowerment is not treated as a token gesture, such as simply inviting participation in a pre-defined project, but rather as a fundamental shift in who holds the authority to define problems and determine solutions. Avelino (2021) reinforces that empowerment must include access to knowledge, legitimacy of diverse perspectives, and real influence over decision-making processes.

When people are empowered, they are more likely to participate meaningfully and sustainably in innovation processes. Empowerment ensures that innovation is not only about novelty but also about justice, ensuring that new systems and structures are responsive to the needs of those most affected by inequality or exclusion.

2.4 Sustainability and Contextual Relevance

Although not cited as a distinct term in every development model, sustainability is deeply embedded in the concepts of innovation, empowerment, and community development. In this context, sustainability refers to the ability of communities to maintain and evolve their development gains over time, in ways that are environmentally sound, economically viable, and socially inclusive.

Sustainable innovation, therefore, must be co-created, adaptive, and grounded in community knowledge systems. It must also build long-term capacity for self-reliance, enabling communities to respond to change proactively and be rooted in their own priorities.

2.5 Integrating the Concepts

Innovation, community development, and empowerment are deeply intertwined. Innovation provides the means to challenge and reshape outdated or unjust systems. Community development offers the structures and relationships that support innovation. Empowerment ensures that innovation is locally controlled and meaningful.

Together, these concepts provide a framework for reimagining development that is inclusive, participatory, and sustainable. They require a rethinking of how knowledge, power, and progress are defined and by whom. By foregrounding these definitions, this chapter sets the stage for an approach to innovation that is led by communities and informed by their strengths, aspirations, and wisdom.

3. LITERATURE REVIEW

The relationship between innovation and community development has undergone a significant transformation in recent years. This literature review synthesises key insights on grassroots innovation, empowerment, and participatory governance, while highlighting conceptual shifts and practical gaps in current research and development practice.

3.1 Shifting Paradigms in Innovation Studies

Traditional innovation frameworks have long emphasised technological advancement, research-based progress, and institutional leadership. These models typically prioritise measurable outputs and market scalability. However, there has been a growing recognition that such approaches often overlook the social and political dimensions of innovation. Newer perspectives frame innovation as a complex, relational, and context-sensitive process that encompasses cultural knowledge, informal practices, and the creative agency of local communities.

These reframing calls attention to the power structures inherent in innovation processes. Who defines innovation? Who benefits from it? And who is excluded? The evolving discourse suggests that innovation must go beyond efficiency and novelty to include justice, equity, and shared control.

3.2 Grassroots Innovation and Local Knowledge

One of the most prominent developments in the field has been the emergence of grassroots innovation. This form of innovation arises from community-level responses to local challenges and is characterised by its bottom-up orientation. Unlike centralised or commercially driven innovation, grassroots efforts are driven by lived experience, collective action, and local resources.

Grassroots innovation is often small-scale, informal, and adaptive. Examples include community farming initiatives, cooperative housing models, indigenous ecological practices, and neighbourhood-based digital networks. These innovations prioritise resilience, well-being, and cultural continuity rather than profitability or rapid replication. While often overlooked in formal innovation policies, they offer rich insights into how communities solve problems using their own knowledge and strengths.

3.3 Empowerment as a Development Strategy

Empowerment has become a central concept in development discourse. It refers to the process by which individuals and communities gain the ability to shape their own lives and influence systems that affect them. Empowerment entails access to resources, participation in decision-making, and the capacity to effect change.

In the context of innovation, empowerment involves more than community consultation, it requires giving communities real authority over how problems are defined, how solutions are designed, and how success is measured. Empowerment ensures that innovation aligns with local priorities and values. It transforms the community from a passive beneficiary into an active agent of development.

When communities are empowered to innovate, the outcomes are not only more relevant but also more sustainable. Empowerment enhances trust, encourages collaboration, and builds the institutional memory required to adapt over time.

3.4 Inclusive and Contextual Governance

Governance structures play a crucial role in shaping how innovation and development unfold. Inclusive governance refers to systems and practices that ensure participation from diverse stakeholders, particularly those traditionally excluded from decision-making processes. It promotes transparency, accountability, and responsiveness to community needs.

There is growing interest in adaptive, locally grounded governance models. These models reject uniform solutions in favour of strategies tailored to specific cultural, environmental, and political contexts. Such approaches recognise that effective development depends not just on delivering services but on building relationships, trust, and shared purpose.

Inclusive governance enables communities to co-create solutions rather than simply adopt externally imposed models. This shift is essential for fostering innovation that is truly empowering and sustainable.

3.5 Evaluation and Metrics of Success

How innovation is measured has significant implications for which projects are supported and scaled. Traditional evaluation methods often focus on cost-effectiveness, scalability, and technological advancement. However, these metrics do not always capture the social value or long-term impact of community-led initiatives.

There is a growing interest in participatory and qualitative approaches to evaluation. These include storytelling, community mapping, and reflective dialogue. These approaches allow communities to define success in their own terms, whether it's increased cohesion, restored trust, improved environmental stewardship, or cultural preservation.

Redefining evaluation also means recognising outcomes that may not be easily quantified but are nonetheless crucial to sustainable development. It encourages funders, researchers, and policymakers to shift from short-term outputs to long-term transformation.

3.6 Challenges and Gaps in the Literature

Despite advances in theory and practice, several challenges persist in the literature and on the ground:

- Many studies focus on short-term or pilot initiatives, with limited attention to how community innovations sustain themselves over time.
- Community voices from the Global South and marginalised regions remain underrepresented in the academic and policy discourse on innovation.
- Intersectional factors such as gender, age, class, and ethnicity are often overlooked in analyses of community development and innovation.
- While participatory language is common in policy frameworks, actual mechanisms for power-sharing and accountability are often weak or absent.

Addressing these gaps will require more inclusive, interdisciplinary, and longitudinal research. There is a need for methodologies that not only document innovation but also facilitate co-learning between communities and institutions.

3.7 Toward a New Understanding

The reviewed literature reveals a growing consensus that innovation, if it is to be sustainable and equitable, must be community-led, empowerment-driven, and contextually grounded. This challenges longstanding assumptions about where innovation originates and how it should be measured or supported.

Future scholarship and practice must continue to explore how local knowledge systems, power dynamics, and cultural frameworks shape innovation in diverse settings. They must also consider how institutions can evolve to support, rather than direct, the innovation processes that communities are already undertaking.

This chapter contributes to that effort by foregrounding the role of empowerment and community agency in innovation. Highlighting how communities are generating solutions to complex challenges builds the case for rethinking innovation as a collaborative and transformative endeavour.

4. THEORETICAL FRAMEWORKS

Understanding innovation as a pathway to community development requires a robust theoretical foundation. This chapter draws on two main theoretical perspectives to explain how innovation, empowerment, and development intersect: power and social change theory and contextual governance. These frameworks illuminate how innovation is influenced not only by technology or economic conditions, but also by relationships, participation, and the structures that enable or restrict community agency.

4.1 Power and Social Change

Power is central to both innovation and community development. It determines who participates, whose knowledge counts, who controls resources, and which outcomes are prioritised. Innovation is often imagined as a neutral process of problem-solving or efficiency improvement, but in practice, it is deeply political. It shapes and is shaped by existing power relations.

A nuanced understanding of power reveals its many forms. "Power over" refers to dominance or control, while "power to" signifies the capacity to act. "Power with" reflects collective strength through collaboration, and "power within" speaks to individual confidence and identity. All four dimensions are relevant in understanding how communities engage in or are excluded from innovation.

In community settings, power often operates subtly. It can manifest in who gets invited to planning meetings, whose ideas are taken seriously, or which groups are funded and supported. The ability of a community to innovate depends not only on access to resources but also on its position within broader power structures, economic, political, institutional, and cultural.

Innovation can either reinforce or disrupt these structures. When externally driven, innovation may impose solutions that communities neither asked for nor control. When community-led, it can challenge dominant systems and offer alternatives that are more equitable, sustainable, and empowering. This makes power analysis essential in any serious study of innovation for development.

4.2 Contextual Governance

Governance refers to the systems, institutions, and processes through which decisions are made and implemented. In the context of innovation and development, governance structures play a key role in shaping opportunities for participation, collaboration, and accountability. A contextual approach to governance recognises that there is no single model that works everywhere. Effective governance depends on how well it aligns with local histories, values, and conditions. It must account for diversity not just across communities, but within them, acknowledging that different groups experience governance and innovation differently.

Traditional governance models often operate in a top-down fashion, with limited engagement from those most affected by decisions. In contrast, contextual governance emphasises inclusivity, adaptability, and shared leadership. It views communities not as passive stakeholders but as active co-creators in shaping innovation and policy. This shift enables more responsive, relevant, and resilient outcomes.

Key characteristics of contextual governance include transparency, flexibility, local legitimacy, and meaningful participation. When communities are engaged early and consistently in governance processes, they are more likely to trust, support, and sustain innovation efforts. Moreover, when local knowledge is integrated into governance systems, solutions are better aligned with actual needs and capacities. This framework is particularly useful in explaining why some community innovations thrive while others struggle. It highlights the importance of enabling environments, policies, relationships, and institutional cultures that support experimentation, learning, and collaboration. Without supportive governance, even the most promising grassroots innovations may falter.

4.3 The Intersection of Power and Governance

While power and governance can be analysed separately, they are deeply interconnected. Governance structures reflect and reinforce power dynamics, while power determines who influences governance. In the context of innovation, these relationships are especially significant because they determine whose vision of development is realised.

When governance is exclusive or technocratic, power remains centralised, and innovation may serve only elite interests. When governance is participatory and context-aware, it redistributes power and makes room for community-driven solutions. This shift allows innovation to become a vehicle for transformation not just in services or infrastructure, but also in rights, relationships, and resilience.

The integration of power and governance perspectives provides a more complete understanding of how innovation operates in real-world settings. It helps explain why innovation cannot be simply transferred from one place to another, and why community engagement is not a box to check but a central component of success.

4.4 Application to the Chapter

This theoretical foundation underpins the analysis in the succeeding sections. It explains why innovation is not neutral, why empowerment is essential, and why development must be participatory to be sustainable. By focusing on power and governance, the chapter examines how communities shape and are shaped by the innovation processes they engage in.

The frameworks also support a critical view of conventional development approaches. They question the assumptions behind top-down planning, highlight the limits of technical fixes, and point to the need for systemic change. Most importantly, they create space for alternative narratives: those that originate in communities, are led by communities, and are evaluated according to community-defined success.

These perspectives guide the interpretation of case examples, stakeholder roles, and the barriers and enablers of local innovation. They serve not only as analytical tools but as normative commitments to equity, justice, and sustainability in development practice.

5. CHAPTER METHOD

This chapter adopts an integrative method, combining a structured literature review with selected case study insights to explore the relationship between innovation and community development through the lens of local empowerment. This dual approach enables a broader understanding of the topic by linking theoretical knowledge with practical community experiences.

The literature review compiles key academic sources that investigate themes such as grassroots innovation, empowerment, participatory governance, and contextual sustainability. These materials form the conceptual basis for understanding how innovation processes operate in different development settings. Alongside this, the chapter includes examples drawn from previously published case studies that document community-led practices across varied geographical and socio-political contexts. These were chosen for their thematic relevance and clarity in demonstrating community agency and adaptive strategies.

This approach is particularly suited for topics like this, where practice and theory are deeply intertwined. The integrative method allows the synthesis of insights from multiple disciplines and avoids the limitations of relying solely on either empirical fieldwork or abstract theory. As highlighted in research methodology literature, such approaches are effective for developing new perspectives and guiding practical applications (Snyder, 2019; Torraco, 2016).

This method supports the chapter's aim to generate insights that are both grounded in academic analysis and reflective of the realities faced by communities striving for innovative, sustainable development.

FINDINGS AND ANALYSIS: COMMUNITY-LED INNOVATION TOWARD INCLUSIVE AND SUSTAINABLE DEVELOPMENT

This section presents the key findings and critical reflections that emerged from the integration of literature, case evidence, and theoretical insights explored in this chapter. It delves into how innovation, when rooted in local agency and supported by enabling structures, can serve as a transformative force for inclusive and sustainable community development. Moving beyond technology-centric and top-down paradigms, the discussion highlights how communities define, lead, and evaluate innovation on their own terms. The subsections that follow examine the reframing of innovation, the role of empowerment, enabling conditions, real-world case studies, institutional systems, evaluation practices, and strategic directions for policy and practice. Together, they illustrate the complex interplay between grassroots action and systemic structures, underscoring the need for participatory, flexible, and equity-driven approaches to development.

6.1 Rethinking Innovation in a Community Context

Conventional models of innovation, often rooted in technology, commercial entrepreneurship, and top-down policy interventions, tend to overlook the everyday creativity and resourcefulness of communities. These mainstream approaches typically prioritise novel products, market scalability, and return on investment. While they may be effective in business or industrial contexts, they often fail to align with the needs, values, and dynamics of local development processes.

In community settings, innovation frequently takes a different shape. It emerges from social relationships, shared responsibilities, and collective problem-solving. It does not always involve cutting-edge technology or breakthrough products. Instead, it often consists of incremental changes, adaptation of traditional practices, or new forms of cooperation that address locally identified needs. This form of innovation is deeply embedded in cultural contexts and rooted in place-based knowledge systems.

Recognising communities as innovators challenges traditional hierarchies of knowledge and agency. It also broadens what is considered "successful" innovation, not just in terms of efficiency or economic gain, but in how well an initiative builds social cohesion, enhances local agency, and supports long-term sustainability. Innovation in this sense is not a one-time intervention but a living, evolving process that reflects the community's capacity to define and drive its own development.

6.2 Empowerment as a Pathway to Sustainability

Sustainability is often described in terms of environmental limits, economic resilience, and institutional reform. However, these dimensions must be matched by a fourth: the capacity of communities to take ownership of their development trajectories. Empowerment, defined here as the ability to make decisions, control resources, and mobilise collective action, is not only an outcome of development but a vital mechanism for ensuring its sustainability.

When people are empowered to lead local initiatives, they are more likely to commit their time, energy, and social capital to sustain those efforts. Empowered communities can adapt more effectively to changing conditions, regenerate local knowledge, and respond to risks with flexibility and cohesion. These capacities are essential for resilience, not simply to bounce back from disruption, but to evolve in ways that reflect community values and aspirations.

Empowerment also supports inclusive innovation, in which diverse perspectives contribute to the creation of meaningful, locally grounded solutions. This inclusion is essential to avoid replicating power imbalances and to ensure that sustainability efforts align with the realities of those most affected by systemic challenges. Engagement of women, youth, and marginalised groups strengthens not just the equity but also the effectiveness of innovation processes (Cornwall, 2016).

At the same time, empowerment must be seen as more than participation in formal projects or consultations. It involves challenging structural barriers, reshaping accountability relationships, and establishing systems that reinforce autonomy. Community resilience, in this context, is not just about recovering from crisis but about transforming in ways that preserve identity while embracing change.

As Copeland et al. (2020) note, there is often a tension between stability and transformation in how social resilience is conceptualised and measured. Empowerment plays a crucial role in navigating this tension. When communities have the tools and legitimacy to determine their own future, resilience is no longer an external goal imposed by others; it becomes a lived, self-defined practice of sustainability.

Empowerment is the connective tissue between vision and implementation. It ensures that sustainability is not merely technocratic or temporary, but deeply rooted in the agency, identity, and priorities of communities themselves.

6.3 Enabling Conditions for Community-Driven Innovation

Community-driven innovation thrives not in isolation but within ecosystems that provide the necessary support structures. These ecosystems encompass institutional frameworks, cultural contexts, political environments, and resource availability. For innovation to be both sustainable and reflective of community priorities, certain enabling conditions must be established.

Inclusive and participatory governance structures are foundational. When communities are actively involved in planning, decision-making, and implementation processes, the resulting innovations are more likely to be relevant and embraced by the community. Such participatory approaches foster transparency, build trust, and enhance the legitimacy of initiatives. Ansell and Gash (2008) emphasise that collaborative governance, characterised by consensus-oriented decision-making involving public agencies and non-state stakeholders, is crucial for addressing complex public issues effectively.

Flexible funding mechanisms are another critical enabler. Traditional funding models often come with rigid requirements and short-term horizons, which can stifle grassroots innovation. In contrast, funding that allows for adaptability and long-term planning empowers communities to experiment, learn, and scale their initiatives. Franz et al. (2012) highlight that social innovations often require financial models that accommodate iterative development and community-specific needs.

Cultural relevance ensures that innovations resonate with the community's values, traditions, and social norms. Innovations that align with local cultures are more likely to be adopted and sustained. Innovations that are responsive to local culture are more likely to gain community acceptance, participation, and long-term support. Thus, culturally grounded approaches are important in designing innovations that are meaningful and sustainable within a particular community context.

Recognition and support of local leadership are pivotal in driving community innovation. Local leaders often possess deep insights into community dynamics and can mobilise resources effectively. Wolfram (2016) discusses the concept of urban transformative capacity, emphasising the importance of leadership in steering urban systems toward sustainable futures. Such leadership is instrumental in fostering environments where community-driven innovations can flourish.

These enabling conditions are interdependent. For instance, participatory governance without flexible funding may limit innovation, while cultural relevance without supportive leadership may hinder implementation. Therefore, a holistic approach that simultaneously addresses these factors is essential for nurturing community-driven innovation.

6.4 Case Studies of Grassroots Innovation

Innovation at the community level often emerges not from institutional programs or corporate laboratories, but from the everyday efforts of people to address challenges in their own contexts. Grassroots innovations are often informal, adaptive, and deeply embedded in local realities. They arise from necessity, resourcefulness, and collective agency, and they offer compelling alternatives to dominant development paradigms. This section presents selected cases from diverse contexts, urban, rural, and informal settlements, to illustrate how communities mobilise knowledge, partnerships, and cultural assets to generate meaningful change.

In urban India, the Self-Employed Women's Association (SEWA) and other community-based efforts have demonstrated how social and economic innovation can emerge from organising the informal sector. In particular, the case of Dholera smart city in Gujarat exemplifies the tension between state-led, technology-driven urban visions and grassroots responses. While Dholera was framed as a symbol of entrepreneurial urbanisation, it also exposed the ways in which top-down models marginalise local needs. Datta (2015) documents how community resistance, negotiation, and adaptation shape the reality of such "smart" projects, highlighting the agency of local actors in challenging or redirecting imposed innovation frameworks.

In South Africa, Cape Town's water governance provides another example of community-driven adaptation. During the severe drought and water crisis of 2015–2018, informal settlements were disproportionately affected. Yet it was in these very areas that residents collaborated with NGOs, researchers, and government bodies to develop decentralised and culturally appropriate water systems. Enqvist and Ziervogel (2019) highlight how communities co-produced sanitation solutions that reflected both environmental constraints and local preferences, revealing a pattern of innovation grounded in justice and participation rather than solely in technology.

In southern Germany, rural communities have pioneered energy cooperatives that put citizens at the center of the renewable energy transition. These cooperatives are not only about generating power—they represent a shift in governance, ownership, and motivation. According to Holstenkamp and Kahla (2016), community energy initiatives allow citizens to influence infrastructure decisions, distribute financial benefits locally, and take collective responsibility for sustainability goals. This decentralised approach counters the narrative that energy transitions must be managed by large utilities or state authorities.

Despite their varied geographies and sectors, these cases share common features. They emphasise collective ownership, contextual relevance, and adaptive learning. Rather than imposing pre-packaged solutions, these initiatives reflect innovation as a relational and negotiated process, in which community actors engage with, and sometimes resist, external systems. They also show that innovation is not always about scale or novelty, but about alignment with values, social trust, and lived experience.

These examples demonstrate that when communities are given the space, resources, and recognition to innovate from within, they produce solutions that are not only effective but sustainable. They reaffirm the view that grassroots innovation is not peripheral to development, it is central to it.

6.5 Innovation Ecosystems: Systems that Support or Hinder

Innovation at the community level does not arise in isolation it is shaped by the surrounding ecosystem of institutions, relationships, policies, and power dynamics. These ecosystems include government bodies, funders, NGOs, universities, and grassroots actors, each playing a role in either enabling or constraining the emergence of community-driven solutions. Understanding how these systems function is essential to fostering inclusive and sustainable innovation.

In supportive ecosystems, public institutions and intermediaries act as enablers rather than gatekeepers. They create environments that welcome local voices, support iterative learning, and decentralise control. A key practice in such systems is co-creation, which involves shared responsibility between institutions and communities in problem definition, solution development, and implementation. According to Voorberg et al. (2015), co-creation and co-production strengthen innovation by fostering trust, increasing legitimacy, and embedding change in local contexts.

However, top-down or technocratic systems often hinder grassroots innovation. Rigid funding structures, narrow success metrics, and centralised decision-making can marginalise local knowledge and suppress creativity. In many development settings, promising community initiatives fail to thrive because the surrounding systems prioritise control, efficiency, or scalability over adaptability and relevance.

Local governments play a pivotal role in shaping the enabling environment. When they adopt participatory governance mechanisms, support decentralised decision-making, and recognise diverse knowledge systems, they shift from delivering services to facilitating community agency. Ansell and Torfing (2016) argue that such "metagovernance" strategies, which govern through collaboration, help balance structure with flexibility and promote long-term resilience.

Intermediary actors, such as NGOs and academic institutions, also help bridge communities and formal institutions. Their effectiveness depends on their ability to listen, adapt, and remain accountable to the communities they serve. Westley et al. (2017) emphasise that social innovation labs and cross-sector partnerships thrive when they prioritise collective learning and redistribute power, rather than merely transferring technical solutions.

A well-functioning innovation ecosystem does not require a proliferation of actors it requires alignment around principles of inclusion, equity, and shared learning. Systems that support grassroots innovation make space for experimentation, respect local autonomy, and adapt institutional practices to meet communities where they are.

When innovation ecosystems shift from extractive to collaborative models, they create the conditions for transformation rooted not in imposed change but in community-defined progress.

6.6 Rethinking Impact and Evaluation

Evaluating innovation in community development requires a shift from conventional metrics like cost-efficiency and output scaling to approaches that value inclusion, adaptability, and transformation. Grassroots innovation is rarely linear or standardised; it evolves within unique socio-cultural contexts and is often more focused on building agency and relationships than producing replicable models.

Developmental evaluation is particularly well-suited for such environments. It supports real-time learning in uncertain and dynamic settings, allowing communities and partners to refine goals, strategies, and actions as they evolve. Patton (2011) emphasises that developmental evaluation strengthens innovation by providing continuous feedback loops that respond to change rather than resist it.

Participatory evaluation is another essential tool. Involving community members in defining success and assessing progress ensures that the evaluation reflects local values and knowledge. Estrella and Gaventa (1998) argue that participatory monitoring and evaluation not only democratise the process but also deepen accountability and learning among all stakeholders. When communities co-create evaluation frameworks, they take greater ownership of both the process and outcomes.

Recent scholarship reinforces the urgency of inclusive evaluation in tackling structural inequities. Ford et al. (2024) demonstrate how participatory evaluation methods were critical to assessing U.S. public health interventions aimed at addressing systemic racism. These approaches centred on lived experience and built trust among historically marginalised groups, factors essential to both evaluation quality and impact.

Institutions are also beginning to respond. The OECD (2023) advocates for evaluation systems that emphasise flexibility, inclusivity, and local ownership. These systems support innovation by enabling decision-makers to consider outcomes such as increased civic participation, stronger networks, or restored cultural practices dimensions often missed by conventional metrics.

Part of this, the Tamarack Institute (2022) provides practical guidance on integrating strategic learning into community-based evaluation, stressing that adaptive evaluation methods are not only more equitable but more effective. When evaluation is seen as a shared learning journey, rather than a top-down judgment, it becomes a tool for empowerment and lasting change.

6.7 Roadmap for Practice and Policy

Creating an enabling environment for community-driven innovation requires deliberate policy choices, inclusive frameworks, and tools that reinforce participation, adaptability, and long-term equity. Over the past five years, institutions, researchers, and civic organisations have offered concrete strategies to embed these values into innovation systems.

1. Embrace Participatory Evaluation and Monitoring Evaluation systems that invite community involvement ensure that innovation initiatives remain grounded in local realities. The OECD (2023) documents how Portugal's National Strategy to Combat Poverty integrates participatory monitoring to align government efforts with citizen priorities. This model of inclusive governance enhances accountability and fosters public trust in institutional innovation.
2. Utilise Digital Platforms for Inclusive Engagement Digital technologies offer new channels for civic participation. The "Voice to Vision" initiative demonstrates how co-designed digital infrastructure can connect community input with

planning outputs, making policymaking more transparent and responsive. Such platforms are critical for ensuring that marginalised voices influence decision-making in real time (Voice to Vision, 2025).

3. Adopt Inclusive Innovation Frameworks Inclusive innovation frameworks help structure how governments and institutions support community engagement. A 2024 report from The Productivity Institute outlines key principles of participation, direction-setting, and distributed governance as anchors for policies aimed at widening access to innovation and making its benefits more equitable (The Productivity Institute, 2024).
4. Align with Mission-Oriented Innovation A mission-oriented approach centres social and environmental goals in innovation strategy. Rather than funding disconnected initiatives, this model ensures coherence by aligning resources with systemic challenges. University College London (2023) proposes a framework for embedding inclusive missions in national and regional innovation systems particularly where historical inequalities persist.

Moving Forward

A roadmap for practice and policy should focus on:

- **Designing inclusive policy instruments** that decentralise decision-making.
- **Funding participatory innovation processes** with long-term flexibility.
- **Building evaluation systems** that recognise learning, adaptation, and transformation.
- **Aligning innovation strategies** with broader missions for sustainability, equity, and resilience.

Innovation becomes transformative when it is co-owned, co-produced, and co-evaluated by the communities it aims to serve.

7. DIRECTIONS FOR FUTURE RESEARCH

While interest in community-driven innovation has grown, important gaps remain in both academic literature and applied research. Future studies must move beyond general advocacy for participation and begin to interrogate the conditions, trade-offs, and power dynamics that shape how innovation is practised and sustained in diverse community settings.

One key direction involves longitudinal research. Much of the current literature documents innovation at a single point in time, often during pilot phases or initial project rollouts. There is a need for sustained observation of how community-led innovations evolve, adapt, or institutionalise over time and how they survive or struggle in shifting political and economic contexts.

Another area for exploration is the intersection of innovation and inequality. While the chapter highlights inclusive approaches, empirical studies are still limited in examining how factors such as gender, ethnicity, class, and geography intersect to shape who participates in innovation, who benefits, and who is excluded. Research that applies intersectional frameworks can deepen our understanding of equity within innovation processes and outcomes.

Future research should also expand methodological experimentation, especially in participatory and transdisciplinary approaches. As innovation is increasingly understood as a relational and social process, scholars must continue developing tools and methods that reflect community-defined indicators of success, qualitative change, and local forms of knowledge. This includes participatory action research, reflexive monitoring, and co-produced evaluation strategies.

The role of intermediary organisations—such as NGOs, innovation labs, or universities—also warrants deeper investigation. Future studies could assess when and how these actors support or hinder genuine community empowerment, and what institutional reforms might strengthen their accountability to local stakeholders.

Finally, there is an emerging need to explore policy integration: how local innovations can inform and reshape mainstream governance frameworks. This includes research on mechanisms for scaling without co-optation, integrating grassroots learning into national innovation strategies, and designing funding structures that accommodate informal, iterative, and locally driven initiatives.

By addressing these gaps, future research can play a pivotal role in advancing not just the theory of innovation, but its practice as a truly inclusive and transformative force in community development.

8. CONCLUSION

Innovation, when decoupled from its community context, often becomes a top-down endeavour focused on efficiency, scale, and replication. This chapter has challenged that dominant narrative by reframing innovation as a relational, inclusive, and empowerment-driven process, anchored in the lived experiences, knowledge systems, and aspirations of communities themselves.

Throughout the discussion, we have seen that innovation is not the sole domain of institutions, experts, or formal research. It also resides in the collective creativity and resilience of ordinary people responding to complex local challenges. Whether through cooperative organising, culturally grounded adaptations, or context-specific problem-solving, communities across the globe continue to demonstrate their role as active agents of transformation.

Key enabling conditions, such as inclusive governance, flexible funding, and support for local leadership, were found to be central to sustaining grassroots innovation. At the same time, we explored how evaluation systems, policy frameworks, and institutional ecosystems must evolve to genuinely support these efforts. Innovation should not be reduced to outputs; it must also be measured in trust built, power shared, and capacities strengthened.

This chapter argues for a shift in how innovation is imagined and operationalised in development contexts. Rather than seeing communities as recipients of innovation, we must recognise them as co-creators of futures not only capable of generating solutions but of defining what meaningful change looks like. Such a shift demands humility, sustained engagement, and structural change from practitioners, funders, and policymakers alike.

Therefore, building sustainable futures depends on more than technology or design. It requires an ethic of partnership and participation where innovation is not imposed but cultivated, and where development is not delivered but co-authored by the people it is meant to serve.

9. RECOMMENDATIONS

To advance innovation that is both sustainable and inclusive, a deliberate shift in practice and policy is essential. Based on the insights explored in this chapter, the following recommendations are offered to guide future work in community development and innovation ecosystems.

1. Prioritise Community Leadership and Ownership

Support initiatives that originate from within communities and reflect their lived experiences. This includes investing in local leadership development, recognising informal networks, and ensuring decision-making authority rests with those closest to the issues.

2. Redesign Funding and Support Mechanisms

Funders should move away from rigid, outcome-driven models and toward flexible, long-term funding structures. These must accommodate iterative processes, allow for uncertainty, and support learning over time. Participatory grantmaking and community-based budgeting are promising models.

3. Institutionalise Inclusive Governance

Governments and organisations must embed inclusive practices into their operational systems. This includes co-design processes, participatory planning, and community representation in advisory or oversight bodies to ensure accountability and relevance.

4. Reframe Evaluation to Reflect Local Values

Evaluation systems should incorporate community-defined indicators of success. Adopt developmental and participatory evaluation methods that capture social transformation, not just material outputs.

5. Strengthen Cross-Sector Collaboration with Clear Power-Sharing

Partnerships among academia, government, civil society, and communities should be built on mutual respect and shared control. Intermediary actors must act as facilitators—not managers—of community-led processes.

6. Align Innovation Policy with Social and Environmental Missions

Innovation strategies at all levels should be anchored in broader goals such as equity, sustainability, and justice. National and local innovation agendas must be responsive to grassroots insights and needs.

By implementing these recommendations, stakeholders can foster innovation ecosystems that are co-created, inclusive, and resilient.

REFERENCES

Ansell, C., & Gash, A. (2008). Collaborative governance in theory and practice. *Journal of Public Administration: Research and Theory*, *18*(4), 543–571. DOI: 10.1093/jopart/mum032

Ansell, C., & Torfing, J. (2016). *Handbook on theories of governance*. Edward Elgar Publishing., DOI: 10.4337/9781782548508

Avelino, F. (2021). Theories of power and social change: Power contestations and their implications for research on social change and innovation. *Journal of Political Power*, *14*(3), 425–448. DOI: 10.1080/2158379X.2021.1875307

Copeland, S., Comes, T., Bach, S., Nagenborg, M., Schulte, Y., & Doorn, N. (2020). Measuring social resilience: Trade-offs, challenges and opportunities for indicator models in transforming societies. *International Journal of Disaster Risk Reduction*, *51*, 101799. DOI: 10.1016/j.ijdrr.2020.101799

Cornwall, A. (2016). Women's empowerment: What works? *Journal of International Development*, *28*(3), 342–359. DOI: 10.1002/jid.3210

Datta, A. (2015). New urban utopias of postcolonial India: 'Entrepreneurial urbanization' in Dholera smart city, Gujarat. *Dialogues in Human Geography*, *5*(1), 3–22. DOI: 10.1177/2043820614565748

Enqvist, J., & Ziervogel, G. (2019). Water governance and justice in Cape Town: An overview. *WIREs. Water*, *6*(4), e1354. DOI: 10.1002/wat2.1354

Estrella, M., & Gaventa, J. (1998). *Who counts reality? Participatory monitoring and evaluation: A literature review*. IDS Working Paper 70. https://www.ids.ac.uk/publications/who-counts-reality-participatory-monitoring-and-evaluation-a-literature-review/

Ford, T. N., Ibe-Lamberts, K., Edmond, S., Abrams, I., Chaudhry, A., Daniels, P., Do, M., Edmiston, B., Fokum, S., Gary, C., Ghebenei, D., Hebert-Beirne, J., Jibrell, H., Jones, J., Kelleher, M. R., Lynch, J., Mahajan, A., Marcus, N., Pinsker, E., & Shaw, B. A. (2024). Challenges and opportunities for participatory evaluation of local public health efforts to address structural racism and advance health equity. *Journal of Participatory Research Methods*, *5*(2). Advance online publication. DOI: 10.35844/001c.118717

Franz, H. W., Hochgerner, J., & Howaldt, J. (Eds.). (2012). *Challenge social innovation: Potentials for business, social entrepreneurship, welfare and civil society*. Springer., DOI: 10.1007/978-3-642-32879-4

Holstenkamp, L., & Kahla, F. (2016). What are community energy companies trying to accomplish? An empirical investigation of investment motives in the German case. *Energy Policy*, *97*, 112–122. DOI: 10.1016/j.enpol.2016.07.010

OECD. (2023). *Evaluation Systems in Development Co-operation 2023*. OECD Publishing., DOI: 10.1787/a255365e-

OECD. (2023). *Monitoring and participatory evaluation of the National Strategy to Combat Poverty 2021–2030 (ENCP)*. OECD Observatory of Public Sector Innovation. https://oecd-opsi.org/innovations/monitoring-and-participatory-evaluation-of-the-national-strategy-to-combat-poverty-2021-2030-encp/

Patton, M. Q. (2011). *Developmental evaluation: Applying complexity concepts to enhance innovation and use*. Guilford Press. https://www.guilford.com/books/Developmental-Evaluation/Michael-Quinn-Patton/9781606238721

Snyder, H. (2019). Literature review as a research methodology: An overview and guidelines. *Journal of Business Research*, *104*, 333–339. DOI: 10.1016/j.jbusres.2019.07.039

Tamarack Institute. (2022). *Participatory Evaluation and Strategic Learning Practices*. https://events.tamarackcommunity.ca/workshop-participatory-evaluation-community-based-assessment-strategic-learning-practices

The Productivity Institute. (2024). *Making innovation more inclusive*. https://www.productivity.ac.uk/wp-content/uploads/2024/11/PIP039-Making-Innovation-Inclusive-FINAL.pdf

Torraco, R. J. (2016). Writing integrative literature reviews: Using the past and present to explore the future. *Human Resource Development Review*, *15*(4), 404–428. DOI: 10.1177/1534484316671606

University College London. (2023). *Towards inclusive innovation systems: Developing a mission-oriented framework*. https://www.ucl.ac.uk/bartlett/sites/bartlett/files/towards_inclusive_innovation_systems_developing_a_mission-oriented_framework_for_no_limits.pdf

Voice to Vision. (2025). *Enhancing civic decision-making through co-designed data infrastructure*. https://arxiv.org/abs/2505.14853

Voorberg, W. H., Bekkers, V. J. J. M., & Tummers, L. G. (2015). A systematic review of co-creation and co-production: Embarking on the social innovation journey. *Public Management Review*, *17*(9), 1333–1357. DOI: 10.1080/14719037.2014.930505

Westley, F., McGowan, K., & Tjörnbo, O. (2017). *The evolution of social innovation: Building resilience through transitions*. Edward Elgar Publishing., DOI: 10.4337/9781786431158

Wolfram, M. (2016). Conceptualizing urban transformative capacity: A framework for research and policy. *Cities (London, England)*, *51*, 121–130. DOI: 10.1016/j.cities.2015.11.011

KEY TERMS AND DEFINITIONS

Capacity Building.: Involves enhancing the skills, knowledge, institutions, and resources that enable communities to organise, innovate, and sustain their own development. It is both a means and an outcome of empowerment and long-term resilience.

Community Development.: Is a participatory process by which individuals and groups work together to improve the social, economic, cultural, and environmental conditions of their locality. It emphasises collaboration, local agency, and the co-creation of solutions that reflect shared goals and values.

Grassroots Innovation.: Describes bottom-up, community-led initiatives that emerge from local knowledge, relationships, and needs. These innovations are typically informal, small-scale, and adaptive, and are rooted in the lived experiences and priorities of marginalised or underserved communities.

Innovation.: In this chapter, innovation refers to a social and relational process through which communities generate context-specific solutions to local challenges. It is not limited to technology or novelty but includes adaptations, collective creativity, and culturally grounded practices that promote social transformation and long-term resilience.

Local Empowerment.: Refers to the ability of communities to make decisions, control resources, and shape development processes that directly affect their lives. It involves strengthening autonomy, enhancing participation, and building local leadership to ensure that innovation efforts are community-driven.

Participatory Governance.: Is a democratic process in which community members actively engage in decision-making, planning, and implementation of policies or programs. It emphasises transparency, accountability, and the sharing of power between institutions and local actors.

Social Equity.: Refers to fairness in the distribution of opportunities, resources, and outcomes across different social groups. This chapter addresses systemic barriers and ensures that innovation and development efforts benefit all, particularly historically marginalised populations.

Sustainability.: This chapter encompasses the capacity of communities to maintain and adapt their social, economic, and environmental systems over time. It involves inclusive, equitable, and locally meaningful practices that promote well-being without compromising the future of future generations.

Chapter 7
Leveraging Indigenous Languages for Economic and Civic Empowerment:
Insights From Kenyan Counties

Margaret Nasambu Barasa
http://orcid.org/0000-0001-9477-5402
Kisii University, Kenya

Galen Sibanda
http://orcid.org/0009-0002-9483-5318
Michigan State University, USA

David Monda
City University of New York, USA

Isaac Orina Nyakirario
Kisii University, Kenya

ABSTRACT

This chapter examines the transformative potential of indigenous languages in fostering local economic development and innovation through civic education in Kenya. With over 40 indigenous languages coexisting alongside English and Kiswahili, the country's linguistic diversity is a powerful yet underutilised resource for sustainable development. Focusing on Kisii and Bungoma counties, this study highlights how linguistic inclusivity can bridge socio-economic gaps, enhance governance, and stimulate grassroots innovation. It proposes strategies for integrating indigenous languages into digital economies, agriculture, and education while drawing com-

DOI: 10.4018/979-8-2600-3325-8.ch007

parisons with global practices. The chapter contributes to global discussions by offering actionable frameworks for leveraging linguistic diversity to drive economic resilience and innovation.

I. THE BACKGROUND OF THE STUDY

Kenya is one of Africa's most linguistically diverse countries, with more than forty indigenous languages spoken alongside the two official languages, English and Kiswahili (Mugambi, 2002; Moseley, 2010). This multilingual environment represents an important cultural asset and offers considerable potential for promoting inclusive governance, community participation, and sustainable socio-economic development. Despite this linguistic richness, indigenous languages remain largely marginalized within formal governance structures, civic education programmes, and development communication (wa Thiong'o, 1986; Bamgbose, 1991). Consequently, many citizens, particularly those living in rural and marginalized communities, experience limited access to information that influences their civic participation and economic well-being.

Civic education plays a fundamental role in strengthening democratic governance by equipping citizens with knowledge of their constitutional rights, public responsibilities, and opportunities for participation in development processes. In Kenya, however, civic education is predominantly delivered through English and Kiswahili, languages that many rural residents do not use as their primary means of communication (Government of Kenya, 2010; Omundi & Okendo, 2018). This linguistic mismatch creates barriers to meaningful participation in governance, limits public understanding of government programmes, and constrains access to economic opportunities. Studies have demonstrated that effective civic education promotes democratic values, citizen participation, and social cohesion, particularly when citizens can engage with information in languages they understand well (Finkel & Smith, 2011; Omundi & Okendo, 2018).

As a result, sections of the population remain excluded from decision-making processes that directly affect their livelihoods.

Beyond communication, indigenous languages function as repositories of local knowledge, cultural values, and community experiences accumulated over generations. They preserve indigenous knowledge systems relating to agriculture, environmental conservation, traditional governance, conflict resolution, health practices, and entrepreneurship (Chisenga, 2002; Wa Mberia, 2015). When these languages receive limited recognition in formal education and public administration, valuable knowledge that could contribute to local innovation and sustainable development is similarly overlooked. The continued marginalization of indigenous languages therefore represents not only a cultural concern but also a developmental challenge (UNESCO, 2003; Prah, 2020).

The growing emphasis on inclusive development, citizen participation, and knowledge-based economies has renewed scholarly and policy interest in the role of language in development. UNESCO (2003; 2022) maintains that education and public communication are more effective when delivered in languages that learners and communities understand well. Similarly, African scholars argue that indigenous languages should be recognized as strategic resources capable of strengthening democratic participation, educational access, social inclusion, and economic transformation rather than being viewed solely as symbols of cultural identity (wa Thiong'o, 2021; Heugh, 2021; Prah, 2020). These perspectives suggest that linguistic inclusivity can strengthen the relationship between citizens and public institutions while creating conditions for grassroots innovation and locally driven development.

Within Kenya, however, relatively little empirical attention has been devoted to examining how indigenous languages simultaneously contribute to civic education and local economic empowerment at the county level. Existing scholarship has primarily focused on language preservation, multilingual education, and language policy (Moseley, 2010; Orao, 2009; Obiero, 2010), with comparatively limited attention to the developmental role of indigenous languages within devolved governance structures established under the Constitution of Kenya (Government of Kenya, 2010). This gap has become increasingly important following the implementation of devolution, which expanded opportunities for citizen participation in governance, planning, and local development.

This chapter addresses this gap by examining how indigenous languages can strengthen civic education and contribute to economic empowerment in Kisii and Bungoma counties. These counties provide an appropriate context because of their linguistic diversity and their experience with county-level governance and citizen participation. Drawing on evidence from the two counties, the study investigates how linguistic inclusivity influences civic participation, local innovation, and economic engagement. It further identifies the challenges associated with integrating indigenous languages into civic education and proposes practical strategies for enhancing inclusive governance and sustainable local development.

By positioning indigenous languages as instruments of both civic empowerment and economic transformation, this study contributes to ongoing scholarly debates on language policy, multilingual governance, and sustainable development in multilingual societies (Freire, 1970; Bamgbose, 1991; UNESCO, 2022). It demonstrates that linguistic diversity should be regarded not merely as cultural heritage but as a strategic developmental resource capable of advancing democratic participation, strengthening community resilience, and promoting equitable economic growth.

2.0 LITERATURE REVIEW

The relationship between language, civic participation, and socio-economic development has attracted increasing scholarly attention over the past several decades. Although indigenous languages have traditionally been studied from linguistic and cultural perspectives, recent scholarship increasingly recognizes them as strategic resources for democratic governance, knowledge production, innovation, and sustainable development. Across multilingual societies, researchers argue that language choice influences citizens' access to information, participation in governance, educational achievement, and economic opportunities (UNESCO, 2003; Bamgbose, 1991; Heugh, 2021).

In the African context, the dominance of colonial languages within public administration and education has continued to shape patterns of social inclusion and exclusion. While English, French, and Portuguese often facilitate national and international communication, their privileged status has frequently marginalized indigenous African languages in governance, formal education, and public discourse (wa Thiong'o, 1986; Prah, 2020). Consequently, many local communities remain unable to participate fully in civic processes because official information is communicated in languages that are not their primary means of everyday interaction.

Scholars further contend that indigenous languages serve functions that extend beyond communication. They preserve indigenous knowledge systems, cultural values, environmental practices, and local innovations that contribute to community resilience and sustainable development (Chisenga, 2002; Wa Mberia, 2015). When such languages are excluded from educational and governance processes, communities risk losing not only their linguistic heritage but also valuable knowledge that supports local development.

Despite growing international recognition of linguistic diversity as a development resource, comparatively little research has examined how indigenous languages simultaneously influence civic education and economic empowerment within Kenya's devolved governance system. Existing studies have largely concentrated on language policy, multilingual education, language maintenance, and language endangerment (Moseley, 2010; Orao, 2009; Ogone, 2010), leaving an important gap regarding the contribution of indigenous languages to county-level governance and grassroots economic transformation. This review therefore examines scholarship relevant to civic education, indigenous languages, multilingual governance, and local economic development in order to establish the conceptual and empirical foundation for the present study.

2.1 Historical Perspective of Civic Education in Kenya

Civic education has evolved considerably in Kenya, reflecting broader political, constitutional, and governance reforms. Before the promulgation of the Constitution of Kenya (2010), civic education initiatives were largely implemented by civil society organizations, religious institutions, and development partners, resulting in fragmented approaches and inconsistent educational content (Omundi & Okendo, 2018). The adoption of the Constitution and subsequent enactment of the County Governments Act (2012) transformed civic education into a fundamental component of democratic governance by emphasizing citizen participation, accountability, transparency, and public engagement.

Section 99 of the County Governments Act establishes civic education as an instrument for strengthening constitutional democracy and enabling citizens to participate effectively in county governance. The legislation seeks to enhance public understanding of constitutional principles, devolved government structures, electoral processes, and the rights and responsibilities of citizens. These provisions recognize that meaningful public participation depends upon citizens' ability to understand governance processes and engage with public institutions in informed ways (Government of Kenya, 2012).

To operationalize these constitutional aspirations, the Government of Kenya introduced the Kenya National Integrated Civic Education (KNICE) Programme to coordinate civic education initiatives across national and county governments. The programme sought to standardize civic education content while promoting consistent delivery mechanisms throughout the country. Civic education has also increasingly been integrated into formal education through curricula that emphasize citizenship, constitutional values, national cohesion, integrity, cultural diversity, and democratic participation (Omundi & Okendo, 2018).

Empirical evidence demonstrates that civic education contributes positively to democratic participation when citizens are actively engaged in discussing governance issues within their communities. Finkel and Smith (2011) found that civic education in Kenya influenced not only individual political knowledge but also facilitated the social transmission of democratic values through interpersonal communication. Their findings further indicate that civic discussions within communities often amplify the effectiveness of formal civic education programmes, particularly among populations with lower levels of formal education.

While these initiatives have strengthened democratic awareness, language remains an important yet insufficiently addressed dimension of civic education in Kenya. Most civic education materials continue to be developed and disseminated primarily in English and Kiswahili despite the country's extensive linguistic diversity. This practice creates barriers for citizens whose primary languages are indigenous languages, thereby limiting comprehension, participation, and effective engagement with governance processes. Consequently, linguistic accessibility has emerged as a critical factor in determining the inclusiveness and effectiveness of civic education within Kenya's devolved governance framework.

The existing literature therefore establishes that civic education plays an indispensable role in democratic governance and citizen empowerment. However, comparatively limited attention has been devoted to understanding how indigenous languages can enhance the accessibility, effectiveness, and developmental impact of civic education at the county level. Addressing this gap provides an important foundation for examining the contribution of indigenous languages to economic empowerment and inclusive local governance in Kisii and Bungoma counties.

2.2 Indigenous Languages in Kenyan Education

Language occupies a central position in education because it serves not only as the medium through which knowledge is transmitted but also as the foundation upon which learners develop identity, critical thinking, and social participation. In multilingual societies such as Kenya, language policy within education has far-reaching implications for educational equity, democratic participation, and socio-economic development. Consequently, debates surrounding the place of indigenous languages in education have increasingly shifted from questions of cultural preservation to broader discussions of inclusive development, knowledge production, and economic transformation (UNESCO, 2003; wa Thiong'o, 2021).

Across Africa, scholars have consistently argued that indigenous languages represent valuable intellectual resources capable of supporting educational achievement, innovation, and sustainable development (Chisenga, 2002; Prah, 2020; Wa Mberia, 2015). These languages preserve indigenous systems of knowledge relating to agriculture, environmental management, health care, conflict resolution, governance, and entrepreneurship. They therefore constitute important repositories of local knowledge that can contribute significantly to community resilience and grassroots economic development when effectively integrated into educational and governance systems.

International scholarship similarly recognizes that learners achieve better educational outcomes when instruction begins in languages they understand well. UNESCO (2003; 2022) maintains that the use of familiar languages during the early years of schooling enhances comprehension, improves literacy development, strengthens learner participation, and facilitates the acquisition of additional languages. Mother-tongue-based education therefore provides both educational and developmental benefits by enabling learners to build new knowledge upon familiar linguistic and cultural foundations.

Despite this growing international consensus, indigenous languages continue to occupy a relatively peripheral position within many African education systems. Colonial language policies established English, French, and Portuguese as languages of prestige, administration, and formal education, creating linguistic hierarchies that continue to influence educational policy long after political independence (wa Thiong'o, 1986; Bamgbose, 1991). As a result, indigenous African languages have frequently been associated with informal domains of communication rather than with academic, scientific, or technological advancement.

Kenya illustrates many of these historical tensions. Although the country is home to more than forty indigenous languages, English and Kiswahili remain the dominant languages of governance, education, and official communication (Mugambi, 2002; Government of Kenya, 2010).

Current language-in-education policies permit the use of local languages during the early years of primary education in linguistically homogeneous rural areas, after which English becomes the principal language of instruction. While this policy acknowledges the educational value of mother-tongue instruction during early childhood, the transition to English substantially reduces the continued use and development of indigenous languages within formal education.

Several scholars argue that this linguistic transition has broader developmental implications beyond classroom instruction. Moseley (2010) observes that many indigenous languages face varying degrees of endangerment as younger generations increasingly adopt dominant languages for education, employment, and urban communication. Language decline consequently threatens the transmission of indigenous knowledge, cultural practices, oral traditions, and locally generated innovations that have historically supported community livelihoods.

The vulnerability of indigenous languages is further reflected in global assessments of language endangerment. UNESCO's Atlas of the World's Languages in Danger (Moseley, 2010) identifies several Kenyan languages as vulnerable, endangered, severely endangered, critically endangered, or extinct. These classifications highlight the urgency of implementing deliberate language revitalization strategies that extend beyond documentation to include meaningful integration of indigenous languages into education, governance, digital technologies, and community development initiatives.

International human rights frameworks reinforce these educational responsibilities. The United Nations Declaration on the Rights of Indigenous Peoples affirms the right of indigenous communities to preserve, develop, and transmit their languages to future generations and to establish educational systems that reflect their linguistic and cultural heritage. These principles underscore the close relationship between language rights, educational inclusion, cultural continuity, and sustainable development.

Within Kenya, numerous educational commissions and policy reviews have acknowledged the importance of indigenous languages in promoting effective learning and national development (Government of Kenya, 1964; 1965; 1976; 1981; 1988; 1999; 2012). Nevertheless, implementation has remained inconsistent, and indigenous languages continue to receive comparatively limited institutional support beyond the lower levels of primary education. This gap between policy aspirations and educational practice has contributed to declining intergenerational language transmission in many communities.

Contemporary African scholars increasingly advocate a decolonial approach to education that recognizes indigenous languages as legitimate vehicles for teaching, research, innovation, and knowledge production rather than simply as symbols of ethnic identity (wa Thiong'o, 2021; Prah, 2020; Wa Mberia, 2015). Such perspectives challenge long-standing assumptions that development and modernization require exclusive reliance on former colonial languages. Instead, they argue that multilingual educational systems can simultaneously promote global engagement while strengthening local knowledge systems and community participation.

Language revitalization has therefore emerged as both an educational and developmental priority. Mufwene (2006) argues that languages decline not because they are inherently inadequate but because social, political, and economic conditions encourage speakers to abandon them in favour of languages perceived to offer greater opportunities. This perspective suggests that successful language revitalization requires creating meaningful economic, educational, technological, and institutional functions for indigenous languages rather than limiting them to symbolic or cultural roles.

Recent scholarship further demonstrates that indigenous languages have an increasingly important role within the digital economy. Advances in information and communication technologies provide new opportunities to develop digital learning resources, mobile applications, online civic education platforms, and electronic knowledge repositories in local languages (UNESCO, 2023). Such innovations have the potential to expand access to educational resources, agricultural information, health communication, and entrepreneurial knowledge among rural populations who are often excluded by language barriers.

The literature therefore demonstrates that indigenous languages contribute substantially to educational quality, cultural continuity, democratic participation, and socio-economic development. However, relatively limited empirical research has examined how these educational functions intersect with civic education and economic empowerment within Kenya's devolved governance framework. This study addresses that gap by examining how indigenous languages can strengthen civic education while simultaneously promoting innovation, inclusive governance, and local economic development in Kisii and Bungoma counties.

2.3 Civic Education and Economic Development

Civic education is widely recognized as a cornerstone of democratic governance and sustainable socio-economic development. Beyond increasing citizens' awareness of their constitutional rights and civic responsibilities, effective civic education equips individuals with the knowledge and skills required to participate meaningfully in public decision-making, hold leaders accountable, and contribute to community development. Consequently, contemporary scholarship increasingly regards civic education as an essential mechanism for promoting social inclusion, good governance, and economic empowerment rather than merely as an instrument of political awareness (Finkel & Smith, 2011; UNESCO, 2022).

The relationship between civic education and economic development is founded on the premise that informed citizens are better positioned to utilize available opportunities, influence public policy, and participate actively in local development initiatives. Communities that understand governance structures, budgeting processes, legal frameworks, and development programmes are more likely to engage in entrepreneurial activities, resource management, environmental conservation, and community-based innovation. Civic education therefore contributes not only to democratic participation but also to the development of social capital that supports sustainable economic growth (Freire, 1970; United Nations, 2023).

Freire's theory of critical pedagogy provides an important perspective for understanding this relationship. Rather than viewing education as the passive transmission of information, Freire (1970; 2020) conceptualizes learning as a participatory process through which individuals develop critical consciousness and acquire the capacity to transform their social and economic realities. Within this framework, civic education becomes a vehicle for empowering citizens to recognize development challenges, question existing inequalities, and participate actively in designing locally appropriate solutions. Such transformative learning is particularly effective when communication occurs in languages that learners understand and identify with.

Empirical studies conducted in Kenya support the developmental significance of civic education. Finkel and Smith (2011) found that civic education programmes contributed significantly to the acquisition of democratic knowledge, political values, and participatory attitudes. Their study further demonstrated that civic learning extended beyond formal training through interpersonal discussions within families, neighbourhoods, and community networks. These findings suggest that civic education produces broader societal benefits when knowledge is shared through familiar social and linguistic environments.

Similarly, Omundi and Okendo (2018) report that civic education contributes to the acquisition of social cohesion competencies among secondary school students by promoting constitutional values, responsible citizenship, national unity, and peaceful coexistence. Their findings reinforce the view that civic education strengthens not only political participation but also the social relationships necessary for inclusive development. Social cohesion, trust, and collective responsibility provide important foundations for community-based economic initiatives and participatory governance.

Despite these positive outcomes, scholars increasingly observe that the effectiveness of civic education depends significantly on linguistic accessibility. Information communicated in unfamiliar languages often reduces comprehension, discourages participation, and excludes marginalized populations from governance processes (Heugh, 2021; Prah, 2020). In multilingual societies, language therefore becomes a determinant of whether citizens can effectively understand public policies, participate in development planning, and benefit from government programmes.

The educational literature likewise demonstrates that language influences both learning outcomes and civic engagement. Learners are more likely to understand complex concepts, retain information, and participate actively in discussions when instruction is delivered in languages that reflect their everyday experiences (UNESCO, 2003; UNESCO, 2022). This principle extends beyond formal education to civic education, where the ability to comprehend information directly influences citizens' capacity to exercise their democratic rights and responsibilities.

Research on culturally responsive education further emphasizes that civic education should acknowledge the linguistic and cultural realities of the communities it serves. Educational materials that incorporate indigenous languages and locally relevant examples are more likely to promote meaningful engagement, encourage dialogue, and strengthen trust between citizens and public institutions (Nyamnjoh, 2021; Freire, 2020). Such approaches recognize language not merely as a communication tool but as a medium through which communities interpret governance, negotiate collective interests, and construct shared solutions to development challenges.

Community participation has consequently emerged as a central principle in contemporary civic education. Studies indicate that collaboration among local leaders, educators, civil society organizations, and community members enhances the effectiveness and sustainability of civic education programmes. Indigenous languages facilitate this collaboration by enabling wider participation among groups that might otherwise be excluded because of language barriers, particularly rural populations, women, and older citizens whose primary languages are not English or Kiswahili (UNDP, 2023).

Comparative studies conducted across multilingual societies further demonstrate that language-inclusive governance contributes to greater transparency, accountability, and public trust. Countries that incorporate indigenous and regional languages into civic communication often experience higher levels of citizen participation, stronger community ownership of development programmes, and improved implementation of public policies (Heugh, 2021; Bamgbose, 1991). These international experiences suggest that multilingual civic education can strengthen democratic governance while simultaneously creating favourable conditions for local economic development.

Although previous studies have established the importance of civic education, language, and community participation independently, relatively few have examined how these factors interact within Kenya's devolved governance system to promote economic empowerment at the county level. Existing literature has tended to focus on educational outcomes, democratic participation, or language policy separately, leaving limited empirical evidence regarding the role of indigenous languages in connecting civic education with grassroots economic transformation. This study addresses that gap by investigating how linguistic inclusivity within civic education influences economic participation, innovation, and inclusive governance in Kisii and Bungoma counties.

2.4 Indigenous Languages, Innovation, and Economic Participation

Recent scholarship has increasingly challenged the traditional perception that indigenous languages are primarily instruments of cultural preservation. Instead, they are now recognized as valuable assets for innovation, entrepreneurship, knowledge creation, and inclusive economic development. Within multilingual societies, indigenous languages facilitate the production, dissemination, and application of locally generated knowledge, thereby enabling communities to develop context-specific solutions to social and economic challenges (Prah, 2020; Bamgbose, 1991).

Innovation is fundamentally a knowledge-driven process that depends upon effective communication, collaboration, and the exchange of ideas. In many rural African communities, indigenous languages provide the principal means through which knowledge relating to agriculture, environmental conservation, health care, conflict resolution, artisanal production, and small-scale enterprise is generated and transmitted across generations (Chisenga, 2002; Wa Mberia, 2015). These knowledge systems constitute an important component of local innovation ecosystems because they enable communities to adapt to changing environmental, technological, and economic conditions using culturally relevant approaches.

The relationship between language and innovation is particularly significant within the context of sustainable development. Indigenous knowledge embedded in local languages often provides practical solutions to challenges relating to food security, climate adaptation, biodiversity conservation, traditional medicine, and natural resource management. Scholars argue that development initiatives become more sustainable when they incorporate local knowledge alongside scientific knowledge, rather than treating the two as mutually exclusive systems (UNESCO, 2022; Prah,

2020). Indigenous languages therefore function not only as communication tools but also as repositories of intellectual capital that support locally driven innovation.

Economic participation similarly depends upon citizens' ability to access information, interpret opportunities, and engage effectively with markets and public institutions. Language plays a critical role in determining whether individuals can understand agricultural extension services, financial literacy programmes, entrepreneurship training, public procurement opportunities, cooperative management, and government development initiatives. Where such information is communicated primarily through unfamiliar languages, many citizens experience barriers that limit their participation in economic activities (Heugh, 2021; UNDP, 2023).

Research on inclusive development consistently demonstrates that linguistic accessibility enhances community participation in economic programmes. Citizens are more likely to adopt new agricultural technologies, participate in savings and credit associations, establish small enterprises, and utilize public services when information is communicated in languages they understand well (UNESCO, 2003; Bamgbose, 1991). This relationship is particularly evident in rural communities, where indigenous languages remain the principal means of everyday communication despite the official status of English and Kiswahili.

Digital transformation has created new opportunities for expanding the functional domains of indigenous languages. Mobile technologies, community radio, digital learning platforms, electronic dictionaries, translation applications, and social media increasingly enable local languages to disseminate educational, civic, and entrepreneurial information to wider audiences (UNESCO, 2023). Such technological innovations demonstrate that indigenous languages can actively support participation in the knowledge economy while strengthening cultural identity and community engagement.

Within Kenya, these developments present significant opportunities for county governments seeking to promote inclusive economic growth. Devolution has increased the demand for effective communication between county administrations and local communities regarding budgeting, agricultural support services, public health, environmental conservation, youth empowerment, and enterprise development (Government of Kenya, 2010; 2012). Integrating indigenous languages into these communication processes can improve citizens' understanding of government programmes, encourage greater public participation, and strengthen accountability within local governance structures.

The contribution of indigenous languages to entrepreneurship extends beyond information dissemination. Local languages facilitate networking among producers, traders, cooperatives, and consumers by fostering trust, social cohesion, and shared cultural values. These social relationships constitute important forms of social capital that support business development, collective marketing, resource mobilization, and community-based enterprises. Consequently, linguistic inclusion contributes to economic participation not only through improved communication but also by strengthening the social institutions upon which local economies depend (Freire, 1970; Nyamnjoh, 2021).

Nevertheless, significant challenges continue to constrain the economic potential of indigenous languages. Limited institutional support, inadequate investment in language development, insufficient educational resources, and the dominance of global languages in science, technology, and commerce restrict opportunities for indigenous languages to function fully within contemporary knowledge economies (Moseley, 2010; wa Thiong'o, 2021). Addressing these constraints requires deliberate language planning, policy implementation, digital innovation, and sustained collaboration among governments, educational institutions, communities, and development partners.

The literature reviewed demonstrates that indigenous languages possess considerable potential to enhance innovation, strengthen entrepreneurial ecosystems, improve access to development information, and promote inclusive economic participation. However, relatively little empirical evidence exists regarding how these relationships operate within Kenya's devolved governance system, particularly at the county level. Existing studies have generally examined language policy, education, or economic development independently, leaving limited understanding of how indigenous languages simultaneously support civic education, innovation, and economic empowerment. This study addresses this gap by investigating these interrelated dimensions in Kisii and Bungoma counties, thereby contributing to broader debates on multilingual governance, sustainable development, and inclusive economic transformation.

3.0 THEORETICAL FRAMEWORK

This study is anchored in Paulo Freire's Critical Pedagogy Theory (Freire, 1970; 2020), which conceptualizes education as a transformative process through which individuals develop critical awareness of their social, political, cultural, and economic realities. Rather than viewing education as the passive transmission of information from teacher to learner, Freire argues that meaningful learning emerges through dialogue, reflection, and collective action. Education therefore becomes a process of empowerment that enables individuals and communities to recognize structural inequalities, question oppressive systems, and participate actively in transforming their societies.

Central to Critical Pedagogy is the concept of critical consciousness (conscientização), which refers to the ability of individuals to critically examine the conditions affecting their lives and to take informed action toward social transformation. Freire contends that education should cultivate independent thinking rather than mere memorization of facts. Learners become active participants in the creation of knowledge by relating educational experiences to their own lived realities. Through dialogue and reflection, education equips citizens with the confidence and capacity to influence decisions affecting their communities and livelihoods.

Dialogue occupies a fundamental place within Freire's theoretical perspective. Unlike traditional models of education that position learners as passive recipients of knowledge, Critical Pedagogy emphasizes reciprocal communication between educators and learners. Such dialogue is most meaningful when it occurs through languages that participants understand and identify with, enabling them to articulate experiences, question assumptions, exchange ideas, and collaboratively develop solutions to shared challenges. Language therefore functions not merely as a medium of communication but as a vehicle for participation, empowerment, and social transformation.

The principles of Critical Pedagogy closely align with the objectives of civic education. Democratic participation requires citizens who can critically evaluate public policies, understand constitutional principles, engage constructively in governance, and hold public institutions accountable. Civic education grounded in dialogue encourages citizens to move beyond passive awareness of rights and responsibilities toward active participation in democratic processes. In multilingual societies, however, such participation depends significantly on linguistic accessibility. When civic education is delivered in unfamiliar languages, opportunities for meaningful dialogue, critical reflection, and inclusive participation are substantially diminished.

The theory is equally relevant to the role of indigenous languages in education and development. Indigenous languages enable communities to discuss local problems using concepts, cultural experiences, and knowledge systems that are familiar to them. They facilitate collective learning by allowing citizens to engage with development information in linguistically and culturally meaningful ways. From the perspective of Critical Pedagogy, excluding indigenous languages from civic education limits opportunities for dialogue and reinforces existing inequalities by restricting access to knowledge among populations that do not communicate primarily in English or Kiswahili.

Critical Pedagogy further recognizes that knowledge is socially situated and that communities possess valuable indigenous knowledge capable of contributing to development. This perspective challenges deficit views that regard local knowledge as inferior to formally institutionalized knowledge. Instead, Freire's framework supports the integration of indigenous knowledge systems into educational and development processes, thereby validating community experiences as legitimate sources of innovation, problem-solving, and socio-economic transformation. Such an approach is particularly relevant to this study, which examines how indigenous languages facilitate the transmission of knowledge relating to entrepreneurship, environmental management, agriculture, health, and community governance.

The theory also provides an appropriate framework for understanding the relationship between language and economic empowerment. Economic participation requires access to information, opportunities, and institutional processes that enable individuals to improve their livelihoods. Citizens who receive civic education through languages they understand are better positioned to interpret development policies, participate in public decision-making, adopt innovative practices, access government programmes, and engage effectively in entrepreneurial activities. Critical Pedagogy therefore links education directly with human agency, demonstrating that learning contributes to development when it enables individuals to become active participants in shaping their economic and social environments.

Although Critical Pedagogy has been applied extensively in educational research, scholars have noted certain limitations. The theory was originally developed within contexts characterized by pronounced social and political oppression and therefore pays comparatively less attention to contemporary challenges associated with globalization, digital transformation, multilingual governance, and rapidly evolving knowledge economies. In addition, the theory does not explicitly address language policy despite the central role that language plays in facilitating dialogue and participation. Nevertheless, these limitations do not diminish its relevance to the present study. Rather, they create opportunities to extend Freire's ideas by examining how indigenous languages enhance civic education and economic participation within Kenya's devolved governance system.

The application of Critical Pedagogy in this study therefore extends beyond formal classroom education. It provides a conceptual lens through which civic education is understood as a participatory and emancipatory process that empowers citizens to engage meaningfully in governance and local development. The theory further explains why indigenous languages constitute essential instruments for facilitating dialogue, strengthening democratic participation, promoting innovation, and enhancing economic empowerment among linguistically diverse communities.

Accordingly, Critical Pedagogy provides an appropriate theoretical foundation for analysing the relationship between indigenous languages, civic education, innovation, and economic participation in Kisii and Bungoma counties. It enables the study to interpret indigenous languages not merely as cultural artefacts but as strategic resources that expand citizens' capabilities, strengthen inclusive governance, and contribute to sustainable socio-economic development.

3.1 Conceptual Framework

The conceptual framework for this study is derived from Freire's Critical Pedagogy Theory and contemporary scholarship on multilingual education, inclusive governance, and sustainable development. It illustrates the interrelationships among indigenous languages, civic education, innovation, and economic empowerment within the context of Kenya's devolved governance system.

The framework conceptualizes indigenous languages as the principal independent variable influencing the effectiveness of civic education and broader development outcomes. Indigenous languages facilitate the dissemination of civic knowledge, enhance communication between public institutions and citizens, strengthen community dialogue, and promote the preservation and transmission of indigenous knowledge systems. By enabling citizens to access information in languages that are linguistically and culturally familiar, indigenous languages create favourable conditions for meaningful participation in governance and local development.

The framework further recognizes several intervening factors that influence the extent to which indigenous languages contribute to civic education and economic development. These include language policy, institutional commitment, educational programmes, community participation, digital technologies, and the availability of learning resources in indigenous languages. These factors may either strengthen or constrain the integration of indigenous languages into governance, education, and development initiatives.

The study also identifies mediating processes through which indigenous languages influence development outcomes. These include dialogue, critical consciousness, knowledge sharing, social inclusion, community participation, and collaborative problem-solving. Drawing from Freire's Critical Pedagogy, the framework assumes that meaningful dialogue enables citizens to develop a critical understanding of their social and economic circumstances and to participate actively in identifying solutions to local development challenges. Indigenous languages facilitate these processes by enabling individuals to communicate confidently, exchange experiences, and collectively generate locally appropriate innovations.

The dependent variables comprise effective civic education, innovation, economic empowerment, inclusive governance, and sustainable community development. Civic education delivered through indigenous languages is expected to improve citizens' understanding of constitutional rights, public responsibilities, and development opportunities. Enhanced understanding is anticipated to increase participation in public decision-making, encourage accountability, strengthen social cohesion, and improve access to government programmes. These outcomes are further expected to stimulate entrepreneurship, local innovation, livelihood diversification, and broader economic participation within communities.

The framework therefore assumes that the relationship between indigenous languages and economic empowerment is not direct but operates through enhanced civic education, increased citizen participation, improved communication, and strengthened community knowledge systems. It further recognizes that supportive institutional policies and effective implementation strategies are necessary for indigenous languages to realize their full developmental potential.

Overall, the conceptual framework positions indigenous languages as strategic developmental resources that facilitate knowledge exchange, democratic participation, innovation, and inclusive economic growth. It provides the analytical structure through which the study examines the contribution of indigenous languages to civic education and economic empowerment in Kisii and Bungoma counties.The conceptual relationships underpinning the study are summarized as follows:

Figure 1. Conceptual Framework

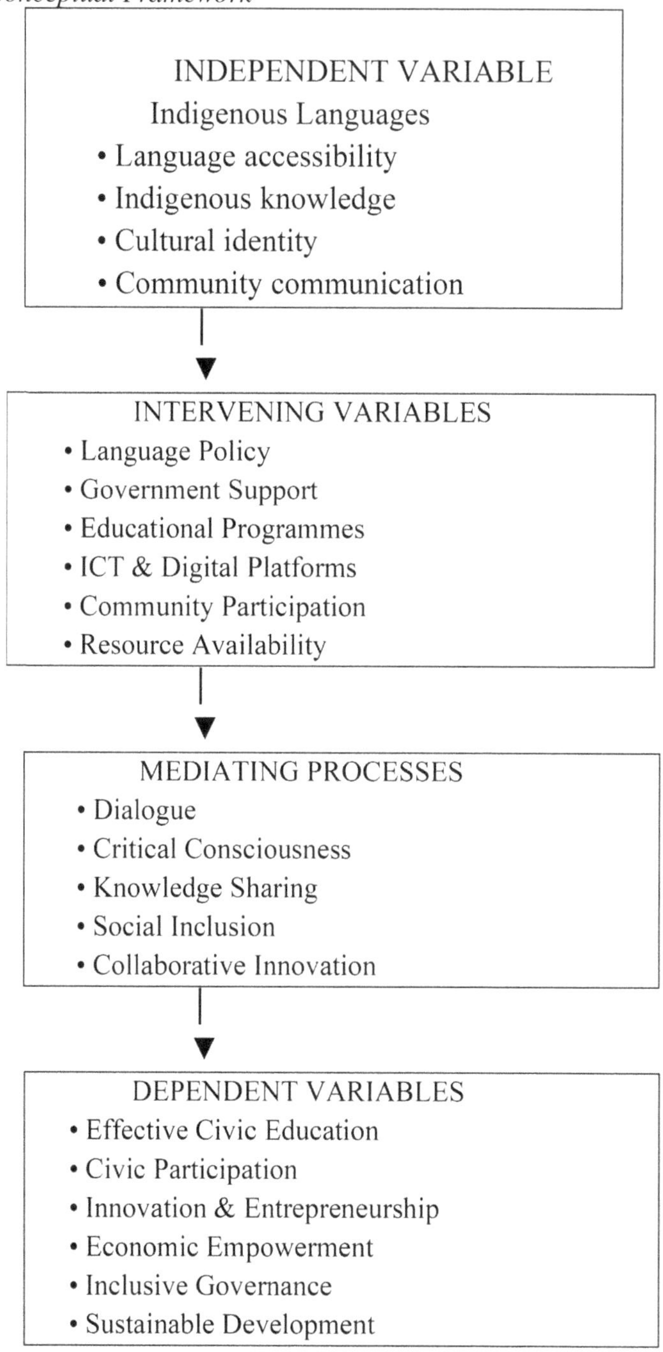

Source: Developed by the author from Freire (1970, 2020), UNESCO (2003, 2022), Bamgbose (1991), Heugh (2021), Prah (2020), and the current study.

The framework proposes that strengthening the use of indigenous languages within civic education enhances dialogue, expands access to development information, promotes active citizen participation, and ultimately contributes to innovation, economic empowerment, and sustainable development.

3.2 Operationalization of the Conceptual Framework

The conceptual framework developed for this study guided the identification of the principal concepts, informed the research questions, and provided the analytical lens through which the findings were interpreted. Drawing upon Freire's Critical Pedagogy Theory, the framework assumes that indigenous languages facilitate meaningful dialogue, enhance civic learning, strengthen community participation, and ultimately contribute to innovation and economic empowerment. These assumptions informed both the design of the study and the interpretation of the empirical evidence collected from Kisii and Bungoma counties.

The independent variable, indigenous languages, was operationalized by examining the extent to which local languages were used in civic education programmes, public participation forums, community meetings, dissemination of government information, and development communication. Particular attention was paid to the accessibility of civic information, the use of indigenous languages by county governments and community organizations, and the perceived influence of local languages on citizens' understanding of governance and development processes.

The study identified several intervening variables that influence the effectiveness of indigenous languages in promoting civic education and economic development. These included national and county language policies, institutional support for multilingual communication, availability of educational materials in indigenous languages, integration of digital technologies, and the level of community participation in civic education initiatives. These contextual factors were analysed to determine how they either facilitated or constrained the developmental use of indigenous languages.

The framework further incorporated mediating processes that explain how indigenous languages influence development outcomes. These processes included dialogue, critical consciousness, knowledge sharing, social inclusion, and collaborative problem-solving. During data collection, participants were invited to describe how communication in indigenous languages affected their understanding of civic issues, their participation in governance, and their ability to engage in community development initiatives. These narratives provided insight into the mechanisms through which language contributes to civic engagement and socio-economic transformation.

The dependent variables were operationalized through indicators relating to civic education, citizen participation, innovation, entrepreneurship, economic empowerment, and inclusive governance. Civic education was assessed in terms of citizens' understanding of constitutional rights, public responsibilities, and government programmes. Economic empowerment was examined through participants' experiences of accessing development information, participating in entrepreneurial activities, utilizing government services, engaging in community-based enterprises, and applying indigenous knowledge to improve livelihoods.

Data analysis was guided by the relationships proposed in the conceptual framework. The analysis examined how the use of indigenous languages influenced dialogue, civic participation, knowledge exchange, and economic opportunities while considering the moderating influence of institutional and policy contexts. Themes emerging from the data were interpreted in relation to Freire's concept of critical consciousness, with particular emphasis on how linguistic accessibility enables citizens to participate actively in governance and local development.

The operationalization of the conceptual framework therefore ensured coherence between the theoretical foundation, research objectives, data collection procedures, and interpretation of findings. It provided a systematic approach for examining the interconnected roles of indigenous languages, civic education, innovation, and economic empowerment within Kenya's devolved governance system. By explicitly linking theory to empirical analysis, the framework strengthens the credibility, transparency, and analytical rigour of the study.

Figure 2. Operational Model Linking Indigenous Languages, Civic Education, Innovation, and Economic Empowerment

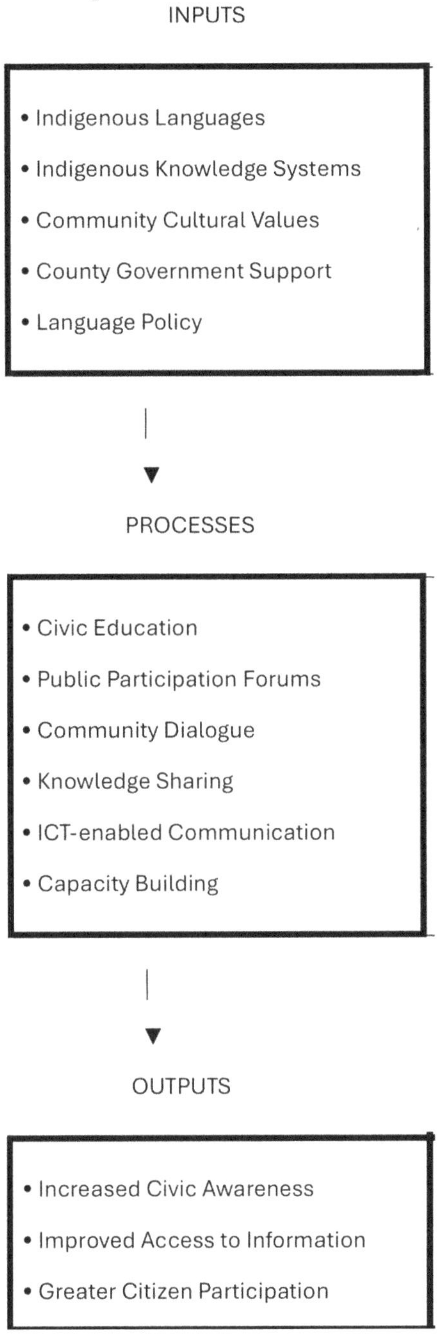

Source: *Developed by the author from Freire (1970, 2020), UNESCO (2003, 2022), Bamgbose (1991), Heugh (2021), Prah (2020), and findings of the present study.*

The operational model illustrates the developmental pathway through which indigenous languages contribute to sustainable socio-economic transformation. The model begins with inputs, comprising indigenous languages, indigenous knowledge systems, cultural values, supportive language policies, and institutional commitment. These inputs provide the foundation for effective communication and community engagement.

The second stage consists of processes through which these inputs are translated into practice. These include civic education, public participation forums, community dialogue, knowledge sharing, ICT-enabled communication, and capacity-building initiatives. Drawing on Freire's Critical Pedagogy Theory, these processes promote critical reflection, active learning, and collaborative problem-solving among citizens.

Successful implementation of these processes generates several outputs, including increased civic awareness, improved access to development information, stronger citizen participation, enhanced knowledge exchange, and greater community innovation. These immediate results create favourable conditions for more inclusive governance and community-driven development.

The outputs subsequently produce broader outcomes, including economic empowerment, entrepreneurship, improved livelihoods, inclusive governance, and strengthened social cohesion. These outcomes collectively contribute to the long-term impact of sustainable community development, democratic participation, poverty reduction, inclusive economic growth, and the revitalization of indigenous languages as strategic resources for development.

The model therefore reinforces the central argument of this study that indigenous languages are not merely cultural symbols but constitute important drivers of civic participation, innovation, and sustainable economic transformation within Kenya's devolved governance system.

4. FINDINGS AND DISCUSSION

The findings of this chapter underscore the critical role of indigenous languages in fostering economic participation, civic engagement, and innovation in Kenya. Using the theoretical frameworks of Freire's critical pedagogy and multilingualism for resilience, and based on the previous literature review, this section examines how linguistic inclusivity addresses socio-economic disparities and drives local development.

4.1 Use of Indigenous Languages in Civic Education and Impact on Local Economic Empowerment

This section addresses the first objective of the study, which sought to examine the role of indigenous languages in civic education and their contribution to local economic empowerment in Kisii and Bungoma counties.

Finding

Participants reported that the use of indigenous languages improved comprehension of civic information and encouraged greater participation in local governance activities. Respondents also noted that communication in local languages strengthened trust between citizens and county leadership.

Discussion

The findings demonstrate that linguistic accessibility enhances participatory governance by reducing communicative exclusion. These findings support Freire's (1970) argument that contextualized communication enhances civic consciousness and participation. Linguistic inclusivity, therefore, serves not only as a communication strategy but also as a mechanism for social empowerment and democratic engagement.

To some extent, the two counties, Kisii and Bungoma, recognized the importance of incorporating indigenous languages in civic education to promote inclusivity, participation, and understanding among all citizens. Respondents indicated that indigenous languages were more accessible to local communities because they reflected everyday communication practices. They are the primary languages spoken by the local populations. The use of these languages helps to maintain and promote the cultural identity of the various indigenous groups within the Counties and for effective communication. Participants reported improved comprehension and retention of civic information when communication occurred in indigenous languages. By doing so, important information about governance, rights, and responsibilities of citizens can be effectively communicated to the citizens.

The following is the impact on local Economic Empowerment:

Underutilization of Indigenous Knowledge Systems

Indigenous languages are deeply intertwined with local knowledge systems, including sustainable agricultural practices, conflict resolution, and environmental management. However, the exclusion of these languages in formal governance and educational settings hinders the transmission of this knowledge, stifling innovation and local problem-solving (Prah, 2009; Mugambi, 2002).

Missed Opportunities in Digital Transformation

Despite the rise of digital tools, the integration of indigenous languages into mobile applications, websites, and social media platforms remains limited. Communities that primarily communicate in Indigenous languages are excluded from accessing critical digital resources such as market prices, farming techniques, and civic updates (Moseley, 2010).

Community Participation and Trust in Governance

The limited use of indigenous languages in civic education creates a disconnect between communities and local governments. Citizens often view governance structures as inaccessible or unresponsive to their needs, leading to reduced participation in decision-making processes (Freire, 1970).

Gender Disparities in Access to Information

Women in rural areas, who are often more fluent in indigenous languages than in English or Kiswahili, are disproportionately affected by linguistic exclusion. This limits their ability to participate in governance and economic activities, further entrenching gender inequalities (Wa Thiong'o, 1986).

Conclusion

Linguistic inclusivity is therefore a strategic development tool for sustainable governance and economic participation.

4.2 Challenges of Using Indigenous Languages in Civic Education and Their Implications for Economic Development

Findings

The participants indicated that there were attempts to incorporate indigenous languages into civic education initiatives in Kisii and Bungoma Counties. The respondents also noted that the engagement was minimal owing to various challenges.

Discussions

There were issues of standardization. Firstly, both counties had numerous languages and dialects, and since none had been standardized as the official dialect, it posed a challenge in developing consistent and accurate civic education materials. Secondly, producing materials in numerous indigenous languages was resource-intensive. This required translation expertise, printing facilities, and distribution networks, which were not always available. Thirdly, in some cases, there were political insensitivities associated with the use of certain indigenous languages. Political dynamics and historical tensions among ethnic groups, to some extent, influenced language policies in civic education.

Both Kisii and Bungoma counties are linguistically diverse, with multiple indigenous languages spoken within their boundaries. Kisii has close to nine indigenous languages, viz: EkeGusii (South Mugirango dialect and the Central Kisii dialect), Kuria, Dholuo, Maragoli (Luhyia dialect), Suba, Nubian, Indians, the Maa, and the Kipsigis. On the other hand, Bungoma has ten indigenous languages, viz: the Luhyia metalanguages, which include (Lubukusu, Tachoni, Marachi, Logoli, Wanga, Banyala, Samia), Saboat and Iteso. It may be challenging to select a single indigenous language to represent the entire population, leading to concerns about inclusivity and equitable representation.

Both Kisii and Bungoma Counties, like the rest of Kenya, recognize Kiswahili and English as the official languages for communication and education. There was a preference for using these languages in civic education materials to ensure consistency and conformity with national language policies.

Perceived effectiveness was another reason for not using indigenous languages in civic education in Kisii and Bungoma Counties. This is because the decision-makers believe that using English and Kiswahili for civic education materials will reach a broader audience and be more effective in conveying important information about governance, rights and responsibilities.

Implications for Economic Development

Resource Limitations: Developing materials in multiple languages is costly and labour-intensive. The high cost of developing civic education materials in multiple indigenous languages remains a significant barrier, limiting their potential for economic empowerment.

Perceptions: Indigenous languages are often undervalued in formal settings, leading to resistance to adopting them for civic and economic programs.

Policy Gaps: The absence of a robust national framework supporting multilingual civic education hinders its integration into economic planning.

Despite the challenges associated with integrating indigenous languages into civic education, both Kisii and Bungoma counties have made varying efforts to promote linguistic inclusivity within their local governance structures. Examining the similarities and differences in these approaches provides deeper insight into how multilingual realities shape civic participation and economic engagement across Counties. The following section, therefore, compares the strategies, experiences, and contextual dynamics influencing the use of indigenous languages in civic education within the two counties.

4.3 Similarities and differences in the use of Indigenous languages for civic education

Finding

The participants indicated that while there may be differences in the specific strategies and approaches employed by the Kisii and Bungoma Counties regarding the use of indigenous languages in promoting civic education, they share common goals of inclusivity, participation, and effective communication within their diverse communities.

Discussions

Both Kisii and Bungoma counties recognize the linguistic diversities within their jurisdictions. They understand the importance of acknowledging and respecting the indigenous languages spoken by their populations. While they may not primarily use the indigenous languages in promoting civic education, both Counties acknowledge the significance of these local languages in local contexts. They incorporated indigenous languages in specific initiatives or programmes targeting certain communities or demographic groups. While both counties demonstrate commitment to inclusivity, their approaches differ according to linguistic composition, administrative priorities, and available resources.

Both counties prioritize the use of English and Kiswahili as official languages. This was in tandem with the national language policies. They recognize these languages for consistency, accessibility, and conformity with broader language standards. Additionally, both Kisii and Bungoma Counties face resource constraints when it comes to producing civic education materials in multiple indigenous languages. Budgetary limitations, translation expertise, and logistical challenges influence the decisions regarding language choice in civic education initiatives.

Despite the emphasis on official languages, both Counties understand the importance of adapting civic education efforts to local contexts. They may employ community outreach programmes, local media or culturally relevant content to effectively engage citizens in civic education, regardless of language.

The comparison between Kisii and Bungoma counties demonstrates that while both counties recognize the importance of indigenous languages, practical implementation remains limited due to policy, financial, and structural constraints. These limitations contribute to broader language barriers that continue to affect citizens' access to civic information and economic opportunities. Consequently, understanding the relationship between language barriers and economic exclusion becomes essential in evaluating the broader developmental implications of linguistic marginalization.

4.4 Language Barriers and Economic Exclusion

Findings

The participants noted that the citizens in Kisii and Bungoma counties face significant challenges in accessing civic and economic information due to the dominance of English and Kiswahili in governance and education. They also noted that indigenous languages, though widely spoken, are rarely used in civic education programs, which limits community understanding of governance processes, resource allocation, and economic opportunities (Government of Kenya, 2010).

Discussions

Language barriers can significantly affect the effectiveness of civic education programmes in Kisii and Bungoma Counties in Kenya in several ways. Firstly, it limits understanding. When civic education materials are presented in languages that citizens do not understand proficiently, it limits their ability to comprehend important information about governance, rights, and responsibilities. This can result in misunderstandings or misinterpretations of civic concepts and processes. Secondly, reduced engagement. People are less likely to actively participate in discussions, ask questions, or seek clarification when the information is presented in a language they are not fluent in. Language barriers disproportionately affect marginalized groups, including ethnic minorities and rural populations who may predominantly speak indigenous languages. These groups may face greater challenges in accessing and benefiting from civic education programmes, leading to their exclusion from important civic processes. Limited access to rights and services is another challenge. It can hinder the citizens' ability to access essential services, participate in democratic processes, and advocate for their interests effectively. Lastly, when citizens encounter language barriers in accessing civic education materials and information, it can undermine their trust in government institutions and democratic processes.

They may perceive the government as inaccessible or indifferent to their needs and concerns. Beyond limiting civic participation, language barriers also carry significant economic consequences for marginalized communities.

Economic Implications

1. Exclusion from Economic Processes/Reduced Market Access: Language barriers limit community participation in local economic initiatives. Citizens unable to access civic information in their native languages
2. Innovation Loss: Marginalizing indigenous knowledge stifles localized innovation.

Struggle to engage with economic opportunities. Innovation Stifling: Excluding indigenous knowledge systems limits the scope of local solutions to community challenges.

The findings on language barriers and economic exclusion reveal that the limited integration of indigenous languages undermines inclusive governance and restricts community participation in development initiatives. Addressing these challenges, therefore, requires deliberate strategies that promote linguistic accessibility, strengthen community engagement, and enhance the role of indigenous languages in civic and economic processes. The following section outlines potential approaches for enhancing civic education through indigenous languages to foster innovation and economic growth.

4.5 Strategies for enhancing civic education through indigenous languages to foster innovation and economic growth.

Findings

The participants indicated that numerous strategies have been employed by the Kisii and Bungoma Counties in overcoming the language-related obstacles in civic education.

Discussions

Firstly, despite the budgetary constraints, there are efforts to prioritize language accessibility by providing materials in Indigenous languages. Secondly, the counties are investing in translation and interpretation services to ensure that civic education materials are accurately translated and effectively communicated to diverse audiences. Thirdly, the counties are engaging the local community leaders, civil society organizations, and grassroots networks to facilitate civic education efforts and bridge language gaps. The two counties have made efforts to incorporate interactive and participatory approaches, such as community forums, drama, and storytelling, to make civic education more engaging and culturally relevant to diverse audiences. They also have strategies to continuously assess and adapt civic education strategies to address the evolving linguistic needs and preferences of the population. In addition to addressing barriers, these strategies also create opportunities for broader community empowerment and innovation.

Opportunities for Empowerment

1. Enhanced Participation: Linguistic inclusivity fosters trust and engagement in governance and economic planning.
2. Grassroots Innovation: Indigenous languages can be platforms for sharing local solutions to economic challenges.
3. Digital Transformation: Mobile apps in native languages can disseminate market prices, farming techniques, and governance updates.
4. Agriculture and Resource Management: Indigenous languages facilitate the transmission of traditional agricultural practices and resource management strategies, essential for climate resilience.
5. . Empowering Marginalized Groups: Women and rural populations, often excluded from mainstream civic processes, can access critical information through localized language initiatives.

4.6 Case Studies In Kenyan Counties

A. Kisii County: Economic Implications of Language Barriers

In Kisii County, respondents indicated that the use of EkeGusii during community forums improved understanding of agricultural policies, resource management, and entrepreneurship initiatives. Farmers expressed greater willingness to participate in county programmes when information was communicated in their indigenous language. However, limited institutional support and a lack of standardized materials constrained broader implementation.

Despite linguistic diversity, the limited use of indigenous languages in civic programs hinders participation in local economic initiatives. The exclusion of indigenous languages in Kisii County has resulted in limited community participation in local economic initiatives. Efforts to integrate native dialects into civic education show potential for improving entrepreneurial engagement.

B. Bungoma County: Successes and Challenges

In Bungoma County, the use of Lubukusu in selected civic education initiatives enhanced community engagement, particularly among rural populations and women. Participants reported improved awareness of governance processes and economic opportunities. Nevertheless, the county faced challenges related to financial resources, multilingual diversity, and policy inconsistencies.

Bungoma County's use of Lubukusu in select civic education programs has enhanced citizen engagement but faces scalability issues due to limited resources. The use of Lubukusu in select programs has improved citizen engagement, though scalability remains a challenge.

The preceding findings demonstrate that indigenous languages play a significant role in enhancing civic participation, economic engagement, and community inclusion in Kisii and Bungoma counties. However, these findings require further interpretation within broader theoretical and scholarly contexts. Drawing on Freire's critical pedagogy and multilingualism frameworks, the following discussion examines how linguistic inclusivity contributes to empowerment, resilience, governance, and sustainable development.

4.7 DISCUSSION

The findings are discussed in light of Freire's critical pedagogy and the multilingualism framework, which highlight the transformative potential of linguistic inclusivity in fostering critical consciousness and economic resilience.

Freire's Critical Pedagogy and Language as Empowerment

Freire (1970) emphasizes that education must be contextual and rooted in the lived realities of learners. In the Kenyan context, indigenous languages provide the foundation for such contextual education, enabling citizens to critically analyze their socio-economic conditions and actively participate in governance. By marginalizing these languages, current civic education practices perpetuate exclusion and limit the agency of rural populations.

The findings support Freire's argument by showing that integrating Indigenous languages into civic education can empower communities to engage with governance processes more effectively. For example, using Lubukusu in Bungoma County and EkeGusii in Kisii County could enhance citizens' understanding of policies related to agriculture, resource management, and local economic initiatives.

Multilingualism and Economic Resilience

The multilingualism framework posits that linguistic diversity enhances community resilience by fostering inclusivity and leveraging local knowledge systems (Prah, 2009; Bamgbose, 1991). The findings reveal that excluding indigenous languages limits the potential for community-driven innovation and economic participation. For instance, traditional farming techniques and water management practices, often preserved in indigenous languages, remain underutilized in formal development initiatives. By promoting multilingual policies, Kenya could harness its linguistic diversity to address local challenges. For example, training programs in indigenous languages could improve farmers' access to climate-resilient practices, thereby enhancing food security and economic stability.Beyond governance and participation, linguistic inclusivity also intersects with emerging technological and digital development opportunities.

Digital Transformation and Linguistic Inclusivity

The rise of digital technologies presents an opportunity to integrate indigenous languages into civic education and economic systems. Mobile applications in local languages could disseminate information on market prices, government programs, and health services, bridging the digital divide and fostering economic inclusion (Moseley, 2010). The findings highlight a missed opportunity in this area, as most digital platforms in Kenya prioritize English and Kiswahili. Incorporating indigenous languages into these platforms could significantly expand their reach and impact, particularly in rural areas. The role of language extends beyond communication alone and significantly influences citizens' perceptions of governance and institutional trust.

Trust and Participation in Governance

Freire's framework also emphasizes the role of language in building trust between communities and governance structures. The findings reveal that the limited use of indigenous languages in civic education diminishes trust in local governments, as citizens perceive them as inaccessible. Enhancing linguistic inclusivity could foster a sense of belonging and encourage active participation in governance (wa Thiong'o, 1986). The findings further reveal that linguistic exclusion disproportionately affects vulnerable groups, particularly women in rural communities.

Addressing Gender Disparities

The findings underscore the importance of linguistic inclusivity in addressing gender disparities. Women in rural areas, often excluded from formal education and governance, could benefit significantly from civic education in indigenous languages. This would enable them to participate in local economic activities and decision-making processes, contributing to gender equality and community development (Nyamnjoh, 2019).

Policy Implications

1. National Language Policy: Establishing a framework that recognizes indigenous languages as critical resources for economic and civic empowerment is essential (Government of Kenya, 2010).
2. Integration into Digital Tools: Developing mobile apps and online platforms in indigenous languages can expand access to critical information and services.
3. Community-Based Programs: Incorporating indigenous languages into community education initiatives can enhance engagement and foster trust.
4. Gender-Sensitive Approaches: Ensuring that women have access to civic education and economic resources in their native languages can address systemic gender inequalities.

The discussion demonstrates that linguistic inclusivity is not merely a cultural concern but a developmental necessity with implications for governance, participation, innovation, and economic resilience. These insights therefore inform the recommendations proposed in the next section, which focus on policy reform, technological integration, community engagement, and inclusive development strategies

4.8 RECOMMENDATIONS

Policy and Governance

Develop a national language policy that recognizes indigenous languages as tools for civic and economic empowerment.

Align multilingual policies with Kenya's Vision 2030 goals.

Technology and Innovation

Develop mobile applications and digital platforms in indigenous languages.

Use audio-visual civic education materials for rural populations.

Community Engagement

Promote storytelling, theatre, and local media in civic education.
Strengthen grassroots participation through local leaders and community networks.

Gender Inclusion

Create language-inclusive programmes targeting women and marginalized groups.
Support women leaders through multilingual communication training.

5. CONCLUSION

Indigenous languages are not merely cultural symbols but strategic resources for inclusive development. Integrating indigenous languages into civic education programs can bridge knowledge gaps, enhance governance, and catalyze local economic development. Kenya's experience provides valuable lessons for other multilingual nations, demonstrating the transformative power of aligning language policy with innovation and sustainability.

The study demonstrates that linguistic inclusivity enhances civic participation, trust in governance, economic engagement, and grassroots innovation. These findings align with global lessons on multilingualism and underscore the transformative potential of embracing linguistic diversity for sustainable development.

The chapter contributes to emerging scholarship linking language policy, development, and indigenous knowledge systems in Africa. It contributes to scholarship on language policy, civic education, and sustainable development by demonstrating how indigenous languages can function as instruments of economic participation and democratic inclusion. Unlike studies that primarily frame indigenous languages as cultural artefacts, this chapter positions them as strategic resources for governance, innovation, and grassroots economic transformation within multilingual African societies.

This chapter highlights the untapped potential of indigenous languages in driving local economic development and innovation in Kenya. By integrating these languages into civic education, the country can empower marginalized communities, foster inclusivity, and stimulate grassroots innovation. The findings emphasize that linguistic diversity, far from being a challenge, is a resource that can be leveraged to enhance governance, trust, and economic participation.

Through the theoretical lenses of Freire's critical pedagogy and multilingualism for resilience, the chapter demonstrates that linguistic inclusivity can address socio-economic disparities, preserve cultural heritage, and catalyze sustainable development. Policies and programs that embrace indigenous languages as tools for civic and economic empowerment have the potential to transform Kenya's development trajectory and serve as a model for other multilingual nations.

In conclusion, Kenya's linguistic diversity is not just a symbol of its cultural richness but also a key to unlocking its economic potential. By prioritizing indigenous languages in civic and economic initiatives, Kenya can build a more inclusive, innovative, and resilient society. Future research should explore digital multilingualism, policy implementation, and comparative county-level language strategies.

REFERENCES

Bamgbose, A. (1991). *Language and the nation: The language question in sub-Saharan Africa.* Edinburgh University Press for the International African Institute.

Chisenga, J. (2002). Indigenous knowledge: Africa's opportunity to contribute to global information content. *South African Journal of Library and Information Science*, *68*(1), 16–20.

Finkel, S. E., & Smith, A. E. (2011). Civic education, political discussion, and the social transmission of democratic knowledge and values in a new democracy: Kenya 2002. *American Journal of Political Science*, *55*(2), 417–435. DOI: 10.1111/j.1540-5907.2010.00493.x

Freire, P. (1970). Pedagogy of the Oppressed. *Continuum.*

Freire, P. (2020). *Pedagogy of the Oppressed* (50th anniversary ed.). Bloomsbury Academic.

Government of Kenya. (1964). *Kenya Education Commission Report (Ominde Report).* Government Printer.

Government of Kenya. (1965). *Sessional Paper No. 10 of 1965: African Socialism and its application to planning in Kenya.* Government Printer. https://new.kenyalaw.org

Government of Kenya. (1976). *Report of the National Committee on Educational Objectives and Policies (Gachathi Report).* Government Printer.

Government of Kenya. (1981). *Second University in Kenya: Report of the Presidential Working Party (Mackay Report).* Government Printer.

Government of Kenya. (1988). *Report of the Presidential Working Party on Education and Manpower Training for the Next Decade and Beyond (Kamunge Report).* Government Printer.

Government of Kenya. (1999). *Totally Integrated Quality Education and Training (TIQET): Report of the Commission of Inquiry into the Education System of Kenya (Koech Report).* Government Printer.

Government of Kenya. (2010). *Constitution of Kenya.* Government Printer. https://new.kenyalaw.org

Government of Kenya. (2012). *County Governments Act, No. 17 of 2012.* Government Printer. https://new.kenyalaw.org

Heugh, K. (2021). Multilingual education policy in Africa. *Language Teaching*, *54*(3), 354–372. DOI: 10.1017/S0261444821000112

Moseley, C. (Ed.). (2010). *Atlas of the world's languages in danger* (3rd ed.). UNESCO Publishing., https://unesdoc.unesco.org

Mufwene, S. S. (2006). Lost tongues and the politics of language endangerment. *University of Chicago Magazine, 98*(3), 24–29. https://mag.uchicago.edu

Mugambi, H. M. (2002). Language choice and shift in Kenya: A look at the changing roles of English, Kiswahili and indigenous languages. *Language, Literacy and Culture Review*, 12–23.

Nyamnjoh, F. B. (2019). *Decolonizing the university in Africa.* Oxford University Press. DOI: 10.1093/acrefore/9780190228637.013.717

Ogone, J. (2010). A case of a mother tongue and another mother tongue in school: Efforts at revitalization of the Olusuba language of Kenya. *Journal of Third World Studies*, *27*(2), 267–291.

Omundi, E., & Okendo, E. (2018). Evaluation of the effectiveness of civic education on acquisition of social cohesion competency among secondary school students in Uasin Gishu County, Kenya. *International Journal of Scientific Research and Management*, *6*(4), EL-249–EL-265. DOI: 10.18535/ijsrm/v6i4.el07

Orao, J. O. (2009). The Kenyan indigenous languages and the mass media: Challenges and opportunities. Stellenbosch papers in linguistics plus, 38(1), 77-86.

Prah, K. K. (2009). *The language of instruction in Africa: The language of instruction conundrum in Africa. Centre for Advanced Studies of African Society*. CASAS.

Prah, K. K. (2020). *The challenge of African languages in education and development*. Centre for Advanced Studies of African Society (CASAS).

South African Government. (2020). *Multilingualism policy framework*. Department of Higher Education and Training. https://www.dhet.gov.za

UNESCO. (2003). *Education in a multilingual world*. UNESCO Publishing. https://unesdoc.unesco.org

UNESCO. (2022). *Global education monitoring report 2022: Inclusion and education*. UNESCO Publishing. https://www.unesco.org/gem-report

UNESCO. (2023). *Digital initiatives for Indigenous languages*. UNESCO. https://www.unesco.org/en/decades/indigenous-languages

United Nations. (2023). *The Sustainable Development Goals Report 2023*. United Nations. https://unstats.un.org

United Nations Development Programme, African Union Commission, United Nations Economic Commission for Africa, & African Development Bank. (2023). *2023 Africa sustainable development report: Accelerating the recovery from the coronavirus disease (COVID-19) and the full implementation of the 2030 Agenda for Sustainable Development and African Union Agenda 2063 at all levels*. United Nations Development Programme. https://www.undp.org/africa/publications/2023-africa-sustainable-development-report

Wa Mberia, K. (2015). Ubuntu: Linguistic exporations. *International Journal of Scientific Research and Innovative Technology*, *2*(1), 103–115.

Wa Thiong'o, Ngugi. (1986). *Decolonising the mind: The politics of language in African literature*. Heinemann Kenya.

Wa Thiong'o. Ngugi. (2021). *The language of languages*. The New Press.

Warschauer, M. (2021). *Technology and social inclusion: Rethinking the digital divide*. MIT Press.

Chapter 8
The Role of Land in Rural Women's Economic Development and Empowerment in KwaZulu-Natal, South Africa

Sibongile Nhlapho
http://orcid.org/0009-0000-9238-2488
University of KwaZulu-Natal, South Africa

Lungile Prudence Zondi
University of KwaZulu-Natal, South Africa

Fikile Mabel Vilakazi-Alberts
University of the Western Cape, South Africa

ABSTRACT

This chapter explores the structural barriers preventing rural women in KZN from accessing land. These barriers arise from a combination of entrenched cultural norms, the marginalization of indigenous knowledge, patriarchal structures, and the stagnation of public policies that fail to amplify the voices of rural women in land access. Utilizing Structuration Theory and Black Feminist Theory, the chapter emphasizes the need to address these structural hindrances to facilitate the implementation of policies that support women's land rights. The analysis is grounded in ethnographic narratives from rural women who are striving to overcome poverty

DOI: 10.4018/979-8-2600-3325-8.ch008

and unemployment. Research findings highlight a strong desire to dismantle these structural barriers so that rural women can fully participate in the democratic process. Currently, they feel excluded from discussions on land access and distribution. Women pointed out the inefficacy of current policies and the legal and customary obstacles hindering their access to land.

INTRODUCTION AND BACKGROUND

Women in many African countries continue to face numerous man-made structural challenges in accessing economic resources, including land, despite bearing a disproportionate responsibility for family support, poverty alleviation, and the pursuit of economic well-being. This gender inequality is often rooted in deeply entrenched cultural practices. In many contexts, patriarchal norms governing gender roles and land ownership become embedded in customary systems that continue to shape access to land despite constitutional guarantees of equality. Although many African countries have adopted legal frameworks promoting gender equality, implementation remains inconsistent because of weak enforcement, conflicting customary practices, and institutional barriers. The persistence of patriarchal customary governance and uneven implementation of land reform means that rural women continue to experience insecure land tenure and unequal inheritance rights, with access to land frequently mediated through relationships with male relatives rather than through independent ownership (Commission for Gender Equality [CGE], 2024; Popoola & Magidimisha, 2019).

Historically, land ownership under customary law emphasised communal ownership, with land inheritance typically passing through the male lineage and reinforced by patriarchal cultural systems. Although women have traditionally participated in and supported customary land tenure systems, many have increasingly asserted their rights to independent land ownership, inheritance, and equal decision-making authority within customary governance structures (Wildschut & Hulbert, 1998; Claassens, 2013; Whitehead & Tsikata, 2003). Research by Claassens and Ngubane (2008) found that women are frequently evicted from their homes following the dissolution of marriage or the death of their husbands. Divorced or widowed women who return to their natal homes often face eviction by their brothers, while unmarried sisters may also be displaced by married brothers after the death of their parents. In many cases, sons assert exclusive inheritance rights to family land, even where a father intended that a daughter should inherit or assume responsibility for the family home.

Customary law underpins the land governance practices of many Indigenous societies, where land is regarded as a collective resource that must be preserved and passed on to future generations. Within these customary systems, disputes over land ownership and control frequently arise. Land is generally held in trust for the community by family heads or traditional leaders, who are predominantly men. These leaders exercise authority over land allocation and use for purposes such as agriculture, hunting, and residential development, often reinforcing patriarchal patterns of land governance that limit women's access to and control over land (Njieassam, 2019).

Although patriarchy remains deeply embedded in many rural communities, patriarchal households may continue to provide women with material and emotional support (Walker, 2003). However, this support often comes at the expense of women's meaningful participation in household and community decision-making, as entrenched patriarchal power relations and hegemonic gender norms continue to reinforce male authority (McEwan, 2005). Under customary land tenure systems, married women frequently experience insecure land rights, with decisions regarding land allocation, use, and inheritance commonly made by male relatives or traditional authorities without their meaningful involvement (Claassens, 2013). The broader evidence demonstrates that the pursuit of gender equality in land ownership extends beyond securing access to land. It requires addressing the historical, cultural, economic, and institutional processes that have systematically constrained women's land rights, thereby positioning land reform as a matter of economic justice, historical redress, cultural recognition, and social transformation.

LITERATURE REVIEW.

This chapter ventures into an exhaustive exploration of literature regarding role of land in rural women’s economic development inequality, drawing upon perspectives that span across continents and around the globe. The goal is to amplify uproar calling for policies designed to obliterate poverty, economic and social development, and inequality, and to champion the cause of land access for women in rural areas.

In South Africa, a range of historical and structural factors continue to undermine women's access to land. Colonial and apartheid legislation, particularly the Natives Land Act 27 of 1913, systematically dispossessed Black South Africans of their land, creating enduring patterns of racial inequality, poverty, and landlessness that continue to shape land ownership today (Presidential Advisory Panel on Land Reform and Agriculture, 2019). Despite democratic reforms, land ownership remains highly unequal. The 2017 National Land Audit found that approximately 79% of the audited land was privately owned, while 14% was state-owned and 7% could not be categorised. The audit further revealed that White South Africans continued to own the largest proportion of individually owned agricultural land, reflecting the persistent legacy of historical dispossession (Department of Rural Development and Land Reform [DRDLR], 2017). These historical inequalities are compounded by contemporary challenges affecting rural women, including insecure tenure rights, limited decision-making authority under customary tenure systems, and unequal access to productive resources (Hall, 2010). Consequently, addressing the structural barriers that hinder rural women's access to land in KwaZulu-Natal is essential for promoting gender equality, sustainable livelihoods, and inclusive economic development.

The legacy of colonialism and apartheid, particularly the Natives Land Act 27 of 1913 and subsequent discriminatory legislation, systematically dispossessed Black South Africans of their land and excluded them from meaningful economic participation, resulting in persistent poverty, landlessness, and socio-economic inequality (Presidential Advisory Panel on Land Reform and Agriculture, 2019; Hall, 2010). Following the democratic transition in 1994, land reform became a central pillar of South Africa's transformation agenda, aimed at addressing historical racial, spatial, and economic injustices through land restitution, redistribution, and tenure reform (Hall, 2010; Walker, 2003). Although the democratic government introduced numerous poverty reduction and rural development programmes alongside an expanded social protection system, structural inequalities in land ownership and access continue to disproportionately affect rural women. Under customary tenure systems, women frequently experience insecure land rights, limited decision-making authority, and restricted access to productive resources, despite constitutional guarantees of equality (Claassens, 2013; Walker, 2003). Consequently, improving rural women's access to land remains fundamental to promoting gender equality, reducing poverty, and achieving sustainable rural development in South Africa (Food and Agriculture Organization [FAO], 2011).

Land ownership is not only a means of economic empowerment and social well-being but also a source of dignity, social recognition, and self-reliance. Njieassam (2019) emphasises that land is fundamental to the livelihoods and cultural identity of millions of people, particularly Indigenous communities, where women play a significant role in agricultural production and household well-being. However, entrenched cultural norms and patriarchal customary practices often reinforce gender inequalities by limiting women's rights to own, inherit, and control land. As a result, Indigenous women experience multiple and intersecting forms of discrimination based on gender, ethnicity, and socio-economic status, which further restrict their access to productive resources and opportunities for sustainable economic development.

Experiences from Latin America demonstrate that legal recognition of women's rights does not automatically translate into gender equality in land ownership. Although land reform programmes have expanded women's legal entitlements in several countries, meaningful gender equality depends on women's effective access to, control over, and ownership of land, as well as their participation in land governance (Deere & León, 2001). Similar challenges have been documented elsewhere in Africa. In Zimbabwe, customary inheritance practices have historically limited divorced and widowed women's rights to land and other productive resources despite their substantial contributions to household livelihoods (Mutangadura, 2004). Likewise, in Rwanda, women's land rights were significantly strengthened through the 1999 Law on Matrimonial Regimes, Liberalities and Successions, which introduced equal inheritance rights for daughters and improved property rights for married women, marking a significant shift from earlier customary practices that largely excluded women from land ownership (Daley, Dore-Weeks, & Umuhoza, 2010).

In Cameroon, as in many African nations, customary law is central to the legal system and is constitutionally recognised, especially in relation to land tenure and governance. These laws and practices are binding within communities. Women in Cameroon, as noted by Njieassam (2019, 8), typically face few obstacles in accessing land for food production. However, the challenge lies in attaining full control and ownership of land. Under customary law, decision-making is dominated by men, leading to discriminatory practices that hinder women's ability to own and control land. Despite their significant contributions to sustainable development, food security, and poverty alleviation, the perception of women as weak and incapable undermines their ability to invest in land.

In South Africa's KwaZulu-Natal Province, patriarchal norms continue to shape customary land governance. Within many rural communities, customary practices often position women as secondary rights holders whose access to land is mediated through male relatives, thereby limiting their autonomy and participation in land-related decision-making despite constitutional guarantees of equality and non-discrimination (Claassens, 2013; Walker, 2003). Following South Africa's democratic transition in 1994, the Ingonyama Trust Act 3 of 1994 transferred approximately 2.8 million hectares of former KwaZulu homeland land to the Ingonyama Trust, to be administered for the benefit of communities living on the land under the custodianship of the Ingonyama (Republic of South Africa, 1994). Since its establishment, several scholars and civil society organisations have argued that the administration of Trust land has often reinforced traditional authority structures and created challenges for women's tenure security and independent land rights (Claassens, 2013; Cousins, 2016). Although land reform programmes have sought to redress historical dispossession and promote equitable access to land, progress in improving rural women's land ownership and tenure security has remained limited (Hall, 2010; Walker, 2003). Against this backdrop of historical land dispossession, persistent poverty, and gendered customary practices, this study examines the challenges that rural women in KwaZulu-Natal continue to face in accessing land and overcoming poverty and inequality.

This study builds on the existing body of scholarship by critically examining whether South Africa's land reform programme has translated its constitutional and legislative commitments into substantive gender justice for women, particularly those residing in rural communities. Although the post-apartheid government introduced land reform as a mechanism for redressing historical inequalities, scholars argue that its implementation has largely failed to transform the gendered patterns of land ownership and control inherited from colonialism and apartheid (Walker, 2003; Cousins, 2016). Access to land remains fundamental to women's livelihoods, providing shelter, food security, agricultural production, income generation, and an asset that can potentially serve as collateral for accessing financial resources (FAO, 2011; World Bank- *Gender in agriculture*, 2009). However, despite these developmental benefits, rural women continue to experience insecure land tenure owing to the intersection of poverty, patriarchal customary practices, and institutional weaknesses that undermine the effective enforcement of land rights (Claassens, 2013; Commission for Gender Equality, 2018).

Against this backdrop, the study adopts a qualitative research approach to generate context-specific evidence capable of informing more gender-responsive land policies and legislative reforms. It specifically investigates the complex interplay between poverty, gender inequality, and women's limited access to land in rural KwaZulu-Natal, where female-headed households continue to experience disproportionately high levels of poverty, unemployment, and food insecurity (Statistics South Africa, 2023). The study further interrogates how historical land dispossession, patriarchal social relations, and the coexistence of customary and statutory land governance systems continue to constrain women's ability to acquire, own, inherit, and exercise secure land rights (Walker, 2003; Claassens, 2013). Rather than assuming that progressive legislation automatically translates into equitable outcomes, the study critically evaluates whether key land reform statutes, including the Extension of Security of Tenure Act 62 of 1997 (ESTA) and the Land Reform (Labour Tenants) Act 3 of 1996 (LTA), have effectively addressed the structural barriers facing rural women. In doing so, it examines the extent to which these legislative instruments have advanced gender justice, reduced poverty and inequality, and strengthened women's tenure security, while recognising that legislative reform alone is insufficient without effective implementation, institutional accountability, and the transformation of patriarchal power relations embedded within customary and local governance systems (Republic of South Africa Constitution, 1996; Republic of South Africa, 1997 *Extension of Security of Tenure Act*; Cousins, 2016; Commission for Gender Equality, 2018).

Various strategies have been developed to address poverty, unemployment, and inequality, with Local Economic Development (LED) emerging as a key approach adopted by governments to stimulate inclusive and sustainable economic growth at the local level. LED is a participatory process through which local governments, businesses, civil society, and communities collaborate to mobilise local resources, attract investment, create employment opportunities, and improve the quality of life of local residents (Rogerson, 2010; World Bank- Local economic development, 2003). In South Africa, LED is recognised as a core developmental responsibility of municipalities, enabling local authorities to create an enabling environment for economic growth while addressing local socio-economic challenges (Republic of South Africa *Land Reform (Labour Tenants) Act 3 of 1996*; Rogerson, 2010). Furthermore, LED initiatives contribute to poverty reduction by supporting entrepreneurship, strengthening local value chains, promoting small enterprises, and improving livelihood opportunities within communities (Meyer, 2014). In rural areas, LED also supports sustainable agriculture and food security by encouraging local production systems, enhancing market access, and strengthening community resilience, thereby reducing dependence on external inputs and promoting inclusive rural development (Food and Agriculture Organization [FAO], 2017).

This study further examines international and continental perspectives on poverty, inequality, and women's access to land through comparative case studies from Cameroon, Latin America, and India. By undertaking a comparative analysis of these contexts alongside South Africa, the study seeks to identify policy and implementation gaps, as well as best practices that have contributed to improving women's land rights and livelihoods in different socio-political settings. The insights generated from this comparative analysis will inform context-specific policy recommendations aimed at strengthening women's access to secure land rights, promoting sustainable livelihoods, and addressing the persistent challenges of poverty and gender inequality in rural South Africa, with particular emphasis on KwaZulu-Natal.

RURAL WOMEN AND LAND ACCESS IN SOUTH AFRICA

Land and its use are fundamental to the livelihoods of rural women, providing access to natural resources that support household food security, income generation, and overall well-being. However, insecure land rights increase the vulnerability of women and girls by limiting their economic opportunities, reducing their tenure security, and constraining their ability to challenge patriarchal power relations. Despite contributing substantially to agricultural production, household labour, and the care economy in South Africa's rural communities, women continue to experience unequal access to land ownership and control because of deeply entrenched patriarchal norms and customary tenure systems (Food and Agriculture Organization [FAO], 2011; Claassens, 2013). Under many customary land tenure arrangements, decisions relating to land allocation, inheritance, and ownership remain predominantly male-centred, resulting in women's continued marginalisation in land governance and widening gender inequalities in land ownership (Claassens, 2013; Walker, 2003).

Women play a central role in agriculture, livestock production, and other sectors of rural economies. However, in many countries, statutory and customary legal systems continue to limit women's ability to exercise secure land rights. Customary land tenure arrangements frequently prevent women from owning or controlling land independently, restricting their inheritance rights and increasing the vulnerability of divorced and widowed women to dispossession despite constitutional and legal commitments to gender equality (Food and Agriculture Organization [FAO], 2011; UN Women, 2020). Studies further demonstrate that women constitute a disproportionate share of the world's rural poor, with agriculture serving as their primary source of livelihood. Consequently, addressing persistent poverty, food insecurity, and gender inequality requires empowering women through equitable access to productive resources while engaging both women and men in transforming unequal gender relations (Doss, 1999; FAO, 2011).

In many African societies, rural women continue to experience the effects of deeply entrenched patriarchal systems that limit their access to power, decision-making, education, productive resources, and economic opportunities, including land and credit. These gendered inequalities reinforce women's dependence within both the household and the wider community, constraining their social, economic, and political participation (Food and Agriculture Organization [FAO], 2011; Kabeer, 1999). Women's experiences are shaped by the intersection of their domestic responsibilities and public roles, resulting in persistent inequalities that undermine their empowerment and limit their ability to exercise agency over productive resources and livelihood decisions (Kabeer, 1999; Agarwal, 1994).

Doss (1999) highlights the persistent challenges experienced by women farmers in Africa, demonstrating how gender inequalities constrain women's access to productive resources, agricultural opportunities, and livelihood security. These challenges are intensified by intersecting forms of disadvantage, including race, class, historical exclusion, and unequal institutional arrangements. In the South African context, Black rural women have experienced particularly severe marginalisation due to the combined effects of colonial and apartheid land dispossession, patriarchal social relations, and unequal access to economic resources (Walker, 2003; Whitehead & Tsikata, 2003). These intersecting inequalities continue to limit women's access to land, markets, education, healthcare, and financial services, thereby reinforcing cycles of poverty and economic dependency (Doss, 1999; FAO, 2011). Although African countries continue to confront complex development challenges, including weak governance, climate change, environmental degradation, and economic insecurity, these challenges are not experienced equally across social groups. Rural women remain disproportionately vulnerable to poverty, food insecurity, and livelihood insecurity because they are often located at the margins of social, economic, and political systems (Doss, 1999; Walker, 2003). Consequently, addressing rural women's poverty requires more than economic interventions; it requires gender-responsive land governance, equitable access to productive resources, and transformative policies capable of challenging the structural inequalities embedded within both statutory and customary land governance systems (Claassens, 2013; Cousins, 2016).

International policy frameworks recognise rural women as central contributors to agricultural production, food security, rural livelihoods, and sustainable development. Rural women play critical roles in farming, household food production, caregiving, and the management of natural resources, making their participation essential for inclusive economic development and poverty reduction (Food and Agriculture Organization [FAO], 2011; International Fund for Agricultural Development [IFAD], 2011). Despite these contributions, rural women continue to shoulder a disproportionate burden of unpaid domestic and care work, including collecting water and fuelwood and caring for children, older persons, and other dependent family members. These responsibilities are often intensified in female-headed households, particularly where male labour migration has shifted household responsibilities to women, thereby increasing their vulnerability to poverty and food insecurity (Food and Agriculture Organization of the United Nations [FAO], 2011). Addressing these challenges is consistent with the objectives of the National Planning Commission, 2012 South Africa's National Development Plan (NDP) 2030, which prioritises poverty reduction, inclusive rural development, gender equality, and equitable access to productive resources as key drivers of sustainable socio-economic transformation.

Despite these challenges, rural women remain the primary contributors to household food production and agricultural activities across much of Africa. However, compared with their urban counterparts, they often face greater barriers to accessing productive resources, basic infrastructure, and essential public services. They also shoulder a disproportionate burden of unpaid domestic and care work, including collecting water and fuelwood and caring for children, older persons, and other dependent family members. These responsibilities increase women's time poverty, limit their opportunities for education and income-generating activities, and reinforce cycles of poverty and food insecurity (Food and Agriculture Organization of the United Nations [FAO], 2011). Addressing these structural inequalities is consistent with the objectives of South Africa's National Development Plan (NDP) 2030, which prioritises poverty reduction, gender equality, inclusive rural development, and equitable access to productive resources as essential pillars of sustainable socio-economic transformation (National Planning Commission, 2012).

Selvan (2017) identifies several interconnected challenges affecting rural girl students, including family responsibilities, restrictive social expectations, financial constraints, and gender discrimination, all of which contribute to higher dropout rates and reduced participation in higher education. These challenges reflect broader patterns of structural inequality that limit rural women's access to transformative opportunities, including education, economic resources, and secure livelihoods. Similar inequalities are evident in the domain of land access, where women often derive fewer benefits from land registration and redistribution programmes due to limited financial resources, discriminatory social norms, and deeply embedded patriarchal practices. Although land reform initiatives have sought to improve tenure security and address historical injustices, scholars argue that many reforms have inadequately engaged with the complexities of African customary land tenure systems, where communal and individual rights often coexist in contested ways (Hall, 2010; Toulmin, 2009). The interaction between statutory and customary land governance has, in many cases, facilitated elite capture of communal resources and weakened women's land rights, leaving rural women vulnerable to dispossession, exclusion from decision-making processes, and competing claims over land ownership (Claassens, 2013; Toulmin, 2009). Consequently, addressing rural women's marginalisation requires an integrated approach that recognises the relationship between education, land rights, and socio-economic empowerment, while developing context-specific interventions that challenge gendered inequalities embedded within households, communities, and governance institutions.

In South Africa, land governance is shaped by both statutory and customary legal systems. The Constitution guarantees men and women equal rights to acquire, own, inherit, and manage property. However, in many rural areas, communal land continues to be administered under customary law, where land allocation and governance are often influenced by patriarchal norms and traditional authority structures. Although customary law has evolved to recognise constitutional principles of equality, its implementation frequently continues to privilege men as primary rights holders while limiting women's independent access to and control over land (Claassens, 2013; Cousins, 2007). Consequently, women remain disadvantaged in matters of land allocation, inheritance, and tenure security despite the legal protections afforded by South Africa's constitutional framework (Mutangadura, 2004; Claassens, 2013).

WOMEN'S REALITIES ON LAND

Land remains one of the most significant livelihood assets for rural communities, particularly among rural dwellers in KwaZulu-Natal, including communities in Estcourt and Pietermaritzburg, where access to land is closely connected to food production, household security, and socio-economic survival. However, the ability of rural households, especially women, to benefit from land is shaped by structural forces, including historical dispossession, poverty, gender inequalities, and unequal access to productive resources. Within this context, indigenous knowledge systems play a critical role in enabling rural communities to sustain livelihoods and respond to environmental and socio-economic challenges. Hart and Vorster (2006), in their study of rural communities in the Eastern Cape and KwaZulu-Natal provinces of South Africa, demonstrate how indigenous knowledge practices assist rural women in adapting to challenges such as drought, seasonal food shortages, and limited agricultural resources. Their findings reveal that the drying and preservation of indigenous leafy vegetables constitute important indigenous food security strategies, allowing households to maintain nutritional availability throughout the year. These practices illustrate that rural women's relationship with land extends beyond ownership and tenure security; it also encompasses the preservation, utilisation, and transmission of indigenous ecological knowledge that supports household resilience and food sovereignty.

Furthermore, Hart and Aliber (2010) and Hart and Vorster (2006) demonstrate that many rural smallholder women farmers in South Africa experience literacy, information, and institutional constraints that limit their access to agricultural knowledge, technologies, innovations, and support services. These challenges are compounded by the marginalisation of Indigenous Knowledge Systems (IKS) within formal agricultural and development frameworks, where local knowledge practices, particularly those held and transmitted by rural women, are often undervalued or excluded from mainstream agricultural extension and policy interventions (Odora Hoppers, 2002; Msuya & Lalika, 2016). Although rural women possess extensive indigenous knowledge related to seed preservation, soil management, biodiversity conservation, food processing, and climate adaptation, unequal power relations within households, communities, and governance institutions often restrict their ability to participate fully in land-based decision-making and agricultural activities (Shackleton & Shackleton, 2004; Walker, 2003). Furthermore, patriarchal interpretations of customary land governance frequently limit women's authority over land use, ownership, and resource management, despite their central role in sustaining rural food systems and household livelihoods (Claassens, 2013; Whitehead & Tsikata, 2003).

Access to reliable agricultural information, gender-responsive extension services, appropriate technologies, and the recognition of Indigenous Knowledge Systems is therefore essential for improving women's agricultural productivity, strengthening household and community food security, and enhancing their participation in local and broader markets (Food and Agriculture Organization [FAO], 2011). However, improving rural women's livelihoods requires more than the provision of technical agricultural support; it necessitates addressing the structural inequalities that continue to marginalise women as land users, agricultural producers, and knowledge holders. Indigenous knowledge practices developed and sustained by rural women represent valuable sources of ecological understanding, climate adaptation strategies, and food system resilience, yet these knowledge systems are frequently overlooked within formal agricultural policies and extension frameworks (Odora Hoppers, 2002; Hart & Vorster, 2006). Consequently, sustainable rural development requires approaches that recognise and integrate women's experiential knowledge alongside scientific and technological innovations. Such recognition is critical not only for reducing poverty and promoting food sovereignty but also for advancing gender-equitable land governance systems that acknowledge rural women as active agents in agricultural development, environmental sustainability, and rural transformation (Claassens, 2013; Walker, 2003). However, recognising women as legitimate land users and knowledge holders requires more than secure land rights alone. It also depends on equitable access to information, education, and lifelong learning opportunities that enable women to exercise agency within agricultural and rural development systems. In this regard, public libraries and community information centres play a significant role in empowering women by providing equitable access to information, digital literacy, lifelong learning, and skills development that enhance livelihoods, social inclusion, and economic participation (International Federation of Library Associations and Institutions [IFLA], 2015). Beyond their traditional educational functions, these institutions serve as community knowledge hubs that reduce information inequalities, facilitate access to public services, and strengthen citizens' capacity to participate meaningfully in local governance and development processes. This function is particularly important in disadvantaged rural communities, where women frequently rely on backyard gardening, small-scale livestock production, and Indigenous Knowledge Systems to strengthen household food security and supplement household incomes. To improve agricultural productivity and livelihood resilience, rural women require timely access to relevant agricultural information, including knowledge relating to sustainable land management, soil conservation, water management, climate adaptation, and pest and disease control (Food and Agriculture Organization [FAO], 2011). Consequently, meaningful rural development cannot be achieved solely through land redistribution or tenure reform; it also requires knowledge systems that enable women to access, generate, and apply information in ways that strengthen their livelihoods and decision-making capacity. As UNESCO (2021) argues, equitable access to information, lifelong learning, and knowledge-sharing constitutes a fundamental pillar of sustainable rural development because it enhances people's capacity to participate fully in social, economic, and community development. Taken together, these perspectives demonstrate that strengthening women's land rights, recognising Indigenous Knowledge Systems, and expanding access to information and lifelong learning are mutually reinforcing processes that are essential for achieving gender equality, sustainable agriculture, and inclusive rural development. Access to relevant information and knowledge is fundamental to empowering women, particularly those living in rural communities where opportunities for education, training, and information are often limited. Knowledge enables women to make informed decisions, adopt improved agricultural and livelihood practices, participate more effectively in community development, and strengthen their economic independence. Furthermore, improving literacy and expanding access to information are critical for enhancing women's capacity to access, interpret, and apply knowledge that supports sustainable livelihoods and social inclusion (United Nations Educational, Scientific and Cultural Organization [UNESCO], 2021; Food and Agriculture Organization [FAO], 2011).

THEORETICAL FRAMEWORK

The study employs Giddens' (1984) structuration theory and Patricia Hill Collins' (2000) black feminist theory to examine the role of land in rural women's economic development. Structuration theory portrays structure as rules and resources structured as facets of social systems, while agency is delineated as individual actions and the constraints and facilitations encountered in their actions. Structuration theory fundamentally asserts that a duality of structure and agency is integral in the perpetuation of social practices, including knowledge sharing. Structure and agency are mutually indispensable. Structure is both the vehicle and result of practice production, while participation in social relationships results from the continual production and reproduction of social systems by members.

Patricia Hill Collins' (2000) concept of the "matrix of domination" illustrates how overlapping forms of oppression are systematically structured. This matrix incorporates various oppressive factors such as race, gender, socioeconomic status, age, and sexuality, which operate across four domains: structural, disciplinary, hegemonic, and interpersonal. While all Black women experience the impact of this matrix of domination, their unique intersection of oppressions results in diverse experiences and perspectives. Building on these theoretical perspectives, the chapter integrates Patricia Hill Collins' Black Feminist Theory with Anthony Giddens' (1984) Structuration Theory to critically examine how historical, cultural, and institutional structures continue to shape rural women's experiences of land ownership, poverty, and socio-economic exclusion in KwaZulu-Natal, while also recognising their agency in challenging these inequalities.

Various approaches have been adopted to understand poverty and devise strategies to eradicate it. Whether individualistic or structural, these methodologies highlight why poverty persists and how different state and non-state actors contribute to its perpetuation. It becomes clear that addressing these issues requires the active involvement of rural women in policy-making and implementation. Giddens asserts that the primary goal of social analysis is to understand human actions. He contends that individual activity matters and that examining practices is essential because they influence outcomes. His concept of social structure encompasses both constraints and opportunities, underscoring the need to account for institutional embeddedness to fully understand human activity. Additionally, Giddens' concept of structuration links structure and agency, providing continuity and potential for structural change.

Within the integrated theoretical framework of Black Feminist Theory (Collins, 2000) and Structuration Theory (Giddens, 1984), the interpersonal domain refers to the everyday social relationships and interactions through which broader structures of power are reproduced or contested. In the context of this study, these structures include cultural norms, customary law, traditional institutions, and the immediate communal environment that shape women's access to land and participation in rural development. Within many rural communities in KwaZulu-Natal, customary land governance and patriarchal cultural norms continue to influence decisions regarding land allocation, inheritance, and ownership. Although these customary institutions remain important for preserving cultural identity and social cohesion, their interpretation and implementation may reinforce gendered inequalities by limiting women's access to productive land and decision-making processes. These gendered power relations mean that rural women frequently experience differential treatment and expectations that reflect historically embedded social norms assigning authority over land and productive resources primarily to men. From the perspective of Structuration Theory (Giddens, 1984), such practices are neither fixed nor inevitable. Rather, they are continuously produced and reproduced through everyday social interactions, institutional arrangements, and customary governance, while simultaneously remaining open to transformation through individual and collective agency. This theoretical perspective demonstrates that although patriarchal structures constrain women's access to land and decision-making processes, they also provide spaces through which rural women can negotiate, contest, and reshape existing power relations. Similarly, Black Feminist Theory highlights that these gendered experiences cannot be understood in isolation from other intersecting forms of inequality, including race, class, and rurality. Together, these theoretical perspectives demonstrate that women's limited access to land is not simply the result of individual discrimination but is embedded within broader social structures that continue to shape economic opportunities, land governance, and rural livelihoods.

Figure 1. Depicting a Map of KwaZulu- Natal.

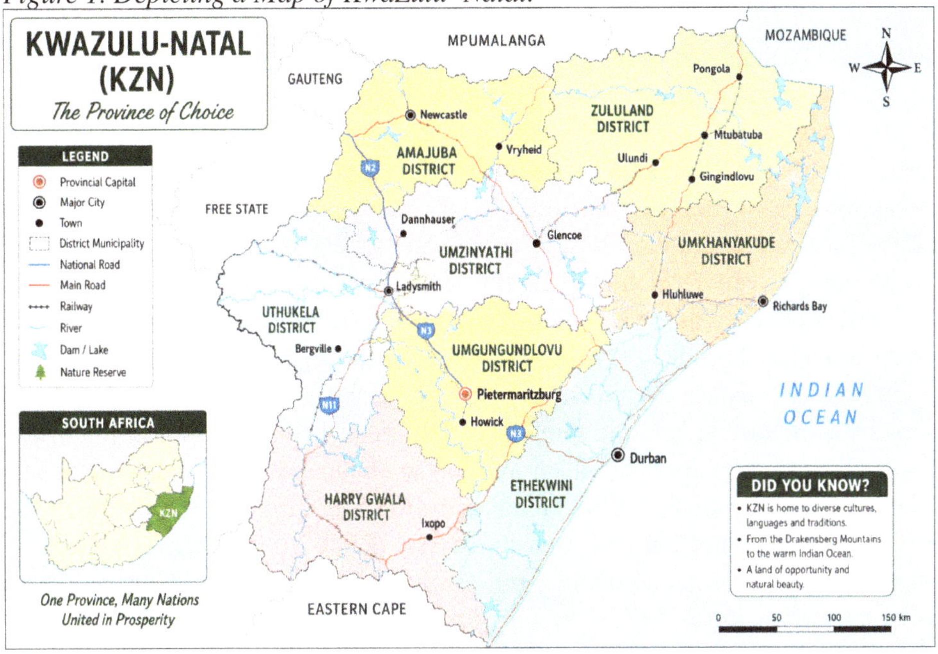

The study was conducted in Pietermaritzburg and Estcourt, located in KwaZulu-Natal Province, South Africa. Although KwaZulu-Natal represents one of the country's most economically significant provinces, it simultaneously reflects the deep contradictions of South Africa's post-apartheid development trajectory, where economic growth coexists with persistent rural poverty, unemployment, and inequality. Many rural communities continue to experience interconnected geographical, structural, and socio-economic constraints, including inadequate infrastructure, limited access to productive resources, climate-related vulnerabilities, and restricted economic opportunities, all of which undermine sustainable livelihood development (Statistics South Africa, 2023). These challenges cannot be understood merely as contemporary development failures but must be situated within the historical context of colonial and apartheid dispossession, which produced enduring inequalities in land ownership, resource distribution, and economic participation.

Following the democratic transition in 1994, the South African government introduced a range of agricultural and rural development policies intended to address historical injustices, improve rural livelihoods, and transform unequal patterns of land ownership and access. However, despite progressive policy commitments, the outcomes of land reform and rural development programmes have remained limited, with scholars attributing these shortcomings to weak institutional capacity, inadequate resources, fragmented implementation, and the persistence of structural inequalities inherited from apartheid (National Planning Commission, 2012 National Development Plan vision 2030; Department of Agriculture, Land Reform and Rural Development [DALRRD], 2022). Furthermore, many rural development interventions have continued to reflect technocratic and top-down approaches that insufficiently engage with local realities, Indigenous Knowledge Systems, and the gendered experiences of rural communities. The cumulative effect of these historical, institutional, and gendered inequalities is that rural households, particularly female-headed households, continue to experience limited access to agricultural information, gender-responsive extension services, financial resources, appropriate technologies, and other productive assets necessary to strengthen sustainable livelihoods and improve agricultural productivity (Food and Agriculture Organization [FAO], 2011).

In KwaZulu-Natal, these challenges are particularly evident in rural communities where smallholder agriculture remains an important livelihood strategy. Female-headed households experience disproportionate vulnerability due to historical and contemporary barriers that restrict their access to land, agricultural credit, financial capital, markets, education, and extension support (FAO, 2011; Aliber & Hall, 2012). Although rural women contribute significantly to food production, household survival, and community resilience through subsistence farming and informal economic activities, their agricultural contributions often remain undervalued within formal development frameworks. Their ability to transition from subsistence production to commercially viable agriculture is constrained by limited access to infrastructure, storage facilities, value-addition opportunities, market networks, and institutional support (DALRRD, 2022). As a result, many households adopt multiple livelihood strategies, including informal trading, wage labour, remittances, and dependence on social grants, not necessarily as indicators of economic diversification, but as responses to structural vulnerability and limited livelihood opportunities (Statistics South Africa, 2023; National Development Plan vision 2030, 2012).

Gender relations within rural communities further shape women's experiences of land access and agricultural participation. While women perform substantial productive and reproductive labour, including food production, household management, and community responsibilities, decision-making authority over land, livestock, and economic resources often remains concentrated among men. In many communal areas, patriarchal interpretations of customary governance systems continue to influence land allocation and inheritance practices, frequently limiting women's ability to exercise secure land rights or participate equally in land-related decision-making processes (Claassens, 2013; Walker, 2003). These gendered power relations demonstrate that women's vulnerability is not simply a consequence of poverty but is produced through the interaction of economic inequality, patriarchal institutions, and governance systems that historically prioritised male authority in land administration.

Therefore, addressing rural livelihood insecurity requires positioning the household as an important analytical entry point while simultaneously recognising the broader institutional and structural conditions that shape household opportunities. Land advocacy and rural development strategies must move beyond treating women as passive beneficiaries of development interventions and instead recognise them as active land users, agricultural producers, knowledge holders, and decision-makers. Meaningful land reform requires the inclusion of rural women in land allocation processes, land claims, governance structures, and development planning to ensure that land redistribution contributes to substantive rather than symbolic gender justice. Development interventions that fail to incorporate women's voices, knowledge systems, and rights risk reproducing existing inequalities rather than transforming them. The cumulative evidence from this study indicates that advancing equitable rural development in KwaZulu-Natal requires a transformative governance approach that extends beyond conventional poverty reduction strategies. Such an approach should strengthen women's substantive land rights, recognise Indigenous Knowledge Systems as essential to sustainable rural development, and challenge the patriarchal institutional and customary power relations that continue to mediate women's access to land, productive resources, and economic opportunities. By addressing these interconnected structural constraints, land reform can move beyond redistributive objectives towards achieving gender justice, sustainable livelihoods, and inclusive rural transformation.

RESEARCH METHODOLOGY

This study adopted a qualitative case study design to examine rural women's experiences of land access, ownership, and economic participation in KwaZulu-Natal, South Africa. A qualitative approach was considered appropriate because the study sought to understand the meanings that women attach to land within historically unequal, culturally embedded, and gendered social contexts. Rather than treating land solely as an economic asset, the study recognises it as a multidimensional resource associated with identity, social belonging, cultural continuity, livelihood security, and intergenerational wellbeing. Consequently, a qualitative methodology provided the depth required to explore how women experience, negotiate, and interpret land-related inequalities within their everyday lives.

The case study design enabled an in-depth examination of the complex relationship between historical land dispossession, customary land tenure, patriarchal governance structures, and contemporary land reform within a specific geographical context. KwaZulu-Natal was purposively selected because of its distinctive history of colonial and apartheid land dispossession, the continued significance of customary land governance, and persistent gender inequalities that shape women's access to land and decision-making processes. Although South Africa's constitutional and legislative framework guarantees equality before the law and promotes equitable access to land, women's everyday experiences frequently reveal tensions between formal legal protections and customary practices governing land allocation, inheritance, and ownership. Situating the study within KwaZulu-Natal therefore provides a context through which broader debates concerning land justice, gender equality, Indigenous Knowledge Systems, and rural transformation can be critically examined.

Purposive sampling was employed to recruit participants with direct experience of land-related challenges and rural livelihoods. The study engaged women from female-headed households, subsistence farming households, labour tenant communities, and women affected by customary land governance systems. This sampling strategy prioritised information-rich participants whose lived experiences could provide detailed insights into the structural barriers influencing women's access to land. The emphasis was therefore placed on analytical depth rather than statistical representativeness, consistent with qualitative inquiry.

Data were generated through semi-structured interviews, participant observation, and narrative accounts, allowing participants to articulate their experiences of land ownership, agricultural production, livelihood insecurity, and interactions with customary and state institutions in their own words. These complementary methods facilitated a deeper understanding of how women navigate complex systems of land governance while simultaneously recognising them as knowledge holders, custodians of Indigenous Knowledge Systems, and active agents who negotiate, contest, and adapt to conditions of social and economic marginalisation.

The qualitative data were analysed using thematic analysis, which enabled the systematic identification and interpretation of recurring patterns across participants' narratives. The analysis focused on themes relating to patriarchal exclusion, customary authority, policy implementation, livelihood insecurity, Indigenous Knowledge Systems, and women's agency. Rather than providing a descriptive account of participants' experiences, the analysis was informed by Anthony Giddens' (1984) Structuration Theory and Patricia Hill Collins' (2000) Black Feminist Theory, enabling a critical examination of the dynamic relationship between structural constraints and individual agency. Structuration Theory facilitated an understanding of how customary institutions, land governance systems, and historical inequalities both constrain and are reproduced through everyday social practices, while Black Feminist Theory illuminated how intersecting systems of gender, race, class, and rurality shape women's lived experiences of land access and economic participation. The integration of these theoretical perspectives strengthened the analytical interpretation by situating participants' experiences within broader debates on social justice, gender equality, and structural transformation.

Ethical considerations were integral to the research process because the study explored sensitive issues relating to poverty, gender inequality, historical land dispossession, and customary governance. Prior to data collection, ethical clearance was obtained from the Humanities and Social Sciences Research Ethics Committee (HSSREC) of the University of KwaZulu-Natal (UKZN). The study adhered to established ethical principles governing research involving human participants, including informed consent, voluntary participation, confidentiality, anonymity, and the protection of participants' dignity, privacy, and Indigenous knowledge. Participants were informed of the purpose of the study, their right to withdraw at any stage without prejudice, and the measures implemented to safeguard their identities and personal information. Given the power asymmetries often associated with research involving marginalised rural communities, the study adopted a reflexive and ethically responsive approach that sought to represent participants' experiences accurately, respectfully, and without reinforcing existing inequalities. Through this methodological framework, the study generated contextually grounded evidence on the relationship between gender, land governance, Indigenous Knowledge Systems, and rural livelihoods. By foregrounding the voices and lived experiences of rural women, the study contributes to ongoing scholarly and policy debates concerning gender-responsive land reform, equitable land governance, and sustainable rural development in South Africa.

FINDINGS AND ANALYSIS

The findings presented in this section are derived from qualitative data collected from twenty-nine (n=29) participants. The participants comprised sixteen (16) women affiliated with the Association for Rural Advancement (AFRA) and thirteen (13) women from the Rural Women's Movement (RWM). These organisations were selected because of their longstanding involvement in land rights advocacy, rural women's empowerment, and struggles for equitable access to land in KwaZulu-Natal. The participants' narratives provide insight into how rural women experience land access, ownership, agricultural participation, and livelihood transformation within historically unequal socio-economic and customary governance systems.

All respondents emphasised the significance of land in their everyday lives. Land was described not only as an economic resource but also as a foundation for social stability, cultural identity, household security, and community belonging. For rural dwellers in KwaZulu-Natal, land remains the ultimate livelihood asset because it provides opportunities for food production, income generation, livestock ownership, and intergenerational continuity. However, the findings also demonstrate that land does not operate as a neutral economic resource; rather, access to and control over land are shaped by historical dispossession, gender relations, customary authority structures, institutional practices, and unequal access to resources.

This finding supports Ribot and Peluso's (2003) theory of access, which argues that the ability to benefit from resources extends beyond formal ownership and is influenced by social, political, and institutional relationships. In the context of rural women in KwaZulu-Natal, possessing a legal claim or living within a land reform environment does not automatically guarantee meaningful access or economic benefit.

Theme 1: Economic Policy Knowledge and Women's Participation in Rural Development

The findings reveal that limited access to economic policy knowledge remains a significant challenge affecting rural women's ability to participate effectively in land-based economic activities. Participants highlighted those historical inequalities in education, limited access to information, and weak communication between government institutions and rural communities continue to constrain women's ability to benefit from development programmes.

The exclusion of Black communities from educational opportunities during apartheid contributed significantly to contemporary patterns of socio-economic inequality. However, the findings suggest that the challenge extends beyond historical educational disadvantage; it also involves the accessibility and relevance of information regarding land reform, agricultural support programmes, markets, and economic opportunities.

The findings suggest that historical inequalities in education continue to shape rural women's participation in agricultural and land governance systems. Fleisch (2008) argues that the legacy of apartheid education has produced persistent disparities in educational attainment and learning outcomes, particularly among historically disadvantaged Black communities. Similarly, Spaull (2013) demonstrates that South Africa's education system continues to reproduce deep socio-economic inequalities inherited from apartheid, limiting opportunities for skills development, employment, and social mobility. Within the context of this study, these historical inequalities are reflected in rural women's limited access to agricultural information, extension services, institutional knowledge, and other resources necessary to engage effectively with formal land governance and agricultural development programmes. From a Structuration Theory perspective (Giddens, 1984), educational disadvantage continues to function as a structural constraint that limits rural women's capacity to exercise agency and derive meaningful economic benefits from land reform initiatives.

One participant explained:

"So, as there is a lack of job opportunities, as a woman, you should be trying anything you can do, but the problem is when you are discouraged from doing

things that are for males. There is none from the government. Some training I only got from AFRA. In the family, I have no experience of discrimination based on being a female."

(RWM/AFRA7)

This narrative illustrates the complexity of gender exclusion. While the participant did not experience direct discrimination within her household, she identified broader structural barriers that discourage women from entering economic spaces traditionally associated with men. This demonstrates that gender inequality is not only reproduced through interpersonal relations but also through institutional arrangements and economic structures.

The participant's experience further highlights the importance of non-governmental organisations such as AFRA and RWM in filling gaps created by limited state outreach. These organisations provide training, advocacy, and knowledge-sharing platforms that enable rural women to engage more effectively with land and agricultural processes.

A Department of Agriculture representative acknowledged government attempts to expand women's participation across agricultural value chains:

"We also have what is called RASET, which ensures that women are participating through the entire value chain from production, processing, up to the market. As a department, we want to focus not only on primary production because there is not much money and job creation at that level, which makes our projects become unsustainable. Currently, the people who make more money are those in the agro-processing and value-added sectors. But we do have all the policies in place to support women in KwaZulu-Natal."

(DoA)

Although these policy initiatives demonstrate the government's commitment to promoting women's economic inclusion, the findings reveal a persistent disconnect between policy aspirations and the lived realities of rural women. Despite their significant contribution to agricultural production, women continue to face systemic barriers to participating effectively in agricultural value chains, including insecure land tenure, limited access to finance, agricultural technologies, markets, and extension services. These findings are consistent with Doss's (1999) argument that gender disparities in agricultural productivity arise primarily from unequal access to productive resources and institutional support rather than differences in women's knowledge, skills, or capabilities. The findings indicate that meaningful economic empowerment cannot be achieved through the existence of gender-responsive policies alone. Rather, it requires effective implementation mechanisms capable of dismantling the structural, institutional, and socio-cultural barriers that continue to constrain women's participation in the rural economy. This study further demonstrates that transformative land reform depends on accessible information systems, accountable and gender-responsive institutions, and inclusive public policies that recognise rural women not merely as beneficiaries of development interventions but as rights holders, land users, knowledge custodians, and economic actors. Such an approach is essential for advancing substantive gender equality, strengthening women's agency in land governance, and promoting sustainable rural livelihoods and inclusive rural transformation.

Theme 2: Public Support, State Intervention, and Implementation Challenges

The findings reveal a contradictory relationship between rural women and state-supported land and agricultural development programmes. Participants acknowledged positive interventions from government institutions, including agricultural training, fencing projects, access to farming inputs, and development programmes. However, they also expressed concerns regarding bureaucratic barriers, inadequate implementation, and limited responsiveness to rural women's circumstances.

One participant acknowledged the positive impact of state intervention:

"A good story is that Land Affairs has fenced our plots with a strong fence. This will save our crops from being destroyed by livestock." (RWM/AFRA5)

This demonstrates that state interventions can contribute positively when they respond directly to practical challenges experienced by rural farmers. However, participants also identified situations where institutional processes created additional barriers.

One participant explained:

"Where I am, there is land. But the municipality is discouraging us as women. I looked for land until I gave up. In the end, they told me the land I was referring to would be advertised, so I must put it out for it in the newspaper. I then decided to just give up, but yes, they are so oppressive."

(RWM/AFRA1)

This narrative reveals the tension between formal policy frameworks and implementation realities. Although land reform policies recognise gender equality and historical redress, administrative procedures may unintentionally exclude women who lack financial resources, information, or institutional support.

Another participant highlighted financial barriers:

"There are challenges we face when we want to acquire land. There is money to pay, and we do not have money." (RWM/AFRA2)

This demonstrates that access to land is influenced not only by availability but also by affordability, institutional processes, and economic inequality.

A Department of Agriculture representative explained:

"We have different policies aimed at empowering women. For instance, we have the Agricultural Development Policy, which we are implementing, and we are aligning all our programmes with it. That policy covers all programmes. It also investigates issues of women's and youth's participation."(DoA)

The contrast between institutional commitments and women's lived experiences demonstrates that progressive policies alone are insufficient. Cousins (2016) argues that South Africa's land reform challenges are strongly linked to implementation weaknesses, institutional fragmentation, and unresolved questions surrounding land governance. Therefore, the findings suggest that effective land reform requires stronger institutional accountability, simplified procedures, and meaningful inclusion of rural women in decision-making processes.

Figure 2. Integrated Implementation Pathway for Transforming Land Access into Rural Women's Economic Empowerment in KwaZulu-Natal

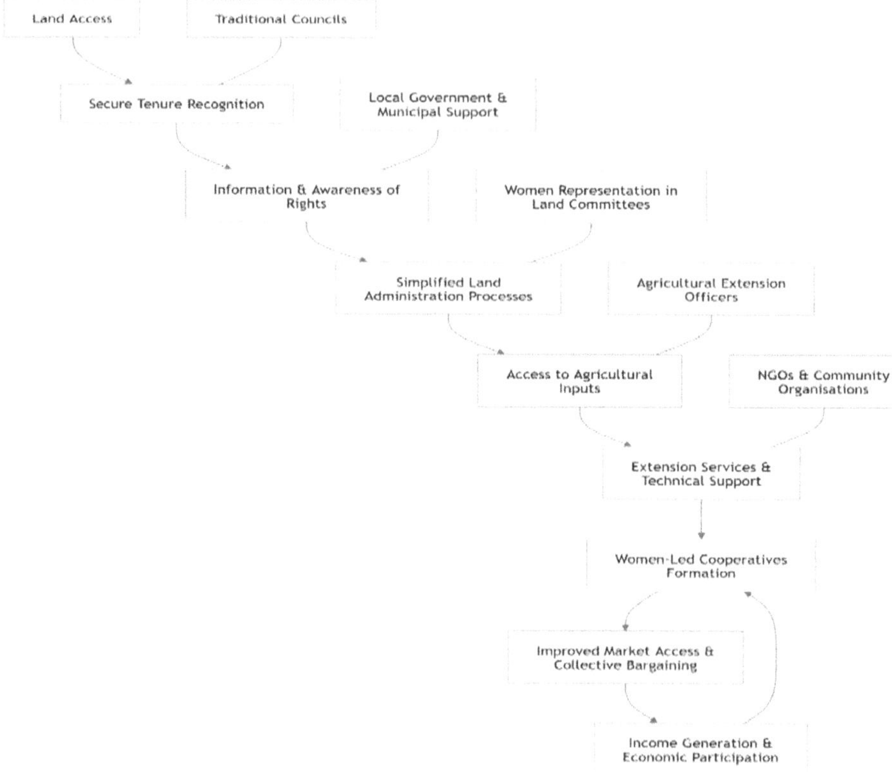

Contributed by Authors: Nhlapho and Zondi

The implementation pathway developed in this study demonstrates that rural women's economic empowerment cannot be achieved through land access alone but requires a multidimensional and interconnected process involving legal recognition, institutional support, productive capacity, and collective agency. The model reconceptualises land as an enabling foundation rather than an ultimate outcome of empowerment, arguing that secure tenure recognition represents only the initial condition through which women can begin to exercise meaningful control over productive resources. However, the pathway also exposes a persistent contradiction within land reform processes: while legislative frameworks may formally recognise women's rights to land, these rights often remain socially and economically ineffective in the absence of accessible information, simplified administrative procedures, responsive institutions, and mechanisms that support women's substantive participation.

Moving beyond a rights-based interpretation of land access, the model advances an understanding of empowerment as a process of converting formal rights into lived economic capabilities. This conversion requires complementary interventions, including access to agricultural inputs, extension services, financial resources, market opportunities, and skills development. These enabling conditions are particularly significant for rural women, whose ability to benefit from land is often constrained by intersecting forms of gendered, historical, and socio-economic exclusion. The inclusion of women-led cooperatives within the pathway highlights the importance of collective organisation as a mechanism through which rural women can overcome individual resource limitations, negotiate market barriers, strengthen social capital, and enhance their participation in local economic systems.

Importantly, the model challenges linear understandings of empowerment by presenting economic transformation as a dynamic and recursive process. Increased productivity and income generation do not represent the final stage of empowerment; rather, they contribute to the strengthening of collective institutions, improved decision-making power, and enhanced capacity to influence future land and development processes. Through the lens of Structuration Theory, this pathway illustrates the continuous relationship between agency and structure, where rural women operate within historically produced institutional and cultural constraints while simultaneously exercising agency to transform these structures through collective practices, knowledge production, and social organisation.

Furthermore, Black Feminist Theory provides an important analytical lens for understanding how rural women's experiences of land access are shaped by intersecting systems of oppression, including race, gender, class, colonial histories, and patriarchal forms of authority. From this perspective, economic empowerment cannot be separated from questions of identity, representation, knowledge legitimacy, and institutional power. The incorporation of Indigenous knowledge systems within the pathway is therefore not an auxiliary component but a critical epistemological foundation for developing land reform interventions that recognise rural women as knowledge holders and active participants in development processes. This challenges technocratic approaches that often position communities as passive beneficiaries rather than co-producers of knowledge and solutions.

The pathway ultimately suggests that the success of land reform depends on moving beyond the redistribution of land towards the creation of enabling ecosystems that support women's sustained control, utilisation, and benefit from land resources. Without coordinated interventions involving government institutions, traditional authorities, community organisations, civil society actors, and women's collective structures, land reform risks remaining institutionally visible but socially and economically transformative only in limited ways. Therefore, achieving gender-equitable land reform requires an approach that integrates legal reform, institutional accountability, Indigenous knowledge systems, and women's collective agency as interconnected components of sustainable rural development.

DIRECTION FOR FUTURE RESEARCH

This study contributes to a deeper understanding of the structural, institutional, and socio-cultural conditions that continue to reproduce poverty, inequality, and gendered disparities in access to land among rural communities in South Africa. By examining the outcomes of land redistribution within rural KwaZulu-Natal, the study highlights the extent to which land reform remains influenced by historical patterns of dispossession, customary governance arrangements, and institutional limitations. The findings suggest that while land reform possesses significant potential as a mechanism for poverty alleviation, livelihood improvement, and tenure security, its transformative capacity depends on the creation of supportive economic, social, and institutional environments that enable women and other marginalised groups to derive meaningful benefits from land resources.

Although this study provides valuable insights into rural KwaZulu-Natal, its geographical focus presents opportunities for comparative investigations across South Africa's former apartheid-era homelands. Future research should examine how variations in historical experiences of dispossession, customary land governance systems, local political economies, and gender relations influence the outcomes of land reform across provinces such as the Eastern Cape, Limpopo, Mpumalanga, North West, and other regions characterised by communal tenure arrangements. Comparative studies would contribute to a more nuanced understanding of how context-specific factors shape women's experiences of land access, ownership, control, and utilisation.

Future scholarship should also move beyond conceptualising land access as a singular measure of empowerment and instead investigate the processes through which land rights are translated into sustainable livelihoods, economic participation, food security, and enhanced decision-making power. Longitudinal research would be particularly valuable in assessing whether land redistribution initiatives generate enduring improvements in household welfare and whether beneficiaries are able to transform land into productive assets over time. Such studies should further explore the role of Indigenous knowledge systems, traditional leadership institutions, community-based organisations, and women's collective initiatives in developing more inclusive and locally grounded models of land governance.

Methodologically, future research would benefit from interdisciplinary and participatory approaches that integrate anthropology, gender studies, development studies, political economy, and Indigenous knowledge scholarship. Participatory methodologies are particularly important because they position rural women and community members not merely as research participants but as active producers of knowledge whose lived experiences can inform policy innovation. Future research should therefore continue examining how land reform can evolve beyond the redistribution of physical resources towards a more inclusive, gender-responsive, and socially transformative framework capable of addressing South Africa's persistent inequalities.

CONCLUSIONS AND RECOMMENDATIONS

The findings demonstrate that land in rural KwaZulu-Natal remains a structurally constrained resource rather than a reliable pathway towards women's economic empowerment. Despite post-apartheid reforms designed to promote land redistribution, tenure security, and gender equality, women's access to and control over land continue to be shaped by the enduring consequences of historical dispossession, patriarchal authority structures, institutional weaknesses, and intersecting inequalities of race, class, gender, and education. The evidence presented in this study demonstrates that land has not yet become a transformative economic asset for most rural women in KwaZulu-Natal. Instead, their engagement with land remains largely confined to subsistence agricultural production, as persistent structural inequalities including insecure land tenure, patriarchal customary governance, limited access to finance, agricultural inputs, extension services, and markets continue to limit opportunities for commercial agriculture, sustainable income generation, and long-term wealth creation. Through the analytical lens of Structuration Theory, the findings reveal how historically embedded social structures continue to influence resource distribution and constrain women's agency, even within a democratic constitutional framework. Although rural women demonstrate resilience and agency through household production, informal economic practices, and community-based survival strategies, their ability to transform land into an economically empowering resource remains restricted by unequal institutional arrangements and gendered systems of authority. Similarly, Black Feminist Theory demonstrates that rural Black women's experiences of land exclusion cannot be understood through gender alone but must be examined through the interconnected realities of race, class, colonial histories, and patriarchal social relations. The limited transformative outcomes of land reform therefore reflect deeper structural inequalities rather than only challenges of policy implementation.

Based on these findings, this study recommends a shift from a narrow focus on land redistribution towards a broader land empowerment approach that integrates secure tenure rights, productive support systems, gender-responsive governance, and institutional accountability. Strengthening women-led cooperatives represents an important strategy for enhancing rural women's participation in the land economy. Cooperative initiatives can reduce production costs, improve access to markets, strengthen collective bargaining power, and provide mechanisms through which women can overcome individual resource constraints. However, the sustainability of these initiatives requires consistent support through agricultural extension services, financial resources, infrastructure development, skills training, and market integration.

Furthermore, greater alignment between customary authorities and formal governance institutions is necessary to address inconsistencies in land allocation, inheritance practices, and decision-making processes that continue to limit women's participation. Constructive dialogue among traditional leaders, municipalities, government departments, civil society organisations, and rural communities can contribute to the development of culturally responsive land governance systems that uphold constitutional commitments to equality and social justice without undermining legitimate customary practices. Such engagement should also recognise Indigenous knowledge systems and rural women's lived experiences as valuable sources of knowledge in shaping sustainable development interventions.

Ultimately, this study concludes that meaningful participation of women in the rural land economy has significant potential to contribute to poverty reduction, food security, and sustainable rural development in KwaZulu-Natal. However, land access alone is insufficient to achieve transformative empowerment. Effective land reform requires an integrated framework that combines secure land rights, institutional support, collective economic strategies, and recognition of women as active agents of development. Moving beyond redistribution towards empowerment-oriented land governance is essential if South Africa's land reform programme is to address enduring inequalities and contribute to more equitable rural futures.

9. REFERENCES

Agarwal, B. (1994). *A field of one's own: Gender and land rights in South Asia.* Cambridge University Press.

Aliber, M., & Hall, R. (2012). Support for smallholder farmers in South Africa: Challenges of scale and strategy. *Development Southern Africa, 29*(4), 548–562. DOI: 10.1080/0376835X.2012.715441

Claassens, A. (2013). Recent changes in women's land rights and contested customary law in South Africa. *Journal of Agrarian Change, 13*(1), 71–92. DOI: 10.1111/joac.12007

Claassens, A. (2013). Recent changes in women's land rights and contested customary law in South Africa. *Journal of Agrarian Change, 13*(1), 71–92. DOI: 10.1111/joac.12007

Claassens, A., & Ngubane, S. (2008). Women, land and power: The impact of the Communal Land Rights Act. In Claassens, A., & Cousins, B. (Eds.), *Land, power and custom: Controversies generated by South Africa's Communal Land Rights Act* (pp. 154–183). University of Cape Town Press.

Collins, P. H. (2000). *Black feminist thought: Knowledge, consciousness, and the politics of empowerment* (2nd ed.). Routledge.

Commission for Gender Equality. (2018). *Women, land and customary law*. Commission for Gender Equality.

Commission for Gender Equality. (2024). *Exploring barriers to women's access to communal land in South Africa*. Commission for Gender Equality.

Cousins, B. (2016). *Land reform in South Africa is sinking: Can it be saved?* Nelson Mandela Foundation.

Daley, E., Dore-Weeks, R., & Umuhoza, C. (2010). Ahead of the game: Land tenure reform in Rwanda and the process of securing women's land rights. *Journal of Eastern African Studies : The Journal of the British Institute in Eastern Africa, 4*(1), 131–152. DOI: 10.1080/17531050903556691

Deere, C. D., & León, M. (2001). *Empowering women: Land and property rights in Latin America*. University of Pittsburgh Press. DOI: 10.2307/j.ctt5hjpf6

Department of Rural Development and Land Reform. (2017). *Land audit report: Phase II—Private land ownership by race, gender and nationality*. Republic of South Africa.

Doss, C. R. (1999). *Twenty-five years of research on women farmers in Africa: Lessons and implications for agricultural research institutions* (Economics Program Paper No. 99-02). International Maize and Wheat Improvement Center.

Fleisch, B. (2008). *Primary education in crisis: Why South African schoolchildren underachieve in reading and mathematics*. Juta.

Food and Agriculture Organization of the United Nations. (2011). [*Women in agriculture—Closing the gender gap for development*. Food and Agriculture Organization of the United Nations.]. *The State of Food and Agriculture*, •••, 2010–2011.

Food and Agriculture Organization of the United Nations. (2011). [*Women in agriculture—Closing the gender gap for development*. Food and Agriculture Organization of the United Nations.]. *The State of Food and Agriculture*, •••, 2010–2011.

Food and Agriculture Organization of the United Nations. (2017). *The state of food and agriculture: Leveraging food systems for inclusive rural transformation*. Food and Agriculture Organization of the United Nations.

Giddens, A. (1984). *The constitution of society: Outline of the theory of structuration*. Polity Press.

Hall, R. (2010). *Land reform in South Africa: A status report 2010*. Institute for Poverty, Land and Agrarian Studies, University of the Western Cape.

Hart, T. G. B., & Aliber, M. (2010). The role of smallholder farmers in food security in South Africa. *Development Southern Africa*, *27*(4), 499–514.

Hart, T. G. B., & Vorster, H. J. (2006). *Indigenous knowledge frameworks and practices for sustainable livelihoods in South Africa*. Human Sciences Research Council.

International Federation of Library Associations and Institutions. (2015). *Public libraries support development through access to information*. International Federation of Library Associations and Institutions.

International Fund for Agricultural Development. (2011). *Rural poverty report 2011: New realities, new challenges: New opportunities for tomorrow's generation*. IFAD.

Kabeer, N. (1999). Resources, agency, achievements: Reflections on the measurement of women's empowerment. *Development and Change*, *30*(3), 435–464. DOI: 10.1111/1467-7660.00125

McEwan, C. (2005). New spaces of citizenship? Rethinking gendered participation and empowerment in South Africa. *Political Geography*, *24*(8), 969–991. DOI: 10.1016/j.polgeo.2005.05.001

Meyer, D. F. (2014). Local economic development (LED), challenges and solutions: The case of the Northern Free State region, South Africa. *Mediterranean Journal of Social Sciences*, *5*(16), 624–634. DOI: 10.5901/mjss.2014.v5n16p624

Msuya, T. S., & Lalika, M. C. S. (2016). The role of indigenous knowledge in managing food security and climate change adaptation among rural communities in Africa. *African Journal of Food, Agriculture, Nutrition and Development*, *16*(3), 11000–11016.

Mutangadura, G. (2004). *Women and land tenure rights in Southern Africa: A human rights-based approach*. United Nations Economic Commission for Africa.

National Planning Commission. (2012). *National Development Plan 2030: Our future—Make it work*. The Presidency, Republic of South Africa.

National Planning Commission. (2012). *National Development Plan 2030: Our future—Make it work*. The Presidency, Republic of South Africa.

Njieassam, E. E. (2019). Gender inequality and land rights: The situation of Indigenous women in Cameroon. *Potchefstroom Electronic Law Journal*, *22*, 4907. Advance online publication. DOI: 10.17159/1727-3781/2019/v22i0a4907

Odora Hoppers, C. A. (Ed.). (2002). *Indigenous knowledge and the integration of knowledge systems: Towards a philosophy of articulation*. New Africa Books.

Popoola, O., & Magidimisha, H. H. (2019). Examining women's access to rural land in UMnini Trust traditional area of KwaZulu-Natal, South Africa. *Journal of Local Government Research and Innovation, 1*, Article 12.

Presidential Advisory Panel on Land Reform and Agriculture. (2019). *Final report of the Presidential Advisory Panel on Land Reform and Agriculture*. Republic of South Africa.

Republic of South Africa. (1994). *Ingonyama Trust Act 3 of 1994*. Government Printer.

Republic of South Africa. (1996). *Constitution of the Republic of South Africa, 1996 (Act No. 108 of 1996)*. Government Printer.

Republic of South Africa. (1996). *Land Reform (Labour Tenants) Act 3 of 1996*. Government Printer.

Republic of South Africa. (1997). *Extension of Security of Tenure Act 62 of 1997*. Government Printer.

Ribot, J. C., & Peluso, N. L. (2003). A theory of access. *Rural Sociology*, *68*(2), 153–181. DOI: 10.1111/j.1549-0831.2003.tb00133.x

Rogerson, C. M. (2010). Local economic development in South Africa: Strategic challenges. *Development Southern Africa*, *27*(4), 481–495. DOI: 10.1080/0376835X.2010.508580

Selvan, A. (2017). Problems of rural girl students in higher educational institution. *Scholarly Research Journal for Humanity Science & English Language*, *4*(23), 5992–5998. DOI: 10.21922/srjhsel.v4i23.9642

Shackleton, C. M., & Shackleton, S. E. (2004). The importance of non-timber forest products in rural livelihood security and as safety nets: A review of evidence from South Africa. *South African Journal of Science*, *100*(11–12), 658–664.

Spaull, N. (2013). Poverty and privilege: Primary school inequality in South Africa. *International Journal of Educational Development*, *33*(5), 436–447. DOI: 10.1016/j.ijedudev.2012.09.009

Statistics South Africa. (2023). *General household survey 2023*. Statistics South Africa.

Toulmin, C. (2009). Securing land and property rights in sub-Saharan Africa: The role of local institutions. *Land Use Policy*, *26*(1), 10–19. DOI: 10.1016/j.landusepol.2008.07.006

United Nations Educational, Scientific and Cultural Organization. (2021). *Reimagining our futures together: A new social contract for education*. UNESCO.

United Nations Entity for Gender Equality and the Empowerment of Women. (2020). *Women's rights to land and productive resources*. UN Women.

Walker, C. (2003). Piety in the sky? Gender policy and land reform in South Africa. *Journal of Agrarian Change*, *3*(1–2), 113–148. DOI: 10.1111/1471-0366.00052

Whitehead, A., & Tsikata, D. (2003). Policy discourses on women's land rights in sub-Saharan Africa: The implications of the return to the customary. *Journal of Agrarian Change*, *3*(1–2), 67–112. DOI: 10.1111/1471-0366.00051

Wildschut, A., & Hulbert, S. (1998). *A seed not a tree: Community perspectives on local governance, land and development*. Community Agency for Social Enquiry (CASE).

World Bank. (2003). *Local economic development: A primer—Developing and implementing local economic development strategies and action plans*. World Bank.

World Bank. (2009). *Gender in agriculture sourcebook*. World Bank.

Chapter 9
Women's Cooperatives as a Social Innovation Model in the Journey of Women's Empowerment:
The Case of Burdur Ball Sewing Cooperative

Özge Kutlu
http://orcid.org/0000-0002-4774-7326
Burdur Mehmet Akif Ersoy University, Turkey

Mehmet Öçal
http://orcid.org/0000-0001-6973-2611
Burdur Mehmet Akif Ersoy University, Turkey

ABSTRACT

Women's empowerment is a crucial element of economic and social development, contributing to gender equality and sustainable growth. This chapter examines the impact of women's cooperatives on economic and social empowerment, focusing on the case of the Burdur Ball Sewing Cooperative in Türkiye. Through qualitative research methods, including in-depth interviews with cooperative members, this study explores how cooperatives contribute to financial independence, expand social networks, and challenge traditional gender roles. The findings indicate that participation in women's cooperatives enhances economic self-sufficiency, strengthens social ties, and promotes gender equality. However, challenges such as financial constraints and social stereotypes persist, necessitating further policy support. The

DOI: 10.4018/979-8-2600-3325-8.ch009

chapter concludes that women's cooperatives serve as an effective tool for social transformation and recommends expanding financial resources, educational programs, and cooperative networks to maximize their impact.

1. INTRODUCTION

The empowerment of women in a society is one of the cornerstones of its economic, social, and sustainable development. The active role of women in all areas of social life (economic, social, political) is not limited to improving the quality of life of individual women, but also increases the welfare of families, communities and society. For this very reason, goals such as eliminating gender inequalities worldwide and increasing women's participation in decision-making mechanisms are a priority within the United Nations Sustainable Development Goals (SDGs) (Yadav, 2023). In particular, the 5th Goal of the United Nations Sustainable Development Goals, “Gender Equality”, and the 8th Goal, “Decent Work and Economic Growth”, are among the determining factors for the economic and social empowerment of women (Suseno & Nataliningsih, 2023). While many factors and tools are effective in empowering women, women's cooperatives stand out as among the most important.

Women's cooperatives are a form of social innovation. Women's cooperatives are platforms that enable women to work collectively, pool their resources, and achieve common goals. In addition to the economic contributions they provide to women, cooperatives enable women to become more visible in both economic and social life. In other words, they accelerate women's participation in social life. At the same time, women's cooperatives encourage a culture of solidarity and cooperation. Women's cooperatives contribute to women's economic and social empowerment, providing sustainable benefits for individuals and communities (Khatri Basnet, 2023). Some of the micro and macro advantages provided by women's cooperatives are the ability to live an economically independent life, gain professional skills and develop existing skills, strengthen social relations, implement new social support mechanisms, and contribute to the local economy. Cooperatives provide women with the opportunity to establish their own businesses, increase their access to financial resources, and strengthen their social status (Datta & Gailey, 2012). In addition, creating a solidarity and support network among women enables important steps towards gender equality across society.

The aim of this study is to examine in depth the effects of women's cooperatives on women's economic independence, gender equality, and social empowerment. Using the Burdur Sewing Ball Cooperative as an example, the processes by which women gain economic freedom, the importance of social solidarity networks, their contributions to the struggle for gender equality, and the difficulties they face in this process are analysed. In this context, the contributions of women's cooperatives to sustainable development and social justice goals are comprehensively evaluated using qualitative research methods.

2. COOPERATIVES: A TOOL AND SOLIDARITY MODEL FOR WOMEN'S EMPOWERMENT

In the globalising world order, while capital and big capitalists have grown stronger with the rise in industrial production and factoryization, their share of the pie has gradually increased. This situation has made it difficult for smaller-scale producers and entrepreneurs to survive in a highly competitive market. On the other hand, the acceleration of urbanisation and the increase in migration from rural to urban areas have caused rural life to lose its appeal and production in rural areas to decrease. Under these difficult conditions, small businesses struggle to survive individually, while cooperatives stand out as a more sustainable production model. Cooperatives offer small producers the opportunity to come together, become collectively stronger, share costs, and become more resilient in the face of market conditions.

Etymologically, the word "cooperative" is derived from the Latin "cooperatio", the origin of the French "cooperer", which means "cooperation". When the word is considered as a verb, it is used as the Latin "cooperari" and means "to work together" or "to cooperate" (Mülayim, 2010). Cooperatives, on the other hand, are a more comprehensive expression and, in a broad sense, refer to a large number of people joining forces, acting together, and working in harmony to achieve a common goal (Çıkın & Karacan, 1994). The International Cooperative Alliance (ICA) defines cooperatives as a human-oriented business model, operated and controlled by cooperative members, to meet the economic, social, and cultural needs of individuals. When we look at the positioning of cooperatives, we see that they are positioned between companies and associations. Cooperatives are a model that allows individuals to organise and conduct their economic activities within a specific structure. Unlike association structures, which pursue a public purpose or public benefit, cooperatives aim to protect and develop their members' interests. In other words, they prioritise the benefit of their partners rather than the public benefit. Cooperatives believe they can achieve this goal through economic activities that lead to production. Compared to the company structure, which is a private formation and aims to make a profit, the main difference between cooperatives is that they are based on individuals coming together rather than a capital partnership. Cooperative members have the right to speak according to the principles of partnership and equality, which can be described as a more egalitarian form of structuring rather than capital contribution. In addition, members' transaction volumes play a decisive role in the profit-sharing of cooperatives, rather than capital contributions (Gönüllü Atakan & Çoban, 2022).

According to Marshall (1999), cooperatives are an alternative organisational model to capitalism, evident in some decentralised approaches to socialism, but also successfully applied within the capitalist system. In today's capitalist economic crisis, where everything is organised along the dimensions of work, labour, producer, and consumer, with the aim of achieving the highest profit, and where production and the producer are almost sanctified, it is possible to see cooperatives as solidarity structures. Cooperatives are not associations, unions or political parties, and they are also distinguished from commercial organisations operating for profit. Cooperatives engage in economic activities, but their primary purpose is not to make a profit. The primary purpose of cooperatives is to provide benefits to their members rather than making a profit (Geray, 2014). It is not right to limit the opportunities provided by cooperatives to economic gains alone. Because cooperatives are also businesses that produce social values. All cooperatives work with their environments by adopting the International Cooperative Principles. Cooperatives, established in various parts of the world to combat poverty, improve social welfare, and enhance employment, support people in establishing sustainable businesses together (ICA, 1995).

The International Cooperative Alliance (ICA) has accepted seven principles as the universal principles of cooperatives (İnan, Kumkale, & Okan, 1999). These seven principles, determined by the ICA in 1995, are as follows:

1. ***Voluntary and Free Entry Principle:*** Participation in cooperatives is free for everyone. Members have the right to join or leave cooperatives at their own will.
2. ***Partner's Democratic Management Principle:*** Each member has equal voting rights. This egalitarian management approach makes it possible for the cooperative's management to be carried out democratically.
3. ***Members' Economic Participation Principle:*** Members contribute to the economic activities of the cooperative. Profits from the cooperative are distributed fairly among the members.
4. ***Principle of Autonomy and Independence:*** Cooperatives have the freedom to make their own decisions. Therefore, they operate independently of external interventions.
5. ***Education, Training and Information Principle:*** Cooperatives support their members' conscious participation in society and the cooperative by providing education and information about cooperatives to their members, employees and communities.

6. ***Principle of Cooperation among Cooperatives:*** Cooperatives become stronger by cooperating with other cooperatives at the local micro level and at the national and international macro level.
7. ***Social Responsibility Principle:*** Cooperatives look after the welfare of communities and their environment. They are sensitive to social problems in their communities and support sustainable development.

These seven principles form the basis of a cooperative, are closely interconnected and represent parts of a whole (ICA, 1995).

As can be understood from the principles of cooperatives, cooperatives are a form of organisation formed by individuals coming together to meet their common economic, social and cultural needs. The cooperative model aims to provide economic benefits to its members through solidarity and partnership, while also contributing to social and community development. Women's cooperatives, which especially encourage women's active participation in economic life, have attracted increasing attention as a "development solution" in recent years. There is general acceptance that women's cooperatives are a functional and effective model for advancing women's development (KEİG, 2015). Although there is no standard definition of women's cooperatives in the international arena, the term is generally used to describe cooperatives founded and operated by women, and led by women (KEİG, 2015).

Women's cooperatives are rapidly gaining popularity today. Women's cooperatives, which can be considered a tool for accelerating women's participation in social life, stand out as a "development solution" in today's world. A study conducted by a committee established to support and develop cooperatives found that women's participation in cooperatives worldwide increased by 75% over the last 20 years (Aksoy Demirci & Günay, 2018). In Türkiye over the last decade, a general consensus has emerged across a wide socio-political landscape that women's cooperatives are a valid and effective model for women's development. Cooperatives established and operated by women offer a way for women and different women's groups to meet their needs in income generation, participation in socio-economic life, employment, and organisation. This is a way out for women, especially in the vicious circle surrounded by a sexist division of labour, where the patriarchal social structure prevails, and women are held responsible only for "private" work (Kutlu & Sütlü, 2024). At the same time, it is considered a means for the state, development organisations, and social movements to express their gender-related goals in a concrete, results-oriented way. The increase in women's cooperatives and cooperativism is perceived as an indicator of a search for a compromise that can bring all stakeholders together, rather than merely reflecting the common preferences of these actors. Thus, women's cooperativism emerges as a fragmented, women-focused development vision that combines various searches and initiatives of different actors but faces uncertainties in practice (KEİG, 2015).

3. WOMEN'S COOPERATIVES IN TÜRKIYE

When cooperatives in Türkiye are examined in a historical context, their history dates back to the Ottoman Empire. Although cooperatives have a deep-rooted history, the establishment of women's cooperatives was not possible until 1999 (Duguid, Durutaş, & Wodzicki, 2015). The establishment of women's cooperatives is based on the declaration titled "Gender Equality in Cooperatives" signed by the International Cooperative Alliance (ICA) with its partners around the world in 1995 (Dalkıran, 2017). The signed document and the developments that have emerged in line with it are considered part of efforts to create an environment that supports women's economic and social empowerment. In particular, women's cooperatives enable women to come together in solidarity, engage in economic activities, and promote gender equality. In this context, the existence of women's cooperatives has the potential to create a significant change in the egalitarian social structure.

The cooperative model emerges as an important tool for re-establishing social balance during the socio-economic fluctuations Türkiye has experienced many times. In this context, it is observed that some important steps have been taken to develop and support cooperatives in Türkiye, especially within the framework of the International Year of Cooperatives. One of these steps was the establishment of the General Directorate of Cooperatives in 2011 to determine policies and develop projects related to cooperatives. Another important step was the preparation of the Turkey Cooperative Strategy and Action Plan for 2012-2016. The said action plan is a multidimensional study that determines policies regarding cooperatives. In other words, it serves as a guide that directs cooperatives in Turkey. The action plan includes measures to enhance women's entrepreneurial skills and organise them within cooperatives, enabling them to play an active role in economic life. In the action plan, three ministries were designated as responsible for measures regarding women's cooperatives: the Ministry of Agriculture and Forestry, the Ministry of Commerce, and the Ministry of Family, Labour and Social Services (Gönüllü Atakan & Çoban, 2022).

There has been a significant increase in the number of women's cooperatives in Türkiye, especially since the early 2010s. The main factors behind this increase include the increasing strength of women's rights movements, the need for women working in both rural and urban areas to organize to market and evaluate the products they produce with their own labor, the encouragement of employment-enhancing projects by the International Labor Organization (ILO) and the International Cooperative Alliance, and the preparation of the articles of association for Women's Enterprise Production and Business Cooperatives by the General Directorate of Cooperatives of the Ministry of Customs and Trade (Duguid, Durutaş, & Wodzicki, 2015). This process, in which women's cooperatives are growing in number, enables women to participate more actively in economic life while also reinforcing social solidarity among women. The women's cooperative movement, which started locally and focused on needs in Turkey, has been adopted over time as a policy for the development of women's employment by public institutions and civil society organisations (Bülbüller, 2022).

When data on women's cooperatives in Turkey are examined, the Marmara region emerges as the region with the highest density. The Marmara region is followed by the Central Anatolia, Black Sea, Mediterranean and Aegean regions. The region with the lowest rate of women's cooperatives is Southeastern Anatolia. When the distribution of women's cooperatives in Turkey is examined according to the Level 2 of the Statistical Regional Units Classification (SRU), it is seen that the TR61 sub-region, which covers the provinces of Antalya, Isparta and Burdur, is the region with the highest number of cooperatives with 64 women's cooperatives (Şahankaya Adar, Dedeoğlu, & Kurtuluş, 2023).

The effort to reveal the current status of women's cooperatives in Turkey addresses the potential of initiatives that support women's participation in economic and social life through these structures, as well as cooperativization, to both empower women and increase women's employment. In this context, understanding the importance of women's cooperatives constitutes a critical step not only for economic development but also for gender equality. When structural characteristics are examined, it is seen that women's cooperatives in Turkey mostly operate in areas known as 'women's work'. In fact, this situation can cause women to be limited to their traditional roles and reproduce gender inequality originating from the existing patriarchal social structure. In addition, it has been determined that the majority of women who are cooperative members or employees have limited access to economic resources. This limited access hinders women's efforts to gain economic independence and reduces the potential of cooperatives (Şahankaya Adar, Dedeoğlu, & Kurtuluş, 2023). The impact of women's cooperatives in Turkey on employment and their potential for women's empowerment are both controversial when the current conditions are taken into account.

4. THE ROLE OF WOMEN'S COOPERATIVES IN WOMEN'S EMPOWERMENT

To a certain extent, women are liberated from gender roles through women's cooperatives. Because cooperatives provide women with the opportunity to leave the private sphere and exist in the public sphere. The production-based structure of cooperatives puts cooperatives in a necessary relationship with capitalism. In this context, while women gain economic gain in return for their work experience, they are also in direct interaction with the exploitation and oppression mechanisms of capitalism (Özar, 2015). Women's cooperatives, which support women's participation in economic life, represent the transformation of women's entrepreneurship from an individual framework to a collective structure.

The adoption of the philosophy of solidarity in cooperatives shows that the organisation's basic driving force is economic. In this context, it is possible to say that women's cooperatives have a unique value. One of the most important distinguishing features of women's cooperatives is that they undertake social functions in addition to their economic functions. While other cooperatives generally focus solely on economic activities, women's cooperatives have a multifaceted structure and attract attention for their social aspects (Duguid, Durutaş, & Wodzicki, 2015). The reasons behind defining women's cooperatives as multi-purpose include meeting women's need for social solidarity, serving as a social support mechanism, enabling them to be active in the public sphere, and generating financial income through participation in economic life. This process enables women to increase their economic independence. When we look at the structure of women's cooperatives in Türkiye, it is noteworthy that most cooperatives are established by women and serve women. Studies show that 80% to 100% of the members in these cooperatives are women (Emiroğlu, 2017). This situation reveals that women's cooperatives play an important role in social life and provide an effective mechanism for women's economic and social empowerment.

Women's cooperatives contribute to women's economic independence and their more effective participation in development processes. Women's cooperatives not only increase women's income potential but also support their integration into socio-economic life, enabling them to take a more active role in social life. Women play an important role in achieving economic freedom, having a greater say in decision-making, and becoming more autonomous in basic areas such as education and health. At this point, women's cooperatives go beyond individual gains, strengthen women's solidarity, and have a positive impact on local communities (Bharti, 2021). In other words, women's cooperatives are considered an important social innovation tool in strengthening gender equality and achieving sustainable development goals.

5. METHODS

5.1. Purpose of the research

The main purpose of this research is to examine in depth the effects of women's cooperatives on women's empowerment in the context of economic and gender equality. The research will analyse the effects of women's cooperatives on women's economic independence, increased employment opportunities, and expanded social networks. The contribution of women's cooperatives to the struggle for gender equality and the potential to strengthen women's participation in decision-making processes will be evaluated.

5.2. Research Questions

The research questions created in line with the research purpose are as follows:

RQ 1: What impact do women's cooperatives have on women's economic independence?
RQ 2: What impact do women's cooperatives have on expanding social networks, and how does this impact contribute to women's empowerment?
RQ 3: In what ways do women's cooperatives contribute to the struggle for gender equality?
RQ 4: How do women's cooperatives change women's perceptions of gender roles?
RQ 5: How do women's experiences in cooperatives affect their leadership and decision-making skills?

5.3. Design and Participants

In this study, the phenomenological research model, a qualitative research method, will be used. Qualitative research focuses on understanding participants' emotional and conceptual perspectives by examining them in depth (Karataş, 2015). The phenomenological approach focuses on phenomena found in routine life that are generally not understood in detail. These phenomena include life experiences, perceptions, tendencies and orientations that people encounter in their daily lives but cannot fully comprehend (Yıldırım & Şimşek, 2016). In this context, it is thought that the phenomenological research model provides a suitable basis for this researcher's purpose.

The study's universe consists of women members of Burdur Top Dikim Women's Production and Business Cooperative. To select the most suitable participants for the study, the purposive sampling method was used to create the sample. This technique, which is frequently used in qualitative research, allows for the most effective use of limited resources and the identification of cases rich in information (Yağar & Dökme, 2018; Cresswell & Plano Clark, 2011). Through purposeful sampling, 10 women members who were thought to be able to convey their experiences with the cooperative in a comprehensive manner were interviewed.

5.4. Data Collection Approach

In this study, the qualitative research method was adopted, using in-depth interviews as the data collection tool. These interviews aimed to gain a comprehensive understanding of participants' thoughts, experiences, and feelings, conducted either face-to-face or over the phone. Each interview lasted approximately 40-50 minutes and was audio recorded with participants' consent. Participants were informed that their responses would be used solely for scientific purposes and that their identities would remain confidential. Thus, the study adhered to ethical principles and ensured participant privacy. Semi-structured questions prepared in advance were asked of the participants during the interviews.

The semi-structured interview questions created in relation to the research questions are as follows:

1. *1. How did you join the cooperative? What were your initial motivations for joining?* **(RQ 1)**
2. *How would you describe your economic situation before joining the women's cooperative? What are the changes after joining the cooperative?* **(RQ 1)**
3. *What can you say about the new friendships and connections you made through the women's cooperative?* **(RQ 2)**
4. *How did these social networks affect your work and life opportunities?* **(RQ 2)**
5. *How did your views on gender equality within the women's cooperative shape you?* **(RQ 3)**
6. *How did your experiences within the cooperative change your perspective on gender roles?* **(RQ 4)**
7. *What were the biggest challenges you faced regarding gender roles, and how did the cooperative support you in this regard?* **(RQ 3)**
8. *How did your interactions with other women in the cooperative affect your understanding of gender roles?* **(RQ 4)**
9. *What were the roles and responsibilities you assumed within the cooperative? How did these roles develop your leadership skills?* **(RQ 5)**
10. *How did being a member of the cooperative contribute to your personal development?* **(RQ 5)**

11. *How do you evaluate the overall impact of cooperative activities on society?* **(RQ 3)**
12. *What were the biggest challenges you faced in your cooperative, and what strategies did you develop to overcome these challenges?* **(RQ 5)**
13. *What are your experiences of collaborating with other women's groups or communities outside of the cooperative?* **(RQ 2)**

5.5. Ethical statement

The study was approved by the Ethical Committee of Burdur Mehmet Akif Ersoy University (GO2024/676) and carried out in accordance with the last declaration of Helsinki.

5.6. Analysis of Data

The research data were analysed using a phenomenological approach, which entails examining individuals' cognitive and emotional experiences holistically. This analysis method involves an interactive process between the researcher and participants, focusing on a deep exploration of emotions and thoughts through discourse (Smith & Eatough, 2007). The process assumes a close relationship between language and individuals' emotional and cognitive states, aiming to interpret and understand these states within the context of their expressions. The gathered data were organised into specific themes, which were then grouped and examined in detail. To facilitate a comprehensive analysis, tables were created based on the research's objectives and primary categories, and responses to similar questions were consolidated in a single document. A thorough and integrative evaluation was then conducted. Throughout this process, participants' identities remained confidential, with personal details anonymised and coded.

5.7. Trustworthiness

Comprehensive strategies were implemented to ensure the trustworthiness of this research, which aims to deeply examine the impact of women's cooperatives on women's empowerment in the context of economic and gender equality. Reliability was supported through triangulation, using multiple data collection methods and perspectives from different researchers to validate the findings and ensure the consistency of interpretations (Creswell & Poth, 2017). Additionally, preliminary themes were shared with participants as part of member checking, allowing them to provide feedback on the accuracy of the findings and ensuring that the themes fully reflected their experiences prior to finalisation.

Confirmability was achieved through steps taken to minimise researcher bias. Researchers carefully identified, documented, and reviewed their biases, continuously working to minimise their influence on the analysis. While developing themes, researchers compared their analysis to the data at each stage, continuing until they believed that data saturation had been reached. These stages contributed to a more accurate and unbiased examination of the data.

Dependability was established by meticulously tracking decision points, changes, and every phase of the analysis process. This documentation created a clear audit trail that allows replication of the study's methods, ensuring that similar results can be achieved in future research using the same approach. Transferability was ensured through detailed descriptions and direct quotes that captured the depth of participants' perspectives, making the findings applicable to similar studies and contexts. Together, these strategies enhanced the credibility and applicability of this research, allowing it to robustly address the effects of women's cooperatives on women's empowerment from both economic and gender equality perspectives.

6. FINDINGS AND DISCUSSION

This study examined the effects of participation in women's cooperatives on women's empowerment, economic independence, social networks, perceptions of gender roles, and leadership skills. Demographic characteristics of the participants are provided in Table 1.

Table 1. Demographic characteristics of the participants

Participant	Age	Level of education	Marital status	Duration of membership in the cooperative	Number of people in the household
Participant 1	38	Associate's degree	Married	4 years	4
Participant 2	47	High school graduate	Married	4 years	4
Participant 3	46	Bachelor's degree	Married	4 years	4
Participant 4	42	Primary school graduate	Married	4 years	3
Participant 5	41	Primary school graduate	Single	3 years	1

continued on following page

Table 1. Continued

Participant	Age	Level of education	Marital status	Duration of membership in the cooperative	Number of people in the household
Participant 6	56	Associate's degree	Married	4 years	4
Participant 7	39	Bachelor's degree	Married	1 years	2
Participant 8	42	High school graduate	Married	4 years	3
Participant 9	41	Associate's degree	Married	4 years	2
Participant 10	36	High school graduate	Single	2 years	3

According to Table 1, the participants' ages range from 36 to 56, with the majority in their 30s and 40s. Their education levels vary; 2 are primary school graduates, 3 are high school graduates, 3 have an associate degree, and 2 have a bachelor's degree. Regarding marital status, 8 are married and 2 are single. The duration of cooperative membership ranges from 1 to 4 years, with the majority of participants having been members for 4 years. Household sizes range from 1 to 4 people, with the majority of participants living in households of 3 or 4.

Four themes emerged from the answers: the journey to economic empowerment, the transformative power of solidarity and social networks, the fight for gender equality, and overcoming challenges to create societal impact. The themes and related questions are listed in Table 2.

Table 2. Matching Questions and Themes

Themes	Questions
The journey to economic empowerment	2-9-11
The transformative power of solidarity and social networks	3-4-13
The fight for gender equality	5-6-7-8
Overcoming challenges to create societal impact	1-11-12

Theme 1: The journey to economic empowerment

Participation in women's cooperatives plays an important role as an individual means for women to become economically independent and as a fundamental tool for economic empowerment in society. This theme examines in depth the economic independence that women gain through cooperatives and how this independence affects every aspect of women's lives. Women members of cooperatives participate in the workforce, gain financial independence, and develop leadership skills through cooperatives. When examined more deeply, participation in women's cooperatives creates resources to combat gender inequality. The roles that women undertake in cooperatives not only improve their economic situation but also contribute to their personal development. While the quality of life of women who find greater social inclusion through cooperatives improves in economic and social terms, cooperatives also strengthen women's economic position.

"I couldn't earn my own money before; I had to get financial support from my husband. But now I've been earning my own money since I joined the cooperative. The happiness of spending the money I earn is very different, very beautiful. Since I joined the cooperative, I've become a more independent person, a stronger woman in economic terms...." **(P1)**

"I have never worked in my life. Since I did not work, I did not feel financially strong. Since I did not have any working experience until this age, I did not think that I would be able to earn money in the future. But now, thanks to the cooperative, we have a job, so I feel financially stronger. I joined the cooperative, and it was really beneficial. I not only earned money, but I also acquired a profession. Thanks to our work, I strengthened both my finances and my spirit. Now I can contribute financially to my family. This makes me very happy." **(P9)**

*"I didn't have economic freedom before. I always had to continue my life by being economically dependent on someone. Thanks to the cooperative, I gained my economic freedom by earning my own money. Before I joined the cooperative, I didn't have a big economic problem; I was making a living. However, with the top sewing cooperative, I realised how important it is to stand on my own feet and have economic freedom. This is really a very valuable thing. A woman, especially a woman who grew up in a village, gaining her own economic independence makes her stronger and freer.."***(P2)**

"....Before joining the cooperative, my wife was our only source of income at home. My wife worked in the factory, and I was at home. Looking at my wife's pocket always made me feel financially dependent. After joining the cooperative, I earned my own money. I can buy the clothes and perfumes I want. I can buy coffee for my friends outside with my own money. Being able to earn my own income gave me a great sense of freedom." **(P7)**

Participants stated that they were economically dependent on their spouses or other family members before joining the cooperative. Joining the cooperative not only provided financial gain but also enabled the participants to gain personal freedom. The statements of P1 and P9 expressed the happiness and strength they felt upon gaining economic independence. P2 stated that the opportunities provided by the cooperative helped her realise the value of economic freedom, especially as someone who grew up in a rural area, by giving her the strength to stand on her own two feet. Similar to the statements of participants P1, P2, and P9, P7 also emphasised that she felt a great sense of relief and freedom, not only financially but also emotionally, when she joined the cooperative. The narratives given above show that, beyond economic empowerment, the cooperative increased the participants' self-confidence and enabled them to become more independent individuals in the social sense. This power gained through the cooperative allows women to contribute more effectively not only to their families but also to their communities.

A study by the International Labour Organisation (ILO) highlighted various obstacles to women's participation in cooperatives in East Africa. Factors such as low levels of education, inadequate skills, cultural perceptions of traditional gender roles, and the concentration of household work on women were cited as obstacles to women's participation in cooperative activities (ILO, 2012). However, the same study also highlighted the positive effects of cooperative membership on women's socio-economic empowerment. Women who participated in cooperatives stated that they earned higher incomes, their living standards improved, they became more effective in production and marketing, they perceived themselves more positively, and they had more say in participating in social processes. Similarly, Koutsou et al. (2003), in their study examining women's cooperatives in Greece, found that participation in women's cooperatives provided women with a source of income, economic freedom, control, and self-confidence. In line with the theme of "The Journey to Economic Empowerment", research findings indicate that cooperative membership helps women gain economic freedom, build self-confidence, and take on their social roles and responsibilities more actively.

Theme 2: The transformative power of solidarity and social networks

The solidarity and social networks that emerge through cooperatives have transformative power, empowering women socially and psychologically. Collective structures such as cooperatives allow individuals to develop themselves, strengthen their social ties and overcome difficulties through solidarity, beyond gaining economic independence. Solidarity and social support mechanisms, especially among women, enable not only women's empowerment but also social change and transformation. Social networks among women increase trust and support relationships among individuals. On the other hand, they reduce the social isolation that women experience when confined to their homes and help individuals feel stronger. Cooperatives, which also support women's functioning, cease to be mechanisms for economic gain and become spaces for learning, sharing, and empowerment for individuals.

"At first, I was worried about whether I could work in the cooperative. Because I had never had a professional career. I was working, but in a day job. When I first started going to the cooperative, it was very difficult for me to be a part of this formation. I had to do other jobs to support my family, and I could not spare much time to join the cooperative. However, after meeting the other women in the cooperative, I realised the power of solidarity. It was as if I revealed the power within myself with the power I received from the women..." **(P4)**

".... It has become much easier to overcome difficulties when we support each other. It is really difficult to struggle alone. But in the cooperative, there are women like me trying to hold on to life on my right and left. You gain strength from the presence of these women, and you understand that you are not alone. Thanks to the cooperative, I have become more economically comfortable and stronger socially. Here, I not only earned money but also found various opportunities to improve myself. I came to this cooperative as a trainee to learn how to sew a ball, and now I can give ball sewing training as an instructor." **(P10)**

".....By working in the cooperative, I not only gained economic freedom but also helped others. I also realised that being here means that women support each other and that we can become stronger with the support we give to each other.." **(P2)**

Similar to the participants' narratives, the study by Çınar et al. (2021) reveals the transformative power of solidarity and social networks in the context of women's cooperatives. The study showed that despite political and social restrictions in Turkey, women's cooperatives make significant contributions to women's economic, psychological, social and organisational empowerment. Beyond providing economic independence, women's cooperatives support women's empowerment at individual and social levels through social solidarity and psychological gains. Women's cooperatives create a collective field of action in the struggle to build a society where women and men are equal and gender inequality is eliminated. In other words, women's cooperatives offer the opportunity for transformation and change through solidarity. The study's findings reveal that solidarity and social networks serve as catalysts not only for individual change in women's lives but also for the struggle for social equality.

Theme 3: The fight for gender equality

Women's cooperatives play an important role in ensuring gender equality. It is obvious that women's cooperatives allow women to contribute to production and, together with production, to earn income. In other words, women's cooperatives increase women's participation in economic life, allowing them to earn income and gain economic independence. At the same time, they support women in developing their entrepreneurial skills, taking on leadership positions and actively participating in decision-making processes. It would be appropriate to say that women's cooperatives facilitate access to the most basic human right, the right to participation. The solidarity-based structure of cooperatives fosters a strong social network among women and raises awareness in the fight against gender-based discrimination. Because the role attributed to women in gender roles is to work unpaid at home. In fact, gender roles are used as a mask for the exploitation of women's labour at home. Women's cooperatives are an important tool for sustainable development, social justice, and women's empowerment, enabling them to take on a more active role in social life as individuals with equal rights.

The effects of women's cooperatives' contributions to gender equality are also clearly evident in the experiences and statements of cooperative members. Participants emphasise that working to be productive and successful gives them both economic and personal strength. Cooperative members who believe that an environment where women can work freely transforms social perceptions that position women at home and away from social life argue that women should be more visible in society during this process. In addition, it is emphasised that demonstrating women's success in many areas is a powerful tool for combating gender-based discrimination. The views that everyone should be able to receive education in line with their abilities and do the job they want, regardless of gender, are a concrete indicator that women's cooperatives are not only an economic platform but also a tool for social transformation.

"After joining the top sewing cooperative, I felt very relieved both financially and spiritually. I felt financially relieved because I started earning income. It is a really great feeling to be both producing and earning. Now, I not only contribute to the household income, but I also feel the power of standing on my own two feet. I hope to inspire other women with this power...." **(P1)**

"I had children at home, and I had to take care of them, so I had a hard time getting a job. If I got a job, the money I earned would go to the children's care. Joining the cooperative offered me the opportunity to earn money while doing my homework and taking care of my children. .....Although it was difficult to achieve this balance at first, thanks to the cooperative's flexibility, I was able to balance my family life with my job. Now I contribute to my family and earn my own money." **(P3)**

"Before I joined the cooperative, I didn't have much chance of finding work outside. There wasn't, because my wife and family weren't keen on me working outside. Both housework and child care meant I had to join the workforce. But here, in the ball sewing cooperative, the fact that women came together, especially in a small city like Burdur, that they achieved this, that they produced balls that they even sent to France, that women earned their own income, gave me a very different perspective on life. We are actually much more than what we think we are...." **(P6)**

Women coming together in cooperatives and participating in production not only allows them to gain economic independence, but also to overcome the boundaries of gender roles. Women who have difficulty participating in the workforce due to traditional responsibilities, such as childcare and housework, can overcome these obstacles through cooperatives. In this way, they can also participate in social life economically. Women's cooperatives not only provide financial contributions to women. In addition to their economic benefits, they increase women's self-confidence by standing on their own two feet and enable them to become active agents in the struggle for social equality. These opportunities offered by cooperatives demonstrate that women's economic independence and social status are important steps toward gender equality. In their research on women's cooperatives in India, Datta and Gailey (2012) stated that women's cooperatives provide women with job opportunities and contribute to women's empowerment. It has also been reported that collective entrepreneurship empowers women through the economy, security, encouragement of entrepreneurial behaviour, and increased economic contributions to the family. Similarly, Gangwar et al. (2004) found that dairy cooperatives in India help women increase their economic independence and self-confidence. The participation of women in economic and social life enables them to know themselves and to be aware of their needs, rights, and responsibilities.

Theme 4: Overcoming challenges to create societal impact

Women's cooperatives are an important tool for bringing about social change despite the difficulties they face. Women's cooperatives encourage women's participation in economic life, allowing them to earn income and gain independence. In addition, they take important steps to overcome deeply rooted structural barriers, such as gender inequality. Overcoming the cultural and structural barriers that women's cooperatives face is an important step toward gender equality. At the macro level, they contribute to social justice and to the Sustainable Development Goals.

"....Now I earn my own money and can spend it however I want. Earning and spending your own money has given me great psychological relief. The cooperative has given me great strength not only economically but also emotionally. While I used to feel useless, I now see myself as a woman who directs her own life..." **(P5)**

" I think the cooperative makes women more visible in social and economic life..." **(P8)**

"...I faced many difficulties in the first days of the cooperative. First of all, there were obstacles such as lack of resources and administrative difficulties. However, these difficulties did not discourage us. On the contrary, we bonded more tightly with each other as women in the cooperative. We produced solutions together

with women to overcome the difficulties. We learned to support each other and turned the difficulties into opportunities...." **(P1)**

Solidarity among women, women's collective participation in production and challenging gender roles increase the empowering effect of cooperatives. Women's cooperatives are solidarity-based structures and enable women to have a stronger presence in social and economic life by working and producing together. This process of existence not only improves women's own lives. In fact, women also have a positive impact on their children and families, as well as on the society and environment in which they live. Women's success in the workplace creates a strong image of women in society. This positive image ignites the fuse for an important transformation in gender equality. This success achieved by women through a cooperative in a relatively small province in Turkey, such as Burdur, is not only a success for women who have gained economic independence, but also a source of inspiration for the communities around them and other women's cooperatives. However, the idea that these successes are not heard enough reveals that women need more opportunities to be heard. Yet, women in these cooperatives are motivated by the positive messages they hear and are making progress toward creating a broader social impact, overcoming barriers such as gender inequality.

Studies clearly show that women's cooperatives have a strong economic and social impact. In a study conducted in Greece, Lassithiotaki and Roubakou (2014) found that joining rural women's cooperatives increased participants' family income, and participants reported that joining the cooperative strengthened their social status and enabled them to spend their free time more efficiently. Similarly, in Turkey, Özdemir (2013) emphasised that women's cooperatives not only provide employment opportunities but also make significant contributions to local development. Women gain self-confidence through unity and solidarity in cooperatives, which in turn contributes to the development of local economies. Barut (2017), on the other hand, using the example of the İzmir Seferihisar Women's Cooperative, explained the contributions of women's cooperatives to the local economy, focusing on basic criteria such as ecological balance, the tourism sector, logistics, women's employment, and increased educational levels. Furthermore, a study on women's cooperatives in Morocco has revealed the important role of generating income in empowering women and its impact on local development (Wafae & Sara, 2021). These studies show that women's participation in economic life not only provides financial gain, but also helps overcome cultural, social and structural barriers and paves the way for women to create a broader social impact.

7. CONCLUSION

Women's cooperatives stand out as an important social innovation model in terms of economic independence, gender equality and social solidarity. The findings of this study reveal that women's participation in cooperatives provides them with economic empowerment and self-confidence at the individual level, while enabling solidarity and expansion of social networks at the social level. Within the scope of the theme “The journey to economic empowerment”, it was observed that women gained financial independence, actively participated in the workforce, and developed leadership skills through their cooperative membership. This process not only improved individuals' economic situations but also enabled them to contribute more effectively to society. The theme “The journey to economic empowerment” showed that cooperatives strengthened women's cooperation and support networks. Solidarity among women catalysed a transformation that not only empowered individuals but also contributed to the struggle for gender equality.

The experiences of cooperative members led to positive changes in their perceptions of gender roles and created a collective space for social equality. From the participants' perspective, these changes and efforts were included under the theme “The fight for gender equality”. Within the scope of the theme “Overcoming challenges to create social impact”, it was concluded that women's cooperatives are effective in overcoming cultural and structural barriers and help women become more visible and powerful individuals in society by providing economic independence. Cooperatives create meaningful changes at both individual and social levels by encouraging women's empowerment. However, for this structure to reach wider audiences, more support mechanisms need to be developed and awareness raised, especially on gender equality.

A number of suggestions can be made to increase the impact of women's cooperatives and make them a sustainable development model. First, expanding financial support mechanisms for women's cooperatives will help them overcome difficulties in accessing financial resources. Expanding training and capacity-building programs can strengthen the effectiveness of cooperatives by increasing women's entrepreneurship, leadership and financial management skills. In addition, increasing awareness of gender equality can encourage women's participation in cooperatives and facilitate their gaining social support. Encouraging cooperation between cooperatives at local and national levels is also important for both sharing experiences and developing marketing opportunities. Finally, establishing regular evaluation mechanisms to measure the impact of women's cooperatives can help build a broader supporter base by making their successes visible.

8. LIMITATIONS AND STRENGTHS

This study has some limitations. First, since participants were selected from a specific geographical region, the generalizability of the findings may be limited. In particular, it should be noted that women's experiences in cooperatives may differ across regions or groups with different demographic characteristics. Another limitation is that the data collection process was carried out within a limited time frame, and resource constraints prevented conducting the research with a larger sample. The study's strengths are highlighted by the in-depth, rich data obtained from participants. Insights into the processes of women's participation in cooperatives and the changes they experience during this process provide important information in the context of women's empowerment and gender equality. The contributions of cooperatives to women's economic independence, increased opportunities, and the development of leadership skills are the most valuable findings of the study. In addition, participants' direct feedback on their cooperative experiences enabled the study to yield important results in both theoretical and practical terms. This study provides a valuable resource for policymakers and social change advocates regarding women's struggle for gender equality and empowerment.

REFERENCES

Aksoy Demirci, A., & Günay, G. (2018). Türkiye'de Kadın Kooperatifçiliği. *Üçüncü Sektör Sosyal Ekonomi*, 77-90.

Barut, Y. (2017). Women's cooperatives contributions to local region economy: Seferihisar agricultural cooperative development model-Turkey. *Management Studies*, 120-127.

Bharti, N. (2021). Role of cooperatives in economic empowerment of women: A review of Indian experiences. *World Journal of Entrepreneurship, Management and Sustainable Development*, •••, 617–631.

Bülbüller, G. (2022). *Türkiye'de Kadın Kooperatiflerinin Sosyal Dayanışma Ekonomisi Kapsamında İncelenmesi: İzmir İli Örneği*. İstanbul Üniversitesi.

Çıkın, A., & Karacan, A. (1994). *Genel Kooperatifçilik*. Ege Üniversitesi Ziraat Fakültesi Yayınları.

Çınar, K., Akyuz, S., Uğur Çınar, M., & Onculer Yayalar, E. (2021). Faces and Phases of Women's Empowerment: The Case of Women's Cooperatives in Turkey. *Social Politics*, *28*(3), 778–805. DOI: 10.1093/sp/jxz032

Cresswell, J., & Plano Clark, V. (2011). *Designing and Conducting Mixed Method Research*. Sage Publications.

Creswell, J., & Poth, C. (2017). *Qualitative inquiry & research design: Choosing among five approaches*. SAGE.

Dalkıran, G. (2017). The support of women work within cooperative enterprises sample of Turkey. *Social Sciences Research Journal*, 1-11.

Datta, P., & Gailey, R. (2012). Empowering women through social entrepreneurship: Case study of a women's cooperative in India. *Entrepreneurship Theory and Practice*, *36*(3), 569–587. DOI: 10.1111/j.1540-6520.2012.00505.x

Datta, P., & Gailey, R. (2012). Empowering Women through Social Entrepreneurship: Case Study of a Women's Cooperative in India. *Entrepreneurship Theory and Practice*, *36*(3), 569–587. DOI: 10.1111/j.1540-6520.2012.00505.x

Duguid, F., Durutaş, G., & Wodzicki, M. (2015). *Türkiye'de Kadın Kooperatiflerinin Mevcut Durumu*. The World Bank.

Emiroğlu, M. (2017). *Kooperatifçilik & Kadın Kooperatifleri.* https://ticaret.gov.tr/data/5d41e48b13b87639ac9e02df/7458fc6b5805cfbbaf4a3f0 d76ad0bf5.pdf adresinden alındı

Gangwar, M., Kandekar, N., Mandai, M., & Kandekar, P. (2004). Empowerment status of rural women: Insights from dairy cooperatives. *Social Change, 34*(1), 112–123. DOI: 10.1177/004908570403400111

Geray, C. (2014). *Kooperatifçilik.* Nika Yayınevi.

Gönüllü Atakan, A., & Çoban, A. (2022). *Türkiye'de Kadınların Kooperatifler Yoluyla Güçlenmesi: Yasal ve Yapısal Stratejiler.* ILO Yayınları: https://dspace.ceid.org.tr/xmlui/bitstream/handle/1/2176/turkiyede-kadinlarinkooperatifler-yoluyla-guclenmesi.pdf?sequence=1&isAllowed=y adresinden alındı

ICA. (1995). *The Cooperative Identity.* https://www.ica.coop/en/media/library/research-and-reviews/review-international-cooperation adresinden alındı

ILO. (2012). *How women fare in East African cooperatives: the case of Kenya, Tanzania and Uganda.* https://www.ilo.org/wcmsp5/groups/public/---ed_emp/---emp_ent/--coop/documents/publication/wcms_735776.pdf adresinden alındı

İnan, İ., Kumkale, İ., & Okan, G. (1999). *Trakya'da Kırsal Kesimin Örgütlenmesinde Tarım Kooperatifleri, Üretici Birlikleri ve Köylere Hizmet Götürme Birliklerinin Rolü.* Türk Kooperatifçilik Kurumu Yayınları.

KEİG. (2015). *Türkiye'de Kadın Kooperatifleşmesi: Eğilimler ve İdeal Tipler.* https://www.keig.org/wp-content/uploads/2016/03/koopwweb.pdf adresinden alındı

Khatri Basnet, R. (2023). Role of Cooperatives in Women Empowerment in the Nepalese Context. *Cognition, 5*(1), 99–105. DOI: 10.3126/cognition.v5i1.55417

Koutsou, S., Iakovidou, O., & Gotsinas, N. (2003). Women's cooperatives in Greece: An ongoing story of battles, successes and problems. *Journal of Rural Cooperation,* •••, 47–57.

Kutlu, Ö. ve Sütlü, S.(2024). Investigation of the Career Development Experiences of Women Managers: An Analysis From a Gender Perspective, M.Haoucha (Ed.), Empowering and Advancing Women Leaders and Entrepreneurs içinde (231-247 ss.), Pennsylvania: IGI Global.

Lassithiotaki, A., & Roubakou, A. (2014). Rural Women Cooperatives at Greece: A retrospective study. *Open Journal of Business and Management,* 127-137.

Marshall, G. (1999). *Sosyoloji sözlüğü.* Bilim ve Sanat Yayınları.

Mülayim, Z. (2010). *Kooperatifçilik*. Yetkin Yayınları.

Özar, Ş. (2015). *Türkiye'de 1980 sonrası dönemde kadın emeği ve istihdamı politikaları: kadın hareketi, sendikalar, devlet ve işveren kuruluşları. A. Makal, & G. Toksöz içinde, Geçmişten günümüze Türkiye'de kadın emeği*. Ankara Üniversitesi Yayınları.

Özdemir, G. (2013). Women's Cooperatives in Turkey. *Procedia: Social and Behavioral Sciences*, *81*, 300–305. DOI: 10.1016/j.sbspro.2013.06.432

Şahankaya Adar, A., Dedeoğlu, S., & Kurtuluş, G. (2023). Türkiye'de Kadın Kooperatifleri: Mevcut Durum Analizi, Kadın Güçlenmesi ve İstihdam Yaratma Potansiyeli. *Çalışma ve Toplum*, 1171-1208.

Suseno, G., & Nataliningsih, N. (2023). The Role of Women's Cooperatives as an Institution to Empower Women in Supporting the Achievement of the SDGs. *International Journal of Ethno-Sciences and Education Research*, 45-53.

Vakoufaris, H., Kizos, T., Spilanis, I., Koulouri, M., & Zacharaki, A. (2007). Women's cooperatives and their contribution to the local development of the North Aegean Region, Greece. *Journal of Rural Cooperation*, •••, 19–41.

Wafae, T., & Sara, R. (2021). Women's rural cooperatives in Morocco: Challenges and collapses. *International Journal of Interdisciplinary Gender Studies*, 85-103.

Yadav, S. (2023). Gender Equality as a Tool for Sustainable Development. *International Journal of Teaching, Learning and Education*, 1-3.

Yağar, F., & Dökme, S. (2018). Niteliksel Araştırmaların Planlanması: Araştırma Soruları, Örneklem Seçimi, Geçerlik ve Güvenirlik. *Gazi Sağlık Bilimleri Dergisi*, 1-9.

Yıldırım, A., & Şimşek, H. (2016). *Sosyal bilimlerde nitel araştırma yöntemleri*. Seçkin Yayıncılık.

Chapter 10
Women's Participation Under Islamic Legal Frameworks:
An Analysis of Social, Political, and Religious Roles in Central Asia

Pooja Srivastava
http://orcid.org/0009-0000-1013-0931
Chanakya National Law University, Patna, India

Ajay Kumar
http://orcid.org/0009-0003-1575-7778
Chanakya National Law University, Patna, India

Shashank Srivastava
Patna University, Patna, India

ABSTRACT

This paper covers the integrated analysis of women's participation in social, political, and religious fields under Islamic law within Central Asia. It takes a step back towards the historical context and newest setbacks and challenges foreseen for women of the region, focusing on the interaction between Islamic law, local customs, and modern legal reforms within this region. It will introduce such study onto how gender roles have changed with the socio-political dynamics since pre-Islamic traditions, Soviet times, and then into the post-Soviet transitions. The attention would be placed on specific areas like family law, political participation, economic empowerment, and religious leadership in respect to a delicate balance between the adherence to

DOI: 10.4018/979-8-2600-3325-8.ch010

traditional values and progressive reforms. Despite impressive steps made in some directions, Central Asian women still face bottlenecks deep down inside patriarchal structures and conservative interpretations of Islamic law.

1. INTRODUCTION

Muslim women's participation in matters related to government and policy has been framed in the literature within discussions of constitutions, Islamic jurisprudence, and gender equality (Mayer, 2013; Mir-Hosseini, 2009). The debates on the compatibility of Islam and gender equality have often been cast in the terms of an opposition between religious tradition and the modernizing discourses of gender equality in Muslim states and constitutions. However, in the Central Asian context, the institutional framework of Islamic law within post-Soviet constitutions is quite distinct, and state control of religious institutions is strong (Fumagalli, 2018). After regaining independence from the USSR in the early 1990s, the constitutions of the Central Asian states enshrined equality before the law and freedom from discrimination on the basis of gender. The constitutions also stress secularism, but the state still regulates religion by requiring registration, applying administrative controls, and centralising religious authority through religious boards (Heathershaw & Montgomery, 2014). Consequently, Islamic institutions do not work as independent legal systems but rather act as institutional structures under the state. Even though equal rights are guaranteed for women in the Constitution, they are not reflected in equal representation in political, public and religious spaces. According to the Inter-Parliamentary Union (IPU, 2023) the proportion of women in national parliaments in the Central Asian countries varies from 17% to 32% and is increasing. Despite legislative gender quotas and gender-sensitive electoral reforms, women are underrepresented in executive leadership roles, senior administrative positions, and in religious institutions (UN Women, 2023). The challenge, therefore, is not only to adopt constitutional equality guarantees but also to identify why these do not lead to equal and consistent substantive participation. Abundant literature has viewed the role of conservative interpretations of Islamic law (Mayer, 2013). However, Islamic jurisprudence is not monolithic; it embraces interpretative pluralism while being grounded on justice (adl), welfare (maslahah), and the dignity of the human person (Kamali, 2008). On the other hand, it has been established that gender-egalitarian interpretations of Islamic legal texts are possible (Mir-Hosseini, 2009); thus, attributing women's under-participation solely to religious doctrine ignores institutional and regulatory contexts in which such interpretations are made. State-recognized muftiates or spiritual boards are the main players who have formal responsibility for religious education and knowledge, as well as the interpretation of Islam in Central

Asia (Fumagalli 2018), and religious governance structures determine who is included and who is excluded from decision-making processes. When institutional authority to bind, interpret, or control doctrine is highly concentrated, and appointments are opaque as well, institutional gatekeeping may exclude women from formal leadership roles, even without a doctrinal prohibition to do so. The contexts illustrate how and why institutional construction is a more compelling explanation for the exclusion of women from the political sphere, even in instances where doctrinal inevitability does not apply. Thus, throughout Central Asia, governance architecture is a more prominent consideration than Islamic legal theory. It locates the analysis of constitutions, gender regulatory regimes, and women's participation indicators within structural mechanisms through which Central Asian states provide legal guarantees of women's right to participate. Thus, it understands institutional mechanisms and principled governance procedures as complementary to constitutional infrastructure. The contributions of this chapter are threefold. SSFirst, it situates Central Asia within the broader gender and Islamic law literature and stresses the post-Soviet institutional context. Second, it employs an institutional governance lens to explain participatory outcomes beyond the doctrinal dimension. Third, it shifts discussions of gender equality from a secular-versus-religious framework towards a dialogue rooted in constitutional accountability and interpretative pluralism. The remainder of the chapter is structured as follows. Section 2 develops the conceptual and theoretical background for the analysis. Research gaps and research question and hypothesis development are described in Section 3. Section 5 describes political, social, and religious trends in selected Central Asian countries. The final chapter discusses implications, future research directions, and recommendations for institutional reform.

Research Gap

This gap in empirical research is important despite the growing scholarly attention paid to women and their rights in Muslim-majority contexts. Most of the existing literature focuses on the Middle East and South Asia (Mir-Hosseini 2009; Bano 2012), while Central Asia has received less scholarly focus partly due to the post-Soviet constitutional context and state-controlled religious institutions. Most existing research on constraints to women's participation relies on doctrinal views of Islamic law (see, e.g., Kamali 2008) and sidestep the institutional and regulatory context.

Although empirical literature on Central Asia stresses parliamentary quotas and descriptive representation (Inter-Parliamentary Union [IPU], 2023), it pays less attention to executive leadership, bureaucratic administration, and governance institutions in Islam. An integrated approach is needed to take into account the interplay between constitutional equality mandates, the local hermeneutics of Islamic jurisprudence, and the modes of bureaucratic governance. This study builds on this work to provide an account of women's participation in Central Asia from a governance perspective.

Recent empirical studies further confirm this gap. Zeinilova (2023) documents that Kazakhstan's current gender regime is shaped by multi-layered processes, including traditionalist social principles, intensive Sovietisation, nation-building dynamics, and a return to patriarchal values, which together constrain women's ascension to senior positions beyond the parliamentary level. Similarly, a cross-country qualitative study of Central Asian states conducted by Nurmagambetova (2024) highlights the CEDAW Committee's expressed concerns about the deep-rooted patriarchal structures in Tajikistan and their continued impact on substantive women's rights, underscoring the need for institutional rather than merely legislative reform. These developments make clear that the governance-centred analytical framework applied in this chapter is supported by the most recent empirical record.

Research Questions

This study is guided by the following research questions:

1. To what extent do constitutional guarantees of equality in Central Asian states translate into substantive participation of women in political, social, and religious institutions?
2. Are participation limitations primarily attributable to Islamic legal doctrine, or do they arise significantly from institutional governance structures and regulatory control mechanisms?
3. What institutional and interpretative reforms could reconcile constitutional equality commitments with religious legitimacy and thereby expand women's substantive participation?

Hypotheses

Based on the research gap and research questions, this study proposes the following hypotheses:

H1: Institutional Authority vs. Doctrinal Text Women's participation in Central Asia is constrained less by specific prohibitions within Islamic doctrine and more by the centralized institutional structures that monopolize how that doctrine is interpreted.

- **Rationale:** Because Islamic jurisprudence inherently allows for diverse interpretations and emphasises justice and equality, religious texts alone cannot explain the current gender disparities.

H2: The Efficacy of Constitutional Guarantees Constitutional promises of gender equality fail to produce substantive results for women and marginalised groups when they are not backed by strong transparency and accountability frameworks.

- **Rationale:** Data confirms that despite the existence of constitutional rights, women remain significantly absent from high-level political and government leadership, indicating a gap between legal promise and practice.

H3: Pathways to Reform Achieving meaningful participation requires institutional reforms that combine enforceable legal safeguards with the acceptance of pluralistic religious interpretations, rather than focusing exclusively on revising religious doctrine.

- **Rationale:** Governance structures and administrative regulations constitute the primary obstacles to inclusion, outweighing the influence of religious texts themselves

2. BACKGROUND

2.1 Conceptual Framework

When discussing women's representation in Central Asia, it is important to note the distinction between formal and substantive representation. The first one refers to presence within legislatures, local government or religious institutions, while the latter refers to the power or influence on decisions and policies (Phillips, 1995). Whilst the principle of equality before the law and the prohibition of discrimination are enshrined in the Central Asian constitutions, formal equality does not ensure substantive participation.

From the perspective of Islamic legal theorists, other than the distinct prohibition recognized by each school, a form of interpretative pluralism exists between the schools of Islamic jurisprudence based on key values such as justice (adl), welfare (maslahah), and others (Kamali, 2008). Modern scholarship shows that doctrinal gender-egalitarian interpretations are doctrinally feasible (Mir-Hosseini, 2009), so doctrinal content cannot explain gender differences in participation.

Nonetheless, the Islamic governance of Central Asia is conducted along state-sponsored lines through the centralized muftiates and administrative jurisdictions (Fumagalli, 2018; Heathershaw & Montgomery, 2014). The present study will employ the following conceptual framework for Islamic governance:

- Constitutional equality guarantees
- Islamic interpretative pluralism
- Institutional governance architecture

Contemporary scholarship has developed and extended Phillips's (1995) foundational distinction in significant ways. Nurbayev, Sultangazy, and Serikbayev (2024) demonstrate through a structural-biographical analysis of Kazakhstani parliamentary elections that women candidates without party affiliation remain structurally excluded from representative bodies, confirming that numerical representation does not translate into substantive access to institutional hierarchies. Lebedeva and Stolyarova (2023) further show that electoral gender quotas in Kyrgyzstan and Uzbekistan contain legal loopholes that permit circumvention, thereby limiting their effectiveness as instruments of substantive inclusion. These findings reinforce the conceptual distinction between descriptive and substantive participation that underpins the analytical framework of this chapter.

Governance design, as the third dimension, is the analytical pivot of this chapter.

2.2 Historical Evolution of Women's Roles

Pre-Islamic Traditions

Prior to the advent of Islam, Central Asian Turkic, Mongol and Persian practices prevailed. For many nomadic Turkic societies, women were involved in economic activities and decision-making (Prior, 2005). However, in some cultures, women had greater autonomy, especially in pastoral societies.

However, public life was more restricted in areas under Persian sedentary influence (Meriwether, 2001), and there was therefore some regional variation and fluidity in gender roles over the course of the Ottoman period.

The Introduction of Islam

The seventh century rise of Islam introduced a codified set of laws in which Muslim women inherited property and had legal rights in marriage and divorce (Ahmed, 1992). By comparison to pre-Islamic traditions, the Islamic provisions were progressive for women.

The establishment of Islamic jurisprudence interacted with local patriarchal systems. Extended male guardianship and certain restrictions on public religious leadership roles may have been extended to women, albeit with variation depending on local conditions (Tucker, 2008).

Soviet Transformation

Under Soviet rule, there was a large-scale shift in gender relations, as literacy and employment opportunities for women rose, and the power of Islamic institutions was curtailed (Kandiyoti, 2007; Khalid, 2021). Women also entered the fields of education, industry, and public administration.

However, the gains were highly mediated by the state, symbolic and mostly limited to Communist Party structures (Fierman, 1991), as the Soviet legacy increased women's visibility and centralized political control.

Post-Soviet Transition

Following independence, Central Asian states experienced both revival of Islamic identity and reassertion of traditional norms. While constitutional equality was retained, institutional enforcement mechanisms weakened in some jurisdictions. The coexistence of secular constitutionalism and religious revival created a hybrid governance environment shaping contemporary participation patterns.

2.3 Islamic Legal Frameworks and Customary Law (Sharia and Adat)

Islamic law, or sharia, and adat (customary law) run concurrently, and women have legal rights with respect to property and marriage under sharia (Ahmed 1992). Customarily, Central Asian adat stresses men's authority and the subordination of women (Paulin, 2005; Kamp, 2006).

In the countryside, bride price payments, religious marriages outside legal sanction, and inheritance practices may come into play even where formal religious courts are in operation. The impact of sharia-adat dualism is mediating cultural practice and institutional enforcement of doctrinal guarantees.

This is particularly seen in family law, where Islamic law gives women the right to divorce and inheritance, but in practice social stigma and local administrative structures limit when and if women can exercise these rights (Tucker, 2008; Khalid, 2021).

Thus, participation deficits in the private and domestic domains are often the result of the usual gaps in enforcement.

2.4 Women's Political Participation under Islamic and Post-Soviet Influence

The unique political histories of Central Asian women also shape their engagement, as few women held formal political positions prior to the Soviet era (Olcott, 1987). Under the Soviet Union, women were better descriptively represented in society thanks to quotas and party membership (Kamp, 2006) . Post-Soviet, gender quotas are often implemented at the national and international levels:

- The candidate quota in Uzbekistan rose to 40%, increasing representation (UN Women, 2024a).
- Kyrgyzstan's 30% local candidate quota improved electoral inclusion (UNDP, 2024).

The most recent data confirm a divergent regional trajectory. According to the UNDP Equal Future platform (2024), Central Asia as a region surpasses the global parliamentary average with approximately 27.4 percent women's representation, yet projections indicate that the sub-region is unlikely to achieve gender parity by 2030 if current trends continue. A Frontiers study (Shkalenko et al., 2025) tracking changes between 2000 and 2024 found that while Uzbekistan registered a 30.8 percent increase in women's share of local parliamentary seats and Kyrgyzstan achieved an 18.8 percent increase, Kazakhstan experienced a significant decline a pattern consistent with the observation that quota-based gains are fragile when unsupported by broader institutional accountability mechanisms. These divergent national trajectories underscore that quota legislation alone is insufficient to deliver sustained substantive representation.

- Regional parliamentary representation averages approximately 27-30% (IPU, 2025).

However, women are underrepresented in high-level positions of party decision-making and leadership. This pattern shows that quota-based representation increases numerical presence, but does not dismantle institutional hierarchies.

2.5 Religious Participation and Interpretative Authority

The domain of religion is the most controlled, with Islamic institutions in Central Asia being centralized in state-recognized muftiates (Fumagalli, 2018).

Women have informally engaged in religious education and community activities as bibi-otuns in parts of Uzbekistan and Tajikistan (Akiner, 1983; Schmitz, 2012), but remain absent from formal religious leadership positions.

Exclusion from religious leadership positions is rarely the result of a statutory prohibition.

- Appointment norms

Recent scholarship in Islamic feminist jurisprudence provides stronger doctrinal grounding for gender-egalitarian interpretations than was available at the time of earlier studies. Mir-Hosseini (2022), in Journeys Toward Gender Equality in Islam, documents how reformist Muslim scholars ground gender equality claims within the maqasid al-shariah framework, arguing that any interpretation producing unequal or unjust outcomes for women contradicts the Islamic legal tradition's foundational commitments to justice and human welfare. Wadud (2021) similarly argues for gender-inclusive Qur'anic hermeneutics as a scholarly practice with deep roots in Islamic tradition, not as an external imposition upon it. Al-Sharmani (2023) further demonstrates that Islamic feminist hermeneutics operates between scholarship and lived realities, providing a bridge between doctrinal flexibility and institutional reform. Together, these contributions confirm that the interpretative pluralism noted by Kamali (2008) is not merely a theoretical possibility but a growing scholarly consensus that directly challenges the institutional monopoly on interpretation held by centralised male-dominated muftiates in Central Asia.

- Institutional custom
- Centralised interpretative authority

It thus supports a key research hypothesis that participation constraints are not doctrinally inevitable, but rather due to governance architecture.

2.6 Socio-Economic Participation and Structural Barriers

Despite a relatively high women's labour force participation in Central Asia (World Bank, 2023), structural gender inequalities remain:

- 15 percentage point gender gap in labour participation

- Women earn approximately 30% less than men (World Bank, 2024)

Women comprise only one-third of entrepreneurs.

Despite Soviet-era integration's increases in education and employment, informal sectors have become vulnerable points since independence (Khalid, 2021).

This is reflected in high levels of sectoral segregation, especially in the energy and industry sectors, which contribute to a lack of access to institutional leadership (OSCE, 2023).

2.7 Contemporary Legal Reforms and Institutional Constraints

Subsequent legal reforms since independence have sought to strengthen women's rights:

- Domestic violence legislation (Human Rights Watch, 2023)
- Gender quotas in politics (International IDEA, 2025)

Several concrete legislative developments since 2022 are relevant to this analysis. The World Bank (2024) reports that in 2022, Uzbekistan amended its Labour Code to ensure equal pay for equal work and removed restrictions on women's employment in previously prohibited industrial occupations. In 2023, Kazakhstan introduced legislative amendments strengthening anti-discrimination enforcement in the public sector (UN Women, 2024). In 2023 and 2024, Tajikistan revised its Law on Prevention of Domestic Violence, expanding women's access to professions that had previously been restricted. Notwithstanding these positive developments, the World Bank's (2024) own surveys on gender norms in Tajikistan and Uzbekistan found that over one-third of respondents agreed that women should earn less than men to maintain family harmony, illustrating the persistent gap between formal legal reform and substantive attitudinal change that enforcement mechanisms must bridge.

- Labour protections and anti-discrimination statutes

The reform trajectory has been stronger in Kazakhstan and Kyrgyzstan than in more unevenly reforming Uzbekistan and Tajikistan.

However, major enforcement gaps remain. While legal guarantees exist on paper, procedural enforcement mechanisms and institutional accountability are lacking in practice.

This overall legal environment results in a structural gap between normative equality and institutional inclusion.

3. METHODOLOGY

Women in Central Asia, participate in political, social and religious institutions in their Central Asian state. The post-Soviet constitutions of Central Asia define the equality of women in the new republics, although this clashes with the implementation of Islamic law in state institutions and social systems in these countries. Instead of Islamic law, this chapter argues that institutionalization, religious regulation, and centralization of religious interpretative authority regulate membership in Central Asia. Through a doctrinal and comparative socio-legal analysis of constitutions, religion laws, and modes of representation, this article shows how quotas have led to women's parliamentary representation in Kazakhstan, Uzbekistan, Kyrgyzstan, and Tajikistan despite male-dominated executive power and religious institutions. This illustrates the structural disjuncture between constitutional gender equality and institutional inclusion across and within different states.

3.1 Doctrinal Legal Analysis

The work begins with an analysis of the "black letter" law i.e. the constitutional text, religious law and gender equality law, though not in isolation, but rather as a whole and complex. The analysis focuses on the interaction between:

- Constitutional equality clauses and non-discrimination mandates;
- The regulatory frameworks that manage religious registration and oversight;
- Relevant family law and inheritance statutes;
- Legislation regarding political representation and gender quotas.

This is the approach that establishes the baseline in formal law terms, because it can distinguish between the more explicit textual commitments to gender equality and legal intentions, tackling Hypothesis 1.

3.2 Institutional and Governance Analysis

Understanding how such legislation translates to action requires consideration of the governance architecture through which it operates. Drawing on institutional theory, this section examines the following dimensions:

- Procedures for appointments within muftiates and religious boards;
- Mechanisms for selecting executive leadership;
- The hierarchy of regulatory control over religious institutions;
- Systems of administrative accountability.

For this analysis, I focus on a potential barrier for women to enter decision-making spaces, namely centralised authority and administrative supervision structures (i.e. Hypotheses 1 and 2).

3.3 Comparative Framework

The study uses a comparative method to analyse regional similarities and national differences between the four selected states. While having a post-Soviet constitutional heritage in common, the four states have progressed differently concerning political liberalisation and regulatory frameworks. This allows for the classification of the types of:

- Inconsistencies in how quotas are implemented;
- Variations in executive representation;
- Contrasting models of religious governance and reform.

This contextualization of national outcomes in a regional perspective has much analytical merit and avoids the pitfalls of analyzing these particularistic legal systems in isolation.

3.4 Secondary Empirical Data

The qualitative legal analysis is supported by secondary quantitative data to provide measurable indicators of socio-economic inclusion and descriptive participation. Data is drawn from established international bodies, including:

- The Inter-Parliamentary Union (IPU) for statistics on parliamentary representation;
- UN Women and the UNDP for gender equality benchmarks;
- The World Bank for labor force participation rates and wage gap data;
- The OSCE for governance assessments.

While this study does not involve primary fieldwork, these datasets provide the evidentiary basis for evaluating substantive outcomes and testing the effectiveness of constitutional provisions (Hypothesis 2).

3.5 Limitations

Since the study draws exclusively on legislative materials and secondary legal analysis, it does not contain ethnographic fieldwork or primary qualitative interview data that can identify informal institutional practices or "unwritten rules." Additionally, the transparency of governance structures in religion in the jurisdictions examined in this study varies widely and, at times, may itself involve possible data deficits. Nevertheless, an analysis of doctrinal, comparative, and institutional methodologies is a suitable lens through which to look at the formal and structural barriers to women's participation.

4. RESULTS / FINDINGS AND ANALYSIS

4.1 Political Participation: Descriptive Progress and Institutional Constraints

In addition to increased presence within leadership, women's descriptive representation within the national legislative bodies of Kazakhstan, Uzbekistan, Kyrgyzstan, and Tajikistan has been improving. Women hold between approximately 17% and 32% of the parliamentary seats of each country (Inter-Parliamentary Union (IPU, 2023)). Uzbekistan and Kazakhstan have had minor increases in women's representation due to legislated quotas and party quotas, while Kyrgyzstan's local government quota has increased representation at the municipal level (UN Women, 2024a; UNDP, 2024).

Table 1. Women's Representation Across Political Branches in Central Asia

Country	Women in Parliament (%)	Women in Cabinet (%)	Quota Mechanism	Substantive Leadership Presence
Kazakhstan	27–30%	Limited	Party quota	Low
Uzbekistan	32%	Limited	40% candidate quota	Low
Kyrgyzstan	20–30%	Limited	30% local quota	Low
Tajikistan	17–25%	Very Limited	Partial quota	Very Low

These findings are confirmed by recent comparative empirical research. A qualitative analysis of alternative strategies for women's political participation across the four states (Frontiers, 2026) identifies institutional gatekeeping, social norms, and party-dominated candidate selection processes as the principal barriers preventing quota-based descriptive gains from translating into substantive leadership. The study finds that in Kyrgyzstan's November 2021 parliamentary elections, only 20.5 percent of seats were held by women despite the existence of a quota mechanism, highlighting the persistent gap between legislative intent and electoral outcome.

Nurbayev et al. (2024) demonstrate through structural analysis of Kazakhstani elections that the 2022 amendment requiring 30 percent representation across three categories — women, youth, and persons with disabilities — contains no mandatory ratio requirement between categories, enabling parties to meet the combined threshold while minimising women's actual presence. These structural loopholes illustrate precisely why constitutional equality clauses require enforceable accountability mechanisms to produce substantive change, as Hypothesis 2 of this study proposes.

Overall, these results suggest that constitutional provisions for equal participation, together with statutory quota laws, have had a positive impact on levels of descriptive representation. Such quota laws also send signals that institutions are recognizing gender-based structural inequalities and wish to address them through the law-making process. Cross-national studies of gender quotas indicate that mandatorily enforceable electoral mechanisms have a positive effect on women's representation (Inter-Parliamentary Union [IPU], 2023).

Although this descriptive representation has not necessarily been translated into substantive representation, as women are regularly under-represented in legislative leadership positions, and often assigned to the committees on social affairs rather than those on finance, defence or the economy, their number in parliament is rising. While UN Women (2023) states numbers are rising, women remain under-represented in leadership roles in many countries.

Centralized parties and executive control of the parliamentary agenda in Central Asia (Heathershaw & Montgomery, 2014) limit the scope for independent policymaking, through mechanisms such as candidate selection methods and party hierarchies. As a result, female legislators may have difficulty implementing gender-responsive policies in political systems where the executive branch dominates the rest of government.

The gap between descriptive representation and substantive influence supports Hypothesis 2: while constitutional provisions and quota-based reform increase representation numerically, they exert less influence where institutional accountability and decision-making power are centralized. This makes the possibility that Islamic doctrinal prohibitions explain these differences unlikely, particularly given that the Central Asian parliamentary systems operate in a secular constitutional framework, and do not have laws regulating electoral eligibility or committee-bidding through religious law (Fumagalli, 2018). It also supports Hypothesis 1, which proposes that differences in participation constraints are mainly associated with governance architecture, rather than doctrine.

In sum, although off-setting legislative quota systems in Central Asia improve descriptive representation, party and institutional structures curtail the potential for substantive representation in legislatures. Though constitutional equality provides a normative foundation, the extent of participation is contingent on the design of governance structures.

4.2 Executive and Administrative Leadership: Vertical Segregation and Governance Architecture

There are even wider disparities when it comes to executive and administrative leadership. Women are underrepresented in the cabinet, in key ministries, and at the top level of the civil service across the selected countries (UN Women, 2023). Despite the fact that women have held ministerial posts in these countries, they have often been in ministries for social protection, education or cultural affairs rather than defence, finance, or energy.

This reflects the vertical segregation and compartmentalization of the state. Political science has found that improved legislative representation does not guarantee a more inclusive executive (Phillips, 1995). In Central Asia, executive positions are generally appointed centrally through elite political networks (Heathershaw & Montgomery, 2014), and can therefore reproduce existing authority structures, which have customarily been hierarchically organized and predominantly male (see above).

The persistence of vertical segregation in executive institutions reflects what Koburtay, Abuhussein, and Sidani (2023) identify as a convergence of cultural norms, religious values, and institutional design that produces exclusionary leadership architectures in Muslim-majority contexts. Their cross-comparative study of female leaders confirms that women are consistently steered toward ministerial portfolios in social, educational, and cultural domains while being effectively excluded from economic, security, and infrastructure ministries. This sectoral channelling is not primarily the product of doctrinal prohibition — none of the states examined operates explicitly religious appointment criteria for civil service roles — but rather of informal institutional norms that reproduce gender hierarchies through discretionary appointment processes. As the UNDP Equal Future platform (2024) notes, without institutionalised accountability frameworks for executive appointments, discretionary powers tend to perpetuate existing gender hierarchies regardless of constitutional equality commitments.

Unlike in the parliament, there is generally no gender parity requirement for members of the executive branch, which shows the limitations of constitutional equality provisions with no enforceable accountability measures. UN Women (2023) reported without institutionalized frameworks for gender parity, discretionary appointment powers often perpetuate gender inequalities.

In addition to the lack of transparency in bureaucratic promotion systems of some of these states, other factors at play include patronage and the centralization of the bureaucracy (Fumagalli 2018), while the stability of institutions in such regimes is another trait that distinguishes them from others.

Table 2. Institutional Constraints in Executive and Administrative Leadership

Institutional Variable	Presence in Central Asia	Effect on Women's Participation
Centralised appointments	High	Restricts access to leadership
Patronage networks	Strong	Reinforces male dominance
Transparency mechanisms	Weak	Limits accountability
Gender parity requirement	Absent	Sustains vertical segregation

This institutional analysis of religious exclusion is reinforced by the most recent comparative scholarship on women's leadership roles in Islamic jurisprudence. Yakar (2022) documents through analysis of two divergent fatwas on women's political leadership that interpretative outcomes are determined not by the texts themselves but by the institutional processes and appointment criteria of those issuing the fatwas — a finding that directly supports this chapter's central argument. Recent scholarship also notes that several Muslim-majority states have begun establishing councils of qualified female scholars to contribute to religious norm-setting, representing an emerging reform trend that provides institutional models for Central Asia (PMC, 2024). The historically documented role of women as authoritative jurists and muhaddithaat in early Islamic scholarship (srdikr.com, 2025) further confirms that contemporary exclusion from formal religious leadership roles reflects socio-political rather than doctrinal evolution, consistent with Hypothesis 1 of this study.

A factor enabling ministers and civil servants to be appointed and transferred without Islamic doctrinal prohibition is the secular constitutions that govern the cabinet and civil service. The absence of elite conflict in the administration of both is another example of the role that institutional design, rather than doctrinal prohibition, plays in constraining substantive participation.

A similar pattern operates in legislative and executive representation (but not judicial representation): formal equality and quotas help ensure descriptive representation, while centralized government weakens material representation. Without political efforts to ensure that appointed bodies systematically justify patronage appointments, constitutional commitments to descriptive representation may not be taken seriously by political actors.

4.3 Religious Governance and Interpretative Authority: Institutional Mediation of Doctrinal Norms

The religious sphere represents the most formal space of women's participation in Central Asia. Yet, while parliamentary bodies are characterised by electoral processes defined by quota systems, religious bodies belong to a set of centralised regulatory systems, operated and managed by the state (Fumagalli, 2018). These systems are important for interpretative authority and access. Islamic structures in Kazakhstan, Uzbekistan, Kyrgyzstan and Tajikistan have a centralised organisation, recognised by the state as a muftiate or spiritual board, which oversees religious education, licensing and provides doctrinal leadership (Heathershaw & Montgomery, 2014). They also oversee the appointment of religious officials in their jurisdictions. However, women's participation within these structures remains limited, particularly in leadership positions. The marginalization of women from apex leadership is rarely articulated as a legal prohibition, and there is no uniform doctrinal prohibition against women giving religious advice or teaching it.

Table 3. Doctrinal vs Institutional Barriers in Religious Governance

Dimension	Doctrinal Prohibition	Institutional Structure	Participation Outcome
Religious leadership	No explicit ban	Centralised muftiates	Exclusion from apex roles
Interpretative authority	Pluralism recognised	Concentrated in male boards	Limited female influence
Informal participation	Permitted	Not institutionally empowered	Symbolic inclusion

According to Kamali (2008), the principles of justice and human welfare are central to Islamic law, and historically, interpretative pluralism has been accepted. Mir-Hosseini (2009) explains the doctrinal legitimacy of gender-equal interpretations. The durability of male religious leadership structures in Central Asia cannot be explained by theological determinism, but rather by a mediating process of the interpretation and implementation of religious doctrine. This supports Hypothesis 1: that participation is constrained by institutional and interpretative structures rather than doctrinal barriers where interpretative authority is concentrated in male hierarchical boards. Women may be responsible at the local level for informal religious education, as well as religious rites, with women religious instructors known as bibi-otuns in Uzbekistan and Tajikistan (Akiner, 1983; Schmitz, 2012). Nevertheless, these roles reveal that women are not entirely excluded from religious formality, despite women's involvement usually being outside the scope of decision-making and devoid of institutional weight to which muftiates are bound. These forms of informal participation and formal exclusion are symptomatic of the governance architecture present: informal positions may have been accepted or even legitimized, but formal institutional leadership was subject to centralized appointment procedures. In contexts where political authorities have granted and oversee permission to religious institutions, interpretative authority is constrained by their officially recognized leaders only (Fumagalli, 2018), thereby limiting plural interpretative possibilities. Furthermore, state regulation of religion in Central Asia is often motivated by stability and security (a regulatory model sometimes called securitised governance of religion, Heathershaw and Montgomery 2014). In contexts of illiberal representation, institutional control is often co-opted into governance priorities, that is, stability of institutions is tied to networks of power. These findings support the view that constitutional guarantees of equality with respect to religion are largely ineffective. Thus, while constitutions may guarantee protection against discrimination based on sex, these provisions are seldom applied to religious organizations. This provides some support for Hypothesis 2: constitutional commitments matter less where accountability frameworks are weak or institutional design favors non-interventionism. This also contradicts more reductionist interpretations of Islamic law as non-inclusive, as doctrinal literature shows interpretative flexibility (Kamali, 2008; Mir-Hosseini, 2009); the more pressing issue is institutional mediation of interpretation. It is, thereby, the governance design, rather than the content of the doctrine, that is relevant where interpretative authority is consolidated. Ultimately, we find that the patterns of religious leadership also roughly follow structural patterns seen in political and executive leadership. In this case, women do not face doctrine-driven barriers, but rather barriers to central access to leadership positions. A focus on simply reforming the doctrine would therefore be unsatisfactory in this case, and more emphasis would have to be placed on the reorganization of institutions, especially the processes of appointment and advice.

4.4 Socio-Economic Participation and Structural Barriers: Equality Commitments and Market Realities

Socio-economic participation in Central Asia is not as straightforward as political and religious participation. For example, women's labour force participation rate has stayed relatively high on several indicators, compared to other Muslim-majority regions (World Bank, 2023). The continued Soviet promotion of women's literacy rates, workforce participation, and subsidised childcare (Kandiyoti, 2007; Khalid,

2021) can obscure structural inequalities that still exist, however, when viewed from a purely statistical perspective.

Despite high participation in the labour force, there is a gender pay gap, and according to the World Bank (2024), women earn considerably less than men in several Central Asian countries. The gender pay gap is estimated to be between 20 and 30 per cent, depending on the sector. Women are more likely to be in low-paid jobs such as education, health care and service sector work, and less likely to work in high-paid sectors like energy, infrastructure and industry (OSCE, 2023).

Table 4: Socio-Economic Participation and Structural Constraints

Recent data from the World Bank (2024) provide empirical specificity to these structural patterns. In Kazakhstan, national statistics reveal a wage gap exceeding 20 per cent in favour of men, with some regions reporting disparities as high as 50 per cent. A 2022 World Bank survey across Central Asia found that over one-third of respondents agreed that women should earn less than men to maintain family harmony, demonstrating that wage discrimination is sustained not only by employer behaviour but also by widely held social norms (World Bank, 2024). In Uzbekistan, the 2022 amendment to the Labour Code equalising pay and lifting employment restrictions on women in industrial sectors represents a significant formal reform, yet the World Bank's own assessments indicate that implementation gaps persist, particularly in rural and informal labour markets (World Bank, 2024). Shkalenko et al. (2025) further show that women's economic representation in senior leadership positions, reaching 31.1 per cent in Kazakhstan and 21.7 per cent in Kyrgyzstan, does not align with their levels of political representation, suggesting that economic and political inclusion follow distinct institutional logics and require correspondingly distinct reform pathways.

Table 1.

Indicator	Observed Trend	Institutional Cause
Labour participation	Relatively high	Soviet legacy
Wage gap (20–30%)	Persistent	Weak pay transparency
Sectoral segregation	High	Structural market reform
Women in corporate boards	Low	Limited governance access

Structural imbalance of entrepreneurship reflects the uneven representation of women in SMEs and their limited access to capital, credit and high-growth enterprises (UN Women, 2023). Participation in the informal economy is more common in rural settings, where customs and familial obligations restrict movements and asset ownership.

These differences indicate that formal equality commitments have proven weak without institutional provisions for their entrenchment and the implementation of economic reform policies, such as regulating labour market segmentation, pay transparency, and access to credit. The findings also provide support for Hypothesis 2, that constitutional equality guarantees are not enough where accountability and regulatory transparency mechanisms are weak.

Socio-economic inequalities in Central Asia do not originate from the Islamic doctrinal model, but economic and liberalization policies, and the post-Soviet reconfiguration of state institutions that shapes labour and protection policies, labour market participation, wage differentials, and occupational segregation (Khalid, 2021). In some contexts, religious revivalism shapes expectations, but economic inequality is associated with structural transition challenges rather than the Islamic model.

Following the collapse of the Soviet Union, the shift towards a market economy and austerity policies eroded decades of social protection. Gender equality gaps, particularly among women in the informal economy in rural areas, persisted (Kandiyoti, 2007), where social protections and anti-discrimination laws do not exist.

Along with political and religious institutions, women are underrepresented in financial regulatory authorities and in corporate boards and other institutions involved in planned economic planning (UN Women, 2023). In this manner too the chapter's central governance-centered thesis appears well-founded in that participation constraints stem from institutional architectures most naturally rather than doctrinal constraints.

Sociologically and socio-economically, despite women's presence in labour markets, community economies, and supply chains, structural barriers limit their potential for upward mobility and leadership. To be fully inclusive and equitable, institutional reform is needed for wage transparency, women's access to economic opportunities, and their pathways to leadership roles.

Ultimately, socio-economic participation is a multi-faceted concept with historical legacies that contribute to generally high levels of workforce participation, but also structural differences stemming from governance structures and economic changes. It adds further empirical weight to Hypotheses 1 and 2 that these outcomes are determined principally by institutional mechanisms not Islamic legal doctrine.

5. DIRECTIONS FOR FUTURE RESEARCH

This article employs a doctrinal and comparative socio-legal approach to analyze women's participation in political, social and religious institutions in selected Central Asian states, allowing a systematic investigation of their constitutional provisions, institutional governance and secondary empirical material. It argues for further investigation in Central Asia within the area of law and gender.

First, deeper primary empirical work via interviews with policymakers, religious authorities, civil society actors, and women leaders in political and religious spaces would be productive. This could include qualitative fieldwork examining informal governance practices and negotiations over appointments and cultural understandings of opportunities for women to participate outside of formal statutory processes.

Second, longitudinal studies of how women candidates' representation develops over time would contribute to research on paths to reform. These time series analyses could investigate whether women's substantive leadership is sustained as a result of contemporary legal reform efforts (e.g., quota legislation, domestic violence legislation, and anti-discrimination legislation). Such analysis could inform whether descriptive gains gradually translate into structural transformation or remain symbolic.

Third, cross-regional works could compare Central Asia to other regions such as Southeast Asia, the Middle East and North Africa, perhaps examining the co-relationship between the regulatory models of religion, such as state or market, and women's forms of political institutionalisation. This would further test the governance-centred hypothesis outlined in this chapter.

Fourth, future research should consider the intra-institutional governance structures of religious organisations in more detail. While the importance of a centralized interpretive authority mechanism is suggested by this study, analyzes of advisory councils, advisory boards, and licensing schemes at a more granular level would further expand our knowledge of whether women are included or excluded by religious governance structures.

Fifth, research on economic participation is increasing but could focus more on energy, extractives and emerging digital economy sectors. Central Asia's calculated economic position also presents opportunities for research on gender inclusion in economic diversification strategies.

Finally, interdisciplinary approaches integrating law with other fields like political economy and sociology could explain the multidimensional phenomenon of participation disparities shaped by law, institutional design, cultural norms and attitudes, and economic change. Future research could develop more integrated approaches to reform bridging these distributional dimensions.

In sum, this chapter offers a governance perspective on women's inclusion in Central Asia; further empirical, comparative, and interdisciplinary work is needed to understand the roles played in institutional change and the scope for long-term women's political engagement.

6. CONCLUSION / RECOMMENDATIONS

Conclusion

This research investigate the political exclusion of women in Central Asia due to Shari'a law or institutional choices that regulate constitutional and religious law. We apply a mixed-methods approach using constitutional and institutional analysis and a quantitative analysis of political participation of women in Kazakhstan, Uzbekistan, Kyrgyzstan, and Tajikistan. In Central Asia, we argue that women's political exclusion is not rooted in Islamic law but rather in governance structures. There was a pattern across systems of political, religious and economic.

- **Political Representation:** While legislative quotas and gender-sensitive electoral reforms have increased women's descriptive (numerical) representation in parliament, this momentum has not been carried through to the executive and administrative branches, where planned posts and high-level decision-making positions are dominated by men. This disparity suggests that constitutional equality clauses may not be effective without mechanisms to hold institutions accountable and ensure transparency.
- **Religious Governance:** Exclusion in this domain rarely finds clear proscription in scripture. Throughout history, Islamic law has encouraged pluralism of interpretations and principles of justice. However, this centralization of state-regulated muftiates creates a bottleneck in which their interpretative power is held by centralized male jurisdictions, supporting the conclusion that institutional design is the primary barrier to women's participation.
- **Socio-Economic Participation:** Despite historical workforce participation, structural inequalities (e.g. wage differences, sectoral segregation) suggest that institutional mechanisms (wage transparency, corporate governance) rather than doctrinal texts determine socio-economic participation. This suggests that the politics of gender inclusion cannot simply be reduced to a contest between secularism and Islam. Rather, it suggests that it is the mediating role of state institutions in the exercise of constitutional rights and religious obligations, and the relationship between authority and accountability that determines women's inclusion.

Recommendations

To bridge the gap between formal equality and substantive inclusion, the following reform pathways are proposed:

1. **Enforceable Accountability:** Constitutional equality clauses must be supported by practical enforcement mechanisms. This includes implementing transparent appointment procedures, establishing gender-balanced advisory bodies, and mandating public reporting to ensure inclusion within executive and administrative institutions.
2. **Beyond Quotas:** While quotas are necessary for numerical representation, genuine political inclusion requires reforms to leadership pathways. Strategies should include formal mentorship programs, transparency in committee allocations, and the democratization of internal party processes.
3. **Institutional Pluralism in Religion:** Religious governance bodies should integrate consultative mechanisms that include qualified female scholars and community representatives. This approach allows for expanded interpretative engagement and inclusivity without challenging religious legitimacy.
4. **Economic Structural Reform:** Policy should move beyond general labor participation to address specific barriers. Priorities must include enforcing wage transparency, diversifying sectoral access, and improving credit availability for female entrepreneurs.
5. **Regional Knowledge Exchange:** Establishing cooperation mechanisms across Central Asian states can facilitate the sharing of best practices, strengthening institutional learning and accountability regarding gender reforms.

Sustainable progress requires a focus on institutional restructuring rather than doctrinal reinterpretation. Since Islamic jurisprudence offers interpretative flexibility and constitutional frameworks offer normative commitments, the deciding factor is governance design. By making institutions more transparent and accountable, Central Asian states can achieve substantive gender equality that honors both legal obligations and religious traditions. This challenge is, fundamentally, one of governance rather than theology.

REFERENCES

Ahmed, L. (1992). *Women and gender in Islam: Historical roots of a modern debate.* Yale University Press.

Akiner, S. (1983). *Islamic peoples of the Soviet Union.* Routledge.

Al-Sharmani, M. (2023). Islamic feminist hermeneutics: Between scholarship and lived realities. *Journal of Feminist Studies in Religion, 39*(2), 95–97. DOI: 10.2979/jfemistudreli.39.2.15

Bano, M. (2012). *The rational believer: Choices and decisions in the Madrasas of Pakistan.* Cornell University Press.

Equal Future Platform, U. N. D. P. (2024). A tapestry of progress and challenges: Women's political participation in Europe and Central Asia. UNDP. https://www.undp.org/eurasia/blog/challenges-womens-political-participation

Fierman, W. (1991). *Language planning and national development: The Uzbek experience.* De Gruyter. (Note: Original publication year is 1991, not 2019.)

Fumagalli, M. (2018). *Religion and politics in Central Asia: Governance, secularism, and Islam.* Routledge.

Heathershaw, J., & Montgomery, D. (2014). The securitisation of Islam in Central Asia. *Europe-Asia Studies, 66*(3), 456–479. DOI: 10.1080/09668136.2014.886567

Human Rights Watch. (2023). *World report 2023: Central Asia.* https://www.hrw.org/world-report/2023

Inter-Parliamentary Union. (2023). *Women in national parliaments: Global data.* https://www.ipu.org

International IDEA. (2025). *Gender quotas database.* https://www.idea.int

Kamali, M. H. (2008). *Shari'ah law: An introduction.* Oneworld Publications.

Kamp, M. (2006). *The new woman in Uzbekistan: Islam, modernity, and unveiling under communism.* University of Washington Press.

Kandiyoti, D. (2007). The politics of gender and the Soviet paradox. *Central Asian Survey, 26*(4), 601–620. DOI: 10.1080/02634930802018521

Khalid, A. (2021). *Central Asia: A new history from the imperial conquests to the present.* Princeton University Press.

Koburtay, T., Abuhussein, T., & Sidani, Y. M. (2023). Women leadership, culture, and Islam: Female voices from Jordan. *Journal of Business Ethics*, *181*(3), 673–689. DOI: 10.1007/s10551-022-05041-0

Lebedeva, M., & Stolyarova, S. (2023). Participation of women in political institutions of post-Soviet countries: Experience of Central Asian countries. International Trends / Mezhdunarodnye Protsessy, 21(1). https://www.intertrends.ru/jour/article/view/188

Mayer, A. E. (2013). *Islam and human rights: Tradition and politics* (5th ed.). Westview Press.

Mir-Hosseini, Z. (2009). *Islam and gender: The religious debate in contemporary Iran*. Princeton University Press.

Mir-Hosseini, Z. (2022). *Journeys toward gender equality in Islam*. Oneworld Academic.

Nurbayev, Z. Y., Sultangazy, G. Z., & Serikbayev, B. S. (2024). A study of political party affiliation as a means to enhance gender equality and women's political participation in Kazakhstan. *Public Administration and Policy*, *27*(1), 45–57. DOI: 10.1108/PAP-07-2023-0095

Nurmagambetova, R. (2024). CEDAW concerns and gender equality in Central Asia: Institutional barriers and reform pathways. *Central Asian Survey*, *43*(2), 210–228.

Olcott, M. B. (1987). *The Kazakhs*. Hoover Institution Press.

Organisation for Security and Co-operation in Europe. (2023). *Gender equality in Central Asia: Economic participation report*. https://www.osce.org

Phillips, A. (1995). *The politics of presence*. Oxford University Press.

Schmitz, A. (2012). Women's informal religious authority in Uzbekistan. *Journal of Muslim Minority Affairs*, *32*(3), 320–338. DOI: 10.1080/13602004.2012.727291

Shkalenko, A., Abenova, D., & Seitkali, M. (2025). Contemporary strategies of women activists in the gender equality movement in Central Asia. *Frontiers in Political Science*, *7*, 1694298. Advance online publication. DOI: 10.3389/fpos.2025.1694298

Tucker, J. (2008). *Women, family, and gender in Islamic law*. Cambridge University Press. DOI: 10.1017/CBO9780511841316

UNDP. (2024). *Local governance and gender inclusion in Kyrgyzstan*. https://www.undp.org

Wadud, A. (2021). Reflections on Islamic feminist exegesis of the Qur'an. *Religions*, *12*(7), 497–508. DOI: 10.3390/rel12070497

Women, U. N. (2023). *Gender equality in Central Asia: Regional overview*. https://www.unwomen.org

Women, U. N. (2024). *Women's political participation in Uzbekistan*. https://www.unwomen.org

World Bank. (2023). *World development indicators: Labour force participation*. https://data.worldbank.org

World Bank. (2024). *Gender wage gap data: Central Asia*. https://data.worldbank.org

Yakar, E. E. (2022). Women's political leadership: One question and two divergent fatwas. *The Journal of Law and Religion*, *37*(2), 332–362. DOI: 10.1017/jlr.2022.15

Zeinilova, A. (2023). Gender regime in Kazakhstan: Multi-layered processes and patriarchal values. *Central Asian Survey*, *42*(1), 105–123.

ADDITIONAL READINGS

Kuehnast, K., & Dudwick, N. (2004). *Better a hundred friends than a hundred rubles? Social networks in transition*. World Bank. DOI: 10.1596/0-8213-5898-7

Rivkin-Fish, M. (2005). *Women's health in post-Soviet Russia: The politics of intervention*. Indiana University Press. DOI: 10.2979/3439.0

KEY TERMS AND DEFINITIONS

Constitutional Equality: Legal principle guaranteeing equal rights and non-discrimination irrespective of gender, typically enshrined in constitutional texts.

Descriptive Participation: Numerical representation of women in political, administrative, or religious institutions without necessarily implying decision-making influence. Substantive Participation: Meaningful involvement in decision-making processes, including agenda-setting authority and policy influence.

Institutional Governance Architecture: The structural design of appointment procedures, accountability mechanisms, and regulatory frameworks that shape participation outcomes.

Interpretative Authority: Institutional power to interpret and operationalise religious or legal norms within formal governance structures.

Maqasid al-Shariah: The higher objectives of Islamic law, including justice, welfare, and protection of human dignity.

Chapter 11

The Impact of Foreign Direct Investment on Local Supply Chains and Small Business Growth

Phathutshedzo Madumi
http://orcid.org/0009-0000-4283-5039
University of Stellenbosch, South Africa

ABSTRACT

Foreign Direct Investment (FDI) plays a significant role in shaping local economic ecosystems by linking domestic suppliers to global value chains and supporting the growth of small and medium-sized enterprises (SMEs). Its benefits, however, vary across sectors and depend on investor strategies and national policies. While FDI can boost productivity, create economic opportunities, and facilitate knowledge transfer, it may also lead to foreign firm dominance and increased dependence on external actors. This chapter examines how FDI influences local supply chains and SMEs in South Africa, assessing both the opportunities it creates—such as access to international markets, improved standards, and enhanced competitiveness—and the challenges it poses, including exclusion from supply networks and unequal power dynamics. It also identifies barriers to effective collaboration between foreign investors and local enterprises and proposes strategies to ensure that FDI contributes to inclusive and sustainable economic growth.

DOI: 10.4018/979-8-2600-3325-8.ch011

1. INTRODUCTION

Foreign direct investment (FDI) is widely considered beneficial for host economies and has been thoroughly examined from diverse perspectives. It plays a crucial role in shaping local economic ecosystems by integrating local suppliers into global value chains and stimulating the growth of small and medium-sized enterprises (SMEs). However, the extent to which FDI benefits local supply chains and SMEs varies significantly across sectors, investor practices, and host-country policies. While FDI can enhance productivity, create business opportunities, and foster technology transfer, it can also pose challenges, including market domination by foreign firms and dependence on external players.

Establishing new businesses is an important part of an economy's development and growth. In recent years, the interaction between multinational corporations and local firms in host countries has arisen as a significant policy concern (Driffield, 1999; UNCTAD, 2001; Giroud, 2007). Furthermore, the linkages have been investigated through a range of theoretical lenses, including industrial economics, development studies, and international business perspectives; however, the study has primarily focused on the manufacturing sector. Even though service links are a significant contributor to inward FDI flow, there is little literature on the subject.

FDI has played and will continue to play an important role in the South African economy. Furthermore, SME investment provides even greater developmental benefits due to its agility, increased reliance on local suppliers and partners, and a lower risk of displacing local enterprises. Importantly, FDI boosts SMEs' productivity and promotes technical innovation, making them more resilient to external shocks. This, in turn, promotes the growth of a vibrant and competitive private sector and speeds up the technical catch-up of emerging countries. Against this background, the objectives of this chapter are to: 1. To analyse how FDI impact the growth and integration of local supply chains; 2. To identify the challenges local businesses face in accessing FDI-driven supply chain opportunities; 3. To assess how policy and regulatory frameworks shape the relationship between FDI, local supply chains, and SMEs.

Existing literature often emphasises the positive spillover effects of FDI, including knowledge transfer, competition, and labour mobility. Yet empirical evidence indicates that these benefits depend critically on domestic conditions, such as institutional quality, policy coordination, and local firms' absorptive capacity. In the absence of these enabling factors, FDI may reinforce structural inequalities, crowd out domestic enterprises, and create dependency on foreign capital.

This chapter addresses this gap by examining how FDI influences local supply chains and SME development in South Africa. It analyses the opportunities created by FDI, identifies the barriers limiting SME participation, and evaluates the role of policy in shaping these outcomes. By integrating global value chain and spillover perspectives, the study provides a more comprehensive understanding of how FDI can be leveraged for inclusive and sustainable economic development.

2. THEORETICAL FRAMEWORK AND CONCEPTUAL MODEL

2.1 Theoretical Foundations

The relationship between FDI, local supply chains, and SMEs development can be understood through two complementary theoretical lenses: Global Value Chain (GVC) theory and FDI spillover theory. GVC theory explains how production processes are fragmented across countries, with multinational enterprises (MNEs) coordinating activities across different locations. Within this framework, domestic firms participate in value chains at varying levels, often depending on their capabilities and the governance structure imposed by lead firms (Gereffi & Fernandez-Stark, 2016). While participation in GVCs can provide opportunities for upgrading, it may also lock local firms into low-value-added activities if they lack the capacity to move up the value chain.

FDI spillover theory focuses on the indirect benefits that domestic firms derive from the presence of foreign firms. These spillovers occur through several channels, including demonstration effects, labour mobility, competition, and supplier linkages (Blomström & Kokko, 2003). However, such spillovers are not automatic; they depend on local firms' absorptive capacity and the broader institutional environment (Javorcik, 2004). By integrating these two perspectives, this study conceptualises FDI not merely as a source of capital but as a mechanism that reshapes production networks and influences the distribution of economic opportunities within the domestic economy (Altenburg & Meyer-Stamer, 1999).

2.2 Conceptual Model

The conceptual model developed in this study explains how FDI influences SME growth through its interaction with local supply chains, while highlighting the mediating and moderating factors that shape this relationship.

Fundamentally, the model conceptualises FDI as the primary independent variable, introducing capital, advanced technologies, and access to global markets. Local supply chain integration functions as the central transmission mechanism, linking multinational enterprises with domestic SMEs. The ultimate outcome of this interaction is reflected in SME growth, particularly through productivity improvements, enhanced innovation capacity, and market expansion. However, this relationship is neither linear nor uniform; rather, it is shaped by a set of mediating and moderating dynamics.

(a) Mediating Mechanism: Local Supply Chain Linkages

The extent to which SMEs benefit from FDI is largely mediated by their ability to integrate into supply chains established or influenced by multinational enterprises. Strong backward linkages—through local sourcing—and forward linkages—through distribution and market channels—create critical pathways for knowledge transfer, technological upgrading, and expanded market access. These linkages enable SMEs to participate more effectively in global value chains, thereby enhancing their productivity, competitiveness, and growth potential (Gereffi, Humphrey, & Sturgeon, 2005).

(b) Moderating Factors

The strength and effectiveness of these linkages, and consequently the impact of FDI on SME development, are contingent upon several moderating factors.

Absorptive Capacity of SMEs: Firms with higher levels of human capital, technological capability, and managerial expertise are better positioned to identify, assimilate, and exploit knowledge from foreign firms, thereby enhancing their ability to benefit from FDI spillovers (Cohen & Levinthal, 1990).

Policy and Institutional Frameworks: Government policies—such as supplier development programmes, local content requirements, and financial support mechanisms—play a crucial role in either enabling or constraining linkages between multinational enterprises and local SMEs (UNCTAD, 2020).

Sectoral Characteristics: The nature of the industry significantly influences the strength of these linkages. Manufacturing sectors, for instance, tend to exhibit stronger supply chain integration and knowledge diffusion compared to capital-intensive extractive industries (OECD, 2013).

Regional Context: Spatial disparities in infrastructure, market access, and institutional networks shape the distribution of FDI benefits, often leading to uneven outcomes across regions (World Bank, 2019).

Figure 1: FDI, Supply Chain Integration, and SME Growth

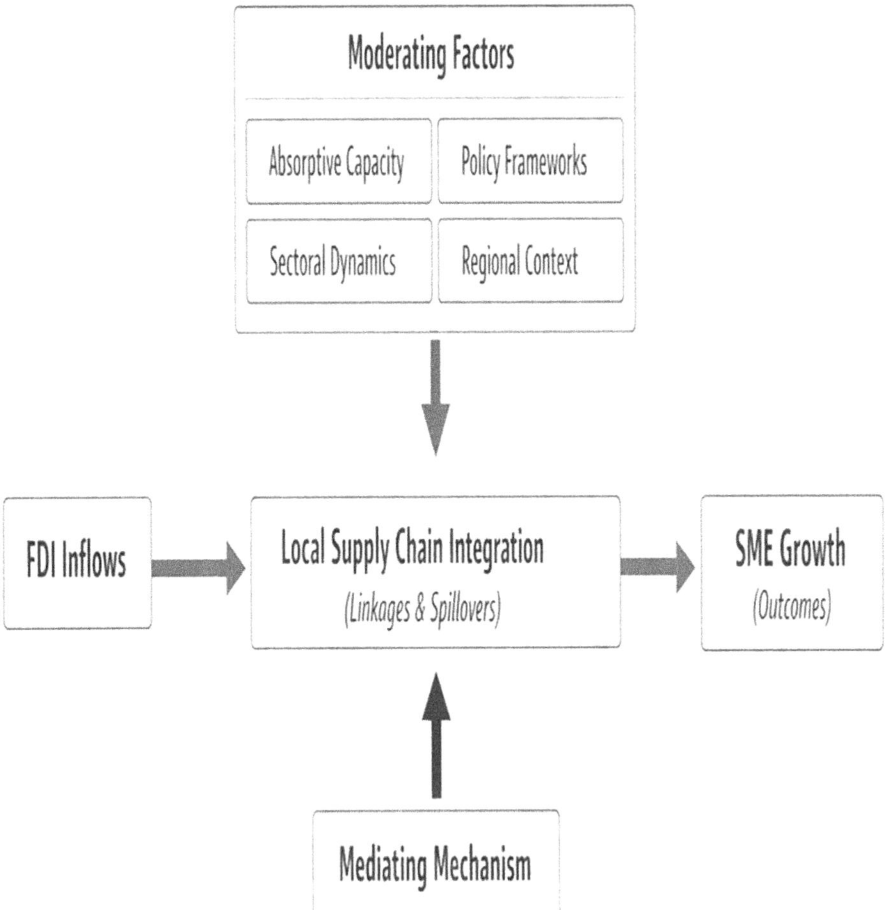

Source: (image by author)

Figure 1 illustrates the pathways through which FDI influences SME growth, highlighting the critical roles of mediating and moderating factors. FDI inflows serve as the primary independent variable, providing capital, advanced technology, managerial expertise, and access to international markets. However, the model underscores that FDI alone is insufficient to generate positive outcomes for domestic firms; the benefits are realised primarily through local supply chain integration, which functions as the mediating mechanism.

Local supply chain integration encompasses both backward linkages, where SMEs supply goods and services to foreign firms, and forward linkages, which facilitate access to distribution networks and broader markets. These linkages enable SMEs to absorb technological and managerial knowledge, improve operational capabilities, and enhance competitiveness, consistent with the tenets of GVC theory and FDI spillover theory (Gereffi & Fernandez-Stark, 2016; Javorcik, 2004).

The diagram also incorporates moderating factors that influence the strength and effectiveness of the FDI–SME growth relationship. Absorptive capacity reflects an SME's human capital, technological competence, and managerial expertise, which are essential for leveraging spillovers (Cohen & Levinthal, 1990). Policy and institutional frameworks, including supplier development programs and local content requirements, shape the conditions under which SMEs can participate in global value chains (UNCTAD, 2020). Sectoral characteristics and regional contexts further determine the extent of integration and the distribution of benefits, acknowledging that manufacturing sectors and well-connected regions are more likely to experience positive spillovers than capital-intensive or geographically isolated contexts (OECD, 2013; World Bank, 2019).

Ultimately, the model emphasises a conditional, multi-level perspective, illustrating that SME growth outcomes—such as enhanced productivity, innovation, and market expansion—emerge from the interplay among FDI, supply chain integration, and contextual factors. By visually mapping these relationships, the diagram highlights the mechanisms through which FDI can foster inclusive domestic economic development while addressing the heterogeneous nature of spillover effects in the South African context.

2.3. Theoretical Contribution

This model contributes to the literature in three important ways. First, it integrates Global Value Chain theory and FDI spillover theory into a unified framework, providing a more comprehensive explanation of how FDI influences domestic economic structures. Second, it moves beyond the assumption of automatic spillovers by explicitly incorporating absorptive capacity and policy conditions as critical determinants of outcomes. Last, it introduces a multi-level perspective that accounts for firm-level, sectoral, and regional variations, thereby offering a more nuanced understanding of FDI impacts in the South African context.

3. OPPORTUNITIES CREATED BY FDI FOR LOCAL SUPPLY CHAINS AND SMES

For many businesses, entering international markets enhances competitiveness and promotes further growth. Internationalisation is regarded as advantageous because it enables businesses to enhance their technological capabilities by acquiring international knowledge and access lower-cost inputs. It also enables businesses to leverage resources in international markets, gain worldwide market influence, and achieve global scale. Additionally, it reduces their volatility via geographical diversification and offers insight into effectively managing operations in international markets by enhancing organisational competencies (Contractor, 2007)

The conceptual framework depicted in Figure 2 illustrates how foreign FDI creates spillovers for domestic SMEs through key diffusion channels, including value chain connections, strategic partnerships, workforce mobility, and competition-driven imitation. It emphasises that the magnitude of these spillovers is strongly reliant on a supporting policy mix that includes innovation, investment promotion, SME growth, and regional development programs. Structural factors, such as the economic structure, SMEs' absorptive capacities, and economic geography, all influence whether domestic enterprises can efficiently absorb and profit from foreign direct investment.

Overall, the model demonstrates that FDI spill-overs are not automatic but require strong policy alignment, capable SMEs, and a favourable economic environment. FDI is vital for helping local companies access global markets. It acts as a bridge connecting local start-ups to the vast opportunities worldwide. FDI offers many advantages that significantly support the global expansion of domestic firms (OECD, 2004; European Central Bank, 2018; Reyes & Atkinson et al., 2018). This research aims to explore the intricate processes by which FDI enables start-ups to access international markets, helping them overcome obstacles related to unfamiliarity and competition.

Figure 2: Understanding FDI-SME spillovers: A conceptual framework

Source: OECD (2023)

This viewpoint supports GVC models, which depict how domestic enterprises occupy places within globally fragmented manufacturing systems. While GVC theories describe where SMEs sit in global production hierarchies and how firm linkages are formed, the FDI spillover theory explains how SMEs gain technological, managerial, and market capabilities through interactions with foreign enterprises.

Accordingly, Javorcik (2004) posits that positive economic benefits stem from both the direct existence of foreign companies and the additional investments they enable.

Similarly, researchers like Blonigen and Piger (2014), Abdouli and Hammami (2018), Baiashvili and Gattini (2020), and Admin (2023) emphasised that FDI is crucial for linking domestic economies to the global market, enhancing technological advancement, and bolstering local entrepreneurial ecosystems. Domestic enterprises may access global networks as subcontractors or suppliers to multinational manufacturers through GVCs, but this does not ensure capability upgrading. The spillover paradigm bridges this gap by emphasising the precise mechanisms, such as knowledge transfer, workforce mobility, and competitive pressure, that allow local firms to transition from low-value to high-value activities. These frameworks operate together to provide a holistic picture of SME development: GVC participation facilitates integration into global markets, whilst FDI spillovers promote functional upgrading, innovation, and productivity growth.

This integrated perspective is particularly significant in South Africa. South Africa intends to industrialise through greater localisation, expanded manufacturing, and increasing engagement in regional and global value chains. Many local SMEs, however, face constraints that limit their capacity to benefit from FDI spill-overs, such as inadequate innovation capabilities, limited access to funding, talent shortages, and technological gaps. Structural and spatial inequalities, as seen by the concentration of industrial activity in Gauteng, the Western Cape, and KwaZulu-Natal, highlight the significance of geographic elements considered in the spillover framework.

Although government measures such as the Industrial Policy Action Plan, Special Economic Zones, supplier development programs, and localisation policies aim to strengthen value chain links and enhance SME skills, gaps in policy coordination and effectiveness persist. According to the framework, improving South Africa's industrialisation outcomes requires aligning FDI attraction strategies with SME upgrading programmes, strengthening regional development interventions, and increasing SME absorptive capacities so that foreign investment results in meaningful productivity gains, technological learning, and inclusive economic development.

Foreign business involvement can fuel the development of staple projects, establish a strong sector-focused presence, improve economic integration across supply chains, boost reinvestment, and foster collaborations that help local enterprises grow and expand. Foreign businesses frequently invest in human resources, expand their operations, and grow their leadership. Innovation has received significant attention from international businesses, both within and outside South Africa. Research and development (R&D) spillovers from wealthy countries are advantageous to the nation. Furthermore, major initiatives in South Africa frequently shape and direct these international businesses' operations.

SMEs can be a real game changer, especially as global competition intensifies for a shrinking pool of large-scale projects and an accelerating trend towards regional economic integration. Numerous studies have found that new firm creation indirectly improves efficiency, accelerates structural change, stimulates innovation, and broadens consumer product options (Schumpeter, 1947; Acs & Audretsch, 1990; Markusen & Venables, 1999; Fritsch & Mueller, 2004). Furthermore, Hutchinson et al. (2009) noted that both huge multinational corporations and smaller businesses are increasingly benefiting from a global marketplace and the substantial potential for corporate expansion and advancement.

Figure 3: Global supply networks, global value chains and backward linkages

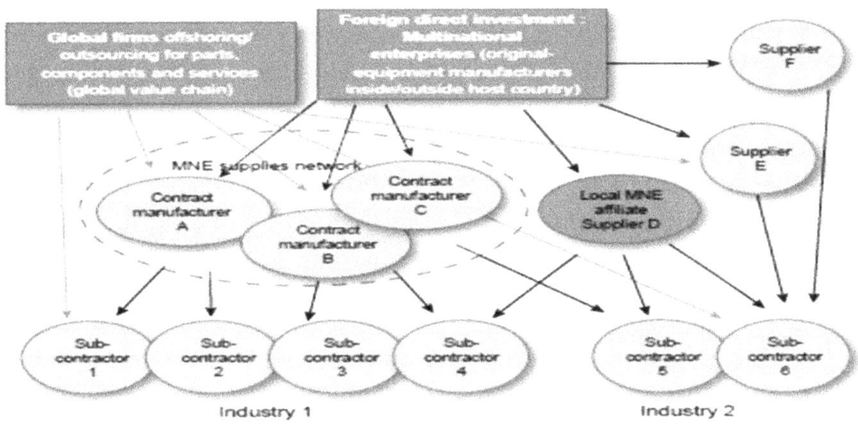

Source: Supapol (1995)

Figure 3 illustrates how global supply networks and value chains operate by depicting the connections among global companies, MNEs, contract manufacturers, and local subcontractors. Global companies outsource and relocate production to contract manufacturers abroad, while MNEs set up regional branches through foreign direct investment, thereby further integrating suppliers in the host country into the network. Contract manufacturers (A, B, and C) manage production and procure components from both international suppliers (E and F) and domestic subcontractors across various industries. This establishes backward linkages, where local businesses, often SMEs, provide inputs to MNE affiliates and contract manufacturers, offering opportunities for technology transfer, skill development, and access to global markets.

To achieve more resilient, sustainable, and inclusive growth, it is crucial to boost productivity and innovation, and to promote their spread across regions to reduce disparities and tackle inequalities. Performance factors that could be improved include SMEs, which are the economic foundation of many areas, and FDI, which contributes to local regions' knowledge base and capital assets. Furthermore, boosting productivity and creativity requires fostering FDI-SME ecosystems. FDI can help SMEs enhance productivity and innovation by promoting knowledge and technology exchanges. SMEs' ability to innovate plays a crucial role in determining FDI location. Finally, strengthening FDI-SME linkages and spillover effects has become increasingly important in the post-COVID-19 recovery, as enterprises, both small and large, strive for competitiveness and resilience in domestic and global value chains.

As noted earlier, inward FDI benefits more than just small and medium-sized enterprises (SMEs). It is widely recognised that FDI supports the economic development of host countries by injecting new capital, generating employment, promoting technology and knowledge transfer, and enabling local firms to integrate into regional and global value chains (UNCTAD, 1999). In essence, this model underscores the complexity of global production systems and the developmental gains that arise when local suppliers are effectively connected to global value chains. Although it is not the primary focus of this chapter, this discussion raises a critical question: what determines the inflow of FDI? Various elements affect the amount of FDI flowing into a nation, including the economic sector engaged. Figure 4 below highlights the main factors influencing FDI as discussed by Alam and Shah (2013)

Figure 4: Determinants of FDI Destination.

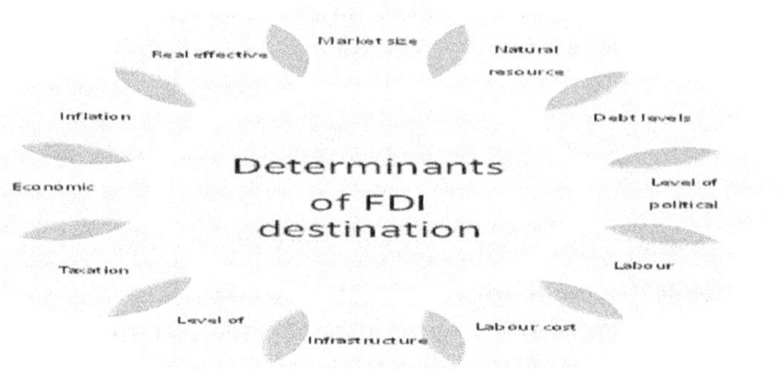

Source: Alam & Shah (2013).

Figure 4 highlights the main factors that affect the direction of FDI flows, as noted by Alam and Shah (2013). These elements represent the economic, political, and structural factors that shape investor trust and decision-making. Market size and economic growth are key factors, as investors favour sizable, growing markets that offer greater returns. The quality of infrastructure is crucial as effective transport, energy, and communication networks reduce business expenses and enhance productivity. Trade openness increases a nation's appeal by facilitating access to local and international markets.

Macroeconomic stability, featuring regulated inflation and stable currency rates, is another crucial element, as it lowers uncertainty and investment risk. Political stability and effective governance are both vital, as consistent policies and robust institutions foster a safe environment for business activities. Finally, factors related to labour, including labour expenses, skill levels, and productivity, affect FDI inflows. Nations with an affordable, skilled labour force are more likely to attract investment, particularly in sectors that rely on labour and technology. This chapter focuses specifically on the key factors that attract foreign investment into particular economic sectors, providing a detailed explanation of how these determinants shape investor decisions.

According to the African Development Bank Outlook (2019), average savings in Southern Africa from 2010 to 2018 were 16.5%, which is lower than those in North Africa (23.5%) and East Africa (17.5%). It also highlights that gross domestic savings (GDS) surpass national savings in the region, signifying negative net foreign savings. At the national level, the scenario is especially worrisome in Lesotho, Malawi, Mozambique, and Zimbabwe. The SADC region continues to face ongoing difficulties, including sluggish economic growth, high poverty levels, and deep inequality. These circumstances impede local growth and diminish the area's appeal to international investors. Lack of growth reduces potential investment returns, whereas elevated poverty and inequality may heighten social unrest and increase operational risks for companies (Asongu & Eita, 2023). Understanding the relationship between these factors and FDI inflows is crucial for policymakers and investors seeking sustainable regional development.

4. CHALLENGES FOR LOCAL SUPPLY CHAINS AND SMES

Although there are large amounts of FDI intended to boost local economic growth, the anticipated advantages for domestic supply chains and the expansion of small businesses remain limited. While FDI can facilitate technology transfer, establish value chain connections, and enhance the competitiveness of small and medium-sized enterprises (SMEs), these positive effects are often weak or inconsistent due to structural challenges in local economies. Many local SMEs lack the capacity to absorb new technologies, are not technologically prepared, and do not have sufficient financial resources to meet the standards set by multinational companies.

Leonidou (2004) observes that SMEs often lack sufficient financial resources to invest in critical capabilities that facilitate market growth. Similarly, Lee et al. (2014) note that SMEs' balance sheets are often too fragile to support such investments.

Consequently, SMEs require significant external funding to facilitate their growth efforts. Additionally, shortages in skilled labour, fragmented industrial policies, and poorly aligned training systems weaken the links between foreign companies and local suppliers. Consequently, foreign investors often procure inputs from outside the local economy, bypassing domestic SMEs and reducing opportunities for their development.

The primary obstacles SMEs face in pursuing FDI include unfair competition, complex regulatory frameworks, lengthy approval processes, corruption, and limited access to funding. SMEs frequently struggle to secure financing for international expansion initiatives due to inadequate collateral, uncertain returns, and information asymmetries. In addition, the exclusion from supply chains due to high entry barriers, such as Unequal power dynamics between foreign investors and local businesses and Risk of dependency and limited long-term sustainability.

Basically, the competitive performance of a business is influenced by various interrelated elements, which comprise: (a) its internal assets like talent, technology, and financial resources; (b) its market position through brand recognition and customer loyalty; (c) its capability to react to rivals and alternative products; (d) its adaptability and innovation potential; (e) its ability to establish new market segments; (f) the broader business landscape, including licensing requirements; (g) the regulatory and policy framework, such as taxation and trade regulations; and (h) the standard of supporting services like infrastructure, logistics, and skills enhancement (Masato, 2009).

Nowadays, globalisation is essential for businesses of all sizes. Increasingly, small- and medium-sized enterprises (SMEs) face global competition and are therefore compelled to contribute to global markets (Onkelinx & Sleuwaegen, 2008). Local startups may face intensified competition from foreign firms, potentially stifling their growth prospects. This means that FDI can create challenges for startups that operate in the same or related sectors as foreign firms, as they may have to compete with them for market share, customers, resources, or talent. For example, foreign firms may have advantages over local startups in terms of scale, technology, quality, or reputation, making it difficult for local startups to match their prices, products, or services.

The South African government has consistently recognised that SMEs face difficulties in accessing markets, and has since implemented supplier development and procurement policies (Department of Trade and Industry, 1995). Equally, foreign firms may also crowd out local startups from accessing finance, suppliers, distributors, or partners, reducing their opportunities and bargaining power. Moreover, FDI can increase the risk of imitation or appropriation of local startups' innovations or intellectual property by foreign firms, undermining their competitive edge and profitability (Branstetter & Chen, 2006; Blalock & Gertler, 2008).

Harrison et al. (2004). Caves (2007), Alfaro and Chen (2012), and Blonigen and Piger (2014) highlight that heavy dependence on foreign investors exposes local startups to significant risks. When startups rely extensively on foreign capital and imported inputs, they become vulnerable to shifts in investor sentiment. Foreign investors may reduce, delay, or withdraw funding due to changes in their strategies, expectations, or external shocks such as political instability, economic crises, or natural disasters. They may also attach various conditions—such as taking equity stakes, influencing decision-making, or shaping pricing policies—that can limit local firms' autonomy. Additionally, reliance on foreign financing introduces exchange-rate risk, as startups must repay foreign-denominated obligations or procure inputs in currencies whose value may fluctuate unpredictably.

Aghion and Tirole (1994) and Dunning (1998) emphasise that asymmetrical power relations often result in unequal partnerships between foreign investors and local startups. Within such dynamics, startups typically possess limited bargaining power, forcing them to accept terms that may be restrictive or unfavourable. Foreign investors may demand high returns, impose low pricing structures, or negotiate exclusive rights, thereby diminishing local firms' profitability and strategic autonomy. In some cases, foreign partners may appropriate local resources, technologies, or innovations without offering equitable compensation or recognition. These imbalances can also lead to various forms of dependency or lock-in, as startups become increasingly reliant on foreign investors for capital, inputs, or market access, thereby compromising their long-term flexibility and capacity to adapt.

Scholars such as Branstetter et al. (2006) and Park and Lippoldt (2008) caution that technology transfer associated with FDI can increase the risk of intellectual property (IP) loss for local startups. When startups share proprietary knowledge, inventions, or innovations with foreign investors, they may inadvertently weaken their competitive advantage or ownership rights. Foreign partners may replicate, leak, or commercially exploit local technologies without proper consent or compensation, and, in some cases, may secure patents or trademarks over innovations developed by local firms, thereby limiting their ability to benefit from their own creations. Furthermore, exposure to multiple international IP regimes can create significant legal and regulatory burdens, as compliance with differing standards across countries is often costly, complex, and

Overall, it may be said that FDI in developing economies often generates uneven and limited benefits for local supply chains and SMEs due to a combination of structural and institutional constraints. Weak linkages between MNEs and domestic firms, driven by reliance on imported inputs and global supplier networks, restrict local participation, while existing connections are typically confined to low-value activities, resulting in enclave-type development. At the firm level, limited absorptive capacity among SMEs, including inadequate skills, technology, and managerial capabilities, further constrains their ability to benefit from knowledge spillovers and supplier opportunities. At the market level, the competitive advantages of MNEs can displace local firms, reinforcing a dualistic economy marked by dominant foreign firms and marginalised domestic enterprises.

These challenges are compounded by power asymmetries within global value chains, where MNEs control high-value segments, and SMEs remain dependent actors with limited value capture. Additionally, weak institutional frameworks, fragmented policies, and infrastructural and financial constraints hinder effective integration of local firms. The spatial and sectoral concentration of FDI further exacerbates inequalities, leaving less-developed regions excluded. Overall, the developmental impact of FDI is highly conditional, with outcomes depending on the interaction between firm capabilities, institutional quality, and the strategic behaviour of foreign investors.

5. SECTORAL AND REGIONAL VARIATIONS IN FDI'S IMPACT

Africa, a continent rich in resources, represents a paradox of enormous promise combined with vulnerability, underdevelopment, and extreme poverty (Okorie et al., 2023; Tukon, 2024). Wöcke and Sing (2013) note that FDI in developing nations typically focuses on the natural resources sector, especially mining and manufacturing, whereas service industries generally attract relatively little FDI. As a result, Africa ranks low on the global economic complexity index and is highly susceptible to changes in global commodity prices.

The manufacturing sector in developing economies is a major recipient of foreign direct investment, with a considerable impact on SME competitiveness. Such investment frequently involves technology transfer, which improves productivity, efficiency, and innovation among local SMEs by utilising innovative machinery, production procedures, and management practices (Johnson & White, 2021). The automobile industry in South Africa has also benefited from foreign direct investment, with major global automakers including BMW, Volkswagen, and Toyota establishing manufacturing plants, creating jobs, and expanding local supply chains (Mqwathi, 2023). Certainly, FDI aids SMEs' integration into global value chains, providing access to international markets and new prospects. However, the presence of foreign enterprises might increase competition, forcing SMEs to invest in expensive technological and operational changes. Furthermore, FDI may result in market concentration, with large foreign enterprises dominating and potentially crowding out smaller domestic businesses.

Ndikumana and Verick (2008) observe that in developing nations, FDI frequently focuses on the primary resources sector, propelled by spikes in commodity prices, whereas market size and economic progress affect sustained investment in wholesale and retail sectors. Nefussi and Schwellnus (2010) investigated whether FDI in manufacturing affects FDI in business services and found no significant differences in location-choice models between manufacturing and service firms. Their findings indicate that these firms' placement decisions are interrelated, since FDI in services increases in response to downstream demand created by manufacturing FDI. This suggests that, while a sector may not directly drive economic growth, its progress might promote growth in other areas, thus boosting the broader economy.

FDI in the services sector, including finance, telecommunications, and healthcare, has benefited small and medium-sized businesses by expanding market opportunities, promoting innovation, and boosting skills training. For example, FDI in telecommunications has improved digital infrastructure, allowing SMEs to better connect and reach global markets, whereas investment in finance has increased credit availability and introduced new financial products. Nonetheless, local SMEs face challenges due to competition from well-funded overseas companies. The intangible nature of services complicates the evaluation of knowledge transfer and skill enhancement, while the prevalence of foreign enterprises may lead to market consolidation and a potential degradation of local corporate identity.

African-Vibes (2021) and Ajide (2025) highlight that the rise of Africa's tech ecosystem, particularly in Kenya, Nigeria, and South Africa, is largely driven by FDI-enabled knowledge transfers. International companies such as Google, Microsoft, and IBM have established R&D centers on the continent, fostering innovation in software development, fintech, and e-commerce. These investments not only enhance technological capacity but also diversify exports and support the production of more sophisticated goods, contributing to overall economic growth. In this case, foreign enterprises contribute to economic progress by creating jobs and promoting seamless integration among industry and supply chain partners. The concentration of foreign subsidiaries in the state's southern region suggests the possibility for a robust ecosystem of businesses, charities, and educational institutions.

Harrison and Rodríguez-Clare (2010), along with Javorcik, & Spatareanu (2011) contend that the commodity boom concealed a significant flaw in Africa's economic transformation: sluggish manufacturing expansion and strong reliance on resource exports. This weakness led to significant downturns in economic performance following major global events, including the end of the commodity supercycle in 2011 and the COVID-19 pandemic in 2020. Throughout these times, Africa's overall GDP growth nearly halved, while per capita growth remained flat, leading the continent into its initial recession. These occurrences have prompted concerns about the sustainability of Africa's development and whether it is underpinned by deeper structural changes (UNECA, 2014; ACET, 2023).

According to Kim & Lee (2019), the renewable energy industry has attracted significant FDI, driven by worldwide trends toward sustainable growth and clean energy. This funding offers SMEs opportunities to engage in eco-friendly initiatives, utilise cutting-edge technologies, and support sustainable growth. Initiatives in solar and wind power, for instance, provide SMEs with fresh business prospects and resources. Nonetheless, the industry presents challenges: its capital-intensive nature might limit SME participation, and competition for essential resources such as land and water could increase alongside foreign investment. Guaranteeing that SMEs have equitable access to and receive assistance is vital to maximising the benefits of FDI in renewable energy.

6. POLICY FRAMEWORKS AND STRATEGIES FOR INCLUSIVE FDI

FDI offers several clear benefits for startups and SMEs. It provides essential capital for growth, research, and market expansion, while also introducing advanced technologies, specialised resources, and managerial expertise that strengthen local entrepreneurial capacity. By leveraging international networks, FDI helps startups access broader markets and attract skilled talent, thereby enriching the local labour pool. Overall, FDI fosters knowledge sharing and exposes entrepreneurs to global best practices, enhancing innovation and competitiveness.

Governments at national and sub-national levels have a crucial role to play in creating the business and policy conditions for stronger FDI-SME linkages and spillovers. Public intervention can take place at the crossroad of investment promotion, innovation, SME and entrepreneurship, and regional development policies, and coordination across the board is key. Effective policy intervention, however, requires a better understanding of how FDI can affect the productivity and innovation of local SMEs, which SMEs can attract quality FDI, and the conditions and policies that can enable greater spillovers and resilience.

Against this background, Doh and Kim (2014) and Gilmore et al. (2013) note that many governments worldwide routinely design and implement initiatives to reduce barriers to entrepreneurship. These efforts typically include support for financing, market access, market information, management capabilities, and compliance requirements—factors that often constrain the growth of Small and Medium Enterprises (SMEs).

In South Africa, nurturing strong SMEs is essential, and their performance should not be hindered by resource gaps or institutional barriers that government intervention can address (Castaño et al., 2016; Heinonen & Hytti, 2014). As in many other countries, South Africa has introduced measures to reduce institutional and regulatory constraints. For example, the adoption of the White Paper on the National Strategy for the Development and Promotion of Small Business in South Africa (Department of Trade & Industry, 1995) established a policy framework to remove barriers faced by SMEs. This made South Africa an appropriate setting for the research. In line with global practice, the White Paper's programmes focus on expanding SME market opportunities to support economic growth, job creation, and poverty reduction.

To help alleviate the difficulties SMEs face in securing external funding, various governments have established grant funding policies (Daskalakis et al., 2013), which may take the form of tax incentives, financing, and grants (Busom et al., 2014). Despite various attempts by governments to offer financial solutions, SMEs, especially in developing countries, remain underfunded (Beck, 2013; Lee & Drever, 2014).

As the global economy becomes more interconnected and economic reforms and liberalisation progress in Africa, local SMEs need to establish networks and partnerships to thrive and compete efficiently. Research indicates that partnerships, clustering, and networking facilitate the growth of small businesses, collaboration with larger enterprises, and access to both national and international markets. Success relies on a customer-centric strategy, collaborative support, and persistent, collective endeavours aimed at ongoing improvement.

On the other hand, research by Vasconcellos and Kish (2013) and Goswami and Haider (2014) indicates that increased political risk reduces FDI inflows, as investors favour stable conditions. Jensen (2013) points out that the race for global capital influences national tax policies, with macroeconomic variables such as inflation, exchange rates, and public debt also playing a role in a nation's appeal to international investors.

The analysis presented in this chapter underscores that the developmental impact of Foreign Direct Investment (FDI) is neither automatic nor uniformly distributed. Instead, it is shaped by the interaction between multinational enterprises (MNEs), domestic firm capabilities, and the broader institutional environment. As such, policy interventions must move beyond a narrow focus on attracting FDI and instead prioritise strategic alignment between foreign investment and local economic development objectives.

Ultimately, a developmental approach to FDI requires shifting from simply attracting investment to embedding it within local economies through stronger linkages with domestic firms. This involves enhancing SME capabilities, facilitating strategic partnerships, and addressing power imbalances in global value chains. Greater policy coherence and institutional coordination are essential to align FDI with industrial and SME development objectives. Targeted interventions are also needed to reduce spatial and sectoral inequalities. Ultimately, FDI should be strategically leveraged as a catalyst for inclusive growth, industrial upgrading, and long-term structural transformation.

7. CONCLUSION AND RECOMMENDATIONS

This chapter examines the relationship between FDI, local supply chains, and the growth of SMEs, with particular emphasis on the mechanisms by which FDI influences domestic economic structures. Drawing on GVC theory and FDI spillover theory, the analysis developed an integrated conceptual framework that highlights the mediating role of firm-level linkages and the moderating influence of institutional and structural factors.

The findings demonstrate that FDI has the potential to generate significant opportunities for local economic development, including supply chain integration, knowledge and technology transfer, market access, and firm-level upgrading. However, these benefits are neither automatic nor uniformly distributed. Instead, they are contingent on the strength of linkages between multinational enterprises and domestic firms, the absorptive capacity of SMEs, and the quality of the policy and institutional environment.

At the same time, the chapter highlights a range of constraints that limit the developmental impact of FDI. These include weak local linkages, limited firm capabilities, competitive displacement, power asymmetries within value chains, and persistent spatial and sectoral inequalities. Together, these challenges underscore the inherently uneven and conditional nature of FDI-led development.

These barriers weaken the potential for upgrading and restrict the movement of knowledge from foreign to local firms. In South Africa, the experiences of provinces like Limpopo, the Eastern Cape, and the Northern Cape demonstrate that significant industrial investments can lead to little local supply chain development if capability gaps and policy inconsistencies are not addressed. This raises important questions about how industrial policy can be redesigned to support SME competitiveness, facilitate local content development, and ensure that foreign investment contributes meaningfully to inclusive economic growth. The discussion, therefore, underscores the need for coordinated strategies that align FDI attraction with SME support, workforce development, and regional economic planning.

The government needs to devise and implement a public policy that promotes the establishment of business networks within a value chain connecting SMEs and large private companies, ensuring that SMEs can obtain adequate private financing, access all essential market data, and participate in confidential purchasing agreements. Moreover, officials, together with relevant stakeholders, should create a supportive regulatory environment through policies and regulations that encourage significant private enterprises to promote SMEs through procurement supply chains or procurement improvement initiatives. In this situation, the government needs to offer incentives and/or financing to major private companies for their involvement in supply chain or procurement progress projects.

These barriers weaken the potential for upgrading and restrict the movement of knowledge from foreign to local firms. In South Africa, the experiences of provinces like Limpopo, the Eastern Cape, and the Northern Cape demonstrate that significant industrial investments can lead to little local supply chain development if capability gaps and policy inconsistencies are not addressed. This raises important questions about how industrial policy can be redesigned to support SME competitiveness, facilitate local content development, and ensure that foreign investment contributes meaningfully to inclusive economic growth. The discussion, therefore, underscores the need for coordinated strategies that align FDI attraction with SME support, workforce development, and regional economic planning.

The government needs to devise and implement a public policy that promotes the establishment of business networks within a value chain connecting SMEs and large private companies, ensuring that SMEs can obtain adequate private financing, access all essential market data, and participate in confidential purchasing agreements. Moreover, officials, together with relevant stakeholders, should create a supportive regulatory environment through policies and regulations that encourage significant private enterprises to promote SMEs through procurement supply chains or procurement improvement initiatives. In this situation, the government needs to offer incentives and/or financing to major private companies to encourage their involvement in supply chain or procurement projects.

REFERENCES

Abdouli, M., & Hammami, S. (2018). Economic Growth, Environment, FDI Inflows, and Financial Development in Middle East Countries: Fresh Evidence from Simultaneous Equation Models. *Journal of the Knowledge Economy*, *11*(2), 479–511. DOI: 10.1007/s13132-018-0546-9

ACET. (2023) African Transformation Index 2023: Tracking Africa's economic successes and setbacks. ACET, Accra. Retrieved from https://acetforafrica.org/ati/

Acs, Z. J., & Audretsch, D. B. (1990). *Innovation and small firms*. MIT Press. DOI: 10.1007/978-94-015-7854-7

Admin. (2023). Foreign Direct Investment (FDI) - definition, types of FDI, FDI in India. UPSC

African Vibes. (2021). "The Top 10 African Tech Hubs." Retrieved from https://africanvibes.com/the-top-10-african-tech-hubs

Aghion, P., & Tirole, J. (1994). The management of innovation. *The Quarterly Journal of Economics*, *109*(4), 1185–1209. DOI: 10.2307/2118360

Ajide, K. B. (2025). Exploring the Relationship between Trade Openness, FDI, and Economic Complexity in Africa. *The International Trade Journal*, *39*(5), 525–551. DOI: 10.1080/08853908.2024.2374739

Alam, A., & Shah, S. (2013). Determinants of foreign direct investment in OECD member countries. *Journal of Economic Studies (Glasgow, Scotland)*, *40*(4), 515–527. DOI: 10.1108/JES-10-2011-0132

Alfaro, L., & Chen, M. X. (2012). Surviving the global financial crisis: Foreign ownership and establishment performance. *American Economic Journal. Economic Policy*, *4*(3), 30–55. DOI: 10.1257/pol.4.3.30

Altenburg, T., & Meyer-Stamer, J. (1999). How to promote clusters: Policy experiences from Latin America. *World Development*, *27*(9), 1693–1713. DOI: 10.1016/S0305-750X(99)00081-9

Baiashvili, T., & Gattini, L. (2020). Impact of FDI on economic growth: The role of country income levels and institutional strength. EIB Working Papers, 2020/02. Retrieved from https://www.eib.org/attachments/efs/economics_working_paper_2020_02_en.pdf

Beck, T. (2013). Bank financing for SMEs: Lessons from the literature. *National Institute Economic Review*, *225*(1), 23–38. DOI: 10.1177/002795011322500105

Blalock, G., & Gertler, P. J. (2008). Welfare gains from foreign direct investment through technology transfer to local suppliers. *Journal of International Economics, 74*(2), 402–442. DOI: 10.1016/j.jinteco.2007.05.011

Blomström, M., & Kokko, A. (2003). The economics of foreign direct investment incentives. NBER Working Paper No. 9489.

Blonigen, B. A., & Piger, J. (2014). Determinants of foreign direct investment. *The Canadian Journal of Economics. Revue Canadienne d'Économique, 47*(3), 775–812. https://onlinelibrary.wiley.com/doi/epdf/10.1111/caje.1209. DOI: 10.1111/caje.12091

Branstetter, L., Fisman, R., & Foley, C. F. (2006). Do stronger intellectual property rights increase international technology transfer? Empirical evidence from U.S. firm-level panel data. *The Quarterly Journal of Economics, 121*(1), 321–349. DOI: 10.1162/qjec.2006.121.1.321

Busom, I., Corchuelo, B., & Martínez-Ros, E. (2014). Tax incentive or subsidies for business R&D? *Small Business Economics, 43*(3), 571–596. DOI: 10.1007/s11187-014-9569-1

Castaño, M. S., Méndez, M. T., & Galindo, M. Á. (2016). The effect of public policies on entrepreneurial activity and economic growth. *Journal of Business Research, 68*(7), 1496–1500. DOI: 10.1016/j.jbusres.2016.04.125

Caves, R. E. (2007). *Multinational enterprise and economic analysis* (3rd ed.). Cambridge University Press. DOI: 10.1017/CBO9780511619113

Cohen, W. M., & Levinthal, D. A. (1990). Absorptive capacity: A new perspective on learning and innovation. *Administrative Science Quarterly, 35*(1), 128–152. DOI: 10.2307/2393553

Contractor, F. J. (2007). Is International Business Good for Companies? The Evolutionary or Multistage Theory of Internationalisation vs. the Transaction Cost Perspective. *International Management Review, 47*(3), 453–475.

Daskalakis, N., Jarvis, R., & Schizas, E. (2013). Financing practices and preferences for micro and small firms. *Journal of Small Business and Enterprise Development, 20*(1), 80–101. DOI: 10.1108/14626001311298420

Department of Trade and Industry. (1995). The White Paper on the national strategy for the development and promotion of small businesses in South Africa.

Doh, S., & Kim, B. (2014). Government support for SME innovations in the regional industries: The case of the government financial support program in South Korea. *Research Policy*, *43*(9), 1557–1569. DOI: 10.1016/j.respol.2014.05.001

Driffield, N. N., A. H. M. (1999). Foreign Direct Investment and Local Input Linkages in Malaysia. *Transnational Corporations*, *8*(3), 1–25.

Dunning, J. H. (1998). Location and the multinational enterprise: A neglected factor? Journal ofInternational Business Studies, 29(1), 45–66.

European Central Bank. (2018). Foreign direct investment and its drivers: A global and EU perspective. *Economic Bulletin*, *4*, •••. https://www.ecb.europa.eu/press/economicbulletin/articles/2018/html/ecb.ebart201804_01.en.html

Fritsch, M., & Mueller, P. (2004). Effects of new business formation on regional development over time. *Regional Studies*, *38*(8), 961–975. DOI: 10.1080/0034340042000280965

Gereffi, G., & Fernández-Stark, K. (2016). *Global value chain analysis: A primer* (2nd ed.). Duke University Centre on Globalisation, Governance & Competitiveness.

Gereffi, G., Humphrey, J., & Sturgeon, T. (2005). The governance of global value chains. *Review of International Political Economy*, *12*(1), 78–104. DOI: 10.1080/09692290500049805

Gilmore, A., Galbraith, B., & Mulvenna, M. (2013). Perceived barriers to participation in R&D programmes for SMEs within the European Union. *Technology Analysis and Strategic Management*, *25*(3), 329–339. DOI: 10.1080/09537325.2013.764987

Giroud, A. (2007). MNE vertical linkages: The experience of Vietnam after Malaysia. *International Business Review*, *6*(2), 159–176. DOI: 10.1016/j.ibusrev.2006.11.003

Goswami, G., & Haider, S. (2014). Does political risk deter FDI inflow? An analytical approach using panel data and factor analysis. *Journal of Economic Studies (Glasgow, Scotland)*, *41*(2), 233–252. DOI: 10.1108/JES-03-2012-0041

Harrison, A., Love, I., & McMillan, M. (2004). Global capital flows and financing constraints. *Journal of Development Economics*, *75*(1), 269–301. DOI: 10.1016/j.jdeveco.2003.10.002

Harrison, A., & Rodríguez-Clare, A. (2010). Trade, foreign investment, and industrial policy for developing countries. Handbook of development economics, 5, 4039–4214.

Heinonen, J., & Hytti, U. (2014). Entrepreneurship mission and content in finish policy programmes. *Journal of Small Business and Enterprise Development*, *23*(1), 149–162. DOI: 10.1108/JSBED-10-2014-0170

Hutchinson, K., Fleck, E., & Llyod-Reason, L. (2009). An investigation into the initial barriers to internationalization: Evidence from small UK retailers. *Journal of Small Business and Enterprise Development*, *16*(4), 544–586. DOI: 10.1108/14626000911000910

Javorcik, B. S. (2004). Does foreign direct investment increase the productivity of domestic firms? In search of spillovers through backward linkages. *The American Economic Review*, *94*(3), 605–627. DOI: 10.1257/0002828041464605

Javorcik, B. S. (2004). Does Foreign Direct Investment Increase the Productivity of Domestic Firms? In Search of Spillovers through Backward Linkages. *The American Economic Review*, *94*(3), 605–627. DOI: 10.1257/0002828041464605

Javorcik, B. S., & Spatareanu, M. (2011). Does it matter where you come from? Vertical spillovers from foreign direct investment and the origin of investors. *Journal of Development Economics*, *96*(1), 126–138. DOI: 10.1016/j.jdeveco.2010.05.008

Jensen, N. M. (2013). Domestic Institutions and the Taxing of Multinational Corporations. *International Studies Quarterly*, *57*(4), 751–759. DOI: 10.1111/isqu.12099

Johnson, P., & White, M. (2021). Foreign direct investment and the growth of SMEs in the manufacturing sector. *International Economic Review*, *47*(2), 123–145.

Kim, Y., & Lee, J. (2019). Sectoral analysis of FDI effects on SMEs in renewable energy markets. *Energy Economics Journal*, *41*(2), 142–160.

Lee, N., & Drever, E. (2014). Do SMEs in deprived areas find it harder to access finance? Evidence from the UK Small Business Survey. *Entrepreneurship and Regional Development*, *26*(4), 337–356. DOI: 10.1080/08985626.2014.911966

Markusen, J. R., & Venables, A. J. (1999). Foreign direct investment as a catalyst for industrial development. *European Economic Review*, *43*(2), 335–356. DOI: 10.1016/S0014-2921(98)00048-8

Masato, A. (2009). Globalization of Production and the Competitiveness of Small and Medium-sized Enterprises in Asia and the Pacific [from United Nations Economic and Social Commission for Asia and the Pacific] [ESCAP]. *Trends and Prospects*, *65*, 33–57.

Mqwathi, H. T. 2023. "Analysing the Impact of Disruptive Events on the Performance of the Automotive Industry Sales in Gauteng, South Africa." Doctoral diss., North-West University (South Africa).

Ndikumana, L., & Verick, S. (2008). The linkages between FDI and domestic investment: Unravelling the developmental impact of foreign investment in Sub-Saharan Africa. *Development Policy Review*, *26*(6), 713–726. DOI: 10.1111/j.1467-7679.2008.00430.x

Nefussi, B., & Schwellnus, C. (2010). Does FDI in manufacturing cause FDI in business services? Evidence from French firm-level data. *The Canadian Journal of Economics. Revue Canadienne d'Économique*, *43*(1), 180–203. DOI: 10.1111/j.1540-5982.2009.01568.x

OECD. (2004). Facilitating SMEs access to international markets. OECD Conference of Ministers Responsible for Small and Medium-Sized Enterprises (SMEs). Retrieved from https://www.oecd.org/industry/smes/31919223.pdf

OECD. (2013). *Interconnected economies: Benefiting from global value chains*. OECD Publishing.

OECD. (2023). Policy Toolkit for strengthening FDI and SME linkages. Retrieved from https://www.oecd.org/en/publications/policy-toolkit-for-strengthening-fdi-and-sme linkages_688bde9a-en.html

Okorie, C., Udoh, E., & Bassey, O. B. (2023). Mirroring the Developmental Challenges of Oil-Rich Nige-ria within the Context of Resource Curse/Dutch Disease and Paradox of Plenty. *TIJER–InternationalResearch Journal*, *10*(4), 818–834.

Onkelinx, J., & Sleuwaegen, L. (2008). Internationalisation of SMEs, Flanders DC. Retrieved from https://repository.vlerick.com/server/api/core/bitstreams/b5e25f8d-0bf2-4223-a455-ca66d58d5248/content

Park, W. G., & Lippoldt, D. (2008). *Technology transfer and the economic implications of the strengthening of intellectual property rights in developing countries (OECD Trade Policy Papers No. 62)*. OECD Publishing., DOI: 10.1787/18166873

Reyes, J. D., & Atkinson, E. (2018). Connecting local businesses with multinational corporations amplifies the development impact of FDI. The Trade Post. Retrieved from https://blogs.worldbank.org/trade/connecting-localbusinesses-multinational-corporations-amplifies-development-impact-fdi

Schumpeter, J. A. (1947). Theoretical problems of economic growth. *The Journal of Economic History*, *7*(S1), 1–9. DOI: 10.1017/S0022050700065189

Supapol, A. B. (1995). Thailand. In *ESCAP and UNCTAD, Transnational Corporations and Backward Linkages in Asian Electronics Industries* (pp. 249–287). United Nations.

Tukon, K. (2024). Examining How Globalization Shapes Africa's Underdevelopment. *Open Journal of Business and Management*, *12*(02), 875–885. DOI: 10.4236/ojbm.2024.122046

UNCTAD. (1998). "The Handbook on Foreign Direct Investment by Small and Medium-Sized Enterprises: Lessons from Asia." Geneva.

UNCTAD (1999). World Investment Report 1999: Foreign direct investment and the challenge

UNCTAD. (2001). World Investment Report: Promoting Linkages. New York, United Nations. https://unctad.org/system/files/official-document/wir2001_en.pdf

UNCTAD. (2020). World investment report 2020: International production beyond the pandemic. *United Nations Conference on Trade and Development*.

UNECA. (2014) Dynamic Industrial Policy in Africa: Innovative Institutions, Effective Processes and Flexible Mechanisms. Retrieved from https://archive.uneca.org/sites/default/files/PublicationFiles/final_era2014_march25_en.pdf

Vasconcellos, G. M., & Kish, R. J. (2013). Cross-Border Mergers and Acquisitions. In Encyclopedia of Finance (pp. 515-523). Springer US. DOI: 10.1007/978-1-4614-5360-4_43

Wöcke, A., & Sing, L. (2013). Inward and Outward FDI Country Profiles. *International Interactions*, *38*(1), 111–139. DOI: 10.1080/03050629.2012.640254

World Bank. (2019). The changing nature of work. World Bank Group. Retrieved from https://documents1.worldbank.org/curated/en/816281518818814423/pdf/2019-WDR

Chapter 12
Circular Economy and Job Creation:
Assessing the Potential for Green Employment.

Phathutshedzo Madumi
http://orcid.org/0009-0000-4283-5039
University of Stellenbosch, South Africa

Humbulani Gilbert Ndou
University of Stellenbosch, South Africa

ABSTRACT

This chapter examines how the circular economy (CE) can support green job creation in South Africa, where unemployment and unsustainable resource use remain major challenges. It presents the CE as a shift from linear production to a system focused on reducing waste, reusing materials, and regenerating natural resources. Through sectoral analysis, the chapter identifies employment opportunities in manufacturing, waste management, water reuse, construction, and renewable energy. It highlights the socioeconomic benefits of circular jobs, including improved skills, resilience, and social inclusion, while acknowledging barriers such as limited infrastructure, high investment costs, technological gaps, and low public awareness. The chapter concludes by outlining policy and business strategies that can expand CE-related employment and promote sustainable development in South Africa.

DOI: 10.4018/979-8-2600-3325-8.ch012

1. INTRODUCTION

One of the major challenges facing the South African government is how to reduce unemployment through effective job creation. Most people in South Africa are unemployed and living in dire conditions, which highlights the urgency for effective policies and initiatives to address the unemployment crisis and improve living standards. It is hardly surprising that South African politicians promise to create thousands of jobs ahead of any general election, as they aim to appear committed to addressing the country's chronic unemployment problem. However, they are failing to keep their commitments. At the same time, it is crucial to acknowledge that investing in job creation presents distinct challenges. Moreover, the full impact of such investments on labour markets is difficult to forecast and quantify, and efforts to create jobs might sometimes conflict with efforts to increase efficiency.

Scholars studying the circular economy (CE) are increasingly examining the relationship between CE and growth. There is a growing recognition that economic growth and development must address environmental and social concerns, particularly in developing countries. For instance, by implementing the circular economy as a development strategy, the nation can grow economically while staying within the bounds of the globe and the environmental constraints required for human activity to be sustainable. The current socioeconomic climate in South Africa provides a favourable foundation for the adoption of circular practices. Through job development, the circular economy offers opportunities to diversify employment in green sectors.

Shifting from the existing linear economic development model to a CE is a popular subject in scholarly articles, public policy discussions, and the business sector. In recent years, scientific and professional circles have paid close attention to the concept of the circular economy (CE) and are placing strong emphasis on implementing its key components, which constitute sustainability (Winans, Kendall, & Deng, 2017). This chapter explores the relationship between green employment and CE, examining how adopting circular practices can support sustainable development and create employment opportunities. It assesses the types of jobs created, the skills required for them, and the potential for inclusion and economic resilience. By identifying key trends and challenges, the chapter aims to provide a comprehensive understanding of the labour market dynamics in a circular economy. The objectives of this chapter are to:

1. To analyse the job creation potential of circular economy initiatives across various sectors.
2. To assess the socioeconomic benefits of green employment, particularly in developing regions.
3. To identify challenges and strategies for scaling circular job opportunities.

The chapter conducts a qualitative literature analysis, primarily utilising key secondary sources and examining relevant information from government and business publications. As previously noted, circular economy practices have the transformative potential to reshape the labour market by creating green jobs, enhancing resilience, and fostering sustainable development. This chapter aims to contribute to the discussion by offering evidence-based perspectives on how this transformation can be leveraged to generate more equitable and inclusive job opportunities.

2. A NEW INDUSTRIAL PARADIGM: THE CIRCULAR ECONOMY

There is growing global awareness that consumption and production patterns at the global, regional, and local levels are unsustainable. Governments, businesses, and individuals are concerned about wasteful behaviours that deplete resources and contribute to pollution, environmental degradation, and severe climate-related impacts. Making the shift to a more environmentally friendly economic system requires a circular economy. It primarily focuses on the physical and material resources within the economy—such as fuel, minerals, water, and biomass—rather than on human well-being or social inclusion. To reduce the use of primary resources, it emphasises recycling, reducing, and reusing material inputs, as well as turning waste into a resource (EEA 2014). In this sense, the circular economy can be viewed as a subset of the broader green growth or green economy framework.

The Circular Economy has been gaining popularity since the late 1970s (Ellen MacArthur Foundation (EMF), 2013). With an emphasis on industrial economics, Stahel and Reday (1976) introduced some aspects of the circular economy. They conceptualised a loop economy to describe industrial strategies for waste prevention, regional job creation, resource efficiency, and dematerialisation of the industrial economy. The most pertinent sustainable business model for a loop economy, according to Stahel (1982), is selling utilisation rather than ownership of goods, which enables industries to make money without externalising the costs and risks associated with waste. Zhai's (2020) conception of a CE emphasises restoration and regeneration over traditional end-of-life concepts. According to Su´arez-Eiroa et al. (2019), a CE seeks to achieve sustainable development, benefiting the economy, environment, and social equity for both current and future generations.

There is currently no widely accepted definition of the circular economy (CE) in the literature (Korhonen et al., 2018). Numerous definitions have been presented by academia and international organisations, each highlighting distinct CE principles such as reuse, redesign, and recycling. For instance, the EMF (2020) describes the circular economy as a socio-economic system that emphasises continuous resource use and minimising waste. It is restorative and regenerative, guided by three principles: eliminating waste and pollution, maintaining products and materials in use via closed-loop systems, and restoring natural ecosystems. Kirchherr et al. (2017) identified 114 definitions of CE, most of which highlight the 3R model—Reduce, Reuse, and Recycle. To achieve "lifecycle extension, sharing, reuse, recycling, remanufacturing, and refurbishing," Homrich et al. (2018, p. 534) define CE as an approach that considers both biological and technical cycles. They note that its successful implementation necessitates rethinking operations management, particularly the lifecycles of goods and services.

Similarly, to accomplish the fundamental objectives of "slowing, closing, and narrowing material and energy loops," Geissdoerfer et al. (2017, p. 759) focused on the regeneration of resources by utilising waste materials and minimising the use of "virgin" resources. Resource efficiency and the circular economy have become increasingly important elements of environmental policy. According to the OECD (2019), if current socioeconomic trends continue, demand for natural resources is expected to more than double by 2060, potentially with severe environmental consequences. The circular economy aims to reduce material, labour, energy, and capital costs in products. By reducing production inputs, such as materials and energy, the circularity of economic processes reduces waste and pollution (Lovins & Michael, 2014; Lacy & Rutqvist, 2016). This results in fewer useless final components, products, and energy remaining at the end of production and consumption cycles. The Ellen MacArthur Foundation (2013) recommends designing finite systems to eliminate waste and material.

To transition from a linear economy to a CE, the EMF (2013) identified four core strategies, which are covered in the entire CE literature. First and foremost, regenerative resource prioritisation should ensure that renewable and reusable resources are efficiently utilised as energy and materials. Second, resource preservation should be achieved through maintenance, repair, and upgrades to maximise resource lifetimes. Thirdly, the use of waste streams as secondary resources should result in the material's useful use. Fourth, the sharing economy should encourage more intensive use and reuse of products. In brief, three key tenets underpin the circular economy: reducing waste and pollution, reusing products and materials, and restoring natural systems.

Figure 1. A concept of the Circular Economy (CE)

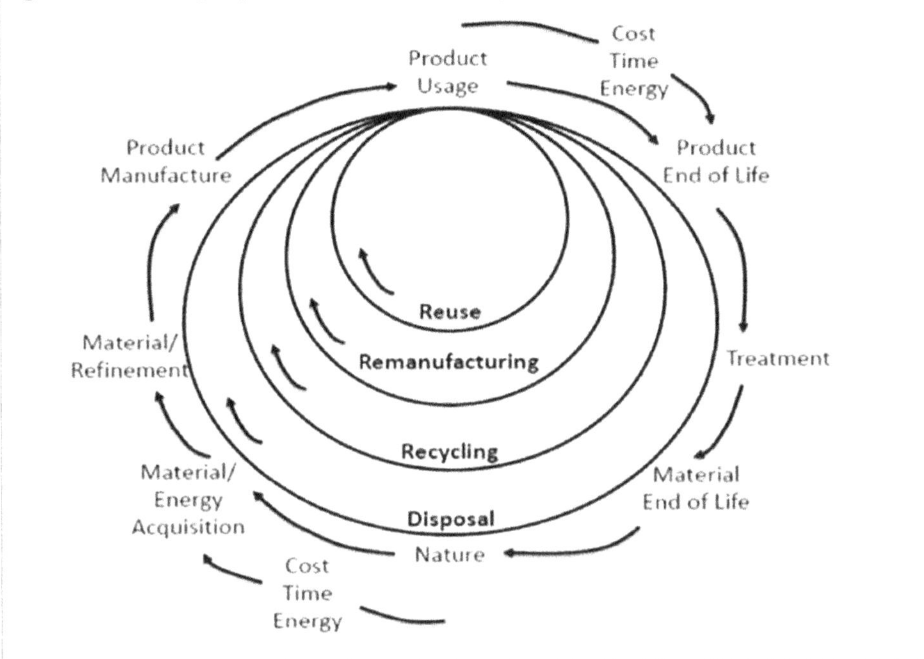

Source: Mihelcic et al. (2003) cited by Horbach, J., & Rammer, C. (2019)

Mihelcic's (2003) approach (Figure 1) emphasises the critical role that enterprises play in developing the circular economy (CE). According to Korhonen (2018:37), “the CE message is that the inner circles demand fewer resources, less energy, and are also more economical.” Optimising these inner circles—by reducing material and energy flows, enhancing recycling, reusing, and remanufacturing, and developing goods with longer lifespans—is significantly dependent on the actions and initiatives of businesses.

Figure 2. Distinctions between circular, reuse, and linear economies.

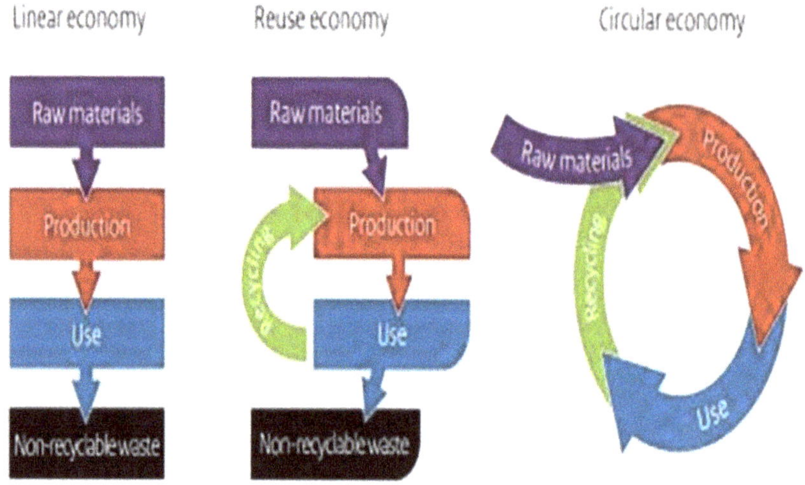

Source: Bonciu (2020).

Figure 2 illustrates the distinctions between a linear economy, a partial recycling or "reuse" economy, and a true circular economy. In a circular economy, products are intentionally designed for extended durability, enabling their reuse and remanufacturing of components. In a linear economy, raw materials are extracted, used in manufacturing, and then consumed. After their use, products generally become non-recyclable waste. This model follows a one-way flow of resources, leading to resource depletion and increased waste. The reuse economy introduces a partial cycle. Although raw materials are still used for production and consumption, some materials or products are recovered through recycling or reuse. This approach reduces waste but still results in a considerable amount of non-recyclable material being discarded. By contrast, the circular economy establishes a closed-loop system. Raw materials are used in production, products are consumed, and at the end of their lifecycle, materials are continuously recycled back into the system. This model minimises waste, lowers reliance on new raw materials, and promotes sustainability by keeping resources in use for as long as possible.

3. SECTORAL ANALYSIS OF JOB CREATION POTENTIAL

According to recent CE research and policy reports, it may generally lead to increased well-being, employment, and economic prosperity. In a recent report by

WRAP (UK), for instance (Morgan & Mitchell, 2015a; Morgan & Mitchell, 2015b), the CE could create 3 million extra jobs and reduce unemployment by 520,000 in EU member states by 2030 (including job offsets in other sectors). On the other hand, mechanisation or automation may replace jobs or restrict job creation, rendering some vocations obsolete in the future (Frey & Osborne, 2017). In general, studies that analyse the net employment effects of renewable energy and energy efficiency, such as those by Blyth et al. (2014) and Meyer and Sommer (2014), often indicate a positive net employment benefit from such an energy transition. When the direct and indirect employment benefits are generally positive, the induced effects may be either positive or negative (Mu et al., 2018). On balance, the CE has a greater potential to produce new jobs in the energy, manufacturing, and service sectors. This chapter identifies the following five sectors as having significant potential for circular economic development:

a. Manufacturing.

South Africa's manufacturing sector is one of the country's largest employers, with over 1.6 million employees as of Q3 2025 (Writer, 2025). The Sector is the fourth-largest contributor to GDP, comprising a diverse range of sub-sectors that depend on various resources and materials. According to Stats SA (2018), the largest contributors include food and beverages (26%), petroleum and chemical products (24%), basic iron and steel (19%), and wood, paper, and printing (11%). Other notable sub-sectors are motor vehicles and parts (7%), glass and non-metallic minerals (4%), textiles and clothing (3%), furniture and other manufactured products (3%), and electrical machinery (2%).

On the contrary, over the last few decades, South Africa's manufacturing sector has deteriorated in line with global trends; however, this has been exacerbated by a variety of other sectoral variables. a heavy reliance on the export of base metals and underutilised natural resources, a lack of demand for South African-made finished goods, bad policymaking, unstable energy supply, and a skilled workforce shortage. Given its mainly linear economic manufacturing method, the local manufacturing sector's long-term viability remains a challenge. These factors have exacerbated the underutilization of industrial sector capacity.

Production and consumption patterns must be altered systematically to enable efficient resource use, achieve long-term economic growth, preserve natural capital, and enhance social welfare. Hendrixson (2020) asserts that the circular economy heavily depends on additive manufacturing because no other production technique provides the same degree of design flexibility or the ability to operate in small, globally dispersed footprints with numerous localised supply chains. This approach has the potential to drastically change manufacturing, causing producers, designers, inventors, and even consumers to reevaluate what they produce, purchase, and utilise. However, the local manufacturing industry in South Africa continues to operate primarily on the linear 'take-make-dispose' economic model, which is plagued by high levels of waste, unsustainable production and consumption patterns, and an excessive demand for resources (Nahman et al., 2021).

The UNEP study on remanufacturing (IRP, 2018) advocates for a revolution in production and consumption, moving from resource-intensive models to low-carbon, efficient processes, with innovation serving as a catalyst for change. Remanufacturing and refurbishing are rigorous, systematic industrial operations that offer the possibility of adding value and extending a product's service life. Repair, refurbishment, and direct reuse are examples of maintenance operations that often occur outside industrial facilities, allowing items to be used for longer periods. Given their contribution to climate goals, the report views these activities as critical to achieving the Sustainable Development Goals, particularly Goal 12: Sustainable Consumption and Production.

b. Waste Management

The Circular Economy (CE), focused on preventing waste creation and reducing waste throughout a resource's value chain, has become a key component of South Africa's National Waste Management Strategy. Godfrey & Oelofse (2017) claim that over the past 40–50 years, South Africa has developed a relatively successful materials recycling industry, covering metals, plastics, paper, and other materials. The National Cleaner Production Centre (NCPC-SA) has also promoted Resource Efficiency and Cleaner Production programs in the manufacturing sector for the past two decades. Additionally, renewable energy technologies have gained momentum in response to load shedding, climate commitments, and supportive policies (NCPC-SA, 2020). Despite these efforts, approximately 107 million tonnes of general waste are generated in South Africa (DFFE, 2020), of which around 90% (84 million tonnes) are sent to landfills or stockpiles. The country is rapidly running out of landfill space due to increasing waste generation and a lack of circular economy and waste-to-resource initiatives. Construction and demolition (C&D) waste is one of the largest waste streams by weight in South Africa, yet it has not been prioritised for recycling or landfill diversion efforts. The waste and recycling industry generated sales revenue of more than £6.5 billion from collection, treatment, disposal, recycling and wholesale of recovered materials, and it employed around 75,000 people.

In South Africa, waste refers to any unwanted, discarded, or legally classified material, encompassing substances from various sectors (Godfrey & Oelofse, 2008). Nevertheless, when a waste stream can be reused, recycled, or recovered, it ceases to be waste and becomes an economic resource. For example, South Africa's primary manufacturers of plastic raw materials are Sasol Polymers and Safripol, supplemented by imports from companies such as Dow Chemicals. In 2018, the nation produced 1.27 million tonnes of virgin plastic, exported 582,000 tonnes, consumed 688,000 tonnes domestically, and imported 856,000 tonnes (WWF SA, 2020). Annually, South Africa generates approximately 2.4 million tonnes of plastic waste, but only 14% of this is recycled. Multilayer plastics (MIC) are seldom recycled due to their high costs and technical challenges. Additionally, recycled plastic faces difficulty competing in the local market because virgin and imported plastics are more affordable (WWF SA, 2020). Moreover, the plastics industry is primarily driven by the packaging sector, which accounts for 52% of the domestic market. The building and construction sector accounts for 13%, and the agricultural sector comprises an additional 8% (PlasticsSA, 2021).

Glass accounts for roughly 4.9% (2.7 million tonnes) of the total waste produced in South Africa (Green Cape, 2022). Glass constitutes about 4.5% of commercial and industrial waste. The primary categories of glass waste in South Africa include packaging glass, such as bottles and jars, and flat or sheet glass, including windows, windscreens, and mirrors (Green Cape, 2022).

Millar et al. (2019) argued that the circular economy cannot achieve environmental sustainability with current technology because certain types of waste cannot be broken down or reused within existing infrastructure. Therefore, from an environmental standpoint, there is a need to foster innovation and upgrade infrastructure to support the development of a circular economy.

Despite these challenges, businesses tend to favour promoting the circular economy, as it encourages innovation and aims to decouple economic growth from resource dependency, a characteristic of the linear economy. In the long term, adopting circular economy principles can help mitigate the risks associated with resource depletion and evolve into a more sustainable development model, whether in the strict sense of sustainable development or from an environmental sustainability perspective (Millar et al., 2019). This raises an additional question: how could these driving factors be applied to the circular economy in South Africa?

c. Water sector

South Africa is a semi-arid country facing water scarcity, with a climate marked by alternating wet and dry periods, including droughts and floods. It ranks among the 30 driest countries globally, with highly variable, unpredictable rainfall and an average annual precipitation of about 460 mm—less than half the global average (DEA, 2011). South Africa's water supplies are under increasing strain due to rising demand for development and socio-economic change. Following a similar line of reasoning, Idrica (2023) suggests that climate change exacerbates water scarcity, causes droughts and floods, and affects all sectors that rely on water. Furthermore, the key challenges confronting the water sector include a lack of prioritisation, insufficient resources, public perception issues, financial limitations, limited awareness of the circular economy, absence of monitoring, compliance, and enforcement, inadequate government support, and corruption.

Due to increasing pressure on our water resources, there is expected to be growing interest in digital technologies and alternative water sources, such as wastewater reuse, decentralisation, and desalination, to optimise water supply management (StartUsInsight, 2023). Reusing water is recognised as an effective way to increase water availability and address severe water shortages. In this context, Saporiti & Robins (2021) argue that water recycling can serve as an important water source for major companies in countries with scarce water resources, such as South Africa. Furthermore, South Africa's water sector, currently reliant on linear approaches, needs to transition to a more resilient, circular water economy where waste and pollution are minimised, water is reused continuously, and natural ecosystems are restored (Mauter & Fiske, 2020). However, Kalebaile et al. (2020) observed that the slow adoption of water reuse in South Africa is due to a complex combination of technological, economic, and socio-political factors. They also highlight that those socio-political factors play a much more significant role in obstructing the broad implementation of planned water reuse.

d. Construction

The construction industry in South Africa offers an opportunity to advance a circular economy by repurposing waste materials for new building projects. The construction sector in South Africa presents a significant opportunity to advance the circular economy by repurposing waste materials in new building projects. According to the Department of Environmental Affairs (DEA) (2012), the country generated approximately 108 million tonnes of waste in 2011, of which 98 million tonnes were disposed of in landfills. Of the total waste produced, an estimated 59 million tonnes (55%) was general waste, 48 million tonnes (44%) remained unclassified at the time, and about 1 million tonnes (1%) was identified as hazardous waste. Only around 10% of the waste generated in 2011 was recycled (DEA, 2012). Similarly, construction and demolition waste accounts for a significant share of South Africa's waste, amounting to 8.1% of total waste generation (DEA, 2018).

For the construction industry, bio-based building materials such as hemp, straw, and wood offer sustainable alternatives. These materials can be responsibly grown, are renewable, and have the added advantage of storing carbon. They provide viable substitutes for conventional materials like steel and cement-based products, which require mining, generate substantial carbon emissions, and produce significant waste. Interest in bio-based materials is growing in South Africa, leading to broader consideration of timber in construction and the development of the world's tallest industrial hemp building, a 12-storey structure located in Cape Town (Bourdin, 2023). Furthermore, Gibberd (2024) asserts that to reduce waste, buildings should be carefully dismantled to rescue and reuse materials and components rather than demolishing structures and sending the rubbish to landfills.

Repurposing materials and products from demolished structures helps keep waste out of landfills and conserves valuable resources. This approach also reduces the use of new resources, minimises transportation-related impacts, and lowers energy consumption by decreasing the need for new building materials. Moreover, reusing construction materials can encourage local business development and generate new job opportunities. While material reuse is common in the informal sector, it is still relatively rare in the formal construction industry. A notable example is the Tsoga Environmental Centre, which incorporated a substantial quantity of reclaimed materials, including reused bricks, into its design (ARG Design, 2024).

e. Energy Sector

Energy plays a significant role in the South African economy, encompassing liquid fuels and electricity. The sector's substantial resource intensity stems from its reliance on coal as the predominant energy source for most operations. Currently, renewable energy sources contribute only 14% to the nation's electricity generation, while coal and thermal power plants account for approximately 80% of the total output (Pierce & Le Roux, 2023). According to SAWEA (2023), the country possesses significant renewable energy resources, especially in onshore wind and solar power. While there are initiatives to expand the use of renewable energy, integrating these sources into the power grid presents certain challenges. One challenge confronting South Africa's energy sector is the availability of water, as previously mentioned. Water is a crucial resource for generating electricity, especially in coal-fired power plants, which require substantial water for cooling.

Since 2012, South Africa has made considerable progress in implementing renewable energy through the government's Renewable Energy Independent Power Producer Procurement Programme (REIPPPP), which has attracted significant investment, primarily in wind and solar energy. By 2021, renewable energy accounted for approximately 13.7% of the nation's electricity generation, with over 6,000 MW of installed capacity (Eskom, 2021b; IPP Office, 2021).

Figure 3. Anaerobic digestion energy value chain.

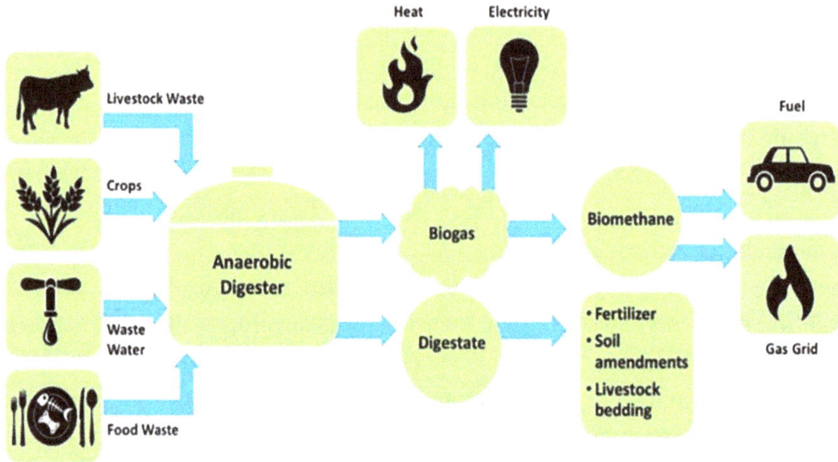

Source: Tanigawa (2017)

Figure 3 illustrates the anaerobic digestion process, which converts various types of organic waste into valuable energy and agricultural products. Materials such as animal manure, crop residues, wastewater, and food scraps are introduced into an anaerobic digester, where microbes decompose the waste in the absence of oxygen. This process generates two main products: biogas and digestate. Biogas, primarily composed of methane, can be used directly to generate heat and electricity or refined into biomethane. This biomethane can then be fed into the gas network or used as a renewable fuel for vehicles. The other product, digestate, is a nutrient-rich substance that can be used as fertiliser, to enhance soil quality, or as bedding for animals. In summary, the value chain shown highlights how anaerobic digestion promotes a circular economy by converting organic waste into renewable energy and beneficial agricultural materials, thereby minimising environmental impact and generating economic benefits.

4. SOCIOECONOMIC BENEFITS OF CIRCULAR JOBS

According to Hergovich and Paprsek (2015), energy efficiency measures are projected to have a favourable impact on net employment, as they increase income, enabling individuals to purchase more products and services. UNEP (2011) and the World Bank (2012) broaden the notion by including a significant social component.

They describe a green economy as one that improves human well-being and social fairness while significantly lowering environmental dangers and ecological scarcity. In its most fundamental form, a green economy is low-carbon, resource-efficient, and socially inclusive (EEA, 2014). Conversely, in certain situations, the linear economic model proves to be extremely wasteful, inefficient, and expensive. For example, air pollution decreases productivity in both the short and long term by reducing available working hours and damaging workers' health. It also exacerbates gender inequality, as women frequently act as caregivers for dependent children affected by these conditions. The International Labour Organisation (ILO) reports that "between 2000 and 2015, an average of 23 million working years were lost annually due to various environmental hazards caused or intensified by human activities" (ILO, 2018).

5. SKILL DEVELOPMENT AND EDUCATION

Researchers like Moreno-Mondejar et al. (2021) and Martínez-del-Río et al. (2012) et al. indicate that participating in circular economy initiatives leads companies to substantially change their human resource management. This is because such practices are typically complex and require advanced skills, which can be developed through comprehensive training or by hiring employees with greater technical expertise. In this instance, local governments also play a key role in integrating skills and environmental policy. In countries such as China, France, the Republic of Korea, the United Kingdom and the United States, local governments integrate skills needs into policy formulation and implementation, due to their familiarity with the regional economy and labour market (ILO, 2018, p. 134). Some countries have successfully integrated skills development into environmental policy, particularly in key priority sectors such as renewable energy and energy efficiency. Policies and programs on skills for the green transition tend to adopt a sectoral approach (ILO, 2018, p. 129).

Sitra recognises that knowledge, skills and training will be challenges in moving towards a circular economy (Sitra, 2016, p. 46). Countries such as Denmark, Estonia, France, Germany, India, the Republic of Korea, the Philippines and South Africa have environmental policies and national development strategies that reference skills development for the green transition (ILO, 2018b, p. 133). Many countries have not identified the skills required for a transition towards a circular economy, as they lack the capacity to collect this data (ILO, 2018, . 4), and training to upgrade skills tends to be short-term and fragmented (ILO, 2018).

6. CHALLENGES IN CIRCULAR JOB CREATION

Recycling is a crucial component of the circular economy, creating significant employment opportunities. Workers in the recycling industry are responsible for collecting, sorting, processing, and converting waste materials into valuable products. These positions encompass both physical labour and sophisticated technology jobs. Furthermore, it is essential to note that the recycling sector is continually evolving, with new technologies and processes being introduced to enhance efficiency and performance. This demands a team trained to operate and maintain advanced recycling gear. As recycling rates increase and technology advances, the demand for experienced professionals in this industry is expected to grow.

Circular economy practices hold significant potential to reshape the labour market by creating green jobs, fostering resilience, and driving sustainable growth. The employment implications of environmental product improvements remain theoretically vague. It is equally important to recognise the difficulties linked to recycling, such as contamination of recyclable materials and the need for improved infrastructure. For example, in 2009, China enacted a law to promote the circular economy, emphasising resource reduction, reuse, and recycling, supported by a development strategy and action plan from 2011 to 2015. The law does not address employment or job effects, and experts suggest that, in China, the circular economy is more of a subject of interest than a concrete action goal (Sitra, 2016, p. 43).

On the one hand, such inventions can increase demand for a company's products by entering new markets or replacing competitors' offerings, thereby positively impacting the firm's employment. At the macroeconomic level, however, the overall effect is uncertain and depends, among other factors, on the labour intensity of the products being replaced. Negative employment effects may also occur if the new product leads to a monopolistic position, ultimately reducing total output (Hall et al., 2006). Overcoming these challenges will necessitate investment in education, training, and technology to ensure that the recycling industry can continue to create jobs and support a more sustainable economy.

7. POLICY AND BUSINESS STRATEGIES FOR GREEN EMPLOYMENT GROWTH

Existing business prospects in the circular economy are primarily found in expanding current operations in the field. One justification for government action is that existing taxation is mostly based on labour income. Labour, considered a renewable factor input, is unfairly taxed in many industrialised countries compared to material and non-renewable inputs, according to economists specialising in resources and labour markets. They advocate shifting the tax burden away from labour and income and toward non-renewable resource use. Furthermore, repairing, refurbishing, disassembling, and remanufacturing products all demand skilled manual labour. However, employers are required to pay substantial payroll taxes and Social Security contributions for each new employee. For circular-economy businesses, this results in a financial disadvantage when they try to act in an environmentally responsible way.

Equally, circularity will develop as a grassroots movement in reaction to growing resource costs and market uncertainty. However, encouraging and supporting entrepreneurship and venture capital will speed the adoption of innovative goods and business models. Improving the education of future entrepreneurs, designers, chemical and industrial engineers, procurement officers, and product managers will be critical to completely rethinking and transforming the current system. In this context, it can be argued that the circular start-up ecosystem can foster technological innovation that supports both economic growth and sustainability (Henry et al., 2021). Henry and colleagues (2021) note that circular start-ups often focus on rapid scaling more than sustainability-oriented entrepreneurs who do not implement circular principles. However, large hyper-scale circular companies remain rare. Still, circular start-ups hold significant potential for promoting sustainability on a broad scale.

Reike et al. (2018) compared the successes of the circular economy in developed countries with those in developing countries. Policies implemented in developed countries to achieve circularity have improved waste recycling by an average of 46%. In developing countries, there is a much greater reliance on informal recycling, which yields less than 3%, particularly in Brazil and South Africa. Further research is needed to determine how developing countries can increase the adoption of circular principles. A lack of public awareness is a significant issue. As is widely recognised, transitioning from traditional, linear economic models to circular ones demands substantial changes in business operations, consumer habits, and societal mindsets.

Additionally, in South Africa and many other developing nations, public acceptance of circular economy principles remains low. Therefore, we believe that altering consumer behaviour and encouraging sustainable consumption necessitate comprehensive education and awareness initiatives. Another challenge is the inadequate infrastructure. Although some progress has been made in recent years through a few companies and startups, South Africa's recycling infrastructure remains underdeveloped, hindering the implementation of more effective circular economy practices. Finally, the high cost of recycling poses a significant obstacle. In many industries, the upfront investment required for recycling infrastructure and technology is substantial, posing a major barrier given the country's limited financial resources.

8. CONCLUSION

Embracing circular economy principles supports sustainable development, preserves natural resources, and generates new economic opportunities. Implementing these principles enables efficient resource use through practices such as recycling, reusing, and minimising waste. This approach encourages reducing waste, reusing materials, and increasing the volume of recyclable resources. Growing populations, along with rising demand from infrastructure, industry, and consumers, are increasing the need for materials, water, and energy. Circular economy methods can help fulfil a large portion of this demand by slowing or even stopping the rise in resource consumption. By adopting these practices, organisations can help prevent resource depletion, climate change, and environmental pollution. A circular economy reduces dependence on resources and their consumption, including energy, which helps lower production costs, decrease market risks, and cut expenses related to resource extraction and manufacturing. It also fosters the creation of cost-effective solutions to reduce pollution and separate hazardous waste from reusable materials. Unfortunately, developing countries such as South Africa often lack the expertise needed to implement resource-efficiency strategies.

The benefits of the circular economy extend beyond individual companies to entire industries and even whole national economies. It fosters cooperation and synergy among businesses, resulting in improved economic, social, and environmental outcomes. As a result, this improves the overall performance of national economies and generates new markets and job opportunities. Moving towards a circular economy provides both environmental sustainability and economic advantages. By emphasising job creation, this chapter demonstrates how circular practices can help reduce unemployment, promote economic inclusion, and support the green transformation of labour markets. It also offers practical recommendations for policymakers and businesses to fully harness the potential of green jobs. For example, most research on circular and green economies has so far concentrated mainly on the environmental and business benefits of improved resource efficiency. The circular economy presents a unique chance to shift towards a deliberate, well-planned, fair, and socially inclusive model. To ensure sustainable reinvestment, researchers should focus on policies that balance environmental, economic, and social objectives, rather than prioritising economic growth alone.

REFERENCES

Blyth, W., Gross, R., Speirs, J., Sorrell, S., Nicholls, J., Dorgan, A., & Hughes, N. 2014. Low Carbon Jobs: the Evidence for Net Job Creation from Policy Support for Energy Efficiency and Renewable Energy. Retrieved from https://www.sciencedirect.com/science/article/pii/S0301421519306342?ref=pdf_download&fr=RR-2&rr=9a7aeb128ff541e2

Bonciu, F. (2020). Is Circular Economy Compatible With Capitalism? *Romanian Economic Business Review, Romanian-American University*, *15*(1), 16–30.

Bourdin, J. (2023). World's tallest 'hemp hotel' to open in Cape Town. Retrieved from: https://mg.co.za/news/2023-05-08-worlds-tallest-hemp-hotel-to-open-in-cape-town/

DEA (Department of Environmental Affairs). (2012). *National Waste Management Strategy*. Department of Environmental Affairs.

DEA (Department of Environmental Affairs). (2018). *South Africa state of waste report. A report on the state of the environment.* Department of Environmental Affairs.

Design, A. R. G. (2024). Architectural Projects, Tsoga Environmental Centre. Retrieved from: https://argdesign.co.za/tsoga.html

DFFE. (2020). National Waste Management Strategy. Retrieved from https://www.dffe.gov.za/sites/default/files/docs/nationalwaste_management_strategy.pdf

Ellen Macarthur Foundation. (2020), The Circular Economy in Detail. Retrieved from https://www.ellenmacarthurfoundation.org/explore/the-circular-economy-indetail

Ellen MacArthur Foundation (EMF). 2013. Towards the Circular Economy, vol. 1 (Isle of Wight). Retrieved from https://www.ellenmacarthurfoundation.org/towards-the-circular-economy-vol-1-an-economic-and-business-rationale-for-an

European Environment Agency (EEA). (2014): Resource-efficient green economy and EU policies EEA Report No 2/2014, Luxembourg. Retrieved from https://www.eea.europa.eu/en/analysis/publications/resourceefficient-green-economy-and-eu

Frey, C.B., Osborne, M.A. (2017). The future of employment: how susceptible are jobs to computerisation? Technol. Forecast. Soc. Chang. Retrieved from https://doi.org/.DOI: 10.1016/j.techfore.2016.08.019

Green Cape. (2022). Waste market intelligence. Retrieved from: https://greencape.co.za/assets/WASTE_MIR_7_4_22_FINAL.pdf

Hall, B. H., Lotti, F., Mairesse, J. (2006): Employment, Innovation and Productivity: Evidence from Italian Microdata. The Institute for Fiscal Studies. Working Paper 24/2006, London

Henry, M., Hoogenstrijd, T., Kirchherr, J. (2021). The rise of the circular entrepreneur: an altruistic spirit and the pursuit of mass-market expansion. Circ. Econ. 127–148. Retrieved from https://doi.org/.DOI: 10.4324/9780367816650-9

Hergovich, S., & Paprsek, M. (2015). Tapping the job potential of green investments in Europe. In Galg'oczi, B. (Ed.), *Europe's Energy Transformation in the Austerity Trap*. ETUI., Retrieved from https://books.google.co.za/books?hl=en&lr=&id=X00oCwAAQBAJ&oi=fnd&pg=PA141&ots=OUHq3e6X9J&sig=WdzzAZTxjBdlHHXFZo1QDAnv8vQ&redir_esc=y#v=onepage&q&f=false

Horbach, J., & Rammer, C. (2019). Employment and performance effects of circular economy innovations, ZEW Discussion Papers, No. 19-016, ZEW - Leibniz-Zentrum für Europäische Wirtschaftsforschung, Mannheim. Retrieved from https://www.econstor.eu/bitstream/10419/196125/1/1664582509.pdf

Idrica (2023). Water trends in water reuse for 2023: Water, from waste to resources. Retrieved fromhttps://www.idrica.com/blog/water-trends-in-water-reuse-for-2023-water-from-waste-to-resource/

International Labour Organization. (2018). World employment and social outlook 2018: Greening with jobs. Retrieved from https://www.ilo.org/wesogreening/documents/WESO_Greening_EN_web2.pdf

IRP. (2018). Re-defining Value – The Manufacturing Revolution. Remanufacturing, Refurbishment, Repair and Direct Reuse in the Circular Economy. Nabil Nasr, Jennifer Russell, Stefan Bringezu, Stefanie Hellweg, Brian Hilton, Cory Kreiss, & Nadia von Gries. A Report of the International Resource Panel. United Nations Environment Programme, Nairobi, Kenya. Retrieved from https://www.resourcepanel.org/sites/default/files/documents/document/media/re-defining_value_-_the_manfacturing_revolution_full_report_for_web.pdf

IWMSA (Institute of Waste Management of Southern Africa). (2019). See not waste, but opportunity on Global Recycling Day. Retrieved from https://cct.mycpd.co.za/IWMSA/IWMSA_Global%20Recycling%20Day%20release_20190308_FINAL.pdf

Kalebaile, N., Ncube, E., Swartz, C., Marais, S., & Lubbe, J. (2020). *Strengthening the implementation of water reuse in South Africa*. Water Research Commission., Retrieved from https://www.wrc.org.za/wp-content/uploads/mdocs/WW%20Sept-Oct%202022_WATER%20REUSE.pdf

Korhonen, J., Honkasalo, A., & Seppälä, J. (2018). Circular economy: The concept and its limitations. *Ecological Economics, 143*, 37–46. DOI: 10.1016/j.ecolecon.2017.06.041

Lacy, P., & Rutqvist, J. (2016). Waste to Wealth: the Circular Economy Advantage, Waste to Wealth: the Circular Economy Advantage.

Lovins, A., & Michael, B. (2014). *A New Dynamic - Effective Business in a Circular Economy, the Business Angle of a Circular Economy – Higher Competitiveness.* Higher Resource Security and Material Efficiency.

Martínez-del-Río, J., Céspedes-Lorente, J., & Carmona-Moreno, E. (2012). High-involvement work practices and environmental capabilities: How HIWPS create environmentally based sustainable competitive advantages. *Human Resource Management, 51*(6), 827–850. DOI: 10.1002/hrm.21505

Mauter, M. S., & Fiske, P. S. (2020). Desalination for a circular water economy. [United Kingdom.]. *Energy & Environmental Science*, •••, 13.

Meyer, I., & Sommer, M. W. (2014). Employment Effects of Renewable Energy Supply A Meta Analysis Employment Effects of Renewable Energy Supply-A Meta Analysis 1–2. Retrieved from https://www.wifo.ac.at/wp-content/uploads/upload2151/sw_2014_WWWforEurope_PP12_47225_-1.pdf

Mihelcic, J. R., Crittenden, J. C., Small, M. J., Shonnard, D. R., Hokanson, D. R., Qiong, Z. H., Sheryla, S., Valentineu, J., Sutherland, J. W., & Schnoor, J. L. (2003). Sustainability science and engineering: The emergence of a new meta discipline. *Environmental Science & Technology, 37*(23), 5314–5324. DOI: 10.1021/es034605h PMID: 14700315

Millar, N., McLaughlin, E., & Börger, T. (2019). The circular economy: Swings and roundabouts? *Ecological Economics, 158*, 11–19. DOI: 10.1016/j.ecolecon.2018.12.012

Moreno-Mondejar, L., Triguero, Á., & Cuerva, M. C. (2021). Exploring the association between circular economy strategies and green jobs in European companies. *Journal of Environmental Management, 297*, 297. DOI: 10.1016/j.jenvman.2021.113437 PMID: 34351301

Morgan, J., & Mitchell, P. (2015a). Opportunities to Tackle Britain's Labour Market Challenges through Growth in the Circular Economy. Retrieved from https://green-alliance.org.uk/wp-content/uploads/2021/12/Opportunities-to-tackle-UK-Labour-Market-Challenges_sgl.pdf

Morgan, J., & Mitchell, P. (2015 b). Employment and the Circular Economy. Job Creation in a More Resource Efficient Britain, vol. 28. Retrieved from https://ecointelligentgrowth.net/wp-content/uploads/2015/02/Employment-and-the-circular-economy-summary.pdf

Mu, Y., Cai, W., Evans, S., Wang, C., & Roland-Holst, D. (2018). Employment impacts of renewable energy policies in China: A decomposition analysis based on a CGE modeling framework. *Applied Energy*, *210*, 256–267. DOI: 10.1016/j.apenergy.2017.10.086

Nahman, A., Godfrey, L., Oelofse, S., & Trotter, D. (2021). Driving economic growth in South Africathrough a low carbon, sustainable and inclusive circular economy, Pretoria: CSIR. Retrieved from http://circulareconomy.co.za/wpcontent/uploads/2021/11/1.-Introduction-CE-BriefingNote.pdf

NCPC-SA. (2020). Annual Report 2020-2021. NCPC: Pretoria. Retrieved from https://www.industrialefficiency.co.za/wpcontent/uploads/2022/01/Annual-Highlights-2020-21.pdf

OECD. (2019). *Global Material Resources Outlook to 2060: Economic Drivers and Environmental Consequences*. OECD Publishing., DOI: 10.1787/9789264307452-

OECD. (2019). Business Models for the Circular Economy: Opportunities and Challenges for Policy. Retrieved from https://www.oecd.org/en/publications/business-models-for-the-circular-economy_g2g9dd62-en.html

Oelofse, S. H. H., & Godfrey, L. (2008). Defining waste in South Africa: Moving beyond the age of 'waste'. *South African Journal of Science*, *104*(7-8), 242–246.

Plastics, S. A. (2021). An analysis of the South African plastics industry data. Retrieved from https://www.plasticsinfo.co.za/wp-content/uploads/2022/12/Plastics-2021-Exec-Summary-30-Nov.pdf

Reike, D., Vermeulen, W. J., & Witjes, S. (2018). The circular economy: New or refurbished as CE 3.0? — Exploring controversies in the conceptualisation of the circular economy through a focus on history and resource value retention options. *Resources, Conservation and Recycling*, *135*, 246–264. DOI: 10.1016/j.resconrec.2017.08.027

REPORTDEA (Department of Environmental Affairs). (2011). South Africa's second national communication under the United Nations Framework Convention on Climate Change. Republic of South Africa, Pretoria.

Saporiti, N., & Robins, E. (2021). Scaling up water reuse: why recycling our water makes sense. Retrieved from https://blogs.worldbank.org/en/climatechange/scaling-water-reuse-why-recycling-our-wastewater-makes-sense

StartUs Insight. (2023). Top 8 water management trends and innovations in 2023. Retrieved from https://www.startus-insights.com/innovators-guide/water-management-trends/

Stats, S. A. (2018). Manufacturing: Production and Sales. Statistical Release P3041.2. Retrieved from http://www.statssa.gov.za/publications/P30412/P30412December2018.pdf

Su'arez-Eiroa, B., Fern'andez, E., M'endez-Martínez, G., & Soto-O˜nate, D. (2019). Operational principles of circular economy for sustainable development: Linking theory and practice. *Journal of Cleaner Production*, *214*, 952–961. DOI: 10.1016/j.jclepro.2018.12.271

The Finnish Innovative Fund Sitra. (2016). Leading the cycle: Finnish roadmap to a circular economy 2016–2025. Retrieved from https://www.sitra.fi/en/publications/leading-cycle

UNEP. (2011): Towards a Green Economy: Pathways to Sustainable Development and Poverty Eradication, Nairobi. Retrieved from https://sustainabledevelopment.un.org/index.php?page=view&type=400&nr=126&menu=35

Winans, K., Kendall, A., & Deng, H. (2017). The history and current applications of the circular economy concept. *Renewable & Sustainable Energy Reviews*, *68*, 825–833. DOI: 10.1016/j.rser.2016.09.123

World Bank. (2012): Inclusive Green Growth. The Pathway to Sustainable Development, Washington. Retrieved from https://siteresources.worldbank.org/EXTSDNET/Resources/Inclusive_Green_Growth_May_2012.pdf

Writer, S. (2025). One of South Africa's biggest employers under siege. Retrieved from https://businesstech.co.za/news/business/845144/one-of-south-africas-biggest-employers-under-siege/

WWF SA. (2020). Plastics: Facts and Futures- Moving Beyond Pollution Management Towards a Circular Plastics Economy in South Africa. Retrieved from https://wwfafrica.awsassets.panda.org/downloads/wwf_plastics_report_final_2nov2020.pdf

Zhai, J. (2020). BIM-Based Building Circularity Assessment from the Early Design Stages. Eindhoven University of Technology. Retrieved from https://pure.tue.nl/ws/portalfiles/portal/165207093/Zhai_1311514.pdf

Chapter 13
The Role and Impact of Local Economic Development Agencies on Poverty and Unemployment Reduction in South Africa

Ndwakhulu Stephen Tshishonga
http://orcid.org/0000-0002-4918-3552
University of KwaZulu-Natal, South Africa

Vukani Urthur Gumede
University of KwaZulu-Natal, South Africa

ABSTRACT

This chapter examines Local Economic Development Agencies (LEDAs) as a strategy for reducing poverty and unemployment in South Africa, focusing on Enterprise iLembe in KwaZulu-Natal. It argues that LEDAs promote inclusive economic development by integrating previously excluded communities into local economies through support for Small, Medium and Micro Enterprises (SMMEs), investment promotion, and strategic partnerships. A qualitative approach based on stakeholder interviews was used in this chapter. The findings show that LEDA initiatives created more than 18,000 jobs and indirectly benefited over 126,000 people, particularly in agriculture, manufacturing, tourism, and construction. However, the chapter also highlights challenges such as limited funding, resource constraints, and inadequate monitoring and evaluation systems. It concludes that although LEDAs are effective

DOI: 10.4018/979-8-2600-3325-8.ch013

instruments for local economic development, their long-term sustainability depends on improved funding models, stronger institutional support, and comprehensive performance assessment frameworks..

INTRODUCTORY BACKGROUND

In South Africa, the twin challenges of poverty and unemployment remain a persistent problem, with 30.4 million persons living in poverty in 2015 (Stats SA, 2017) and 32.6% of the population, or 7.8 million persons, unemployed in the second quarter of 2021 (Stats SA, QLFS; Q2, 2021; the Presidency, 2019). The unemployment rate among black Africans (36.7%) population group remains higher than the national average and other population groups (Stats SA, QLFS; Q1:2021: 25). Attempts to uproot poverty and unemployment in particular saw the introduction of various programmes such as the Rural Sustainable Development Programme (ISRDP), the Urban Renewal Programme (URP), A National Poverty Relief Programme, Expanded Public Works Programme (EPWP) and Community Work Programmes (CWP). The EPWP and CWPs (see Khan, 2010; Tshishonga & Matsiliza, 2021; and the Presidency, 2014). The aim of EPWP and CWP was to provide short-term safety nets for the unemployed, semi-skilled and unskilled citizens (Tshishonga & Matsiliza, 2021). Both programmes had limited successes because participants could not sustain themselves even after gaining skills and training in agriculture that could enable them to start their own gardens and open vegetable stalls (Kobedi, 2021, p. 8). On the other hand, these programmes suffered from a plethora of challenges ranging from lack of active participation of the unemployed and host communities, poor coordination, inadequate infrastructure and resources to run the programmes effectively, as well as limited access to resources, assets and skills that can be jointly used to sustain the economy (Tshishonga & Matsiliza, 2021). For Tshishonga and Matsiliza (2021), the interface of poverty, unemployment and inequality not only undermines South Africa's potential to become a developmental state, but also perpetuates the skewed distribution of resources for economic development. These challenges persist despite the policy and programme interventions introduced by the African National Congress (ANC)-led democratic government.

Legislative frameworks such as the Constitution of the Republic of South Africa (1996) and the White Paper on Local Government (1998) were used to create an enabling environment for municipalities to operate. This was further reiterated by Masuku, Jili and Selepe (2016:2), who add that local governments have an essential role in creating favourable environments for business success and job creation. Importantly, Meyer (2013) pointed out that to achieve dynamic local development, all aspects of local communities, including the economy, social, welfare, environmental, and political issues, need to be addressed in an integrated and holistic manner. Although municipalities have a developmental role to play, implementing LED initiatives has become difficult because local authorities lack the capacity and understanding to do so (Ackron & Auriacombe, 2016).

In 2012, the KZN Cabinet Lekgotla resolved to establish LEDAs (UMEDA, 2016) due to their location within a local governance space. LEDAs are well-positioned to address local governance challenges and opportunities, and they are also well-located to offer flexible, participatory, and widely tested local governance instruments for reducing poverty and for proximity to the private sector (Rogerson, 2018). LEDAs were thus rooted in engaging in social dialogue (Khambule, 2015), while Nene (2015) supports local innovation, and Mncwabe (2008) supports skills development for Local Economic Development (LED) as a poverty alleviation tool.

However, the assessment of LEDAs has not extended beyond project beneficiaries; hence, no study has examined how LEDA activities contribute to poverty and unemployment reduction. Therefore, this study assesses the role and impact of LEDAs on poverty and unemployment reduction, with particular focus on the iLembe District Municipality in the KwaZulu-Natal Province, South Africa. The iLembe District Municipality consists of four (4) local municipalities, namely: KwaDukuza Local Municipality, Mandeni Local Municipality, Maphumulo Local Municipality, and Ndwedwe Local Municipality. The iLembe District lies between King Cetshwayo District Municipality in the north and eThekwini Metropolitan City in the south, and is bordered by UMgungundlovu District Municipality and UMzinyathi District Municipality.

LITERATURE REVIEW

Conceptualised Framing of Key Terms

Local Economic Development (LED):

There are numerous definitions of Local Economic Development (LED), with no single one unanimously accepted as the common denominator with similar characteristics (Pavel & Moldovan, 2019, p. 2; Ndlovu, 2021). These characteristics are territory-based on the development of a particular region or a locality in which people live. External stakeholders, such as the private and non-governmental sectors, are encouraged to participate through LED approaches that empower the local community for the future. The second characteristic pertains to participation as a core to LED's success. Various stakeholders which include the public and the private sectors and the community (Kanayo et al., 2021) are encouraged to work together since they come with different expertise like local knowledge from the community, the private sector with LED technical experience and skills like accessing funding (writing business plans) and government for development facilitation to achieve local economic development potential of employment creation and economic growth to reduce the twin challenges of poverty and unemployment (Dyosi, 2016). The service delivery triangle is the most favoured LED and is encouraged by the performance of LEDAs in local government. Participation involves all stakeholders concerned in the locality sharing a common goal or vision. Akudugu and Laube (2013), in Selepe et al. (2016), confirm that LED becomes more effective when local stakeholders and authorities partner with national planning agencies and international donors to jointly design and implement initiatives to improve the local economy. Eroglu (2020:56) asserts that developing co-operation between the public, private, and NGO sectors of the region to achieve regional development goals and promote the region's business and investment opportunities at the national and international levels. LED is a multi-faceted concept with various connotations that seeks to address local challenges to achieve sustained development and poverty alleviation (Mashamaite & Lethoko, 2018, p. 118).

LED is about local people taking control and responsibility for job growth and the economic well-being of their community, thereby reducing poverty (Masuku, Jili & Selepe, 2016). LED emerged as the process through which public, business and non-governmental sector partners can work collectively to create better conditions for economic growth and employment generation (Wekwete, 2014; Nel & Rogerson, 2017). LED is also understood as an outcome-based, locally initiated, and stakeholder-driven approach that involves identifying and using local resources, ideas, and skills to stimulate economic growth and development. (Makhathini, Mlambo and Mpanza, 2020). Within government circles, LED is regarded as an adaptive and responsive process through which government, public sector entities, citizens, business, and non-governmental sector partners work collectively to create better conditions for innovation-driven, inclusive economic development (Mthimkhulu & Mpanza, 2021). Furthermore, Mthimkhulu and Mpanza (2021:28) argue that this process is characterised by knowledge transfer and competence building; employment generation; capacity development; investment attraction and retention; image enhancement and revenue generation in a local area to improve its economic future and the quality of life for all.

The LED method creates employment opportunities and enables poverty reduction (Agholor et al., 2021). LED is a tool for stimulating economic growth and alleviating poverty (Costa & Parker, 2016). Local Economic Development is the process of economic development at the local level in both developed and developing nations (Masikane, 2021). In South Africa, LED emerged during the political transition and was perceived as a strategy to include the majority of South Africans in the economy. Through LED, the public, businesses, and non-governmental sector partners create better conditions for economic growth and employment generation in a particular community. Masikane (2021) and Mncwabe (2013) argue that LED is an interdisciplinary field of study which encompasses physical planning, economics, and marketing. Quality-of-life improvements are achieved through the creation of job opportunities for local people, poverty alleviation, and the redistribution of resources and opportunities to the benefit of all residents (Mokoena, 2019).

The above definitions identify LED's core focus by emphasising concepts or elements of participation, locality, and economic growth. It can be deduced that LED is based on a bottom–up rather than a top-down approach. Dyosi (2016) re-affirms that LED cannot succeed without the involvement of the local community. LED contributes to the reduction of twin challenges of poverty and unemployment (Kanayo et al., 2020; Masuku et al., 2016; Costa & Parker, 2016). LED is a result of the failure of the top-down development approach to address local needs (Ateljevic et al., 2013; Rogerson, 2018). Therefore, a bottom-up development approach was adopted to decentralise development to local government and its constituencies. This is promoted worldwide (Ateljevic et al., 2013).

Table 1: Difference between Top-Down and Bottom–up Approaches

Top-Down Development Approach	Bottom-Up Development Approach
Decision-making is centralised	Decision-making decentralised
Development issues are administered centrally	Development issues are negotiated between social partners
Development is done through sectors	The locality is the main driver of development
Biasness towards established businesses	Biasness towards locality/territorial development
Incentives and financial assistance as investment attractors	Provision of infrastructure /basic services for easy access to economic activity

Source: Khambule (2015:48)

Conceptualising Local Economic Development Agencies (LEDAs)

There are very few definitions of LEDAs, yet there is a common understanding that they play an important role in addressing territorial LED challenges and building partnerships. LED is a programme well executed by LEDAs due to their skills, experience, and innovation. It is believed that Local Development Agencies (LDAs) play a leading role in LED and mobilising local resources (Ateljevic et al.,

2013). There are a few authors on LEDAs, although LEDAs began after the 2nd World War, around the 1950s (Pretorius & Blauuw, 2008). Hence, the definitions of LEDAs employed in this study are mainly drawn from Khambule (2019, 2020), Khambule & Gerwel-Proches (2019), and Lawrence and Rogerson (2019). In Europe, LEDAs were used for re-industrialisation, and in Mexico, they were used to re-industrialise cities facing economic decline. It was through international experience and institutional challenges at the local government level that LEDAs in South Africa have been used to implement projects to grow the economy, attract investment to the local area, and capacitate local communities. Unemployment and poverty are still crucial issues in South Africa (Herta, 2018).

LEDAs are structured organisations established at the local level to promote sustainable economic growth, local income, employment, and decent jobs (Eddine-Maliki et al., 2016). LEDAs are independent organisations, shaped by public and private institutions, to implement strategies of shared territorial development, with particular emphasis on expanding access to the most marginal portions of a population to opportunities for income and decent employment (Blaauw & Pretorius, 2008). LEDAs are institutional agents with the sole mandate to strengthen LED arrangements (Khambule & Gerwel-Proches, 2019).

SOUTH AFRICAN PERSPECTIVE ON LEDAS

Background of LEDAs

In South Africa, LEDAs were established during the new democratic dispensation with the hope of redressing past imbalances, such as creating equal access to the mainstream economy. The national government first enacted the National Development Agency Act No.108 of 1998 (Khambule, 2015) to stimulate sustainable co-operation between the government and communities. This is the first wave of the establishment of LEDAs in South Africa through international partnerships between the Italian government, the United Nations Development Programme (UNDP), the United Nations Office for Project Services (UNOPS), the Department of Trade and Industry, and the Department of Economic Affairs (Pretorius & Blaauw, 2008). The second wave occurred at the local and regional levels, with municipalities establishing LEDAs to stimulate co-operation between municipalities and local communities, economic growth, and job creation. This meant that a parent municipality was responsible for institutional arrangements between the LED Units and LEDAs, and for financing LEDAs' operations for a period of 3 years. In South Africa, Local Economic Development Agencies (LEDAs) were established as municipal entities under the Companies Act of 1978, the Municipal Systems Act

(MSA) No. 32 of 2000, and the Municipal Finance Management Act (MFMA) No. 56 of 2003. Co-operation was important for harnessing and building trust between the state, the market sector, and citizens.

Emergence of LEDAs in South Africa

Since the 1950s through to the late 1990s, numerous LEDAs were established in Europe, North America, East Asia, and later in Africa, with South Africa in particular. Based on the Western experience, LEDAs were perceived as a response to the ever-increasing triple challenges of unemployment, poverty and inequality ravaging our country. Most black people in the colonies did not have equal access to the mainstream economy. Hence, LEDAs were established in South Africa to address unemployment, poverty and inequality (Khambule & Mtapuri, 2018). In South Africa, the first wave of LEDAs came about in the late 1990's through joint co-operation between the Italian government, United Nations Development Programme (UNDP), United Nations Office for Project Services (UNOPS), the Department of Trade and Industry and the Department of Economic Affairs (Pretorius & Blaauw, 2008).

LEDAs, through the UNDP programme, were based on a local-level participatory development model, since it involved local people in the development that affected them. The main aim was to promote and attract investment in catalyst projects with a multiplier effect. The projects were located mainly in small rural towns to stimulate economic activity and create employment (Pretorius & Blaauw, 2008). The first wave of LEDAs is marked by projects implemented in four (4) provinces, namely, the Eastern Cape Province, Northern Cape Province, Mpumalanga Province, and Limpopo Province, with 18 municipalities and four (4) District Municipalities in each province (Pretorius & Blaauw, 2008). The international experience reveals that LEDAs address a variety of problems, such as i) fighting social exclusion and poverty, and Local Economic Development as Social Dialogue: (Pretorius & Blaauw, 2008; Khambule, 2015); ii) reconstruction and development of economies; iii) development of SMMEs and promoting innovation (Nene, 2015; Pretorius & Blaauw, 2008). The success of the LED programme is best handled by LEDAs. The most recognised successes of develop-

Local experience also reveals that LED projects implemented by LEDAs in South Africa are a resounding success, such as LOREDA (Lower Orange Economic Development) in the province of Northern Cape; NKEDU (Nkomazi Economic Development Unit) in the province of Mpumalanga, ORTEDA (OR Tambo Economic Development Agency) in the province of the Eastern Cape and VHEDA (Vhembe Economic Development Agency) in the Limpopo province (Pretorius & Blaauw, 2008) and their existence shows that they have a role to play in society. One institutional arrangement that presents a unique opportunity to support the objectives and garner increased attention is LEDA (Lawrence & Rogerson, 2018). Through LEDAs, the LED programmes are in capable hands.

Sectoral agencies are based on Public-Private Partnerships, as they promote localities and economic activities, and their focus is on project implementation and management (Pretorius & Blaauw, 2008). LEDAs are known to be a relevant vehicle for implementing LED because they possess experience and capacity to plan, and the skills to attract investments and implement large catalyst projects. The IDC adopted the LEDA approach to assist local municipalities in achieving their LED mandate (Nene, 2015). Similarly, Khambule (2018:96) states that the failure of municipalities to champion and lead LED prompted the establishment of LEDAs in South Africa to focus on municipalities' institutional and capacity arrangements. LEDAs can also attract international development institutions focusing on LED to finance projects (Lawrence & Rogerson, 2019).

The current challenge for LEDAs is that they are not positioned to sustain themselves, as all identified projects depend solely on funding from the UNDP and the Italian government (Khambule & Mtapuri, 2018). The projects undertaken by the LEDAs were more oriented towards identifying viable development projects, sustainable development and making an impact in addressing the triple challenges (Khambule & Mtapuri, 2018). Inaccessibility of funding led to the collapse of the first wave of LEDAs, and subsequently, this led to the development of the second wave of LEDAs, now under the guidance of the Industrial Development Corporation as a champion through the dedicated Agency Development and Support to support LEDAs institutionally and operationally (Khambule & Mtapuri, 2018, p. 444). In the province of KwaZulu-Natal, LEDAs were introduced to the KZN Cabinet through IDC and Co-operative Governance and Traditional Affairs (Cogta) in 2012. This was followed by the Cabinet Lekgotla Resolution that all municipalities must establish LEDAs. The UMgungundlovu Economic Development Agency was established in 2016 (UMEDA, 2022). LEDAs still exist due to two (2) principles: one, to use LEDAs to implement capital projects because municipalities are failing to champion LED due to a lack of funding and capacity to plan and implement LED projects; and two, to attract investments, promote economic growth, and create jobs. The third wave of LEDAs is unknown in South Africa, since it has not been thoroughly investigated. Most documented research focused mainly on the early stages, initially supported by international donor agencies and two (2) South African government departments, the Department of Trade and Industry and the Department of Economic Affairs (Pretorius & Blaauw, 2008).

While previous studies on LEDAs focused on the role of LEDAs (Khambule & Mtapuri, 2018) and the capacity of Local Government to Support LEDAs in South Africa (Lawrence, 2017). This study sought to assess the role and impact of LEDAs in reducing the twin challenges of poverty and unemployment.

The Role of Local Economic Development Agencies (LEDAs)

According to the White Paper on Developmental Local Government (1998), municipalities are empowered to provide essential services such as water, electricity, housing and infrastructure and to coordinate social and economic activities within their jurisdiction. However, the failure of local government to implement LED necessitated the establishment of LEDAs to address challenges facing local economies and to drive LED (Khambule, 2020). LEDAs create favourable conditions by targeting marginalised communities through social dialogue between government and non-government stakeholders, and by building public-private partnerships to stimulate funding for the district, thus creating access to opportunities for income and decent employment (Khambule, 2015; Khambule & Mtapuri, 2018; Lawrence & Rogerson, 2019). Hence, they address the country's worsening poverty and unemployment sits at 36% (Khambule & Mtapuri, 2018; Stats SA, 2021). The role of LEDAs is to reduce the twin challenges of poverty and unemployment through the employment of specific strategies like social dialogue, innovation, revitalising local economies after internal conflicts, and technical and financial assistance to support small and medium enterprises (Suarez et al., 2015; Khambule, 2015; Nene, 2016). This depends on each region's priority.

THEORETICAL FRAMEWORK

A theoretical framework is the blueprint for the whole research study and can be regarded as a guiding tool that shapes and builds the study (Colley & Hulley, 2021). It assists in developing the hypothesis and serves as a guide for identifying logical relationships among variables (Mkhwanazi, 2019). The theoretical frameworks guiding this study are Entrepreneurship Development, based on Joseph Schumpeter's research and development model; Resource-Based Entrepreneurship Development, based on McClelland's innovation model; and Human Capital Development Theory (education, training, and innovation).

Entrepreneurship Development Theory

The Entrepreneurship Development Theory was first developed by Joseph Schumpeter in 1912 (Mehmood et al., 2019). He was the first scholar to theorise about entrepreneurship. This theory initially puts firms and entrepreneurs at the centre of the growth process, placing greater emphasis on research and development. According to Allen (1991), Schumpeter's model of growth is dependent on innovation, and innovation is a result of investment in education, research and development, whereby firms invest in skills development of the workers to compete in the global market. Creative destruction means that innovations tend to render old technologies and skills outdated (Gubik & Buah, 2019). Innovations replace old technologies, and new technological skills acquired through training will eventually replace old ones.

For any economy to grow and develop, it requires not only a general workforce, but also infrastructure and basic services such as water, buildings, transport and technology to compete in the global market; hence, the local economy will grow. Infrastructure investment promotes economic growth (Makhathini et al., 2020). Tourism, manufacturing, community services, mining, agriculture, trade, business and finance are key sectors that contribute to local development (Garidzirai, Meyer and Muzindutsi, 2019:21; Enterprose iThemba, 2022; iLembe District Municipality, 2020). The provision of basic infrastructure facilitates entrepreneurial activity, leading to job creation, employment generation, and, most importantly, economic growth and development (Gubik & Buah, 2019).

The success of industrial development, regional growth and employment generation depends on entrepreneurial development (Naji, 2019). The combination of entrepreneurship and innovation results in innovative entrepreneurship, whereby new firms are established based on new ideas (Ayandibu & Houghton, 2017).

Innovation in this regard is a process that moves from subsistence production of goods to the entrepreneurial /invention of new goods using modern or advanced technology (Lowrey & Xie, 2019). Innovation is when people develop new and better ways of doing things by using their resources and their initiative (Nene, 2015). Innovation is the key to a company, region, or country's economic development (Mehmood et al., 2019). Enterprise iLembe promotes innovation by assisting in the establishment and market access of a cleaning detergents and cosmetics manufacturing company led by Gift Mbalane (iThemba, 2020). Today, this company sells its products beyond the iLembe District. Most of the basic training for Kuhle Konke Enterprise was conducted through Enterprise iLembe's Business Incubator in KwaDukuza/Stanger. Most LEDAs provide entrepreneurship training to their clients or project members to successfully manage their businesses. In turn, such businesses create jobs, improving living standards and reducing poverty.

MF Mabhala (Pty) Ltd employs more than 26 people (iThemba, 2020). Ebiringa (2012 in Abubakar et al., 2017) reaffirms that "countries with increased entrepreneurial activities tend to have experienced a greater decrease in unemployment rates as well as recorded sustained increase in the standard of living", and it helps to reduce the unemployment problem in the country (Abubakar et al., 2017). This theory resonates with small business development, and this is what LEDAs are known for. The Entrepreneurship theory enables small businesses to be independent and able to successfully compete in the world of work.

Resource-Based Entrepreneurship Development Theory

According to Hakami (2021:157), Resource-Based Entrepreneurship Theory emphasises access to resources as an essential element of opportunity-based entrepreneurship and new experience. David McClelland's development model emphasises innovation as a core of economic growth (Gubik & Buah, 2019) and suggests that the state can prosper if the number of entrepreneurs is at least 2% of the population (Herta, 2018, p. 127). South Africa's population is approximately 60 million, and 2% of that is 1,2 million people. The number of 1.2 million entrepreneurs with two (2) employees might result in approximately 2,4 million people having an opportunity to get employment. The informal business sector employs more than 75% of people when compared to the formal business sector (Mehmood et al., 2019, p. 2). Informal/SMMEs are the backbone of the growing economy; hence, the government needs to invest and nurture this sector.

Hakami (2021) adds that Resource-Based Entrepreneurship emphasises access to financial, social and human resources. This theory resonates with what LEDAs do to access funding, provide technical skills, and network on behalf of their clients (Suarez et al., 2015; UMEDA; Enterprise iThemba, 2022). This can also be referred to internationally: LEDAs in IXCAN in Guatemala, Nariño in Colombia, and in Africa, LEDAs from Mozambique (Sofala, Manica, and Maputo), and in South Africa, Enterprise iLembe (Ei) and UMgungundlovu Economic Development Agency, to name a few. Resource-based Entrepreneurship Theory focuses more on financial assistance in the form of aid or loans, networking with LEDAs on behalf of clients to access the market, and assistance and training to help clients manage their businesses. (Hakami, 2021) states that this theory emphasises three theoretical elements: access to financial, social, and human resources. The first element is: financial resources refer to the ability to access financial aid or assistance for the business.

The second element concerns networking, people's knowledge, and the acceptance of goods and services by customers or the market (Hakami, 2021). The ability and willingness to offer the services required by the market are also important. Providing required services creates trust, loyalty, and a strong bond with customers (Hakami, 2021). The third element concerns the development of human capital, including individual technical skills, experience, and education required to easily grasp and implement new technology.

It is crucial to develop skills, expertise and knowledge of people who are value creators (Adekoya, 2018). However, Schumpeter's model encourages research and development. The McClelland theory (1917-1998) states that the entrepreneur has three (3) unique characteristics: a desire to take personal responsibility for decisions, a preference for decisions that involve risk, and an interest in concrete knowledge of the results of decisions. (Gubik and Buah, 2019:8) point out that this should be inculcated in the child-rearing system so that individuals will grow up with a strong need for achievement, and, by so doing, economic development will eventually take place. As part of a longer–term strategy, the household may also invest in the education of younger members to generate higher future income (Vandenberg, 2006). The Training programme requires the conference venue, transport, and the supply of a qualified or professional individual to impart the necessary skills. Capacity building requires a relevant workforce or personnel, along with the training and funding (conference venue, travel costs, refreshments, and the trainer) for the programme.

Vocational training, entrepreneurship development and access to microfinance contribute to poverty reduction (Vandenberg, 2006). Where there is an increase in research and development, entrepreneur obtains new ideas to enable him to produce a variety of goods, with a variety of goods consumption will increase and output will increase leading to economic growth and development (Gubik and Buah, 2021). The upskilling of entrepreneurs results in the increase of income levels, conducting business in ways that are compatible with current trends and promote local or national economic growth.

Human Capital Development Theory

There are no universally accepted definitions of Human Capital Development Theory. Human Capital Development refers to the stock of a nation's human skills and expertise at a particular point in time. Human Capital Theory is represented by the aggregation of investment in activities such as education, health, on-the-job training, and migration that enhance an individual's productivity in the labour market (Adeyinka & Usman, 2019). It relates to skills, qualifications, education, work experience and communication skills. Human Capital Development can result in the development of networking or influencing skills, self-esteem, resilience, and social capital, where an individual has a better understanding of, knowledge about, and norms and rules governing patterns of interaction that groups of individuals bring to a recurrent activity (Bayat, 2005, p. 3). Education is key to success as training enables people to develop new skills such as networking and operating a new machine.

Human Capital is defined as knowledge, skills, competencies, and attributes embodied in individuals that facilitate the creation of personal, social, and economic well-being (Alhajjar & Alnachef, 2017, 1154). Human Capital implies the totality of knowledge and skills which have been accumulated during life, through education, training and work experience which influence labour productivity (Adeyinka & Usman, 2019). Human capital is defined as the competencies, skills, knowledge, and attributes that individuals possess, enabling them to create social, personal, and economic value (Muathe & Khayinga, 2018). Human capital is an important factor in increasing labour efficiency and productivity (Adekoya, 2018). Human capital is a stock of competencies, knowledge and personality attributes embodied in the ability to perform labour to produce economic value (Hoa, 2021).

Human Capital Development theory may lead to the development of effective leadership, decision-making influence, creativity, and problem-solving. From the definitions above, one can deduce that human capital comprises skilled, experienced, and self-esteem-driven people who are determined to work with the poor to improve their standard of living by imparting skills and knowledge.

This approach emphasises developing human capital within the economic system to foster long-term economic growth. Upskilling small enterprises reduces poverty and unemployment, as they are major employers (Ayandibu & Houghton, 2017). The more educated people are, the less unemployment there is. Human capital is associated with productivity and higher salaries (Alhajjar & Alnachef, 2017). Human capital emphasises the role of education in the development of both individuals and nation-states. Investment in education offers long-term economic and social benefits for both individuals and society at large (Hoa, 2021).

Investment in education, training, and enhanced benefits will improve the quality and level of production (Adekoya, 2018). Education leads to employment, satisfaction and better performance, which may result in better salaries. In this instance, Enterprise iLembe assisted Gift Mabalane to open a cleaning detergents and cosmetics manufacturing company called Kuhle Konke Enterprise operating in the eNkukhwini /Gledhow area under KwaDukuza Local Municipality and Pink Print Farm Produce owned by a 24-year-old lady by the name of Nokwanda Mchunu, processing meat products such as Boerewors, Burger Patties, Cheese Wors, Flavoured Sausages and Mincemeat in Maphumulo Local Municipality, both operate within iLembe District municipal boundaries(iThemba, 2020). It benefits the company, the community, and individuals by increasing productivity and improving income. Each organisation, when investing, expects a better return on its investment, which is creativity, good leadership, flexibility and adaptability, and the enhancement of individual competencies, organisational competencies, and individual employability (Alhajjar & Alnachef, 2017, p. 1155). The acquired skills are beneficial to the worker and to society as a whole and can be compared to machines; they must be invested in, but they yield a return after sufficient time (George-Anokwuru & Ubi-Abai, 2018).

BACKGROUND OF LEDA AT ILEMBE DISTRICT MUNICIPALITY

The Enterprise iLembe is a private company, an entity of iLembe District Municipality, established under the Companies Act of 1978, the Municipal Systems Act of 2000 (section 86c), and the Municipal Finance Management Act of 2003. In 2012, the KwaZulu-Natal Cabinet Lekgotla took a resolution that municipalities should establish Economic Development Agencies (UMEDA, 2022). It is a particular implementation vehicle created by the iLembe District Municipality to achieve its common objectives; as such, the district municipality has delegated the implementation of economic projects to the Enterprise iLembe. The economic development agency is not mandated to create policy but rather to implement the policies as adopted by the Council (iLembe IDP, 2021/2022:89).

LEDAs can influence the development of local development strategies such as Integrated Development Planning (IDP). LED strategies, amongst others, are empowered to implement such policies in ways that benefit and suit the local communities they serve. In short, LEDAs do not serve as referees or players. In this case, a parent municipality is responsible for decision-making. iLembe District Municipality is bordered by the districts of uMgungundlovu and uMzinyathi, as well as the eThekwini Metro. iLembe District comprises four Local Municipalities: Mandeni, KwaDukuza, Ndwedwe and Maphumulo. At 3,260 km^2, it is the smallest of KZN's 10 District Municipalities. The seat of the District Municipality is in Stanger, KwaDukuza (iLembe District Municipality, 2020). The 2019 Community Survey shows that the population in the iLembe District has grown to 678,048, and that those most affected by poverty are those with little or no formal education.

The district's economic drivers are agriculture, which contributes about 8% to the province of KwaZulu-Natal's total agricultural yield, and manufacturing, tourism, and commerce. Agriculture is the main economic sector for the ILembe District Municipality (iLembe District Municipality, 2020:6 & 21). The priorities of LEDAs differ from region to region and locality to locality; hence, they have different roles and functions, depending on the reasons for their introduction. Sectoral agencies are commonly found in the Global South since they are based on public-private partnerships (PPP). Public-Private Partnerships promote localities and economic activities, with a focus on project implementation and management (Pretorius & Blaauw, 2008; Khambule, 2019). LEDAs provide a customised service to their local clients, including transportation of goods and services (UMEDA, 2022). The UMgungundlovu Enterprise Development Agency (UMEDA) provided seedling support to 76 emerging farmers, training and mentorship, market access, and technical advice (UMEDA, 2022, p. 4). Enterprise iLembe also established the iLembe Business Incubation Programme to support local SMMEs by training the community to ensure they experience growth. The Incubation programme focuses on manufacturing, construction, agriculture, ICT, tourism and renewable energy (Enterprise iThemba, 2022).

The beneficiaries of the Incubation Programme are Taste KZN Café, Kuhle Konke Enterprise, Lucent Media, Luko Designs, Pink Print Farm Produce, Amabomvu Lounge, Thamiso Creations, Godide Engineering, Azowell Farming, MF Mabhala (PTY) Ltd, Amatshitsh'oqobo Poultry Farm, Mlamula Tunnels, Youth Enterprise

Park, KwaDukuza Mobile Tyre Repairs, Sisimeme Civil & Building Contractors, Dokodweni Farming Project, Thushu Berries and Nqobizitha Farm. Enterprise iLembe's priority is to reduce poverty through the implementation of territorial marketing and SMME Development (capacity building and financial assistance). Territorial marketing (networking) includes Tourism Programmes such as the Rand Easter Show, the Africa Travel Indaba, and the Trade and Investment Seminar and Exhibition. Tourism is one of the major contributors to employment in the district. In 2021, tourism attracted 954 visitors, generating R 1,002 634 037 in local income, with a total contribution of R1 billion to GDP and creating more than eight thousand (8000) job opportunities. The Enterprise iLembe Economic Development Agency organised a workshop to assist informal traders and SMMEs affected by the July 2021 unrest in accessing the Business Relief Fund. The informal traders benefited from getting R8,000 in grant funding in March 2022. Enterprise iLembe conducted contract-meeting sessions with Afrimax Potato Market to introduce SMMEs to the potato market (Enterprise iThemba, 2022).

The ongoing partnership with Latter Day Saints (LDS) charities benefited 5 (five) projects, and this partnership dates back to 2016. Through the agency's Business Incubator Project, Endless Day Trading t/a Tyre Solutions and Lady M Cosmetics have directly benefited from the programme (Enterprise iThemba, 2022). LEDAs offer financial and non-financial training, using collaborative means to assist local businesses. Training helps entrepreneurs draft business plans that meet financial institutions' requirements, enabling them to access funding. AgriSeta and Enterprise iLembe, in partnership with iThunga Development, conducted a 12-month agricultural training programme that benefited eighty (80) emerging farmers and also conducted financial management capacity building for small enterprises, with the help of Economic Development, Tourism and Environmental Affairs (KZNEDTEA) (Enterprise iThemba, 2022). The provision of basic infrastructure facilitates entrepreneurial activity, drives job creation, and, most importantly, promotes economic growth and development (Buah & Gubik, 2019). LEDAs like Semilla are also financed by the Ford Foundation, which supports basic infrastructure, creates job opportunities during implementation, and facilitates economic growth (Suarez et al., 2015). During project implementation, local people benefit from job opportunities created by basic service projects and also develop skills and a sense of ownership of the project. Hence, the project would be adequately maintained after completion.

Background to the study site

The study was conducted at Enterprise iLembe, located in the iLembe District Municipality, with its offices in Balitto, KwaZulu-Natal, South Africa (iLembe District Municipality, 2020:6 21). iLembe is bordered by the districts of uMgungundlovu and uMzinyathi, as well as the eThekwini Metro. iLembe District is divided into four Local Municipalities: Mandeni, KwaDukuza, Ndwedwe and Maphumulo. At 3,260 km^2, it is the smallest of the 10 District Municipalities of KZN. The seat of the District Municipality is in Stanger, KwaDukuza (iLembe District Municipality, 2020). The 2019 Community Survey shows that the population in the iLembe District has grown to 678,048, and that those most affected by poverty are those with little or no formal education. The district's economic drivers are agriculture, which accounts for about 8% of the province of KwaZulu-Natal's total agricultural yield, followed by manufacturing, tourism, and commerce. Agriculture is the main economic sector for the iLembe District Municipality (iLembe District Municipality, 2020).

The iLembe District Municipality consists of four (4) local municipalities: KwaDukuza, Mandeni, Maphumulo, and Ndwedwe. The iLembe District lies between King Cetshwayo District Municipality in the north and eThekwini Metropolitan City in the south, and it is bordered by UMgungundlovu District Municipality and UMzinyathi District Municipality. Below, Figure 1.1. shows the map of the iLembe District Municipality and the location of each local municipality.

Figure 1. ILembe District Map.

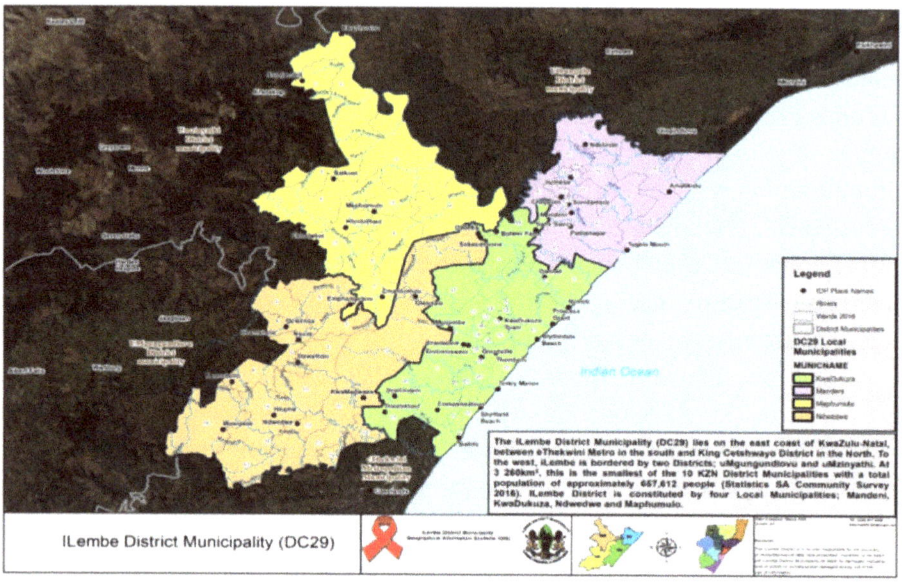

Source IDP iLembe 2022-2027

Establishment of Enterprise iLembe

Enterprise iLembe (Pty) Ltd is an Economic Agency entirely owned by the iLembe District Municipality. The agency is registered in terms of section 86C of the Municipal Systems Act, and thus its existence and operations are governed by the Municipal Finance Management Act and the Companies Act. Enterprise iLembe was envisioned and adopted by iLembe District as a special implementing agent of the economic development strategies for the four Local Municipalities within its jurisdiction, namely Mandeni, KwaDukuza, Ndwedwe, and Maphumulo, and by other stakeholders to achieve the common economic development objectives. The economic development agency is not mandated to create policy but rather to implement the policies as adopted by the Council. The core role of Enterprise iLembe is to implement the economic development strategy promoting trade and investment within the iLembe District as set out in the Integrated Development Plan (IDP) (iLembe IDP, 2022-2027).

LEDAs that are formed as municipal entities are informed by Section 86B of the Municipal Systems Act, which provides for three different types of municipal entities:

- A private company, which includes a process of integration in terms of the Companies Act 61 of 1973.
- A service mechanism founded by the use of a by-law.
- A multi-jurisdictional agreement consisting of written agreements between two or more municipalities.

That Enterprise iLembe is an economic development mechanism of cooperation is further attested to by the agency's philosophy.

FINDINGS AND ANALYSIS

Emergence of LEDAs in South Africa

Since the 1950s through to the late 1990s, numerous LEDAs were established in Europe, North America, East Asia, and later in Africa, with South Africa in particular. In the Western experience, LEDAs were perceived as a response to the ever-increasing triple challenges of unemployment, poverty and inequality ravaging our country. The majority of black people in the colonies did not have equal access to the mainstream economy. Hence, LEDAs were established in South Africa to address unemployment, poverty and inequality (Khambule & Mtapuri, 2018).

In South Africa, the first wave of LEDAs came about in the late 1990's through joint co-operation between the Italian government, United Nations Development Programme (UNDP), United Nations Office for Project Services (UNOPS), the Department of Trade and Industry and the Department of Economic Affairs (Pretorius & Blaauw, 2008). LEDAs under the UNDP programme were based on a local-level participatory development model since it involved local people in the development that affected them. The main aim was to promote and attract investments in catalyst projects with a multiplier effect. The projects were located mainly in small, rural towns to stimulate economic activity and employment creation (Pretorius & Blaauw, 2008).

The first wave of LEDAs is also marked by projects implemented in four (4) provinces, namely the Eastern Cape Province, Northern Cape Province, Mpumalanga Province, and Limpopo Province, with 18 municipalities and four (4) District Municipalities, one district in each province (Pretorius & Blaauw, 2008). The international experience reveals that LEDAs address a variety of problems, such as i) fighting social exclusion and poverty, and Local Economic Development as Social Dialogue: (Pretorius & Blaauw, 2008; Khambule,2015); ii) reconstruction and development of economies; iii) development of SMMEs and promoting innovation (Nene, 2015; Pretorius & Blaauw, 2008). The success of the LED programme is best handled by LEDAs. The most recognised successes of develop-

Local experience also reveals that LED projects implemented by LEDAs in South Africa are a resounding success, such as LOREDA (Lower Orange Economic Development) in the province of Northern Cape; NKEDU (Nkomazi Economic Development Unit) in the province of Mpumalanga, ORTEDA (OR Tambo Economic Development Agency) in the province of the Eastern Cape and VHEDA (Vhembe Economic Development Agency) in the Limpopo province (Pretorius & Blaauw, 2008) and their existence shows that they have a role to play in society. One institutional arrangement that presents a unique opportunity to support the objectives and garner increased attention is LEDA (Lawrence & Rogerson, 2018). LED programmes are secure under LEDA.

Sectoral agencies are based on Public-Private Partnerships, as they promote localities and economic activities, and their focus is on project implementation and management (Pretorius & Blaauw, 2008). LEDAs are known to be a relevant vehicle for implementing LED because they possess experience and capacity to plan, and the skills to attract investments and implement large catalyst projects. The IDC adopted the LEDA approach to assist local municipalities in achieving their LED mandate (Nene, 2015). Similarly, Khambule (2018:96) states that the failure of municipalities to champion and lead LED prompted the establishment of LEDAs in South Africa to focus on municipalities' institutional and capacity arrangements. LEDAs can also attract international development institutions focusing on LED to finance projects (Lawrence & Rogerson, 2019). The current challenge for LEDAs was that they were not positioned to sustain themselves, as all identified projects were solely dependent on funding from the UNDP and the Italian government (Khambule & Mtapuri, 2018). The projects undertaken by the LEDAs were more oriented towards identifying viable development projects, sustainable development and making an impact in addressing the triple challenges.

Inaccessibility of funding led to the collapse of the first wave of LEDAs, and subsequently, this led to the development of the second wave of LEDAs, now under the guidance of the Industrial Development Corporation as a champion through the dedicated Agency Development and Support to support LEDAs institutionally and operationally (Khambule & Mtapuri, 2018). In the province of KwaZulu-Natal, LEDAs were introduced to the KZN Cabinet through IDC and Co-operative Governance and Traditional Affairs (Cogta) in 2012. LEDAs still exist for two (2) reasons: one, to implement capital projects because municipalities are failing to champion LED due to a lack of funding and capacity to plan and implement LED projects; and two, to attract investments, promote economic growth, and create jobs. The third wave of LEDAs is unknown in South Africa, since it has not been thoroughly investigated. Most documented research focused mainly on the early stages, initially supported by international donor agencies and two (2) South African government departments, the Department of Trade and Industry and the Department of Economic Affairs (Pretorius & Blaauw, 2008). While previous studies on LEDAs focused on the role of LEDAs (Khambule & Mtapuri, 2018) and the capacity of Local Government to Support LEDAs in South Africa (Lawrence, 2017). This study sought to assess the role and impact of LEDAs in reducing the twin challenges of poverty and unemployment.

The Role of Local Economic Development Agencies (LEDAs)

According to the White Paper on Developmental Local Government (1998), municipalities are empowered to provide essential services such as water, electricity, housing, and infrastructure, and to coordinate social and economic activities within their jurisdiction.

However, the failure of local government to implement LED necessitated the establishment of LEDAs to address challenges facing local economies while also driving LED (Khambule, 2021). LEDAs create favourable conditions by targeting marginalised communities through social dialogue between government and non-government stakeholders, and by building public-private partnerships to stimulate funding for the district, thus creating access to opportunities for income and decent employment (Khambule, 2015; Khambule & Mtapuri, 2018; Lawrence & Rogerson,

2019). Hence, they address the country's worsening poverty and unemployment sits at 36% (Khambule & Mtapuri, 2018; Stats SA, 2021). The role of LEDAs is to reduce the twin challenges of poverty and unemployment through the employment of specific strategies like social dialogue, innovation, revitalising local economies after internal conflicts, and technical and financial assistance to support small and medium enterprises (Suarez et al., 2015; Khambule, 2015; Nene, 2016). This depends on each region's priority.

LEDA at iLembe District Municipality

The Enterprise iLembe is a private company, an entity of iLembe District Municipality, established under the Companies Act of 1978, the Municipal Systems Act of 2000 (section 86c), and the Municipal Finance Management Act of 2003. In 2012, the KwaZulu-Natal Cabinet Lekgotla took a resolution that municipalities should establish Economic Development Agencies (UMEDA, 2016). It is a particular implementation vehicle created by the iLembe District Municipality to achieve its common objectives; as such, the district municipality has delegated the implementation of economic projects to the Enterprise iLembe. The economic development agency is not mandated to create policy but rather to implement policies adopted by the Council (iLembe IDP, 2021/2022:89). LEDAs can influence the development of local development strategies, such as Integrated Development Planning (IDP). LED strategies, amongst others, are empowered to implement such policies in ways that benefit and suit the local communities they serve. In short, LEDAs do not play the roles of referee or player. In this case, a parent municipality is responsible for decision-making.

iLembe District Municipality is bordered by the districts of uMgungundlovu and uMzinyathi, as well as the eThekwini Metro. iLembe District comprises four Local Municipalities: Mandeni, KwaDukuza, Ndwedwe and Maphumulo. At 3,260 km^2, it is the smallest of the 10 District Municipalities of KZN. The seat of the District Municipality is in Stanger, KwaDukuza (iLembe District Municipality, 2020). The 2019 Community Survey shows that the population in the iLembe District has grown to 678,048 people, and the most affected by poverty are people with less or no formal education. The district's economic drivers are agriculture, which contributes about 8% to the province of KwaZulu-Natal's total agricultural yield, and manufacturing, tourism, and commerce. Agriculture is the main economic sector for the ILembe District Municipality (iLembe District Municipality, 2020).

The priorities of LEDAs differ from region to region and locality to locality; hence, they have different roles and functions, depending on the reasons for their introduction. Sectoral agencies are commonly found in the global South because they are based on public-private partnerships (PPPs). Public-Private Partnerships promote localities and economic activities, with a focus on project implementation and management (Pretorius & Blaauw, 2008; Khambule, 2019). LEDAs provide a customised service to their local clients, including transportation of goods and services (UMEDA, 2022:6). The UMgungundlovu Enterprise Development Agency (UMEDA) provided seedling support to 76 emerging farmers, training and mentorship, market access and technical advice (UMEDA, 2022), and Enterprise iLembe also established the iLembe Business Incubation Programme to support local SMMEs by training the community to ensure that they experience growth. The Incubation programme focuses on manufacturing, construction, agriculture, ICT, tourism and renewable energy (Enterprise iThemba, 2022). The beneficiaries of the Incubation Programme are: Taste KZN Café, Kuhle Konke Enterprise, Lucent Media, Luko Designs, Pink Print Farm Produce, Amabomvu Lounge, Thamiso Creations, Godide Engineering, Azowell Farming, MF Mabhala (PTY) Ltd, Amatshitsh'oqobo Poultry Farm, Mlamula Tunnels, Youth Enterprise Park, KwaDukuza Mobile Tyre Repairs, Sisimeme Civil & Building Contractors, Dokodweni Farming Project, Thushu Berries and Nqobizitha Farm.

Enterprise iLembe's priority is reducing poverty through the implementation of territorial marketing, SMME Development (capacity building and financial assistance). Territorial marketing (networking) includes Tourism Programmes such as the Rand Easter Show, the Africa Travel Indaba, and the Trade and Investment Seminar and Exhibition.

Tourism is one of the major contributors to employment in the district. In 2021, tourism attracted 954 visitors worth R 1,002 634 037 local income, with a total contribution of R 1billion to the GDP and created more than eight thousand (8000) job opportunities. The Enterprise iLembe Economic Development Agency organised a workshop to assist informal traders and SMMEs affected by the July 2021 unrest in accessing the Business Relief Fund. The informal traders benefited from getting R8,000 in grant funding in March 2022. The Enterprise iLembe conducted contract meeting sessions with Afrimax Potato Market to introduce SMMEs to the potato market (Enterprise iThemba, 2022, p. 8). The ongoing partnership with Latter Day Saints (LDS) charities benefited 5 (five) projects, and this partnership dates back to 2016. Endless Day Trading t/a Tyre Solutions and Lady M Cosmetics have directly benefited from the programme from the agency's Business Incubator Project (Enterprise iThemba, 2022).

LEDAs offer financial and non-financial training, using collaborative means to assist local businesses. Training helps entrepreneurs draft business plans that meet financial institutions' requirements, enabling them to access funding. AgriSeta and Enterprise iLembe, in partnership with iThunga Developments, conducted a 12-month agricultural training programme that benefited eighty (80) emerging farmers and also conducted financial management capacity building for small enterprises, with the help of Economic Development, Tourism and Environmental Affairs (KZNEDTEA) Enterprise (Enterprise iThemba, 2022). The provision of basic infrastructure facilitates entrepreneurial activity, leading to job creation, employment generation and most importantly, economic growth and development (Buah & Gubrik, 2019). LEDA-like Semilla, funded by the Ford Foundation, is also involved in providing basic infrastructure, as it creates job opportunities during implementation and facilitates economic growth (Suarez et al., 2015). During project implementation, local people benefit from job opportunities created by basic service projects and also develop skills and a sense of ownership of the project. Hence, the project would be adequately maintained after completion.

Actors for LED Strategies

The shortcomings of the top-down development approach led to the emergence of the bottom-up approach, which is perceived as people-centred because it allows communities to have greater say in programmes that address their problems and challenges. Anyway, the major aim of LED programmes is to support local participation and build to determine economic and social benefit initiatives for the whole area and the community (Maliki et al, 2008).

This means that for LED programmes to succeed, the participation of the recipient community is central, since it requires them to maintain their services when the project is completed. Currently, the prominent stakeholders are those that represent the community, followed by the private and public (government) sectors, and they remain actors in LED. The successful LED depends on the collective efforts of the public, private, and societal sectors (Eddine-Maliki et al., 2016). These sectors are referred to as the service delivery triangle to LED (Meyer, 2014).

Figure 2. Service delivery triangle regarding to LED

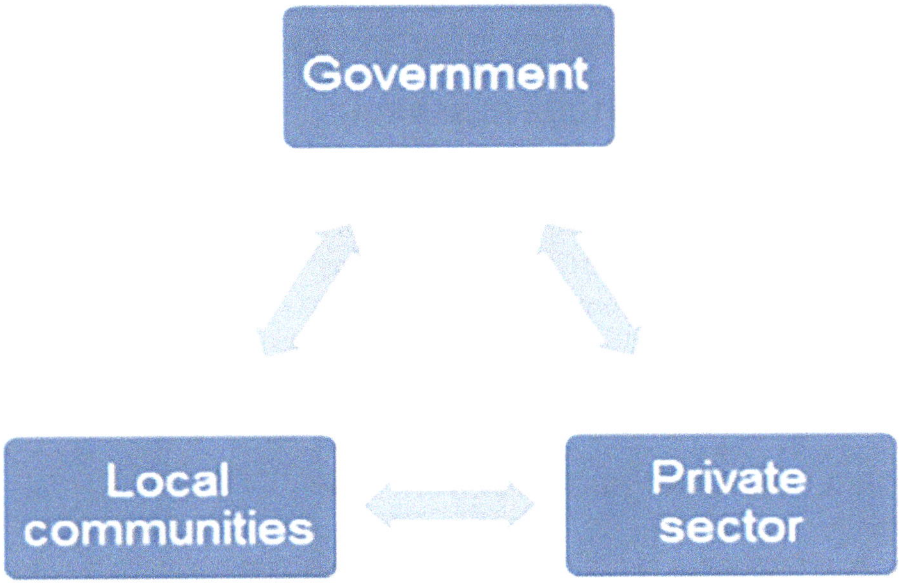

Source: Meyer 2014

All these sectors have relevant roles to play and work as equal partners in planning, decision-making, and implementation. Each sector has a role to play. The role of the public sector is to create a conducive environment for businesses to thrive, including the provision of basic services such as water, roads, electricity, schools, health care, and housing. The role of the private sector is to invest in the area to create employment and boost the local economy (Nene, 2015). Communities are usually represented by NGOs, civil organisations, or other structures that possess knowledge and understanding of local community issues. Due to LED, the range of actors involved in development matters has increased to include community-based organisations (CBOs), non-governmental organisations (NGOs), private enterprises, and government structures (Mncwabe, 2013). Every sector represents the constituency they account to. Community-based organisations represent communities, the private sector represents the interests of established businesses and investors, and the public sector is concerned with fulfilling its mandate of creating a conducive environment for business to thrive, by making policies to attract investment that would create jobs for local people. The role of LED is to uplift the local economy through the cooperation and participation of all relevant stakeholders. Cooperation among stakeholders can reduce poverty and unemployment by fostering skills development and innovation. The combination of entrepreneurship and innovation yields innovative entrepreneurship, in which new firms are established based on new ideas and technologies (Ayandibu & Houghton, 2017).

DIRECTIONS FOR FUTURE RESEARCH

This study was undertaken to explore the role and impact of LEDAs in reducing poverty and unemployment in the iLembe District Municipality. Although the study had limitations, there is a need for broader research on the benefits of reducing poverty and unemployment across other development agencies. This type of research could yield more coordinated, impact-driven initiatives and interventions that better affect residents or the population.

CONCLUSION AND RECOMMENDATIONS

The perceived role of LEDAs stemmed from municipalities' inability to lead LED activities, resulting in the delegation of LED matters to development agencies. The role of LEDAs can range from encouraging social dialogue and participation to fostering innovation, attracting investment, creating employment, and imparting skills. Development Agencies operate according to the territory they serve, including the nature of government policies. Through their expertise and support, LEDAs can reduce unemployment and poverty (twin challenges) by implementing jointly agreed projects in the locality they serve. The LEDAs play a pivotal role by ensuring that SMMEs have access to financial assistance, by networking on behalf of their clients, and by offering relevant training.

LEDAs have a role to play in the development of society, particularly in South Africa. In South Africa, LEDAs are involved in the implementation of economic development projects by developing and capacitating small enterprises, and by providing social networking and market intelligence on behalf of their clients. Local Economic Development Agencies (LEDAs) continue to face financial constraints and theft when supporting development projects. Parent municipalities do not contribute adequate financial support, and it has been suggested that local municipalities should also contribute to projects executed in their jurisdictions. Municipalities have a constitutional mandate to provide basic services to fast-track service delivery and create a conducive environment for thriving. The private sector is not willing to financially support LEDAs due to the corruption stigma attached to them. It should be noted that other countries receive direct funding from the national government and have organised national structures responsible for Development Agencies.

Recommendations

The LEDAs are better positioned to lead the implementation of Local Economic Development programmes and have proven expertise in the field. However, they face a multitude of challenges in areas such as funding, theft, business concessions, the provision of adequate basic services, corruption stigma, and the diversification or withdrawal of programmes such as NSNP, which inhibit them from implementing more economical projects. Training has featured prominently across all themes and findings/responses, along with strategies employed by LEDAs, challenges encountered during implementation, and recommendations to remedy or improve the situation. The research recommends the following:

1. The municipal entities were established through the Companies Act and Municipal Finance Management Act, which allow them to get external funding; hence, financial policies /prescripts governing the management of LEDAS should be reviewed or relaxed to allow LEDAs to receive external financial assistance. Relevant funding streams can include the National Lottery, relevant SETAs, the private sector, and the public sector. This will aid in attracting/recruiting and retaining personnel with the requisite skills to efficiently implement economic development projects and venture into new spaces in renewable energy to generate income that would make the agency self-sustainable without solely relying on a single source of income, such as an equitable share from a parent municipality.
2. The benefiting municipalities should inject some form of assistance, either in the form of capital, human resources, provision of land, equipment and tools, etc.
3. Encourage the use of the Intergovernmental Relations (IGR) /District Development Model (DDM) to share information and resources.
4. Municipalities should give competitive business concessions/ rebates (water, electricity and municipal rates) to attract and retain investors.
5. The government should resuscitate economic projects that create massive employment, such as the National School Nutrition Programme (NSNP) under the auspices of the Enterprise iLembe (EiEDA), since it has proven itself in the past to reduce the twin challenges of poverty and unemployment through this programme. In the past, it employed 500 farmers who produced fresh produce, and with local transport, they consistently supplied the agency with it.
6. Such projects should also involve other government departments like Health and Correctional Services to consistently supply hospitals and correctional facilities with fresh farm produce. This will create more employment across the province/s if replicated well.

7. Municipalities should create an investor-friendly environment, so that there is uninterrupted provision of basic services such as water, electricity, security, roads, and refuse collection.

REFERENCES

Ackron, J., & Auriacombe, C. J. (2016). A critical analysis of the approach to local economic development (LED) in South Africa. *Administratio Publica, 24*(3), 141–165.

Adekoya, O. D. (2018). Impact of human capital development on poverty alleviation in Nigeria. *Scholars Journal of Economics, Business and Management*, *5*(10), 904–915. DOI: 10.36347/sjebm.2018.v05i10.002

Adeyinka, O.-B., & Usman, F. K. (2019). Effects of human capital development on the economic growth of ECOWAS member states. *Advances in Sciences and Humanities*, *5*(1), 27–42. DOI: 10.11648/j.ash.20190501.14

Alhajjar, A., & Alnachef, T. (2017). Effects of human capital on organisational performance: A literature review. *International Journal of Science and Research*, *6*(8), 1154–1158. https://www.ijsr.net/

Ateljevic, J., O'Rourke, T., & Poljasevic, B. Z. (2013). Local economic development in Bosnia and Herzegovina: Role of local development agencies. *Journal of Balkan & Near Eastern Studies*, *15*(3), 280–305. DOI: 10.1080/19448953.2013.789319

Ayandibu, A. O., & Houghton, J. (2017). The role of small and medium-scale enterprises in local economic development (LED). *The Journal of Business and Retail Management Research*, *11*(2), 133–139. DOI: 10.24052/JBRMR/262

Bayat, A. (2005). *Defining Social Capital: A brief overview of the key aspects and debates*. Policy Management, Governance and Poverty Alleviation in the Western Cape.

Buah, A.-S., & Gubik, A. S. (2019). The role of entrepreneurship in economic growth: The picture according to literature. In T. Kékesi (Ed.), *MultiScience – XXXIII. microCAD International Multidisciplinary Scientific Conference* (Paper No. 2019.105). University of Miskolc. https://doi.org/DOI: 10.26649/musci.2019.105

Costa, K., & Parker, G. D. (2016). *Enhancing capacity for local economic development in creating vibrant, productive and sustainable rural communities*. Global Centre for Academic Research. https://africarxiv.ubuntunet.net/handle/1/1026

Dyosi, F. S. (2016). *A study of local economic development in the town of Stutterheim* (Master's dissertation, University of Cape Town). OpenUCT. https://open.uct.ac.za/

Enterprise iLembe. (2022). *Enterprise iLembe iThemba newsletter: Local economic development and enterprise development initiatives*. Enterprise iLembe. https://www.enterpriseilembe.co.za/images/ilembe/files/Ei_iThemba_Newsletter _- June_2022_rev_5.pdf

Enterprise ILembe Economic Development Agency. (2020), Bringing Hope. Www .enterpriseilembe.co.za. accessed 18 October 2021.

Eroglu, M. (2020). *A study of science –policy interfaces in Climate Change Policy Making: IZMAR and ISTANBUL DEVELOPMENT AGENCIES*. Istanbul Technical University, Graduate School of Arts and Social Sciences.

Garidzirai, R., Meyer, D. F., & Muzindutsi, P. F. (2019). Impact of economic sectors on local economic development: A case of the Capricorn Region, Limpopo Province, South Africa. *International Journal of Economics and Finance Studies, 11*(2), 1–16. https://www.sobiad.org/eJOURNALS/journal_IJEF/archieves/IJEF -2019-2_1/r_garidzirai.pdf. DOI: 10.34109/ijefs.201911202

George-Anokwuru, C.C., and Ubi-Abai, I.P. (2018). Empirical Analysis of Determinants of Human Capital Formation: Evidence from the Niger Delta, Journal of World Economic Research, Vo. 17, No.2:173-81.

Gubik, A. S., & Buah, A. (2019). The Role of Entrepreneurship in Economic Growth: The picture according to literature, International Multidisciplinary Scientific Conference, ISN978-963-358-177-3.

Hakami, S. (2021). The role of social entrepreneurship in community development: A case study of social entrepreneurship in Saudi Arabia. *Psychology and Education, 58*(2), 154–161. https://www.psychologyandeducation.net/

Herta, S. A. (2018). Entrepreneurship education as the molding of entrepreneurial attitudes: A case study. *International Journal of Economics and Business Administration, 6*(3), 127–135. DOI: 10.35808/ijeba/172

Hoa, N. O. (2021). Human capital and productivity growth in agriculture in Vietnam. *Journal of Science, 50*(2B), 43–54.

iLembe District Municipality. (2020). *Draft integrated development plan 2019/2020*. https://www.enterpriseilembe.co.za/images/ilembe/files/archive/ilembe%20idp/IDP -REVIEW-2-2019-2020.pdf

Kanayo, O., Ndlovu, P., & Agholor, I. (2021). Impact of local economic development programmes on livelihood: Evidence from Mpumalanga, South Africa. *International Journal of Economics and Financial Issues, 11*(4), 105–114. DOI: 10.32479/ijefi.11589

Khambule, I. (2021). Decentralisation or deconcentration: The case of regional and local economic development in South Africa. *Local Economy*, *36*(1), 22–41. DOI: 10.1177/0269094221101 8427

Khambule, I., & Gerwel-Proches, C. (2019). Exploring the role of social dialogue in local economic development: A case of a South African Local Economic Development Agency. *Progress in Development Studies*, *19*(1), 36–54. DOI: 10.1177/1464993418806126

Khambule, I., & Mtapuri, O. (2018). Assessing the role of Local Economic Development Agencies in KwaZulu-Natal, South Africa. *Local Economy*, *33*(4), 438–455. DOI: 10.1177/0269094218773933

Khambule, I., & Mtapuri, O. (2018). Interrogating the Institutional Capacity of Local Government to Support Local Economic Development Agencies in KwaZulu/Natal Province of South Africa. *African Journal of Public Affairs*, *10*(1).

Khambule, I. B. (2015). *Local economic development as a social dialogue: A case of Enterprise iLembe* (Master's dissertation, University of KwaZulu-Natal, Graduate School of Business and Leadership). University of KwaZulu-Natal. http://hdl.handle.net/10413/14217

Khan, F. (2010). The Community Work Programme: Building a society that works. In Turok, B. (Ed.), *Wealth Doesn't Trickle Down: The Case for a Developmental State in South Africa* (pp. 181–193). Jacana Media.

Kobedi, K. C. S. (2021). *Local economic assessment of community work programmes as a job creation mechanism* (Master's dissertation, University of Johannesburg). University of Johannesburg Institutional Repository. https://hdl.handle.net/10210/485211

Lawrence, F. (2017). *Local economic development agencies in South Africa: Evolution, organisation and progress* (Doctoral dissertation, University of Johannesburg). University of Johannesburg Institutional Repository. https://hdl.handle.net/10210/270030

Lawrence, F., & Rogerson, C. M. (2018). Local economic development agencies and place-based development: Evidence from South Africa. *Bulletin of Geography. Socio-Economic Series*, *41*(41), 29–43. DOI: 10.2478/bog-2018-0024

Lawrence, F., & Rogerson, C. M. (2019). Local economic development agencies and peripheral small town development: Evidence from Somerset East, South Africa. *Urbani Izziv*, *30*(30, Supplement), 144–157. DOI: 10.5379/urbani-izziv-en-2019-30-supplement-010

Makhathini, M. S. M., Mlambo, V. H., & Mpanza, S. (2020). Infrastructure provision as a catalyst for local economic development in South Africa. *Strategic Review for Southern Africa, 42*(1), 105–126. https://www.up.ac.za/strategic-review-for-southern-africa

Maliki, S. B.-E., Amine, M. M., Metaiche, F. T., & Ziani, T. (2008). *The role of local economic development agencies (LEDA) in territorial development and the whole macro-economic goals achievement. Les Cahiers du MECAS, 4*(1), 68–84. https://www.asjp.cerist.dz/en/article/9688

Maliki, S. B.-E., Metaiche, M. A., Metaiche, F. T., & Ziani, T. (2008). The role of local economic development agencies (LEDA) on territorial development and the whole macroeconomic goals achievement. *Les Cahiers du MECAS, 4*(1), 68–84. https://asjp.cerist.dz/en/article/9688

Mashamaite, K., & Lethoko, M. (2018). Role of the South African local government in local economic development. *International Journal of eBusiness and eGovernment Studies, 10*(1), 114–128. https://dergipark.org.tr/en/pub/ijebeg/issue/36107/535456

Masikane, S. (2021). *Local economic development as an employment strategy in eMkhazane rural area (Ward 21), Ulundi Municipality* (Master's dissertation, University of KwaZulu-Natal). University of KwaZulu-Natal ResearchSpace. https://researchspace.ukzn.ac.za/handle/10413/19835

Masuku, M. M., Jili, N. N., & Selepe, B. M. (2016). The implementation of local economic development initiatives towards poverty alleviation in Big 5 False Bay Local Municipality. *African Journal of Hospitality, Tourism and Leisure*, *5*(4), 1–11. https://www.ajhtl.com/

Mehmood, T., Alzoubi, H. M., Alshurideh, M., Al-Gasaymeh, A., & Ahmed, G. (2019). Schumpeterian entrepreneurship theory: Evolution and relevance. *Academy of Entrepreneurship Journal*, *25*(4), 1–10. https://www.abacademies.org/articles/Schumpeterian-entrepreneurship-theory-evolution-and-relevance-

Meyer, D. F. (2014). Local economic development (LED), challenges and solutions: The case of the Northern Free State region, South Africa. *Mediterranean Journal of Social Sciences*, *5*(16), 624–634. DOI: 10.5901/mjss.2014.v5n16p624

Mkhwanazi, M. N. (2019). *An investigation of challenges affecting the implementation of project management practices: A case study of Msunduzi Expanded Public Works Programme clearing project* (Master's dissertation, University of KwaZulu-Natal). University of KwaZulu-Natal ResearchSpace. https://researchspace.ukzn.ac.za/

Mncwabe, L. (2013). *The role of skills development initiatives in promoting local economic development (LED) in South African townships: A case study of Cato Manor, Durban* (Master's dissertation, University of KwaZulu-Natal). University of KwaZulu-Natal ResearchSpace. https://researchspace.ukzn.ac.za/

Mokoena, S. K. (2019). The role of local economic development on small, medium and micro enterprises. *Acta Universitatis Danubius. Œconomica, 15*(1), 59–83. https://journals.univ-danubius.ro/index.php/oeconomica

Mthimkhulu, S., and Mpanza, S. (2021). The role of local economic development agencies and non-profit organisations in local economic development: South African case studies.

Muathe, S., & Khayinga, L. M. (2018). Human capital development and organisational performance: Review and critique of literature and research agenda. *International Journal for Innovation Education and Research*, *6*(2), 144–153. DOI: 10.31686/ijier.vol6.iss2.959

Naji, A. A. H. (2019). *Factors influencing entrepreneurship development*. ResearchGate. https://www.researchgate.net/publication/332255136_Factors_Influencing_Entrepreneurship_Development

Ndlovu, C. (2021). *Pro-poor local economic development (LED): The case of Umzinyathi District Municipality, KwaZulu-Natal* (Master's dissertation, University of the Free State). University of the Free State. http://hdl.handle.net/11660/11628

Nel, E., and Rogerson. (2017) Local Economic Development in the Developing World: The experience of Southern Africa. http:/tayloandfrancis.com.

Nene, O. J. (2015). *The role of local economic development agencies in supporting local innovation* (Master's research report, University of the Witwatersrand). Wits Business School. http://hdl.handle.net/10539/20936

Nene, O. J. (2016). *The role of local economic development agencies (LEDAs) in supporting local innovation* (Research report, Wits Business School, University of the Witwatersrand). University of the Witwatersrand. https://wiredspace.wits.ac.za/items/95122b68-05b7-4421-a07b-fae6402c5ec1

Pavel, A., & Moldovan, O. (2019). Determining Local Economic Development in the Rural Areas of Romania. Exploring the Role of Exogenous Factors. *Sustainability (Basel), 2019*(11), 282. . DOI: 10.3390/su11010282

Pretorius, A. M., & Blaauw, P. F. (2008). Local economic development agencies in South Africa: Six years later. *The South African Journal of Economic History*, *23*(1–2), 155–183. DOI: 10.1080/10113430809511210

Republic of South Africa. (1996). *Constitution of the Republic of South Africa, Act 108 of 1996*. Government Gazette.

Republic of South Africa. (1998). White Paper on Local Government, 9 March 1998, Pretoria: Government Gazette.

Republic of South Africa. (2014). *KwaZulu-Natal Poverty Eradication Master Plan*. KwaZulu-Natal Office of the Premier. https://www.kznonline.gov.za/images/Downloads/Publications/Poverty%20Eradication%20Master%20Plan.pdf

Statistics South Africa. (2017). *Quarterly Labour Force Survey (QLFS): Quarter 2, 2017* (Statistical Release P0211). Statistics South Africa. https://www.statssa.gov.za/?page_id=1854

Statistics South Africa. (2021). *Quarterly Labour Force Survey (QLFS): Quarter 1, 2021* (Statistical Release P0211). Statistics South Africa. https://www.statssa.gov.za/?page_id=1854

Statistics South Africa. (2021). *Quarterly Labour Force Survey (QLFS): Quarter 2, 2021* (Statistical Release P0211). Statistics South Africa. https://www.statssa.gov.za/?page_id=1854'

Suarez, F. J. T., Chicas, O. A., Troshani, R., & Coelho, J. (2015). *Local economic development agencies for governance and internationalisation of local economies*. IDEASS. https://www.ideassonline.org/public/pdf/BrochureAdelENG.pd

The Presidency. (2014). *Medium-Term Strategic Framework 2014–2019*. Republic of South Africa. https://www.gov.za/documents/medium-term-strategic-framework-2014-2019-3-aug-2014-0000

Tshishonga, N., & Matsiliza, N. S. (2021). Addressing the twin challenges of poverty and unemployment through community work programmes in South Africa. *African Journal of Development Studies*, *11*(2), 217–235. DOI: 10.31920/2634-3649/2021/v11n2a12

Vandenberg, P. (2006). *Poverty reduction through small enterprises: Emerging consensus, unresolved issues and ILO activities* (SEED Working Paper No. 75). International Labour Organization. https://www.ilo.org/publications/poverty-reduction-through-small-enterprises-emerging-consensus-unresolved

Wekwete, K. (2014). Local Government and Local Economic Development in Southern Africa, Commonwealth Local Government Forum.

Xie, D., & Lowrey, Y. (2019). A Theory of Entrepreneurial Work. *Theoretical Economics Letters*, *9*(5), 1507–1517. DOI: 10.4236/tel.2019.95097

Compilation of References

Abdouli, M., & Hammami, S. (2018). Economic Growth, Environment, FDI Inflows, and Financial Development in Middle East Countries: Fresh Evidence from Simultaneous Equation Models. *Journal of the Knowledge Economy*, *11*(2), 479–511. DOI: 10.1007/s13132-018-0546-9

Aboelnour, A., & Abuelela, M. H. (2019). Increase adherence to waste management policy at healthcare facility in Egypt. *Bulletin of the National Research Center*, *43*(29), 1–11. DOI: 10.1186/s42269-019-0065-2

ACET. (2023) African Transformation Index 2023: Tracking Africa's economic successes and setbacks. ACET, Accra. Retrieved from https://acetforafrica.org/ati/

Ackron, J., & Auriacombe, C. J. (2016). A critical analysis of the approach to local economic development (LED) in South Africa. *Administratio Publica*, *24*(3), 141–165.

Acs, Z. J., & Audretsch, D. B. (1990). *Innovation and small firms*. MIT Press. DOI: 10.1007/978-94-015-7854-7

Adekoya, O. D. (2018). Impact of human capital development on poverty alleviation in Nigeria. *Scholars Journal of Economics, Business and Management*, *5*(10), 904–915. DOI: 10.36347/sjebm.2018.v05i10.002

Adeyinka, O.-B., & Usman, F. K. (2019). Effects of human capital development on the economic growth of ECOWAS member states. *Advances in Sciences and Humanities*, *5*(1), 27–42. DOI: 10.11648/j.ash.20190501.14

Admin. (2023). Foreign Direct Investment (FDI) - definition, types of FDI, FDI in India. UPSC

African Vibes. (2021). "The Top 10 African Tech Hubs." Retrieved from https://africanvibes.com/the-top-10-african-tech-hubs

Agamuthu, P., & Hansen, J. A. (2007). Universities in capacity building in sustainable development: Focus on solid waste management and technology. *Waste Management & Research, 25*(3), 241–246. DOI: 10.1177/0734242X07079155 PMID: 17612324

Agarwal, B. (1994). *A field of one's own: Gender and land rights in South Asia*. Cambridge University Press.

Ager, A., & Strang, A. (2008). Understanding integration: A conceptual framework. *Journal of Refugee Studies, 21*(2), 166–191. DOI: 10.1093/jrs/fen016

Aghion, P., & Tirole, J. (1994). The management of innovation. *The Quarterly Journal of Economics, 109*(4), 1185–1209. DOI: 10.2307/2118360

Ahmad, I., & Islam, M. R. (2024). Empowerment and participation: Key strategies for inclusive development. In *Building strong communities: Ethical approaches to inclusive development* (pp. 47–68). Emerald Publishing Limited. DOI: 10.1108/978-1-83549-174-420241003

Ahmed, L. (1992). *Women and gender in Islam: Historical roots of a modern debate*. Yale University Press.

Ahmed, S. A., & Ali, S. M. (2006). People as partners: Facilitating people's participation in public–private partnerships for solid waste management. *Habitat International, 30*(4), 781–796. DOI: 10.1016/j.habitatint.2005.09.004

Ajide, K. B. (2025). Exploring the Relationship between Trade Openness, FDI, and Economic Complexity in Africa. *The International Trade Journal, 39*(5), 525–551. DOI: 10.1080/08853908.2024.2374739

Akbar, T. (2025). Power and resistance: exploring the conceptions and experiences of gender and career aspirations of young people in Bangladesh (Doctoral dissertation, University of Glasgow)

Akiner, S. (1983). *Islamic peoples of the Soviet Union*. Routledge.

Aksoy Demirci, A., & Günay, G. (2018). Türkiye'de Kadın Kooperatifçiliği. *Üçüncü Sektör Sosyal Ekonomi*, 77-90.

Alam, A., & Shah, S. (2013). Determinants of foreign direct investment in OECD member countries. *Journal of Economic Studies (Glasgow, Scotland), 40*(4), 515–527. DOI: 10.1108/JES-10-2011-0132

Alesina, A., & La Ferrara, E. (2005). Ethnic diversity and economic performance. *Journal of Economic Literature, 43*(3), 762–800. DOI: 10.1257/002205105774431243

Alfaro, L., & Chen, M. X. (2012). Surviving the global financial crisis: Foreign ownership and establishment performance. *American Economic Journal. Economic Policy*, *4*(3), 30–55. DOI: 10.1257/pol.4.3.30

Alhajjar, A., & Alnachef, T. (2017). Effects of human capital on organisational performance: A literature review. *International Journal of Science and Research*, *6*(8), 1154–1158. https://www.ijsr.net/

Aliber, M., & Hall, R. (2012). Support for smallholder farmers in South Africa: Challenges of scale and strategy. *Development Southern Africa*, *29*(4), 548–562. DOI: 10.1080/0376835X.2012.715441

Al-Sharmani, M. (2023). Islamic feminist hermeneutics: Between scholarship and lived realities. *Journal of Feminist Studies in Religion*, *39*(2), 95–97. DOI: 10.2979/jfemistudreli.39.2.15

Altenburg, T., & Meyer-Stamer, J. (1999). How to promote clusters: Policy experiences from Latin America. *World Development*, *27*(9), 1693–1713. DOI: 10.1016/S0305-750X(99)00081-9

Altowayti, W. A. H., Shahir, S., Othman, N., Eisa, T. A. E., Yafooz, W. M., Al-Dhaqm, A., Soon, C. Y., Yahya, I. B., Che Rahim, N. A. N., Abaker, M., & Ali, A. (2022). The role of conventional methods and artificial intelligence in the wastewater treatment: A comprehensive review. *Processes (Basel, Switzerland)*, *10*(9), 1832. DOI: 10.3390/pr10091832

Ameh, B. (2024). Digital tools and AI: Using technology to monitor carbon emissions and waste at each stage of the supply chain, enabling real-time adjustments for sustainability improvements. *Int J Sci Res Arch*, *13*(1), 2741–2754. DOI: 10.30574/ijsra.2024.13.1.1995

Amin, T. (2024). Globalization and cultural homogenization: A critical examination. *Kashf Journal of Multidisciplinary Research*, *1*(03), 10–20.

Andeobu, L., Wibowo, S., & Grandhi, S. (2022). Artificial intelligence applications for sustainable solid waste management practices in Australia: A systematic review. *The Science of the Total Environment*, *834*, 155389. DOI: 10.1016/j.scitotenv.2022.155389 PMID: 35460765

Angima, B. M. (2021). Effects of Anthropogenic Activities on the Diversity of Macrophytes and Water Quality in Sironga and Kapkatet Wetlands, Kenya (Master's dissertation, KISII UNIVERSITY).

Ansell, C., & Gash, A. (2008). Collaborative governance in theory and practice. *Journal of Public Administration: Research and Theory*, *18*(4), 543–571. DOI: 10.1093/jopart/mum032

Ansell, C., & Torfing, J. (2016). *Handbook on theories of governance*. Edward Elgar Publishing., DOI: 10.4337/9781782548508

Arnstein, S. (2025). A Ladder of Citizen Participation. Journal of the American Institute of Planners (1969). In *The City Reader* (pp. 306–321). Routledge. DOI: 10.4324/9781003519508-36

Arya, B., & Bassi, B. (2011). Corporate social responsibility and broad-based black economic empowerment legislation in South Africa: Codes of good practice. *Business & Society*, *50*(4), 674–695. DOI: 10.1177/0007650309332261

Ateljevic, J., O'Rourke, T., & Poljasevic, B. Z. (2013). Local economic development in Bosnia and Herzegovina: Role of local development agencies. *Journal of Balkan & Near Eastern Studies*, *15*(3), 280–305. DOI: 10.1080/19448953.2013.789319

Avelino, F. (2021). Theories of power and social change: Power contestations and their implications for research on social change and innovation. *Journal of Political Power*, *14*(3), 425–448. DOI: 10.1080/2158379X.2021.1875307

Ayandibu, A. O., & Houghton, J. (2017). The role of small and medium-scale enterprises in local economic development (LED). *The Journal of Business and Retail Management Research*, *11*(2), 133–139. DOI: 10.24052/JBRMR/262

Baiashvili, T., & Gattini, L. (2020). Impact of FDI on economic growth: The role of country income levels and institutional strength. EIB Working Papers, 2020/02. Retrieved from https://www.eib.org/attachments/efs/economics_working_paper_2020_02_en.pdf

Bakker, K. (2012). Water Security: Research Challenges and Opportunities. *Science*, *337*(6097), 914–915. DOI: 10.1126/science.1226337 PMID: 22923564

Bamgbose, A. (1991). *Language and the nation: The language question in sub-Saharan Africa*. Edinburgh University Press for the International African Institute.

Bano, M. (2012). *The rational believer: Choices and decisions in the Madrasas of Pakistan*. Cornell University Press.

Barry, L., & Victor, S. (2011). Water Rights and Water Fights: Preventing and Resolving Conflicts Before They Boil Over. *American Journal of Public Health*, *101*(5), 778–780. DOI: 10.2105/AJPH.2010.194670 PMID: 21421949

Bartram, J., & Cairncross, S. (2010). Hygiene, sanitation, and water: Forgotten foundations of health. *PLoS Medicine*, *7*(11), e1000367. DOI: 10.1371/journal.pmed.1000367 PMID: 21085694

Barut, Y. (2017). Women's cooperatives contributions to local region economy: Seferihisar agricultural cooperative development model-Turkey. *Management Studies*, 120-127.

Bayat, A. (2005). *Defining Social Capital: A brief overview of the key aspects and debates*. Policy Management, Governance and Poverty Alleviation in the Western Cape.

Beck, T. (2013). Bank financing for SMEs: Lessons from the literature. *National Institute Economic Review*, *225*(1), 23–38. DOI: 10.1177/002795011322500105

Bendel, P. (2020). *Integration policies and practices in Austria: A comprehensive review*. Springer.

Berry, J. W. (1997). Immigration, acculturation, and adaptation. *Applied Psychology = Psychologie Appliquée*, *46*(1), 5–34. DOI: 10.1111/j.1464-0597.1997.tb01087

Bhabha, H. K. (1994). *The Location of Culture*. Routledge.

Bharti, N. (2021). Role of cooperatives in economic empowerment of women: A review of Indian experiences. *World Journal of Entrepreneurship, Management and Sustainable Development*, •••, 617–631.

Biermann, F., & Boas, I. (2010). Preparing for a warmer world: Towards a global governance system to protect climate refugees. *Global Environmental Politics*, *10*(1), 60–88. DOI: 10.1162/glep.2010.10.1.60

Blalock, G., & Gertler, P. J. (2008). Welfare gains from foreign direct investment through technology transfer to local suppliers. *Journal of International Economics*, *74*(2), 402–442. DOI: 10.1016/j.jinteco.2007.05.011

Blomström, M., & Kokko, A. (2003). The economics of foreign direct investment incentives. NBER Working Paper No. 9489.

Blonigen, B. A., & Piger, J. (2014). Determinants of foreign direct investment. *The Canadian Journal of Economics. Revue Canadienne d'Économique*, *47*(3), 775–812. https://onlinelibrary.wiley.com/doi/epdf/10.1111/caje.1209. DOI: 10.1111/caje.12091

Blyth, W., Gross, R., Speirs, J., Sorrell, S., Nicholls, J., Dorgan, A., & Hughes, N. 2014. Low Carbon Jobs: the Evidence for Net Job Creation from Policy Support for Energy Efficiency and Renewable Energy. Retrieved from https://www.sciencedirect.com/science/article/pii/S0301421519306342?ref=pdf_download&fr=RR-2&rr=9a7aeb128ff541e2

Bolong, N., Ismail, A. F., Salim, M. R., & Matsuura, T. (2009). A review of the effects of emerging contaminants in wastewater and options for their removal. *Desalination, 239*(1-3), 229–246. DOI: 10.1016/j.desal.2008.03.020

Bonciu, F. (2020). Is Circular Economy Compatible With Capitalism? *Romanian Economic Business Review, Romanian-American University, 15*(1), 16–30.

Boschi-Pinto, C., Velebit, L., & Shibuya, K. (2008). Estimating child mortality due to diarrhoea in developing countries. *Bulletin of the World Health Organization, 86*(9), 710–717. DOI: 10.2471/BLT.07.050054 PMID: 18797647

Bourdieu, P. (1990). *The Logic of Practice*. Stanford University Press. DOI: 10.1515/9781503621749

Bourdin, J. (2023). World's tallest 'hemp hotel' to open in Cape Town. Retrieved from: https://mg.co.za/news/2023-05-08-worlds-tallest-hemp-hotel-to-open-in-cape-town/

Branstetter, L., Fisman, R., & Foley, C. F. (2006). Do stronger intellectual property rights increase international technology transfer? Empirical evidence from U.S. firm-level panel data. *The Quarterly Journal of Economics, 121*(1), 321–349. DOI: 10.1162/qjec.2006.121.1.321

Buah, A.-S., & Gubik, A. S. (2019). The role of entrepreneurship in economic growth: The picture according to literature. In T. Kékesi (Ed.), *MultiScience – XXXIII. microCAD International Multidisciplinary Scientific Conference* (Paper No. 2019.105). University of Miskolc. https://doi.org/DOI: 10.26649/musci.2019.105

Bülbüller, G. (2022). *Türkiye'de Kadın Kooperatiflerinin Sosyal Dayanışma Ekonomisi Kapsamında İncelenmesi: İzmir İli Örneği*. İstanbul Üniversitesi.

Buruma, I., & Margalit, A. (2004). *Occidentalism: The West in the Eyes of Its Enemies*. Penguin.

Busom, I., Corchuelo, B., & Martínez-Ros, E. (2014). Tax incentive or subsidies for business R&D? *Small Business Economics, 43*(3), 571–596. DOI: 10.1007/s11187-014-9569-1

Byrne, J.. (2016). Renewable energy and climate change mitigation in developing countries. [Volume, issue, and page numbers required]. *Climate Policy*.

California State Government Report. (2020). *Immigrant Investment Program*. State of California. Search CA.gov | CA.gov

Carr, G. M., & Neary, J. P. (2008). *Water Quality for Ecosystem and Human Health*. UNEP/Earthprint.

Castaño, M. S., Méndez, M. T., & Galindo, M. Á. (2016). The effect of public policies on entrepreneurial activity and economic growth. *Journal of Business Research, 68*(7), 1496–1500. DOI: 10.1016/j.jbusres.2016.04.125

Caves, R. E. (2007). *Multinational enterprise and economic analysis* (3rd ed.). Cambridge University Press. DOI: 10.1017/CBO9780511619113

Cesari, J. (2019). *Islam, secularism, and liberal democracy: Toward a democratic theory for Muslim societies*. Oxford University Press.

Checkley, W., Epstein, L. D., Gilman, R. H., Figueroa, D., Cama, R. I., Patz, J., & Black, R. E. (2000). Effects of El Nino and ambient temperature on hospital admissions for diarrhoeal diseases in Peruvian children. *Lancet, 355*(9197), 442–450. DOI: 10.1016/S0140-6736(99)06215-7 PMID: 10841124

Chellaney, B. (2013). *Water, Peace, and War: Confronting the Global Water Crisis*. Rowman & Littlefield.

Chisenga, J. (2002). Indigenous knowledge: Africa's opportunity to contribute to global information content. *South African Journal of Library and Information Science, 68*(1), 16–20.

Chiswick, B. R., & Miller, P. W. (2015). The economics of immigration. In J. C. M. (Ed.), International Encyclopedia of the Social & Behavioral Sciences (2nd ed., pp. 153-160). Elsevier. https://doi.org/DOI: 10.1016/B978-0-08-097086-8.81026-6

Christian Aid. (2007). Human tide: The real migration crisis. *Christian Aid Report*.

Çıkın, A., & Karacan, A. (1994). *Genel Kooperatifçilik*. Ege Üniversitesi Ziraat Fakültesi Yayınları.

Çınar, K., Akyuz, S., Uğur Çınar, M., & Onculer Yayalar, E. (2021). Faces and Phases of Women's Empowerment: The Case of Women's Cooperatives in Turkey. *Social Politics, 28*(3), 778–805. DOI: 10.1093/sp/jxz032

Cissé, G. (2019). Food-borne and water-borne diseases under climate change in low- and middle-income countries: Further efforts needed for reducing environmental health exposure risks. *Acta Tropica, 194*, 181–188. DOI: 10.1016/j.actatropica.2019.03.012 PMID: 30946811

Claassens, A. (2013). Recent changes in women's land rights and contested customary law in South Africa. *Journal of Agrarian Change, 13*(1), 71–92. DOI: 10.1111/joac.12007

Claassens, A., & Ngubane, S. (2008). Women, land and power: The impact of the Communal Land Rights Act. In Claassens, A., & Cousins, B. (Eds.), *Land, power and custom: Controversies generated by South Africa's Communal Land Rights Act* (pp. 154–183). University of Cape Town Press.

Clemens, M. A., & Hunt, J. (2017). The labor market effects of refugee waves: Reconciling conflict and evidence. *The Review of Economic Studies, 84*(2), 1533–1558. DOI: 10.1093/restud/rdx021

Cohen, W. M., & Levinthal, D. A. (1990). Absorptive capacity: A new perspective on learning and innovation. *Administrative Science Quarterly, 35*(1), 128–152. DOI: 10.2307/2393553

Collins, P. H. (2000). *Black feminist thought: Knowledge, consciousness, and the politics of empowerment* (2nd ed.). Routledge.

Commission for Gender Equality. (2018). *Women, land and customary law*. Commission for Gender Equality.

Commission for Gender Equality. (2024). *Exploring barriers to women's access to communal land in South Africa*. Commission for Gender Equality.

Contractor, F. J. (2007). Is International Business Good for Companies? The Evolutionary or Multistage Theory of Internationalisation vs. the Transaction Cost Perspective. *International Management Review, 47*(3), 453–475.

Copeland, S., Comes, T., Bach, S., Nagenborg, M., Schulte, Y., & Doorn, N. (2020). Measuring social resilience: Trade-offs, challenges and opportunities for indicator models in transforming societies. *International Journal of Disaster Risk Reduction, 51*, 101799. DOI: 10.1016/j.ijdrr.2020.101799

Cornwall, A. (2016). Women's empowerment: What works? *Journal of International Development, 28*(3), 342–359. DOI: 10.1002/jid.3210

Cornwall, A., & Brock, K. (2005). What do buzzwords do for development policy? A critical look at 'participation', 'empowerment' and 'poverty reduction'. *Third World Quarterly*, *26*(7), 1043–1060. DOI: 10.1080/01436590500235603

Costa, K., & Parker, G. D. (2016). *Enhancing capacity for local economic development in creating vibrant, productive and sustainable rural communities*. Global Centre for Academic Research. https://africarxiv.ubuntunet.net/handle/1/1026

Cousins, B. (2016). *Land reform in South Africa is sinking: Can it be saved?* Nelson Mandela Foundation.

Cresswell, J., & Plano Clark, V. (2011). *Designing and Conducting Mixed Method Research*. Sage Publications.

Creswell, J., & Poth, C. (2017). *Qualitative inquiry & research design: Choosing among five approaches*. SAGE.

Daily Nation, (2018). Outraged residents demand solution for filthy, stinking Kisii Town.

Daley, E., Dore-Weeks, R., & Umuhoza, C. (2010). Ahead of the game: Land tenure reform in Rwanda and the process of securing women's land rights. *Journal of Eastern African Studies : The Journal of the British Institute in Eastern Africa*, *4*(1), 131–152. DOI: 10.1080/17531050903556691

Dalkıran, G. (2017). The support of women work within cooperative enterprises sample of Turkey. *Social Sciences Research Journal*, 1-11.

Daskalakis, N., Jarvis, R., & Schizas, E. (2013). Financing practices and preferences for micro and small firms. *Journal of Small Business and Enterprise Development*, *20*(1), 80–101. DOI: 10.1108/14626001311298420

Datta, A. (2015). New urban utopias of postcolonial India: 'Entrepreneurial urbanization' in Dholera smart city, Gujarat. *Dialogues in Human Geography*, *5*(1), 3–22. DOI: 10.1177/2043820614565748

Datta, P., & Gailey, R. (2012). Empowering women through social entrepreneurship: Case study of a women's cooperative in India. *Entrepreneurship Theory and Practice*, *36*(3), 569–587. DOI: 10.1111/j.1540-6520.2012.00505.x

Davis, A. P., Hunt, W. F., Traver, R. G., & Clar, M. (2009). Bioretention technology: Overview of current practice and future needs. *Journal of Environmental Engineering*, *135*(3), 109–117. DOI: 10.1061/(ASCE)0733-9372(2009)135:3(109)

DEA (Department of Environmental Affairs). (2012). *National Waste Management Strategy*. Department of Environmental Affairs.

DEA (Department of Environmental Affairs). (2018). *South Africa state of waste report. A report on the state of the environment.* Department of Environmental Affairs.

Deborah, B. (2022). *How Does Population Growth Affect Water Scarcity?* Healing Water International.

Deere, C. D., & León, M. (2001). *Empowering women: Land and property rights in Latin America.* University of Pittsburgh Press. DOI: 10.2307/j.ctt5hjpf6

Dempsey, N., Bramley, G., Power, S., & Brown, C. (2011). The social dimension of sustainable development: Defining urban social sustainability. *Sustainable Development (Bradford), 19*(5), 289–300. DOI: 10.1002/sd.417

Department of Rural Development and Land Reform. (2017). *Land audit report: Phase II—Private land ownership by race, gender and nationality.* Republic of South Africa.

Department of Trade and Industry. (1995). The White Paper on the national strategy for the development and promotion of small businesses in South Africa.

Design, A. R. G. (2024). Architectural Projects, Tsoga Environmental Centre. Retrieved from: https://argdesign.co.za/tsoga.html

DFFE. (2020). National Waste Management Strategy. Retrieved from https://www.dffe.gov.za/sites/default/files/docs/nationalwaste_management_strategy.pdf

Dharmaraj, S., Ashokkumar, V., Pandiyan, R., Munawaroh, H. S. H., Chew, K. W., Chen, W. H., & Ngamcharussrivichai, C. (2021). Pyrolysis: An effective technique for the degradation of COVID-19 medical wastes. *Chemosphere, 275*, 130092. DOI: 10.1016/j.chemosphere.2021.130092 PMID: 33984908

Doh, S., & Kim, B. (2014). Government support for SME innovations in the regional industries: The case of the government financial support program in South Korea. *Research Policy, 43*(9), 1557–1569. DOI: 10.1016/j.respol.2014.05.001

Doss, C. R. (1999). *Twenty-five years of research on women farmers in Africa: Lessons and implications for agricultural research institutions* (Economics Program Paper No. 99-02). International Maize and Wheat Improvement Center.

Driffield, N. N., A. H. M. (1999). Foreign Direct Investment and Local Input Linkages in Malaysia. *Transnational Corporations, 8*(3), 1–25.

Duguid, F., Durutaş, G., & Wodzicki, M. (2015). *Türkiye'de Kadın Kooperatiflerinin Mevcut Durumu.* The World Bank.

Dunning, J. H. (1998). Location and the multinational enterprise: A neglected factor? Journal ofInternational Business Studies, 29(1), 45–66.

Dushkova, D., & Ivlieva, O. (2024). Empowering communities to act for a change: A review of the community empowerment programs towards sustainability and resilience. *Sustainability (Basel), 16*(19), 8700. DOI: 10.3390/su16198700

Dustmann, C., & Frattini, T. (2014). The fiscal impact of immigration to the UK. *Economic Journal (London), 124*(580), F293–F343. DOI: 10.1111/ecoj.12181

Dyosi, F. S. (2016). *A study of local economic development in the town of Stutterheim* (Master's dissertation, University of Cape Town). OpenUCT. https://open.uct.ac.za/

Ebregt, A., & Greve, P. D. (2000). Buffer zones and their management. Policy and best practices for terrestrial ecosystems in developing countries. Theme Studies Series, 5.

Effler, E., Isaacson, M., Arntzen, L., Heenan, R., Canter, P., Barrett, T., Lee, L. C., Mambo, C., Levine, W., Zaidi, A., & Griffin, P. M. (2001). Factors contributing to the emergence of Escherichia coli O157 in Africa. *Emerging Infectious Diseases, 7*(5), 812–819. DOI: 10.3201/eid0705.017507 PMID: 11747693

El Hammoumi, A., Seghyar, N., Gouiouez, M., Amane, M., & Berdi, A. (2024). The adoption of a qualitative approach in management science: An exploratory survey on the effects of big data on the performance of companies. In *Applying qualitative research methods to management science* (pp. 283–309). IGI Global. DOI: 10.4018/979-8-3693-5543-5.ch011

Ellen MacArthur Foundation (EMF). 2013. Towards the Circular Economy, vol. 1 (Isle of Wight). Retrieved from https://www.ellenmacarthurfoundation.org/towards-the-circular-economy-vol-1-an-economic-and-business-rationale-for-an

Ellen Macarthur Foundation. (2020), The Circular Economy in Detail. Retrieved from https://www.ellenmacarthurfoundation.org/explore/the-circular-economy-indetail

Emiroğlu, M. (2017). *Kooperatifçilik & Kadın Kooperatifleri.* https://ticaret.gov.tr/data/5d41e48b13b87639ac9e02df/7458fc6b5805cfbbaf4a3f0 d76ad0bf5.pdf adresinden alındı

Engel, K., Jokiel, D., Kraljevic, A., Geiger, M., & Smith, K. (2011). Big Cities, Big Water, Big Challenges: Water in an Urbanizing World. World Wildlife Fund, Koberich.

Enqvist, J., & Ziervogel, G. (2019). Water governance and justice in Cape Town: An overview. *WIREs. Water, 6*(4), e1354. DOI: 10.1002/wat2.1354

Enterprise ILembe Economic Development Agency. (2020), Bringing Hope. Www .enterpriseilembe.co.za. accessed 18 October 2021.

Enterprise iLembe. (2022). *Enterprise iLembe iThemba newsletter: Local economic development and enterprise development initiatives.* Enterprise iLembe. https://www.enterpriseilembe.co.za/images/ilembe/files/Ei_iThemba_Newsletter _- June_2022_rev_5.pdf

EPA. (1992). Guidelines for Water Reuse. Washington, DC, Environmental Protection Agency. *Technical Report no.* EPA/625/R-92/004).

Equal Future Platform, U. N. D. P. (2024). A tapestry of progress and challenges: Women's political participation in Europe and Central Asia. UNDP. https://www .undp.org/eurasia/blog/challenges-womens-political-participation

Eroglu, M. (2020). *A study of science –policy interfaces in Climate Change Policy Making: IZMAR and ISTANBUL DEVELOPMENT AGENCIES.* Istanbul Technical University, Graduate School of Arts and Social Sciences.

Escobar, A. (1995). *Encountering development: The making and unmaking of the Third World.* Princeton University Press.

Estrella, M., & Gaventa, J. (1998). *Who counts reality? Participatory monitoring and evaluation: A literature review.* IDS Working Paper 70. https://www.ids.ac .uk/publications/who-counts-reality-participatory-monitoring-and-evaluation-a -literature-review/

Etim, E. (2024). Leveraging public awareness and behavioural change for entrepreneurial waste management. *Heliyon, 10*(21), e40063. DOI: 10.1016/j.heliyon.2024. e40063 PMID: 39553649

European Central Bank. (2018). Foreign direct investment and its drivers: A global and EU perspective. *Economic Bulletin, 4,* •••. https://www.ecb.europa.eu/press/ economicbulletin/articles/2018/html/ecb.ebart201804_01.en.html

European Commission. (2015). *Circular Economy Action Plan.* https://ec.europa.eu

European Environment Agency (EEA). (2014): Resource-efficient green economy and EU policies EEA Report No 2/2014, Luxembourg. Retrieved from https://www .eea.europa.eu/en/analysis/publications/resourceefficient-green-economy-and-eu

Eurostat. (2020). *Immigrant workforce in the European Union.* https://ec.europa .eu/eurostat

Faludi, A. (2000). *The performance of spatial planning.* Routledge. DOI: 10.1080/713691907

Fang, B., Yu, J., Chen, Z., Osman, A. I., Farghali, M., Ihara, I., Hamza, E. H., Rooney, D. W., & Yap, P. S. (2023). Artificial intelligence for waste management in smart cities: A review. *Environmental Chemistry Letters*, *21*(4), 1959–1989. DOI: 10.1007/s10311-023-01604-3 PMID: 37362015

FAO. (2017). The Future of Food and Agriculture – Trends and Challenges. https://www.fao.org/3/a-i6583e.pdf

Fierman, W. (1991). *Language planning and national development: The Uzbek experience*. De Gruyter. (Note: Original publication year is 1991, not 2019.)

Finkel, S. E., & Smith, A. E. (2011). Civic education, political discussion, and the social transmission of democratic knowledge and values in a new democracy: Kenya 2002. *American Journal of Political Science*, *55*(2), 417–435. DOI: 10.1111/j.1540-5907.2010.00493.x

Fleermuys, F., Nakusera, F., Shangula, F., & Steytler, J. (2007). Overview of Broad-Based Economic Empowerment in Namibia. In *Bank of Namibia 9th Annual Symposium Publication* (pp. 13-63).

Fleisch, B. (2008). *Primary education in crisis: Why South African schoolchildren underachieve in reading and mathematics*. Juta.

Food and Agriculture Organization of the United Nations. (2011). [*Women in agriculture—Closing the gender gap for development*. Food and Agriculture Organization of the United Nations.]. *The State of Food and Agriculture*, •••, 2010–2011.

Food and Agriculture Organization of the United Nations. (2017). *The state of food and agriculture: Leveraging food systems for inclusive rural transformation*. Food and Agriculture Organization of the United Nations.

Food and Agriculture Organization. (2019). *Water-efficient agriculture in arid regions*. FAO.

Ford, T. N., Ibe-Lamberts, K., Edmond, S., Abrams, I., Chaudhry, A., Daniels, P., Do, M., Edmiston, B., Fokum, S., Gary, C., Ghebenei, D., Hebert-Beirne, J., Jibrell, H., Jones, J., Kelleher, M. R., Lynch, J., Mahajan, A., Marcus, N., Pinsker, E., & Shaw, B. A. (2024). Challenges and opportunities for participatory evaluation of local public health efforts to address structural racism and advance health equity. *Journal of Participatory Research Methods*, *5*(2). Advance online publication. DOI: 10.35844/001c.118717

Fourie, M. (2003). Beyond the ivory tower: service learning for sustainable community development.

Franz, H. W., Hochgerner, J., & Howaldt, J. (Eds.). (2012). *Challenge social innovation: Potentials for business, social entrepreneurship, welfare and civil society*. Springer., DOI: 10.1007/978-3-642-32879-4

Freire, P. (2020). *Pedagogy of the Oppressed* (50th anniversary ed.). Bloomsbury Academic.

Freire, P. (1970). Pedagogy of the Oppressed. *Continuum.*

Frey, C.B., Osborne, M.A. (2017). The future of employment: how susceptible are jobs to computerisation? Technol. Forecast. Soc. Chang. Retrieved from https://doi.org/.DOI: 10.1016/j.techfore.2016.08.019

Fritsch, M., & Mueller, P. (2004). Effects of new business formation on regional development over time. *Regional Studies*, *38*(8), 961–975. DOI: 10.1080/0034340042000280965

Fumagalli, M. (2018). *Religion and politics in Central Asia: Governance, secularism, and Islam*. Routledge.

Gangwar, M., Kandekar, N., Mandai, M., & Kandekar, P. (2004). Empowerment status of rural women: Insights from dairy cooperatives. *Social Change*, *34*(1), 112–123. DOI: 10.1177/004908570403400111

Garg, M. C., Kumari, S., & Agarwal, S. (2024). The integration of artificial intelligence in advanced wastewater treatment systems. In The AI Cleanse: Transforming Wastewater Treatment Through Artificial Intelligence (pp. 1–27). Springer. DOI: 10.1007/978-3-031-67237-8_1

Garidzirai, R., Meyer, D. F., & Muzindutsi, P. F. (2019). Impact of economic sectors on local economic development: A case of the Capricorn Region, Limpopo Province, South Africa. *International Journal of Economics and Finance Studies*, *11*(2), 1–16. https://www.sobiad.org/eJOURNALS/journal_IJEF/archieves/IJEF-2019-2_1/r_garidzirai.pdf. DOI: 10.34109/ijefs.201911202

Geertman, S. (2020). *Smart Cities and Urban Sustainability: Opportunities and Challenges*. Springer.

Geertz, C. (1973). *The Interpretation of Cultures*. Basic Books.

George-Anokwuru, C.C., and Ubi-Abai, I.P. (2018). Empirical Analysis of Determinants of Human Capital Formation: Evidence from the Niger Delta, Journal of World Economic Research, Vo. 17, No.2:173-81.

Geray, C. (2014). *Kooperatifçilik*. Nika Yayınevi.

Gereffi, G., & Fernández-Stark, K. (2016). *Global value chain analysis: A primer* (2nd ed.). Duke University Centre on Globalisation, Governance & Competitiveness.

Gereffi, G., Humphrey, J., & Sturgeon, T. (2005). The governance of global value chains. *Review of International Political Economy, 12*(1), 78–104. DOI: 10.1080/09692290500049805

German Federal Office for Migration and Refugees. (2020). *Germany's integration course statistics*. Federal Office for Migration and Refugees. https://www.bamf.de

Gesimba, L. (2020). A Critical Analysis of the Cooperative Frameworks on Shared Natural Resources in the East African Community: a Case Study of Lake Victoria (Doctoral dissertation, University of Nairobi).

Gichaba, M. A., Ogendi, G., Peletz, R., Khush, R., & Kumpel, E. (2017). Can sanitary surveys replace water quality testing? Evidence from Kisii, Kenya. *International Journal of Environmental Research and Public Health, 14*(2). PMID: 28178226

Giddens, A. (1984). *The constitution of society: Outline of the theory of structuration*. Polity Press.

Gilmore, A., Galbraith, B., & Mulvenna, M. (2013). Perceived barriers to participation in R&D programmes for SMEs within the European Union. *Technology Analysis and Strategic Management, 25*(3), 329–339. DOI: 10.1080/09537325.2013.764987

Giroud, A. (2007). MNE vertical linkages: The experience of Vietnam after Malaysia. *International Business Review, 6*(2), 159–176. DOI: 10.1016/j.ibusrev.2006.11.003

Gkotsis, P. K., Banti, D. C., Peleka, E. N., Zouboulis, A. I., & Samaras, P. E. (2014). Fouling issues in membrane bioreactors (MBRs) for wastewater treatment: Major mechanisms, prevention and control strategies. *Processes (Basel, Switzerland), 2*(4), 795–866. DOI: 10.3390/pr2040795

GOK, (2010). Laws of Kenya National Council for Law Reporting.

Gönüllü Atakan, A., & Çoban, A. (2022). *Türkiye'de Kadınların Kooperatifler Yoluyla Güçlenmesi: Yasal ve Yapısal Stratejiler*. ILO Yayınları: https://dspace.ceid.org.tr/xmlui/bitstream/handle/1/2176/turkiyede-kadinlarinkooperatifler-yoluyla-guclenmesi.pdf?sequence=1&isAllowed=y adresinden alındı

Gössling, S., & Peeters, P. (2022). Tourism and environmental sustainability. *Journal of Sustainable Tourism, 30*(4), 789–804.

Goswami, G., & Haider, S. (2014). Does political risk deter FDI inflow? An analytical approach using panel data and factor analysis. *Journal of Economic Studies (Glasgow, Scotland), 41*(2), 233–252. DOI: 10.1108/JES-03-2012-0041

Government of Kenya. (1964). *Kenya Education Commission Report (Ominde Report)*. Government Printer.

Government of Kenya. (1965). *Sessional Paper No. 10 of 1965: African Socialism and its application to planning in Kenya*. Government Printer. https://new.kenyalaw.org

Government of Kenya. (1976). *Report of the National Committee on Educational Objectives and Policies (Gachathi Report)*. Government Printer.

Government of Kenya. (1981). *Second University in Kenya: Report of the Presidential Working Party (Mackay Report)*. Government Printer.

Government of Kenya. (1988). *Report of the Presidential Working Party on Education and Manpower Training for the Next Decade and Beyond (Kamunge Report)*. Government Printer.

Government of Kenya. (1999). *Totally Integrated Quality Education and Training (TIQET): Report of the Commission of Inquiry into the Education System of Kenya (Koech Report)*. Government Printer.

Government of Kenya. (2010). *Constitution of Kenya*. Government Printer. https://new.kenyalaw.org

Government of Kenya. (2012). *County Governments Act, No. 17 of 2012*. Government Printer. https://new.kenyalaw.org

Government of South Africa. (2012). National Development Plan: Vision for South Africa's Future - Unlocking Our Potential: Creating Work Opportunities for All [online]. Available at: https://www.ndp.gov.za/ [Accessed: 3 March 2023]

Green Cape. (2022). Waste market intelligence. Retrieved from: https://greencape.co.za/assets/WASTE_MIR_7_4_22_FINAL.pdf

Greenpeace Africa. (2023). *Kenya's poisoned waters*. Retrieved from https://www.greenpeace.org/africa/en/

Gubik, A. S., & Buah, A. (2019). The Role of Entrepreneurship in Economic Growth: The picture according to literature, International Multidisciplinary Scientific Conference, ISN978-963-358-177-3.

Guest, G., Namely, E. E., and Mitchell, M. L. (2013). Collecting Qualitative Data: A Field Manual for Applied Research. Sage Publications. United State of America

Haas, H. (2018). *Successful integration policies: Lessons from Austria*. Routledge.

Hakami, S. (2021). The role of social entrepreneurship in community development: A case study of social entrepreneurship in Saudi Arabia. *Psychology and Education*, *58*(2), 154–161. https://www.psychologyandeducation.net/

Hall, B. H., Lotti, F., Mairesse, J. (2006): Employment, Innovation and Productivity: Evidence from Italian Microdata. The Institute for Fiscal Studies. Working Paper 24/2006, London

Hall, R. (2010). *Land reform in South Africa: A status report 2010*. Institute for Poverty, Land and Agrarian Studies, University of the Western Cape.

Hall, S. (1997). Representation: Cultural Representations and Signifying Practices. *Sage (Atlanta, Ga.)*.

Hanna, N. K. (2010). Transforming government and building the information society: Challenges and opportunities for the developing world.

Harrison, A., & Rodríguez-Clare, A. (2010). Trade, foreign investment, and industrial policy for developing countries. Handbook of development economics, 5, 4039–4214.

Harrison, A., Love, I., & McMillan, M. (2004). Global capital flows and financing constraints. *Journal of Development Economics*, *75*(1), 269–301. DOI: 10.1016/j.jdeveco.2003.10.002

Hart, T. G. B., & Aliber, M. (2010). The role of smallholder farmers in food security in South Africa. *Development Southern Africa*, *27*(4), 499–514.

Hart, T. G. B., & Vorster, H. J. (2006). *Indigenous knowledge frameworks and practices for sustainable livelihoods in South Africa*. Human Sciences Research Council.

Haughton, G., & Hunter, C. (1994). *Sustainable cities*. Jessica Kingsley Publishers.

Healey, P. (2006). *Collaborative planning: Shaping places in fragmented societies* (2nd ed.). Macmillan. DOI: 10.1007/978-1-137-08600-6

Heathershaw, J., & Montgomery, D. (2014). The securitisation of Islam in Central Asia. *Europe-Asia Studies*, *66*(3), 456–479. DOI: 10.1080/09668136.2014.886567

Heinonen, J., & Hytti, U. (2014). Entrepreneurship mission and content in finish policy programmes. *Journal of Small Business and Enterprise Development*, *23*(1), 149–162. DOI: 10.1108/JSBED-10-2014-0170

Henry, M., Hoogenstrijd, T., Kirchherr, J. (2021). The rise of the circular entrepreneur: an altruistic spirit and the pursuit of mass-market expansion. Circ. Econ. 127–148. Retrieved from https://doi.org/.DOI: 10.4324/9780367816650-9

Hergovich, S., & Paprsek, M. (2015). Tapping the job potential of green investments in Europe. In Galg'oczi, B. (Ed.), *Europe's Energy Transformation in the Austerity Trap*. ETUI., Retrieved from https://books.google.co.za/books?hl=en&lr=&id=X00oCwAAQBAJ&oi=fnd&pg=PA141&ots=OUHq3e6X9J&sig=WdzzAZTxjBdlHHXFZo1QDAnv8vQ&redir_esc=y#v=onepage&q&f=false

Herta, S. A. (2018). Entrepreneurship education as the molding of entrepreneurial attitudes: A case study. *International Journal of Economics and Business Administration, 6*(3), 127–135. DOI: 10.35808/ijeba/172

Hettiarachchi, H., Meegoda, J. N., & Ryu, S. (2018). Organic waste buyback as a viable method to enhance sustainable municipal solid waste management in developing countries. *International Journal of Environmental Research and Public Health, 15*(11), 2483. DOI: 10.3390/ijerph15112483 PMID: 30405058

Heugh, K. (2021). Multilingual education policy in Africa. *Language Teaching, 54*(3), 354–372. DOI: 10.1017/S0261444821000112

Hill, D. D., Owens, W. E., & Tchounwou, P. B. (2006). The impact of rainfall on fecal coliform bacteria in Bayou Dorcheat (North Louisiana). *International Journal of Environmental Research and Public Health, 3*(1), 114–117. DOI: 10.3390/ijerph2006030013 PMID: 16823083

Hoa, N. O. (2021). Human capital and productivity growth in agriculture in Vietnam. *Journal of Science, 50*(2B), 43–54.

Hoffmann, C. (2020). *Counter-radicalization and integration policies in Europe: A comparative analysis*. Routledge.

Hofste, W., Reig, R., & Schleifer, L. (2019). 17 countries, home to one-quarter of the world's population, face extremely high-water stress. World Resources Institute. https://www.wri.org/blog/2019/08/17-countries-home-one-quarter-world - population-face-extremely-high-water-stress

Holstenkamp, L., & Kahla, F. (2016). What are community energy companies trying to accomplish? An empirical investigation of investment motives in the German case. *Energy Policy, 97*, 112–122. DOI: 10.1016/j.enpol.2016.07.010

Horbach, J., & Rammer, C. (2019). Employment and performance effects of circular economy innovations, ZEW Discussion Papers, No. 19-016, ZEW - Leibniz-Zentrum für Europäische Wirtschaftsforschung, Mannheim. Retrieved from https://www.econstor.eu/bitstream/10419/196125/1/1664582509.pdf

Horwitz, F. M., & Jain, H. (2011). An assessment of employment equity and broad based black economic empowerment developments in South Africa. *Equality, Diversity and Inclusion*, *30*(4), 297–317. DOI: 10.1108/02610151111135750

Hossain, M. I. (2024). Creation of 'other'in their own country, politicized identity-based division, and the rise of hostility toward 'out-group'in a multi-ethnic, poly-cultural world: A study on genocide prevention, human security, and peacebuilding. *Social Identities*, *30*(2), 88–109. DOI: 10.1080/13504630.2024.2342613

Hossain, M. I. (2025). Gender Inequality, Deprivation and Seclusion of Indian Muslim Women: Reflections on the 'Intersectionality'of Marginalization. *Hawwa*, *23*(1), 94–116. DOI: 10.1163/15692086-12341433

Huang, B. C., He, C. S., Fan, N. S., Jin, R. C., & Yu, H. Q. (2020). Envisaging wastewater-to-energy practices for sustainable urban water pollution control: Current achievements and future prospects. *Renewable & Sustainable Energy Reviews*, *134*, 110134. DOI: 10.1016/j.rser.2020.110134

Human Rights Watch. (2023). *World report 2023: Central Asia*. https://www.hrw.org/world-report/2023

Hutchinson, K., Fleck, E., & Llyod-Reason, L. (2009). An investigation into the initial barriers to internationalization: Evidence from small UK retailers. *Journal of Small Business and Enterprise Development*, *16*(4), 544–586. DOI: 10.1108/14626000911000910

ICA. (1995). *The Cooperative Identity*. https://www.ica.coop/en/media/library/research-and-reviews/review-international-cooperation adresinden alındı

Idrica (2023). Water trends in water reuse for 2023: Water, from waste to resources. Retrieved fromhttps://www.idrica.com/blog/water-trends-in-water-reuse-for-2023-water-from-waste-to-resource/

iLembe District Municipality. (2020). *Draft integrated development plan 2019/2020*. https://www.enterpriseilembe.co.za/images/ilembe/files/archive/ilembe%20idp/IDP-REVIEW-2-2019-2020.pdf

ILO. (2012). *How women fare in East African cooperatives: the case of Kenya, Tanzania and Uganda*. https://www.ilo.org/wcmsp5/groups/public/---ed_emp/---emp_ent/--coop/documents/publication/wcms_735776.pdf adresinden alındı

Immigration, Refugees and Citizenship Canada. (2020). *Settlement program report*. Retrieved from https://www.canada.ca/en/immigration-refugees-citizenship.html

İnan, İ., Kumkale, İ., & Okan, G. (1999). *Trakya'da Kırsal Kesimin Örgütlenmesinde Tarım Kooperatifleri, Üretici Birlikleri ve Köylere Hizmet Götürme Birliklerinin Rolü*. Türk Kooperatifçilik Kurumu Yayınları.

International Federation of Library Associations and Institutions. (2015). *Public libraries support development through access to information*. International Federation of Library Associations and Institutions.

International Fund for Agricultural Development. (2011). *Rural poverty report 2011: New realities, new challenges: New opportunities for tomorrow's generation*. IFAD.

International IDEA. (2025). *Gender quotas database*. https://www.idea.int

International Labour Organization. (2018). World employment and social outlook 2018: Greening with jobs. Retrieved from https://www.ilo.org/wesogreening/documents/WESO_Greening_EN_web2.pdf

International Migration Organization. (2020). *Global GDP and immigration integration*. International Migration Organization. https://www.iom.int

International Renewable Energy Agency. (2018). *Renewable energy outlook*. IRENA.

International Renewable Energy Agency. (2022). *Renewable energy in Africa: Challenges and opportunities*. IRENA Publications.

Inter-Parliamentary Union. (2023). *Women in national parliaments: Global data*. https://www.ipu.org

IOM. (2012). *International dialogue on migration 18: climate change, environmental degradation and migration*. IOM.

IPCC. (2014). Climate change 2014: synthesis report. In Pachauri, R. K., & Meyer, L. A. (Eds.), *Contribution of working groups I, II and III to the fifth assessment report of the intergovernmental panel on climate change* (pp. 1–168). Academic Press.

IRP. (2018). Re-defining Value – The Manufacturing Revolution. Remanufacturing, Refurbishment, Repair and Direct Reuse in the Circular Economy. Nabil Nasr, Jennifer Russell, Stefan Bringezu, Stefanie Hellweg, Brian Hilton, Cory Kreiss, & Nadia von Gries. A Report of the International Resource Panel. United Nations Environment Programme, Nairobi, Kenya. Retrieved from https://www.resourcepanel.org/sites/default/files/documents/document/media/re-defining_value_-_the_manfacturing_revolution_full_report_for_web.pdf

IWMSA (Institute of Waste Management of Southern Africa). (2019). See not waste, but opportunity on Global Recycling Day. Retrieved from https://cct.mycpd.co.za/IWMSA/IWMSA_Global%20Recycling%20Day%20release_20190308_FINAL.pdf

Japan Ministry of Health. (2020). *The role of immigrant workers in Japan's economy*. Ministry of Health, Labour and Welfare. https://www.mhlw.go.jp

Javorcik, B. S. (2004). Does foreign direct investment increase the productivity of domestic firms? In search of spillovers through backward linkages. *The American Economic Review, 94*(3), 605–627. DOI: 10.1257/0002828041464605

Javorcik, B. S., & Spatareanu, M. (2011). Does it matter where you come from? Vertical spillovers from foreign direct investment and the origin of investors. *Journal of Development Economics, 96*(1), 126–138. DOI: 10.1016/j.jdeveco.2010.05.008

Jensen, N. M. (2013). Domestic Institutions and the Taxing of Multinational Corporations. *International Studies Quarterly, 57*(4), 751–759. DOI: 10.1111/isqu.12099

Jiménez, B., & Asano, T. (2008). *Water Reuse: An International Survey of Current Practice, Issues and Needs*. IWA., DOI: 10.2166/9781780401881

Johnson, M., & Lee, K. (2022). Advanced Filtration Technologies for Water Treatment. *Water Research, 78*(4), 456–467.

Johnson, P., & White, M. (2021). Foreign direct investment and the growth of SMEs in the manufacturing sector. *International Economic Review, 47*(2), 123–145.

Kabeer, N. (1999). Resources, agency, achievements: Reflections on the measurement of women's empowerment. *Development and Change, 30*(3), 435–464. DOI: 10.1111/1467-7660.00125

Kalebaile, N., Ncube, E., Swartz, C., Marais, S., & Lubbe, J. (2020). *Strengthening the implementation of water reuse in South Africa*. Water Research Commission., Retrieved from https://www.wrc.org.za/wp-content/uploads/mdocs/WW%20Sept-Oct%202022_WATER%20REUSE.pdf

Kamali, M. H. (2008). *Shari'ah law: An introduction*. Oneworld Publications.

Kamali, M., Suhas, D. P., Costa, M. E., Capela, I., & Aminabhavi, T. M. (2019). Sustainability considerations in membrane-based technologies for industrial effluents treatment. *Chemical Engineering Journal, 368*, 474–494. DOI: 10.1016/j.cej.2019.02.075

Kamau, J., & Njoroge, W. (2024). AI-Driven Pollution Monitoring in Nairobi River. *Kenya Environmental Review, 15*(1), 34–50.

Kamp, M. (2006). *The new woman in Uzbekistan: Islam, modernity, and unveiling under communism*. University of Washington Press.

Kanayo, O., Ndlovu, P., & Agholor, I. (2021). Impact of local economic development programmes on livelihood: Evidence from Mpumalanga, South Africa. *International Journal of Economics and Financial Issues, 11*(4), 105–114. DOI: 10.32479/ijefi.11589

Kandiyoti, D. (2007). The politics of gender and the Soviet paradox. *Central Asian Survey, 26*(4), 601–620. DOI: 10.1080/02634930802018521

Kapilashrami, A., Quinn, N., & Das, A. (2025). 'Communities', power, and participation: unpacking concepts from praxis. In *Advancing Health Rights and Tackling Inequalities* (pp. 44–66). Policy Press. DOI: 10.1332/policypress/9781447361398.003.0003

Karanja, M., Wambui, N., & Njenga, M. (2020). The impact of the polluter pays principle on waste management in Kenya. *Environmental Economics and Policy Studies, 22*(4), 789–805. DOI: 10.1007/s10018-020-00267-3

Kariuki, P., & Ngugi, J. (2018). The Water Act 2016: Implications for water resource management in Kenya. *Water Policy Journal, 20*(2), 215–230. DOI: 10.2166/wp.2018.001

Kaza, S., Yao, L., Bhada-Tata, P., & Van Woerden, F. (2018). *What a Waste 2.0: A Global Snapshot of Solid Waste Management to 2050.* World Bank Publications. DOI: 10.1596/978-1-4648-1329-0

Kebaso, B. M. (2015). The effects of hydrological characteristics of the river Nyakomisaro on the water supply of Kisii municipality, Kenya (Doctoral dissertation, Kenyatta University).

KEİG. (2015). *Türkiye'de Kadın Kooperatifleşmesi: Eğilimler ve İdeal Tipler.* https://www.keig.org/wp-content/uploads/2016/03/koopwweb.pdf adresinden alındı

Kenya Marine and Fisheries Research Institute. (2022). *Annual report 2022*. KMFRI.

Kenya National Bureau of Statistics. (2019). Kenya Population and Housing Census Volume II: Distribution of Population by Administrative Units. p. 252.

Kerich, E., & Ndege, F. (2020). Sources of Water Pollution and Selected Physico-chemical Parameters of the Nyakomisaro River in Kisii County, Kenya. *American Journal of Biological and Environmental Statistics, 6*(2), 17–23. DOI: 10.11648/j.ajbes.20200602.11

Khalid, A. (2021). *Central Asia: A new history from the imperial conquests to the present*. Princeton University Press.

Khambule, I. B. (2015). *Local economic development as a social dialogue: A case of Enterprise iLembe* (Master's dissertation, University of KwaZulu-Natal, Graduate School of Business and Leadership). University of KwaZulu-Natal. http://hdl.handle.net/10413/14217

Khambule, I. (2021). Decentralisation or deconcentration: The case of regional and local economic development in South Africa. *Local Economy*, *36*(1), 22–41. DOI: 10.1177/02690942211018427

Khambule, I., & Gerwel-Proches, C. (2019). Exploring the role of social dialogue in local economic development: A case of a South African Local Economic Development Agency. *Progress in Development Studies*, *19*(1), 36–54. DOI: 10.1177/1464993418806126

Khambule, I., & Mtapuri, O. (2018). Assessing the role of Local Economic Development Agencies in KwaZulu-Natal, South Africa. *Local Economy*, *33*(4), 438–455. DOI: 10.1177/0269094218773933

Khambule, I., & Mtapuri, O. (2018). Interrogating the Institutional Capacity of Local Government to Support Local Economic Development Agencies in KwaZulu/Natal Province of South Africa. *African Journal of Public Affairs*, *10*(1).

Khan, F. (2010). The Community Work Programme: Building a society that works. In Turok, B. (Ed.), *Wealth Doesn't Trickle Down: The Case for a Developmental State in South Africa* (pp. 181–193). Jacana Media.

Khatri Basnet, R. (2023). Role of Cooperatives in Women Empowerment in the Nepalese Context. *Cognition*, *5*(1), 99–105. DOI: 10.3126/cognition.v5i1.55417

Kibuika, F. M., & Wanyoike, D. (2012). Assessment of Factors Affecting Sustainability of Rural Water Supply Schemes in Nyandarua County, Kenya: A Case of Kangui Water Scheme. [IJSR]. *International Journal of Science and Research*, *3*, 578–584.

Kimani, J., & Wanjiku, M. (2023). Biodegradable Materials and Their Impact on Aquatic Environments. *Journal of Environmental Protection*, *14*(2), 112–128.

Kimani-Murage, E. W., & Ngindu, A. M. (2007). Quality of water the slum dwellers use: The case of a Kenyan slum. *Journal of Urban Health : Bulletin of the New York Academy of Medicine*, *84*(6), 829–838. DOI: 10.1007/s11524-007-9199-x PMID: 17551841

Kim, Y., & Lee, J. (2019). Sectoral analysis of FDI effects on SMEs in renewable energy markets. *Energy Economics Journal*, *41*(2), 142–160.

Kiptum, C. K., & Ndambuki, J. M. (2012). Well water contamination by pit latrines: A case study of Langas. *Int. J. Water Res. Environ. Eng.*, *4*(2), 35–43.

Kitaka, N., Omondi, L. A., Mureithi, P. W., Bauer, A., Melcher, A., & Ssanyu, G. A. (2024). A critical review of biomonitoring in East African rivers: Fostering community-based collaboration for environmental change observation. *Frontiers in Water*, *6*, 1360941. DOI: 10.3389/frwa.2024.1360941

KNBS. (2019). Kenya Population and Housing Census, Volume II: Distribution of Population by Administrative Units. KNBS, Nairobi.

Kobedi, K. C. S. (2021). *Local economic assessment of community work programmes as a job creation mechanism* (Master's dissertation, University of Johannesburg). University of Johannesburg Institutional Repository. https://hdl.handle.net/10210/485211

Koburtay, T., Abuhussein, T., & Sidani, Y. M. (2023). Women leadership, culture, and Islam: Female voices from Jordan. *Journal of Business Ethics*, *181*(3), 673–689. DOI: 10.1007/s10551-022-05041-0

Korhonen, J., Honkasalo, A., & Seppälä, J. (2018). Circular economy: The concept and its limitations. *Ecological Economics*, *143*, 37–46. DOI: 10.1016/j.ecolecon.2017.06.041

Koutsou, S., Iakovidou, O., & Gotsinas, N. (2003). Women's cooperatives in Greece: An ongoing story of battles, successes and problems. *Journal of Rural Cooperation*, ●●●, 47–57.

Kristian, A., Goh, T. S., Ramadan, A., Erica, A., & Sihotang, S. V. (2024). Application of ai in optimizing energy and resource management: Effectiveness of deep learning models. *International Transactions on Artificial Intelligence*, *2*(2), 99–105. DOI: 10.33050/italic.v2i2.530

Kumar, S., Pratap, B., Dubey, D., & Dutta, V. (2022). Integration of Constructed Wetland Technology as a Decentralised Wastewater Treatment Facility and Water Reuse in Agriculture. In *Environmental Studies and Climate Change* (pp. 565–582). CRC Press. DOI: 10.1201/9781003220824-39

Kung'u, M. N. (2023). Challenges and Possible Solutions for Effective Solid Waste Management in Githunguri Town, Kiambu County (Doctoral dissertation, University of Nairobi).

Kuppan, N., Padman, M., Mahadeva, M., Srinivasan, S., & Devarajan, R. (2024). *A comprehensive review of sustainable bioremediation techniques: Eco-friendly solutions for waste and pollution management*. Waste Management Bulletin.

Kurniawan, T. A., Maiurova, A., Kustikova, M., Bykovskaia, E., Othman, M., & Goh, H. H. (2022). Accelerating sustainability transition in St. Petersburg (Russia) through digitalisation-based circular economy in waste recycling industry: A strategy to promote carbon neutrality in the era of Industry 4.0. *Journal of Cleaner Production, 363*, 132452. DOI: 10.1016/j.jclepro.2022.132452

Kutlu, Ö. ve Sütlü, S.(2024). Investigation of the Career Development Experiences of Women Managers: An Analysis From a Gender Perspective, M.Haoucha (Ed.), Empowering and Advancing Women Leaders and Entrepreneurs içinde (231-247 ss.), Pennsylvania: IGI Global.

Kymlicka, W. (2018). Multiculturalism and immigrant integration in Canada. In Triandafyllidou, A. (Ed.), *Handbook of migration and globalization* (pp. 97–112). Edward Elgar Publishing.

Lacy, P., & Rutqvist, J. (2016). Waste to Wealth: the Circular Economy Advantage, Waste to Wealth: the Circular Economy Advantage.

Lane, B. (1994). Sustainable rural tourism strategies. *Journal of Sustainable Tourism, 2*(1-2), 102–112. DOI: 10.1080/09669589409510687

Lanzieri, G. (2014). *The demographic impact of migration in Europe*. Eurostat.

Lassithiotaki, A., & Roubakou, A. (2014). Rural Women Cooperatives at Greece: A retrospective study. *Open Journal of Business and Management*, 127-137.

Laurence, J. (2020). Discrimination and integration in France. In Kaufmann, E., & Goodwin, P. (Eds.), *The integration of migrants: Challenges and policies* (pp. 67–88). Routledge.

Lawrence, F. (2017). *Local economic development agencies in South Africa: Evolution, organisation and progress* (Doctoral dissertation, University of Johannesburg). University of Johannesburg Institutional Repository. https://hdl.handle.net/10210/270030

Lawrence, F., & Rogerson, C. M. (2018). Local economic development agencies and place-based development: Evidence from South Africa. *Bulletin of Geography. Socio-Economic Series, 41*(41), 29–43. DOI: 10.2478/bog-2018-0024

Lawrence, F., & Rogerson, C. M. (2019). Local economic development agencies and peripheral small town development: Evidence from Somerset East, South Africa. *Urbani Izziv, 30*(30, Supplement), 144–157. DOI: 10.5379/urbani-izziv-en-2019-30-supplement-010

Lebedeva, M., & Stolyarova, S. (2023). Participation of women in political institutions of post-Soviet countries: Experience of Central Asian countries. International Trends / Mezhdunarodnye Protsessy, 21(1). https://www.intertrends.ru/jour/article/view/188

Lee, N., & Drever, E. (2014). Do SMEs in deprived areas find it harder to access finance? Evidence from the UK Small Business Survey. *Entrepreneurship and Regional Development*, *26*(4), 337–356. DOI: 10.1080/08985626.2014.911966

Levy, K., Smith, S. M., & Carlton, E. J. (2018). Climate Change Impacts on Waterborne Diseases: Moving Toward Designing Interventions. *Current Environmental Health Reports*, *5*(2), 272–282. DOI: 10.1007/s40572-018-0199-7 PMID: 29721700

Lieder, M., & Rashid, A. (2016). Towards circular economy implementation: A comprehensive review in the context of the manufacturing industry. *Journal of Cleaner Production*, *115*, 36–51. DOI: 10.1016/j.jclepro.2015.12.042

Liu, L., Johnson, H. L., Cousens, S., Perin, J., Scott, S., Lawn, J. E., Rudan, I., Campbell, H., Cibulskis, R., Li, M., Mathers, C., & Black, R. E. (2012). Global, regional, and national causes of child mortality: An updated systematic analysis for 2010 with time trends since 2000. *Lancet*, *379*(9832), 2151–2161. DOI: 10.1016/S0140-6736(12)60560-1 PMID: 22579125

Livesley, S. J., McPherson, G. M., & Calfapietra, C. (2016). The urban forest and ecosystem services: Impacts on urban water, heat, and pollution cycles at the tree, street, and city scale. *Journal of Environmental Quality*, *45*(1), 119–124. DOI: 10.2134/jeq2015.11.0567 PMID: 26828167

Lovins, A., & Michael, B. (2014). *A New Dynamic - Effective Business in a Circular Economy, the Business Angle of a Circular Economy – Higher Competitiveness.* Higher Resource Security and Material Efficiency.

Luiz, S., & Van Der Linde, K. (2006). Broad-based Economic Empowerment: Some Challenges in Measuring Ownership of Companies. *S. Afr. Mercantile LJ*, *18*, 473.

Lybbert, T. J., & Sumner, D. A. (2020). Agriculture in North Africa: Adaptive strategies for climate change. *Agricultural Economics*, *51*(2), 207–219.

Lyons, M., Smuts, C., & Stephens, A. (2001). Participation, empowerment and sustainability:(How) do the links work? *Urban Studies (Edinburgh, Scotland)*, *38*(8), 1233–1251. DOI: 10.1080/00420980125039

Maalouf, A., & Mavropoulos, A. (2023). Re-assessing global municipal solid waste generation. *Waste Management & Research*, *41*(4), 936–947. DOI: 10.1177/0734242X221074116 PMID: 35075952

Madzivhandila, T., Maloka, C. (2014). Community Participation in Local Government Planning Processes: A Paramount Step Towards a Successful Service Delivery.

Makhathini, M. S. M., Mlambo, V. H., & Mpanza, S. (2020). Infrastructure provision as a catalyst for local economic development in South Africa. *Strategic Review for Southern Africa, 42*(1), 105–126. https://www.up.ac.za/strategic-review-for-southern-africa

Makwana, G., & Elizabeth, H. (2022). The Concept of the Indian Marginalized Communities. *Madhya Bharti Manviki Evam Samaj Vigyan Shodh Patrika*, *82*(2), 166–174.

Maliki, S. B.-E., Amine, M. M., Metaiche, F. T., & Ziani, T. (2008). *The role of local economic development agencies (LEDA) in territorial development and the whole macro-economic goals achievement. Les Cahiers du MECAS, 4*(1), 68–84. https://www.asjp.cerist.dz/en/article/9688

Maliki, S. B.-E., Metaiche, M. A., Metaiche, F. T., & Ziani, T. (2008). The role of local economic development agencies (LEDA) on territorial development and the whole macroeconomic goals achievement. *Les Cahiers du MECAS, 4*(1), 68–84. https://asjp.cerist.dz/en/article/9688

Maphumulo, L. S. (2025). Empowering Traditional Leadership for Effective Community Development. African Journal of Religion. *Philosophy and Culture*, *6*(3), 213.

Markusen, J. R., & Venables, A. J. (1999). Foreign direct investment as a catalyst for industrial development. *European Economic Review*, *43*(2), 335–356. DOI: 10.1016/S0014-2921(98)00048-8

Marshall, G. (1999). *Sosyoloji sözlüğü*. Bilim ve Sanat Yayınları.

Martínez-del-Río, J., Céspedes-Lorente, J., & Carmona-Moreno, E. (2012). High-involvement work practices and environmental capabilities: How HIWPS create environmentally based sustainable competitive advantages. *Human Resource Management*, *51*(6), 827–850. DOI: 10.1002/hrm.21505

Masato, A. (2009). Globalization of Production and the Competitiveness of Small and Medium-sized Enterprises in Asia and the Pacific [from United Nations Economic and Social Commission for Asia and the Pacific] [ESCAP]. *Trends and Prospects*, *65*, 33–57.

Mashamaite, K., & Lethoko, M. (2018). Role of the South African local government in local economic development. *International Journal of eBusiness and eGovernment Studies, 10*(1), 114–128. https://dergipark.org.tr/en/pub/ijebeg/issue/36107/535456

Masikane, S. (2021). *Local economic development as an employment strategy in eMkhazane rural area (Ward 21), Ulundi Municipality* (Master's dissertation, University of KwaZulu-Natal). University of KwaZulu-Natal ResearchSpace. https://researchspace.ukzn.ac.za/handle/10413/19835

Massey, D. S., Arango, J., Hugo, G., Kouaouci, A., Pellegrino, A., & Taylor, E. J. (1993). Theories of international migration: A review and appraisal. *Population and Development Review*, *19*(3), 431–466. DOI: 10.2307/2938462

Masuku, M. M., Jili, N. N., & Selepe, B. M. (2016). The implementation of local economic development initiatives towards poverty alleviation in Big 5 False Bay Local Municipality. *African Journal of Hospitality, Tourism and Leisure*, *5*(4), 1–11. https://www.ajhtl.com/

Mauter, M. S., & Fiske, P. S. (2020). Desalination for a circular water economy. [United Kingdom.]. *Energy & Environmental Science*, •••, 13.

Mawere, M. (2024). *Mawere: Culture, Indigenous Knowledge and Develo*. African Books Collective.

Mayer, A. E. (2013). *Islam and human rights: Tradition and politics* (5th ed.). Westview Press.

McEwan, C. (2005). New spaces of citizenship? Rethinking gendered participation and empowerment in South Africa. *Political Geography*, *24*(8), 969–991. DOI: 10.1016/j.polgeo.2005.05.001

McKinsey Global Institute. (2017). *The economic value of cultural diversity in firms*. McKinsey & Company. https://www.mckinsey.com

MEA. (2005). *Millennium Ecosystem Assessment: Ecosystems and human well-being: Synthesis*. Island Press.

Mehmood, T., Alzoubi, H. M., Alshurideh, M., Al-Gasaymeh, A., & Ahmed, G. (2019). Schumpeterian entrepreneurship theory: Evolution and relevance. *Academy of Entrepreneurship Journal*, *25*(4), 1–10. https://www.abacademies.org/articles/Schumpeterian-entrepreneurship-theory-evolution-and-relevance-

Meissner, D. (2019). Public-private partnership models for science, technology, and innovation cooperation. *Journal of the Knowledge Economy*, *10*(4), 1341–1361. DOI: 10.1007/s13132-015-0310-3

Meyer, I., & Sommer, M. W. (2014). Employment Effects of Renewable Energy Supply A Meta Analysis Employment Effects of Renewable Energy Supply-A Meta Analysis 1–2. Retrieved from https://www.wifo.ac.at/wp-content/uploads/upload2151/sw_2014_WWWforEurope_PP12_47225_-1.pdf

Meyer, D. F. (2014). Local economic development (LED), challenges and solutions: The case of the Northern Free State region, South Africa. *Mediterranean Journal of Social Sciences*, *5*(16), 624–634. DOI: 10.5901/mjss.2014.v5n16p624

Mihelcic, J. R., Crittenden, J. C., Small, M. J., Shonnard, D. R., Hokanson, D. R., Qiong, Z. H., Sheryla, S., Valentineu, J., Sutherland, J. W., & Schnoor, J. L. (2003). Sustainability science and engineering: The emergence of a new meta discipline. *Environmental Science & Technology*, *37*(23), 5314–5324. DOI: 10.1021/es034605h PMID: 14700315

Mikkelsen, B. (2005). *Methods for Development Work and Research: A New Guide for Practitioners*. Sage Publications. DOI: 10.4135/9788132108566

Millar, N., McLaughlin, E., & Börger, T. (2019). The circular economy: Swings and roundabouts? *Ecological Economics*, *158*, 11–19. DOI: 10.1016/j.ecolecon.2018.12.012

Millennium Ecosystem Assessment. (2005). *Ecosystems and human well-being: Synthesis*. Island Press.

Ministry of the Environment. Morocco. (2017). *Politique nationale de développement durable*. Government of Morocco.

Minkov, M., Kaasa, A., & Welzel, C. (2021). Economic development and modernization in Africa homogenize national cultures. *Journal of Cross-Cultural Psychology*, *52*(8-9), 801–821. DOI: 10.1177/00220221211035495

Mir-Hosseini, Z. (2009). *Islam and gender: The religious debate in contemporary Iran*. Princeton University Press.

Mir-Hosseini, Z. (2022). *Journeys toward gender equality in Islam*. Oneworld Academic.

Mironga, J. M. (2006). Degradation of wetland ecosystems: A case study of Kisii District, western Kenya. *Biodiversity (Nepean)*, *7*(3-4), 3–16. DOI: 10.1080/14888386.2006.9712806

Mitch, A. A., Gasner, K. C., & Mitch, W. A. (2010). Feacal coliform accumulation within a river subject to seasonally-disinfected wastewater discharges. *Water Research*, *44*(16), 4776–4782. DOI: 10.1016/j.watres.2010.05.060 PMID: 20580053

Mkhize, M. L. (2017). The role of sense of community in promoting community based entrepreneurship in rural KwaZulu-Natal, South Africa: an exploratory study of agricultural co-operatives (Doctoral dissertation, University of KwaZulu-Natal, Howard College).

Mkhize, S., Mlatsheni-Mathebula, T., & Mashaba-Nkosi, L. (Eds.). (2017). Community Based Participatory Research: A Guide for Practitioners [online]. Available at: https://www.researchgate.net/publication/334644677_Community_Based_Participatory_Research_A_Guide_for_Practitioners [Accessed: 3 March 2023]

Mkhwanazi, M. N. (2019). *An investigation of challenges affecting the implementation of project management practices: A case study of Msunduzi Expanded Public Works Programme clearing project* (Master's dissertation, University of KwaZulu-Natal). University of KwaZulu-Natal ResearchSpace. https://researchspace.ukzn.ac.za/

Mncwabe, L. (2013). *The role of skills development initiatives in promoting local economic development (LED) in South African townships: A case study of Cato Manor, Durban* (Master's dissertation, University of KwaZulu-Natal). University of KwaZulu-Natal ResearchSpace. https://researchspace.ukzn.ac.za/

Modood, T. (2019). Multiculturalism and integration in the UK. *Journal of Ethnic and Migration Studies*, *45*(8), 1315–1331.

Mogaka, E. (2022). Project Planning on Implementation of Solid Waste Management Practices in Kisii Central Sub-County, Kisii County, Kenya (Doctoral dissertation, University of Nairobi).

Mohamed, A. M. O., Mohamed, D., Fayad, A., & Al Nahyan, M. T. (2024). Enhancing decision making and decarbonation in environmental management: A review on the role of digital technologies. *Sustainability (Basel)*, *16*(16), 7156. DOI: 10.3390/su16167156

Mokoena, S. K. (2019). The role of local economic development on small, medium and micro enterprises. *Acta Universitatis Danubius. Œconomica, 15*(1), 59–83. https://journals.univ-danubius.ro/index.php/oeconomica

Momanyi, M. D. (2021). Land-use Transformation and Changes in Peri-urban Livelihoods in Kisii Municipality, Kisii County, Kenya (Doctoral dissertation, University of Nairobi).

Mongkolnchaiarunya, J. (2005). Promoting a community-based solid-waste management initiative in local government: Yala municipality, Thailand. *Habitat International*, *29*(1), 27–40. DOI: 10.1016/S0197-3975(03)00060-2

Moosa, I. A. (2023). *The West Versus the Rest and The Myth of Western Exceptionalism*. Palgrave Macmillan. DOI: 10.1007/978-3-031-26560-0

Moreno-Mondejar, L., Triguero, Á., & Cuerva, M. C. (2021). Exploring the association between circular economy strategies and green jobs in European companies. *Journal of Environmental Management, 297*, 297. DOI: 10.1016/j.jenvman.2021.113437 PMID: 34351301

Morgan, J., & Mitchell, P. (2015 b). Employment and the Circular Economy. Job Creation in a More Resource Efficient Britain, vol. 28. Retrieved from https://ecointelligentgrowth.net/wp-content/uploads/2015/02/Employment-and-the-circular-economy-summary.pdf

Morgan, J., & Mitchell, P. (2015a). Opportunities to Tackle Britain's Labour Market Challenges through Growth in the Circular Economy. Retrieved from https://green-alliance.org.uk/wp-content/uploads/2021/12/Opportunities-to-tackle-UK-Labour-Market-Challenges_sgl.pdf

Mor, S., & Ravindra, K. (2023). Municipal solid waste landfills in lower- and middle-income countries: Environmental impacts, challenges and sustainable management practices. *Process Safety and Environmental Protection, 174*, 510–530. DOI: 10.1016/j.psep.2023.04.014

Mosago, F. A. (2010). *Factors influencing solid waste management in Kisii Municipal Council*. University of Nairobi., https://erepository.uonbi.ac.ke/handle/11295/4938

Moseley, C. (Ed.). (2010). *Atlas of the world's languages in danger* (3rd ed.). UNESCO Publishing., https://unesdoc.unesco.org

Mosoti, R. D., Obed, N., Albert, G., Reuben, O., Paul, O., & Argwings, O. (2024). *Phytoplankton Diversity and Heavy Metal Accumulation: A Case of Suneka Wastewater Treatment Plant*.

Moulai, S., & Boukrif, M. (2018). The choice of successor in family SMEs. *Revue Africaine de Management, 1*(3).

Mqwathi, H. T. 2023. "Analysing the Impact of Disruptive Events on the Performance of the Automotive Industry Sales in Gauteng, South Africa." Doctoral diss., North-West University (South Africa).

Msuya, T. S., & Lalika, M. C. S. (2016). The role of indigenous knowledge in managing food security and climate change adaptation among rural communities in Africa. *African Journal of Food, Agriculture, Nutrition and Development, 16*(3), 11000–11016.

Mthimkhulu, S., and Mpanza, S. (2021). The role of local economic development agencies and non-profit organisations in local economic development: South African case studies.

Muathe, S., & Khayinga, L. M. (2018). Human capital development and organisational performance: Review and critique of literature and research agenda. *International Journal for Innovation Education and Research*, *6*(2), 144–153. DOI: 10.31686/ijier.vol6.iss2.959

Mufwene, S. S. (2006). Lost tongues and the politics of language endangerment. *University of Chicago Magazine, 98*(3), 24–29. https://mag.uchicago.edu

Mugambi, H. M. (2002). Language choice and shift in Kenya: A look at the changing roles of English, Kiswahili and indigenous languages. *Language, Literacy and Culture Review*, 12–23.

Mungai, E. (2022). An Evaluation of the Effectiveness of Alternative Water Supply: A Case Study of Nairobi Water Central Region, Zone 1 (Doctoral dissertation, University of Nairobi).

Munir, M. T., Li, B., & Naqvi, M. (2023). Revolutionising municipal solid waste management (MSWM) with machine learning as a clean resource: Opportunities, challenges and solutions. *Fuel*, *348*, 128548. DOI: 10.1016/j.fuel.2023.128548

Mutangadura, G. (2004). *Women and land tenure rights in Southern Africa: A human rights-based approach*. United Nations Economic Commission for Africa.

Mutua, E., & Wambua, J. (2024). Overcoming Challenges in Waste Management: A Kenyan Perspective. *Journal of Environmental Policy*, *17*(1), 45–60.

Mutua, J., Kariuki, P., & Ngugi, J. (2020). Kenya Vision 2030 and environmental sustainability. *Sustainable Development Review*, *28*(3), 345–359. DOI: 10.1002/sd.2045

Mu, Y., Cai, W., Evans, S., Wang, C., & Roland-Holst, D. (2018). Employment impacts of renewable energy policies in China: A decomposition analysis based on a CGE modeling framework. *Applied Energy*, *210*, 256–267. DOI: 10.1016/j.apenergy.2017.10.086

Mwangi, A., & Otieno, D. (2023). Integrated Waste Management Strategies in Kenya. *Journal of Sustainable Development*, *11*(2), 78–92.

Mwangi, H., Otieno, P., & Omondi, R. (2020). Application of AI in monitoring urban river pollution in Nairobi. *Environmental Monitoring and Assessment*, *192*(5), 1–12. DOI: 10.1007/s10661-020-08311-5

Naftal, M. O., Mutua, B. K., & Moronge, J. M. (2023). Existing Governance Structures for Sustainable Solid Waste Management in Kisii Town, Kenya. *Water Technology*, *11*(2), 102–111.

Nahman, A., Godfrey, L., Oelofse, S., & Trotter, D. (2021). Driving economic growth in South Africathrough a low carbon, sustainable and inclusive circular economy, Pretoria: CSIR. Retrieved from http://circulareconomy.co.za/wpcontent/uploads/2021/11/1.-Introduction-CE-BriefingNote.pdf

Naji, A. A. H. (2019). *Factors influencing entrepreneurship development*. ResearchGate. https://www.researchgate.net/publication/332255136_Factors_Influencing_Entrepreneurship_Development

Najlis, P., & Edwards, A. (1991). The international drinking water supply and sanitation decade in retrospect and implications for the future. *Natural Resources Forum*, *15*(2), 110–117. DOI: 10.1111/j.1477-8947.1991.tb00121.x

National Bureau of Economic Research. (2019). *Immigrant entrepreneurs and job creation*. https://www.nber.org

National Environment Management Authority (NEMA). (2023). *Environmental best practices in waste management*. Retrieved from https://www.nema.go.ke

National Planning Commission. (2012). *National Development Plan 2030: Our future—Make it work*. The Presidency, Republic of South Africa.

NCPC-SA. (2020). Annual Report 2020-2021. NCPC: Pretoria. Retrieved from https://www.industrialefficiency.co.za/wpcontent/uploads/2022/01/Annual-Highlights-2020-21.pdf

Ndebele, N. (2013). Decolonising the University: The Wits Experience [online]. Available at: https://www.witsuniversitypressscholarshiponline.com/view/titlepage/witsup-978-1-77614-468-5 [Accessed: 3 March 2023]

Ndegwa, S., & Karanja, T. (2023). Anaerobic Digestion and Pyrolysis: Waste to Energy Solutions. *Renewable Energy Journal*, *22*(4), 299–315.

Ndikumana, L., & Verick, S. (2008). The linkages between FDI and domestic investment: Unravelling the developmental impact of foreign investment in Sub-Saharan Africa. *Development Policy Review*, *26*(6), 713–726. DOI: 10.1111/j.1467-7679.2008.00430.x

Ndlovu, C. (2021). *Pro-poor local economic development (LED): The case of Umzinyathi District Municipality, KwaZulu-Natal* (Master's dissertation, University of the Free State). University of the Free State. http://hdl.handle.net/11660/11628

Neene, V. (2017). Mobile GIS for enhanced property tax collection: a case of Lusaka province local authorities (Doctoral dissertation, The University of Zambia).

Nefussi, B., & Schwellnus, C. (2010). Does FDI in manufacturing cause FDI in business services? Evidence from French firm-level data. *The Canadian Journal of Economics. Revue Canadienne d'Économique*, *43*(1), 180–203. DOI: 10.1111/j.1540-5982.2009.01568.x

Nel, E., and Rogerson. (2017) Local Economic Development in the Developing World: The experience of Southern Africa. http:/tayloandfrancis.com.

Nene, O. J. (2015). *The role of local economic development agencies in supporting local innovation* (Master's research report, University of the Witwatersrand). Wits Business School. http://hdl.handle.net/10539/20936

Nene, O. J. (2016). *The role of local economic development agencies (LEDAs) in supporting local innovation* (Research report, Wits Business School, University of the Witwatersrand). University of the Witwatersrand. https://wiredspace.wits.ac.za/items/95122b68-05b7-4421-a07b-fae6402c5ec1

Ngubane, N., & Makua, M. (2021). Ubuntu pedagogy–transforming educational practices in South Africa through an African philosophy: From theory to practice. *Inkanyiso*, *13*(1), 1–12. DOI: 10.4102/ink.v13i1.9

Ni, W., Ding, G., Li, Y., Li, H., Liu, Q., & Jiang, B. (2014). Effects of the floods on dysentery in north central region of Henan Province, China from 2004 to 2009. *The Journal of Infection*, *69*(5), 430–439. DOI: 10.1016/j.jinf.2014.05.016 PMID: 24955987

Njenga, M., Mutua, J., & Kariuki, P. (2021). National solid waste management strategy: Achievements and challenges. *Waste Management Journal*, *34*(1), 67–79. DOI: 10.1016/j.wasman.2021.01.012

Njieassam, E. E. (2019). Gender inequality and land rights: The situation of Indigenous women in Cameroon. *Potchefstroom Electronic Law Journal*, *22*, 4907. Advance online publication. DOI: 10.17159/1727-3781/2019/v22i0a4907

Novovic, G. (2022). Can Agenda 2030 bring about "localization"? Policy limitations of Agenda 2030 in the broader global governance system. *Development Policy Review*, *40*(4), e12587. DOI: 10.1111/dpr.12587

Nowak, D. J., Hirabayashi, S., Bodine, A., & Greenfield, E. (2018). Tree and forest effects on air quality and human health in the United States. *Environmental Pollution*, *193*, 119–129. DOI: 10.1016/j.envpol.2014.05.028 PMID: 25016465

Ntsebeza, L., & Hall, R. (2007). *The land question in South Africa: The challenge of transformation and redistribution*. HSRC Press.

Nurbayev, Z. Y., Sultangazy, G. Z., & Serikbayev, B. S. (2024). A study of political party affiliation as a means to enhance gender equality and women's political participation in Kazakhstan. *Public Administration and Policy, 27*(1), 45–57. DOI: 10.1108/PAP-07-2023-0095

Nurmagambetova, R. (2024). CEDAW concerns and gender equality in Central Asia: Institutional barriers and reform pathways. *Central Asian Survey, 43*(2), 210–228.

Nussbaum, M. C. (1997). *Cultivating Humanity: A Classical Defense of Reform in Liberal Education*. Harvard University Press.

Nyamache, C. M. (2021). Challenges in the Use and Conservation of Urban Green Spaces: a Case of Kisii Municipality, Kisii County, Kenya (Doctoral dissertation, University of Nairobi).

Nyamache, T. J. (2018). The Effects of Solid Waste Dumping on Infrastructures and Human Health: Dandora Dump Site, Nairobi County (Doctoral dissertation, University of Nairobi).

Nyamnjoh, F. B. (2019). *Decolonizing the university in Africa*. Oxford University Press. DOI: 10.1093/acrefore/9780190228637.013.717

Ochieng, P., & Mutiso, S. (2023). Bioremediation in Lake Victoria: Successes and Challenges. *African Journal of Environmental Science, 12*(3), 210–225.

Odada, E. O., Olago, D. O., Kulindwa, K., Ntiba, M., & Wandiga, S. (2004). Mitigation of pollution in Lake Victoria, East Africa: Causal chain and policy options analyses. *Ambio, 33*(1-2), 13–23. DOI: 10.1579/0044-7447-33.1.13 PMID: 15083646

Odhiambo, L., & Achieng, M. (2024). Buffer Zones and Their Role in Pollution Control. *Environment Conservation Journal, 19*(1), 56–70.

Odora Hoppers, C. A. (Ed.). (2002). *Indigenous knowledge and the integration of knowledge systems: Towards a philosophy of articulation*. New Africa Books.

OECD. (2004). Facilitating SMEs access to international markets. OECD Conference of Ministers Responsible for Small and Medium-Sized Enterprises (SMEs). Retrieved from https://www.oecd.org/industry/smes/31919223.pdf

OECD. (2013). *Interconnected economies: Benefiting from global value chains*. OECD Publishing.

OECD. (2017). Making integration work: Refugees and others in need of protection. OECD Publishing. Making Integration Work | OECD

OECD. (2018). *Skills proficiency and the labour market outcomes of migrants*. OECD Publishing. Skills proficiency and the labour market outcomes of migrants | OECD

OECD. (2019). Business Models for the Circular Economy: Opportunities and Challenges for Policy. Retrieved from https://www.oecd.org/en/publications/business-models-for-the-circular-economy_g2g9dd62-en.html

OECD. (2019). *Global Material Resources Outlook to 2060: Economic Drivers and Environmental Consequences*. OECD Publishing., DOI: 10.1787/9789264307452-

OECD. (2021). *The economic impact of immigration.* OECD Publishing. Economic impact of migration | OECD

OECD. (2023). *Evaluation Systems in Development Co-operation 2023*. OECD Publishing., DOI: 10.1787/a255365e-

OECD. (2023). *Monitoring and participatory evaluation of the National Strategy to Combat Poverty 2021–2030 (ENCP)*. OECD Observatory of Public Sector Innovation. https://oecd-opsi.org/innovations/monitoring-and-participatory-evaluation-of-the-national-strategy-to-combat-poverty-2021-2030-encp/

OECD. (2023). Policy Toolkit for strengthening FDI and SME linkages. Retrieved from https://www.oecd.org/en/publications/policy-toolkit-for-strengthening-fdi-and-sme linkages_688bde9a-en.html

OECD. (2024). *Climate change, demography and migration*. OECD Publishing. Climate change, demography and migration | OECD

Oelofse, S. H. H., & Godfrey, L. (2008). Defining waste in South Africa: Moving beyond the age of 'waste'. *South African Journal of Science*, *104*(7-8), 242–246.

Ogechi, B. O. I. (2023). *Influence of anthropogenic activities on Nyangongo wetland in Nyaribari Chache sub-county*. Kisii County.

Ogendi, G. M. (2022). Effects of Anthropogenic Activities on the Water Quality of River Nyakomisaro-Riana, Kisii, Kenya. *European Journal of Applied Sciences*, *10*(5), 171–190.

Ogendi, G. M. (2022). Effects of nutrients on the water quality and the algal community of River Nyakomisaro-Riana, Kisii, Kenya. *International Journal of Fisheries and Aquatic Studies*, *10*(5), 111–118. DOI: 10.22271/fish.2022.v10.i5b.2734

Ogendi, G. M. (2023). Climate Change and Its Implications on School Education in Kenya. In Keengwe, J., & Nyatuka, B. O. (Eds.), *Climate Change Education for Sustainable Development* (pp. 144–167). IGI Global., DOI: 10.4018/978-1-6684-9099-0.ch007

Ogone, J. (2010). A case of a mother tongue and another mother tongue in school: Efforts at revitalization of the Olusuba language of Kenya. *Journal of Third World Studies*, *27*(2), 267–291.

Okorie, C., Udoh, E., & Bassey, O. B. (2023). Mirroring the Developmental Challenges of Oil-Rich Nige-ria within the Context of Resource Curse/Dutch Disease and Paradox of Plenty. *TIJER–InternationalResearch Journal*, *10*(4), 818–834.

Okotto-Okotto, J., Okotto, L., Price, H., Pedley, S., & Wright, J. (2015). A longitudinal study of long-term change in contamination hazards and shallow well quality in two neighbourhoods of Kisumu, Kenya. *International Journal of Environmental Research and Public Health*, *12*(4), 4275–4291. DOI: 10.3390/ijerph120404275 PMID: 25898406

Okullo, J. O., Moturi, W. N., & Ogendi, G. M. (2017). Open Defeacation and Its Effects on the Bacteriological Quality of Drinking Water Sources in Isiolo County, Kenya. *Environmental Health Insights*, *11*, 1–8. DOI: 10.1177/1178630217735539 PMID: 29051705

Olaopa, O. R., & Ayodele, O. A. (2022). Building on the strengths of African indigenous knowledge and innovation (AIKandI) for sustainable development in Africa. *African Journal of Science, Technology, Innovation and Development*, *14*(5), 1313–1326. DOI: 10.1080/20421338.2021.1950111

Olcott, M. B. (1987). *The Kazakhs*. Hoover Institution Press.

Olds, H. T., Corsi, S. R., Dila, D. K., Halmo, K. M., Bootsma, M. J., & McLellan, S. L. (2018). High levels of sewage contamination released from urban areas after storm events: A quantitative survey with sewage specific bacterial indicators. *PLoS Medicine*, *15*(7), e1002614. DOI: 10.1371/journal.pmed.1002614 PMID: 30040843

Omarova, A., Tussupova, K., Hjorth, P., Kalishev, M., & Dosmagambetova, R. (2019). Water Supply Challenges in Rural Areas: A Case Study from Central Kazakhstan. *International Journal of Environmental Research and Public Health*, *16*(5), 688. DOI: 10.3390/ijerph16050688 PMID: 30813591

Omosa, E. K. (2005). *The Impact of Water Conflicts on Pastoral Livelihoods The Case of Wajir District in Kenya. International Institute for Sustainable Development*. IISD.

Omundi, E., & Okendo, E. (2018). Evaluation of the effectiveness of civic education on acquisition of social cohesion competency among secondary school students in Uasin Gishu County, Kenya. *International Journal of Scientific Research and Management*, *6*(4), EL-249–EL-265. DOI: 10.18535/ijsrm/v6i4.el07

Omweno, J., Opiyo, S., Omondi, A., & Zablon, W. (2021). Natural and anthropogenic changes threatening the ecological and limnological integrity of Lake Baringo, Kenya: A Review. Pan Africa Science Journal.

Ondara, C. O., Nyachong'i, B. O., & Orucho, V. O. (2019). Prevalence and predisposing factors associated to gastro intestinal protozoan infections among diarrheal children under 5 years in Kisii county, Kenya. *Research Square*, pp 1-11. DOI: 10.21203/rs.2.13014/v1

Ondemo, F., Getabu, M. A., Gichana, Z., & Omweno, J. O. (2022). Length-weight relationships (LWRs) and condition factor of seven fish species in River Nyangweta Tributary, Kenya. *Journal of Engineering Research and Sciences*, *1*(3), 193–199. DOI: 10.55708/js0103020

Ondieki, C., & Kebaso, B. (2017). Water Supply Challenges and Storm Water Management in Kisii Municipality, Nyakomisaro Sub Catchment, Kenya. *OAlib*, *4*(9), 1–12. DOI: 10.4236/oalib.1103769

Ondieki, J. K., Akunga, D. N., Warutere, P. N., & Omanga, K. (2022). Socio-demographic and water handling practices affecting quality of household drinking water in Kisii Town, Kisii County, Kenya. *Heliyon*, *8*(5), e09419. DOI: 10.1016/j.heliyon.2022.e09419 PMID: 35600434

Onjala, J., Ndiritu, S. W., & Stage, J. (2014). Risk perception, choice of drinking water and water treatment: Evidence from Kenyan towns. *Journal of Water, Sanitation, and Hygiene for Development : a Journal of the International Water Association*, *4*(2), 268–280. DOI: 10.2166/washdev.2014.131

Onkelinx, J., & Sleuwaegen, L. (2008). Internationalisation of SMEs, Flanders DC. Retrieved from https://repository.vlerick.com/server/api/core/bitstreams/b5e25f8d-0bf2-4223-a455-ca66d58d5248/content

Onyango Ouma, S. (2025). Rethinking of Development in the Twenty-First-Century Africa: Development Strategies, Governance, and Foreign Aid. In *Indigenous Systems, Colonialism, Colonial Legacies, and Africa's Economic Challenges: Why is Africa Failing?* (pp. 139–163). Springer Nature Switzerland. DOI: 10.1007/978-3-032-00317-1_6

Orao, J. O. (2009). The Kenyan indigenous languages and the mass media: Challenges and opportunities. Stellenbosch papers in linguistics plus, 38(1), 77-86.

Organisation for Economic Co-operation and Development. (2020). *Sustainable development goals in emerging economies*. OECD Publishing.

Organisation for Security and Co-operation in Europe. (2023). *Gender equality in Central Asia: Economic participation report*. https://www.osce.org

Oseko, M. B. (2023). Assessing Land Use Suitability in Relation to Ecologically Sensitive Areas-a Case of Kisii Central Ward in Kisii County (Doctoral dissertation, University of Nairobi).

Otieno, P., & Omondi, R. (2022). Localised waste management strategies in Nairobi and Kisumu. *Urban Environmental Studies, 15*(3), 45–60. DOI: 10.1007/s11252-022-01134-5

Otiso, K. M. (1993). Urban environmental problems: the case of solid waste pollution and management in Kisii Town, Kenya (Master's thesis, Ohio University).

Özar, Ş. (2015). *Türkiye'de 1980 sonrası dönemde kadın emeği ve istihdamı politikaları: kadın hareketi, sendikalar, devlet ve işveren kuruluşları. A. Makal, & G. Toksöz içinde, Geçmişten günümüze Türkiye'de kadın emeği*. Ankara Üniversitesi Yayınları.

Özdemir, G. (2013). Women's Cooperatives in Turkey. *Procedia: Social and Behavioral Sciences, 81*, 300–305. DOI: 10.1016/j.sbspro.2013.06.432

Park, W. G., & Lippoldt, D. (2008). *Technology transfer and the economic implications of the strengthening of intellectual property rights in developing countries (OECD Trade Policy Papers No. 62)*. OECD Publishing., DOI: 10.1787/18166873

Pataki, D. E., Carreiro, M. M., Cherrier, J., Grulke, N. E., Jennings, V., Pincetl, S., & Zipperer, W. C. (2011). Coupling biogeochemical cycles in urban environments: Ecosystem services, green solutions, and misconceptions. *Frontiers in Ecology and the Environment, 9*(1), 27–36. DOI: 10.1890/090220

Patel, L., & Graham, L. (2012). How broad-based is broad-based black economic empowerment? *Development Southern Africa, 29*(2), 193–207. DOI: 10.1080/0376835X.2012.675692

Patton, M. Q. (2011). *Developmental evaluation: Applying complexity concepts to enhance innovation and use*. Guilford Press. https://www.guilford.com/books/Developmental-Evaluation/Michael-Quinn-Patton/9781606238721

Pavel, A., & Moldovan, O. (2019). Determining Local Economic Development in the Rural Areas of Romania. Exploring the Role of Exogenous Factors. *Sustainability (Basel), 2019*(11), 282. . DOI: 10.3390/su11010282

Perkins, R. (2017). *Migration and the economy: Economic impacts of migration on the UK economy*. Palgrave Macmillan.

Petersen, T. M., Rifai, H. S., Suarez, M. P., & Stein, A. R. (2005). Bacteria loads from point and nonpoint sources in an urban watershed. *Journal of Environmental Engineering, 131*(10), 1414–1425. DOI: 10.1061/(ASCE)0733-9372(2005)131:10(1414)

Pfeiffer, C., & Nentwig, T. (2019). *Integration through education: Evidence from Austria*. Cambridge University Press.

Phillips, A. (1995). *The politics of presence*. Oxford University Press.

Pike, A., Puchert, J., & Chinyamurindi, W. T. (2018). Analysing the future of Broad-Based Black Economic Empowerment through the lens of small and medium enterprises. *Acta Commercii, 18*(1), 1–10. DOI: 10.4102/ac.v18i1.566

Plastics, S. A. (2021). An analysis of the South African plastics industry data. Retrieved from https://www.plasticsinfo.co.za/wp-content/uploads/2022/12/Plastics-2021-Exec-Summary-30-Nov.pdf

Popoola, O., & Magidimisha, H. H. (2019). Examining women's access to rural land in UMnini Trust traditional area of KwaZulu-Natal, South Africa. *Journal of Local Government Research and Innovation, 1*, Article 12.

Porter, M. E. (1998). *On competition*. Harvard Business Review Press.

Portes, A., & Rumbaut, R. G. (2014). *Immigrant America: A portrait*. University of California Press.

Prah, K. K. (2020). *The challenge of African languages in education and development*. Centre for Advanced Studies of African Society (CASAS).

Prah, K. K. (2009). *The language of instruction in Africa: The language of instruction conundrum in Africa. Centre for Advanced Studies of African Society*. CASAS.

Presidential Advisory Panel on Land Reform and Agriculture. (2019). *Final report of the Presidential Advisory Panel on Land Reform and Agriculture*. Republic of South Africa.

Pretorius, A. M., & Blaauw, P. F. (2008). Local economic development agencies in South Africa: Six years later. *The South African Journal of Economic History, 23*(1–2), 155–183. DOI: 10.1080/10113430809511210

Pretty, J. (2003). Social capital and the collective management of resources. *Science*, *302*(5652), 1912–1914. DOI: 10.1126/science.1090847 PMID: 14671287

Rahman, A., Ai Ping, T., Mubeen, S. K., Mahmud, I., & Abbasi, G. A. (2022). What influences home gardeners' food waste composting intention in high-rise buildings in DHAKA MEGACITY, BANGLADESH? An integrated model of TPB and DMP. *Sustainability (Basel)*, *14*(15), 9400. DOI: 10.3390/su14159400

Rahman, M. A., Moser, A., Gold, A., Rötzer, T., & Pauleit, S. (2015). Vertical air temperature gradients under the shade of two contrasting urban tree species during different types of summer days. *The Science of the Total Environment*, *633*, 100–111. DOI: 10.1016/j.scitotenv.2018.03.168 PMID: 29573677

Rayori, D. M. (2023). Assessment of Efficiency of Wastewater Treatment Based on Physico-Chemical and Biological Parameters of Kisii Town Wastewater Treatment Plant, Kenya (Doctoral dissertation, Kisii University).

Reike, D., Vermeulen, W. J., & Witjes, S. (2018). The circular economy: New or refurbished as CE 3.0? — Exploring controversies in the conceptualisation of the circular economy through a focus on history and resource value retention options. *Resources, Conservation and Recycling*, *135*, 246–264. DOI: 10.1016/j.resconrec.2017.08.027

REPORTDEA (Department of Environmental Affairs). (2011). South Africa's second national communication under the United Nations Framework Convention on Climate Change. Republic of South Africa, Pretoria.

Republic of South Africa. (1994). *Ingonyama Trust Act 3 of 1994*. Government Printer.

Republic of South Africa. (1996). *Constitution of the Republic of South Africa, 1996 (Act No. 108 of 1996)*. Government Printer.

Republic of South Africa. (1996). *Constitution of the Republic of South Africa, Act 108 of 1996*. Government Gazette.

Republic of South Africa. (1996). *Land Reform (Labour Tenants) Act 3 of 1996*. Government Printer.

Republic of South Africa. (1997). *Extension of Security of Tenure Act 62 of 1997*. Government Printer.

Republic of South Africa. (1998). White Paper on Local Government, 9 March 1998, Pretoria: Government Gazette.

Republic of South Africa. (2014). *KwaZulu-Natal Poverty Eradication Master Plan*. KwaZulu-Natal Office of the Premier. https://www.kznonline.gov.za/images/Downloads/Publications/Poverty%20Eradication%20Master%20Plan.pdf

Reyes, J. D., & Atkinson, E. (2018). Connecting local businesses with multinational corporations amplifies the development impact of FDI. The Trade Post. Retrieved from https://blogs.worldbank.org/trade/connecting-localbusinesses-multinational-corporations-amplifies-development-impact-fdi

Ribot, J. C., & Peluso, N. L. (2003). A theory of access. *Rural Sociology*, *68*(2), 153–181. DOI: 10.1111/j.1549-0831.2003.tb00133.x

Ritchie, H., & Roser, M. (2021). Deforestation and forest loss. Our World in Data. https://ourworldindata.org/deforestation

Rockström, J., & Falkenmark, M. (2021). Water resilience for agriculture in semi-arid regions. *Science*, *374*(6566), 375–380.

Rogerson, C. M. (2010). Local economic development in South Africa: Strategic challenges. *Development Southern Africa*, *27*(4), 481–495. DOI: 10.1080/0376835X.2010.508580

Royer, C., Baribeau, C., & Duchesne, A. (2009). Individual interviews in social science research in Quebec: Where do we stand? Un panorama des usages. *Recherches Qualitatives*, *7*, 64–79.

Saaida, M., and Saaidah, I. (2023). Understanding the Dynamics of Failure Development in Marginalized Areas: A Comprehensive Analysis.

Sachs, J. (2015). *The Age of Sustainable Development*. Columbia University Press. DOI: 10.7312/sach17314

Şahankaya Adar, A., Dedeoğlu, S., & Kurtuluş, G. (2023). Türkiye'de Kadın Kooperatifleri: Mevcut Durum Analizi, Kadın Güçlenmesi ve İstihdam Yaratma Potansiyeli. *Çalışma ve Toplum*, 1171-1208.

Said, E. W. (1978). *Orientalism*. Pantheon Books.

Saporiti, N., & Robins, E. (2021). Scaling up water reuse: why recycling our water makes sense. Retrieved from https://blogs.worldbank.org/en/climatechange/scaling-water-reuse-why-recycling-our-wastewater-makes-sense

Schmidt, E., & Bader, M. (2018). *Vocational training and employment support for immigrants in Austria*. Palgrave Macmillan.

Schmitz, A. (2012). Women's informal religious authority in Uzbekistan. *Journal of Muslim Minority Affairs*, *32*(3), 320–338. DOI: 10.1080/13602004.2012.727291

Schnitzler, J., Benzler, J., Altmann, D., Mucke, I., & Krause, G. (2007). Survey on the population's needs and the public health response during floods in Germany 2002. *Journal of Public Health Management and Practice*, *13*(5), 461–464. DOI: 10.1097/01.PHH.0000285197.23932.3e PMID: 17762689

Schumpeter, J. A. (1947). Theoretical problems of economic growth. *The Journal of Economic History*, *7*(S1), 1–9. DOI: 10.1017/S0022050700065189

Sebunya, J., & Gichuki, A. (2024). The impact of participatory planning on sustainable development: A literature review. *Journal of Strategy and Management*, *4*(4), 1–9.

Seckler, D., Barker, R., & Amarasinghe, U. (1999). Water Scarcity in the Twenty-First Century. *International Journal of Water Resources Development*, *15*(1-2), 29–42. DOI: 10.1080/07900629948916

Selvan, A. (2017). Problems of rural girl students in higher educational institution. *Scholarly Research Journal for Humanity Science & English Language*, *4*(23), 5992–5998. DOI: 10.21922/srjhsel.v4i23.9642

Sen, A. (2006). *Identity and Violence: The Illusion of Destiny*. Norton.

Shackleton, C. M., & Shackleton, S. E. (2004). The importance of non-timber forest products in rural livelihood security and as safety nets: A review of evidence from South Africa. *South African Journal of Science*, *100*(11–12), 658–664.

Sharpley, R., & Telfer, D. J. (2021). *Tourism and development in the developing world* (2nd ed.). Routledge.

Shkalenko, A., Abenova, D., & Seitkali, M. (2025). Contemporary strategies of women activists in the gender equality movement in Central Asia. *Frontiers in Political Science*, *7*, 1694298. Advance online publication. DOI: 10.3389/fpos.2025.1694298

Showers, K. B. (2002). Water Scarcity and Urban Africa: An Overview of Urban-Rural Water Linkages. *World Development*, *30*(4), 621–648. DOI: 10.1016/S0305-750X(01)00132-2

Singh, A., Sawant, M., Kamble, S. J., Herlekar, M., Starkl, M., Aymerich, E., & Kazmi, A. (2019). Performance evaluation of a decentralised wastewater treatment system in India. *Environmental Science and Pollution Research International*, *26*(21), 21172–21188. DOI: 10.1007/s11356-019-05444-z PMID: 31119547

Singh, K. (2007). *Quantitative Social Research Methods*. Sage Publications. DOI: 10.4135/9789351507741

Smith, J., & Brown, L. (2023). Bioremediation of Oil Spills: A Review. *Environmental Science Journal*, *45*(2), 123–135.

Snyder, H. (2019). Literature review as a research methodology: An overview and guidelines. *Journal of Business Research*, *104*, 333–339. DOI: 10.1016/j.jbusres.2019.07.039

Soja, E. (2010). *Seeking Spatial Justice*. University of Minnesota Press. DOI: 10.5749/minnesota/9780816666676.001.0001

Sondarjee, M. (2021). Collective learning at the boundaries of communities of practice: Inclusive policymaking at the World Bank. *Global Society*, *35*(3), 307–326. DOI: 10.1080/13600826.2020.1835833

Souch, C. A., & Souch, C. (1993). The effect of trees on summertime below canopy urban climates: A case study, Bloomington, Indiana. *Arboriculture & Urban Forestry*, *19*(5), 303–312. DOI: 10.48044/jauf.1993.049

South African Government. (2020). *Multilingualism policy framework*. Department of Higher Education and Training. https://www.dhet.gov.za

Sovacool, B. K., & Griffiths, S. (2021). Renewable energy in Sub-Saharan Africa: Emerging lessons for sustainable development. *Renewable & Sustainable Energy Reviews*, *137*, 110600.

Spaull, N. (2013). Poverty and privilege: Primary school inequality in South Africa. *International Journal of Educational Development*, *33*(5), 436–447. DOI: 10.1016/j.ijedudev.2012.09.009

Spivak, G. C. (1988). Can the subaltern speak? In Nelson, C., & Grossberg, L. (Eds.), *Marxism and the Interpretation of Culture* (pp. 271–313). University of Illinois Press.

StartUs Insight. (2023). Top 8 water management trends and innovations in 2023. Retrieved from https://www.startus-insights.com/innovators-guide/water-management-trends/

Statistics Canada. (2020). *Immigrant entrepreneurs in Canada: Economic impact*. Statistics Canada. https://www.statcan.gc.ca

Statistics South Africa. (2017). *Quarterly Labour Force Survey (QLFS): Quarter 2, 2017* (Statistical Release P0211). Statistics South Africa. https://www.statssa.gov.za/?page_id=1854

Statistics South Africa. (2021). *Quarterly Labour Force Survey (QLFS): Quarter 1, 2021* (Statistical Release P0211). Statistics South Africa. https://www.statssa.gov.za/?page_id=1854

Statistics South Africa. (2021). *Quarterly Labour Force Survey (QLFS): Quarter 2, 2021* (Statistical Release P0211). Statistics South Africa. https://www.statssa.gov.za/?page_id=1854'

Statistics South Africa. (2023). *General household survey 2023*. Statistics South Africa.

Stats, S. A. (2018). Manufacturing: Production and Sales. Statistical Release P3041.2. Retrieved from http://www.statssa.gov.za/publications/P30412/P30412December2018.pdf

Su'arez-Eiroa, B., Fern'andez, E., M'endez-Martínez, G., & Soto-O˜nate, D. (2019). Operational principles of circular economy for sustainable development: Linking theory and practice. *Journal of Cleaner Production*, *214*, 952–961. DOI: 10.1016/j.jclepro.2018.12.271

Suarez, F. J. T., Chicas, O. A., Troshani, R., & Coelho, J. (2015). *Local economic development agencies for governance and internationalisation of local economies*. IDEASS. https://www.ideassonline.org/public/pdf/BrochureAdelENG.pd

Sultana, F. (2010). Living in hazardous waterscapes: Gendered vulnerabilities and experiences of floods and disasters. *Environmental Hazards*, *1*(1), 43–53. DOI: 10.3763/ehaz.2010.SI02

Supapol, A. B. (1995). Thailand. In *ESCAP and UNCTAD, Transnational Corporations and Backward Linkages in Asian Electronics Industries* (pp. 249–287). United Nations.

Suseno, G., & Nataliningsih, N. (2023). The Role of Women's Cooperatives as an Institution to Empower Women in Supporting the Achievement of the SDGs. *International Journal of Ethno-Sciences and Education Research*, 45-53.

Swedish Ministry of Education. (2018). *Educational outcomes for immigrant students*. Ministry of Education and Research. https://www.regeringen.se

Swierczewski, B. E., Odundo, E. A., Koech, M. C., Ndonye, J. N., Kirera, R. K., Odhiambo, C. P., Cheruiyot, E. K., Shaffer, D. N., Ombogo, A. N., & Oaks, E. V. (2013). Enteric pathogen surveillance in a case-control study of acute diarrhoea in the town of Kisii, Kenya. *Journal of Medical Microbiology*, *62*(Pt 11), 1774–1776. DOI: 10.1099/jmm.0.059139-0 PMID: 23842139

Tamarack Institute. (2022). *Participatory Evaluation and Strategic Learning Practices*. https://events.tamarackcommunity.ca/workshop-participatory-evaluation-community-based-assessment-strategic-learning-practices

Thakur, T. K., Barya, M. P., Dutta, J., Mukherjee, P., Thakur, A., Swamy, S. L., & Anderson, J. T. (2023). Integrated phytobial remediation of dissolved pollutants from domestic wastewater through constructed wetlands: An interactive macrophyte-microbe-based green and low-cost decontamination technology with prospective resource recovery. *Water (Basel), 15*(22), 3877. DOI: 10.3390/w15223877

The Finnish Innovative Fund Sitra. (2016). Leading the cycle: Finnish roadmap to a circular economy 2016–2025. Retrieved from https://www.sitra.fi/en/publications/leading-cycle

The Presidency. (2014). *Medium-Term Strategic Framework 2014–2019*. Republic of South Africa. https://www.gov.za/documents/medium-term-strategic-framework-2014-2019-3-aug-2014-0000

The Productivity Institute. (2024). *Making innovation more inclusive*. https://www.productivity.ac.uk/wp-content/uploads/2024/11/PIP039-Making-Innovation-Inclusive-FINAL.pdf

Tilman, D., Cassman, K. G., Matson, P. A., Naylor, R., & Polasky, S. (2002). Agricultural sustainability and intensive production practices. *Nature, 418*(6898), 671–677. DOI: 10.1038/nature01014 PMID: 12167873

Torraco, R. J. (2016). Writing integrative literature reviews: Using the past and present to explore the future. *Human Resource Development Review, 15*(4), 404–428. DOI: 10.1177/1534484316671606

Toulmin, C. (2009). Securing land and property rights in sub-Saharan Africa: The role of local institutions. *Land Use Policy, 26*(1), 10–19. DOI: 10.1016/j.landusepol.2008.07.006

Troeger, C., Colombara, D. V., Rao, P. C., Khalil, I. A., Brown, A., Brewer, T. G., Guerrant, R. L., Houpt, E. R., Kotloff, K. L., Misra, K., Petri, W. A.Jr, Platts-Mills, J., Riddle, M. S., Swartz, S. J., Forouzanfar, M. H., Reiner, R. C.Jr, Hay, S. I., & Mokdad, A. H. (2018). Jr, Platts-Mills, J., Riddle, M.S., Swartz, S.J., Forouzanfar, M.H., Reiner, R.C. Jr., Hay, S.I., & Mokdad, A.H. (2018). Global disability-adjusted life-year estimates of long-term health burden and undernutrition attributable to diarrhoeal diseases in children younger than 5 years. *The Lancet. Global Health, 6*(3), 255–269. DOI: 10.1016/S2214-109X(18)30045-7

Troeger, C., Forouzanfar, M., Rao, P. C., Khalil, I., Brown, A., Reiner, R. C.Jr, Fullman, N., Thompson, R. L., Abajobir, A., Ahmed, M., Alemayohu, M. A., Alvis-Guzman, N., Amare, A. T., Antonio, C. A., Asayesh, H., Avokpaho, E., Awasthi, A., Bacha, U., Barac, A., & Mokdad, A. H.GBD. (2017). Diarrhoeal Diseases Collaborators. Estimates of global, regional, and national morbidity, mortality, and aetiologies of diarrhoeal diseases: A systematic analysis for the Global Burden of Disease Study 2015. *The Lancet. Infectious Diseases*, *17*(9), 909–948. DOI: 10.1016/S1473-3099(17)30276-1 PMID: 28579426

Tshishonga, N., & Matsiliza, N. S. (2021). Addressing the twin challenges of poverty and unemployment through community work programmes in South Africa. *African Journal of Development Studies*, *11*(2), 217–235. DOI: 10.31920/2634-3649/2021/v11n2a12

Tucker, J. (2008). *Women, family, and gender in Islamic law*. Cambridge University Press. DOI: 10.1017/CBO9780511841316

Tukon, K. (2024). Examining How Globalization Shapes Africa's Underdevelopment. *Open Journal of Business and Management*, *12*(02), 875–885. DOI: 10.4236/ojbm.2024.122046

Turok, I. (2011). Cities and economic development: A polarisation view. In Parnell, S., & Pieterse, E. (Eds.), *Africa's urban revolution: Policy press scholarship online* (pp. 119–134). University of Cape Town Press.

Turok, I., Visagie, J., & Scheba, A. (2021). Social inequality and spatial segregation in Cape Town. In *Urban socio-economic segregation and income inequality: A global perspective* (pp. 71–90). Springer International Publishing. DOI: 10.1007/978-3-030-64569-4_4

UN. (2015). *Transforming our world: The 2030 agenda for sustainable development*. United Nations.

UNCTAD (1999). World Investment Report 1999: Foreign direct investment and the challenge

UNCTAD. (1998). "The Handbook on Foreign Direct Investment by Small and Medium-Sized Enterprises: Lessons from Asia." Geneva.

UNCTAD. (2001). World Investment Report: Promoting Linkages. New York, United Nations. https://unctad.org/system/files/official-document/wir2001_en.pdf

UNCTAD. (2020). World investment report 2020: International production beyond the pandemic. *United Nations Conference on Trade and Development*.

UNDP. (2024). *Local governance and gender inclusion in Kyrgyzstan*. https://www.undp.org

UNECA. (2014) Dynamic Industrial Policy in Africa: Innovative Institutions, Effective Processes and Flexible Mechanisms. Retrieved from https://archive.uneca.org/sites/default/files/PublicationFiles/final_era2014_march25_en.pdf

UNEP. (2011). *Towards a Green Economy: Pathways to Sustainable Development and Poverty Eradication*. United Nations Environment Programme.

UNEP. (2011): Towards a Green Economy: Pathways to Sustainable Development and Poverty Eradication, Nairobi. Retrieved from https://sustainabledevelopment.un.org/index.php?page=view&type=400&nr=126&menu=35

UNESCO. (2003). *Education in a multilingual world*. UNESCO Publishing. https://unesdoc.unesco.org

UNESCO. (2022). *Global education monitoring report 2022: Inclusion and education*. UNESCO Publishing. https://www.unesco.org/gem-report

UNESCO. (2023). *Digital initiatives for Indigenous languages*. UNESCO. https://www.unesco.org/en/decades/indigenous-languages

UN-Habitat. (2019). *The Future of Sustainable Cities: Urbanization and Development*. United Nations Human Settlements Programme.

UN-Habitat. (2023). Kenya's Kisii Town validates draft solid waste management strategy. UN-Habitat. https://unhabitat.org/kenyas-kisii-town-validates-draft-solid-waste-management-strategy

United Nations Development Programme, African Union Commission, United Nations Economic Commission for Africa, & African Development Bank. (2023). *2023 Africa sustainable development report: Accelerating the recovery from the coronavirus disease (COVID-19) and the full implementation of the 2030 Agenda for Sustainable Development and African Union Agenda 2063 at all levels*. United Nations Development Programme. https://www.undp.org/africa/publications/2023-africa-sustainable-development-report

United Nations Educational, Scientific and Cultural Organization. (2021). *Reimagining our futures together: A new social contract for education*. UNESCO.

United Nations Entity for Gender Equality and the Empowerment of Women. (2020). *Women's rights to land and productive resources*. UN Women.

United Nations Environment Programme (UNEP). (2021). The sixth Global Environment Outlook (GEO) for Cities report. UN-Habitat. https://unhabitat.org/the-sixth-global-environment-outlook-geo-for-cities-report

United Nations Environment Programme (UNEP). (2023). *Harnessing data, awareness, and investment to tackle Africa's wastewater woes*. Retrieved from https://www.unep.org

United Nations Environment Programme. (2021). *Global Environment Outlook 6: Healthy Planet, Healthy People*. UNEP.

United Nations Global Compact. (2017). *Achieving SDGs through sustainable business practices*. United Nations Global Compact.

United Nations Human Settlements Programme (UN-Habitat). (2022). World Cities Report 2022: Envisaging the Future of Cities. UN-Habitat. https://unhabitat.org/sites/default/files/2022/06/wcr_2022.pdf

United Nations Human Settlements Programme (UN-Habitat). (2024). World Cities Report 2024: Cities and Climate Action. UN-Habitat. https://unhabitat.org/world-cities-report-2024-cities-and-climate-action

United Nations. (2023). *The Sustainable Development Goals Report 2023*. United Nations. https://unstats.un.org

University College London. (2023). *Towards inclusive innovation systems: Developing a mission-oriented framework*. https://www.ucl.ac.uk/bartlett/sites/bartlett/files/towards_inclusive_innovation_systems_developing_a_mission-oriented_framework_for_no_limits.pdf

UN-World Water Assessment Programme. (2009). *Water in a Changing World*. Earthscan.

UNWTO. (2019). *The economic impact of cultural tourism*. World Tourism Organization. Economic contribution of Tourism and beyond: Data on the economic contribution of Tourism

Urama, K. C., & Ozor, N. (2010). Impacts of climate change on water resources in Africa: the role of adaptation. https://www.researchgate.net/publication/267218899_Impacts_of_climate_change_on_water_resources_in_Africa_the_role_of_adaptation#fullTextFileContent

USGCRP. (2018). Impacts, Risks, and Adaptation in the United States: Fourth National Climate Assessment, Volume II [Reidmiller, D.R., C.W. Avery, D.R. Easterling, K.E. Kunkel, K.L.M. Lewis, T.K. Maycock, and B.C. Stewart (eds.)]. U.S. Global Change Research Program, Washington, DC.

Vakoufaris, H., Kizos, T., Spilanis, I., Koulouri, M., & Zacharaki, A. (2007). Women's cooperatives and their contribution to the local development of the North Aegean Region, Greece. *Journal of Rural Cooperation*, •••, 19–41.

Vandenberg, P. (2006). *Poverty reduction through small enterprises: Emerging consensus, unresolved issues and ILO activities* (SEED Working Paper No. 75). International Labour Organization. https://www.ilo.org/publications/poverty-reduction-through-small-enterprises-emerging-consensus-unresolved

Varwell, S. (2022). A Literature Review of Arnstein's Ladder of Citizen Participation: Lessons for contemporary student engagement. Exchanges. *The Interdisciplinary Research Journal*, *10*(1), 108–144. DOI: 10.31273/eirj.v10i1.1156

Vasconcellos, G. M., & Kish, R. J. (2013). Cross-Border Mergers and Acquisitions. In Encyclopedia of Finance (pp. 515-523). Springer US. DOI: 10.1007/978-1-4614-5360-4_43

Vergunst, F., & Berry, H. L. (2022). Climate Change and Children's Mental Health: A Developmental Perspective. *Clinical Psychological Science*, *10*(4), 767–785. DOI: 10.1177/21677026211040787 PMID: 35846172

Vertovec, S. (2007). Super-diversity and its implications. Centre on Migration, Policy and Society.

Vigneswaran, S. (2006). *Quantity and Quality of Drinking Water Supplies*. University of Technology.

Voice to Vision. (2025). *Enhancing civic decision-making through co-designed data infrastructure*. https://arxiv.org/abs/2505.14853

Voorberg, W. H., Bekkers, V. J. J. M., & Tummers, L. G. (2015). A systematic review of co-creation and co-production: Embarking on the social innovation journey. *Public Management Review*, *17*(9), 1333–1357. DOI: 10.1080/14719037.2014.930505

Vymazal, J. (2011). Constructed wetlands for wastewater treatment: Five decades of experience. *Environmental Science & Technology*, *45*(1), 61–69. DOI: 10.1021/es101403q PMID: 20795704

Wa Mberia, K. (2015). Ubuntu: Linguistic exporations. *International Journal of Scientific Research and Innovative Technology*, *2*(1), 103–115.

Wa Thiong'o. Ngugi. (2021). *The language of languages*. The New Press.

Wa Thiong'o, Ngugi. (1986). *Decolonising the mind: The politics of language in African literature*. Heinemann Kenya.

Wachira, J. M. (2023). Molecular characterisation of denitrifying Bacteria and their potential in the reduction of nitrogenous Compounds In Lake Victoria, Kenya (Doctoral dissertation, UoEm).

Wächter, T. (2021). *Language barriers in immigrant integration: A comparative analysis*. Routledge.

Wade, T. J., Sandhu, S. K., Levy, D., Lee, S., LeChevallier, M. W., Katz, L., & Colford, J. J. (2004). Did a severe flood in the Midwest cause an increase in the incidence of gastrointestinal symptoms? *American Journal of Epidemiology*, *159*(4), 398–405. DOI: 10.1093/aje/kwh050 PMID: 14769644

Wadud, A. (2021). Reflections on Islamic feminist exegesis of the Qur'an. *Religions*, *12*(7), 497–508. DOI: 10.3390/rel12070497

Wafae, T., & Sara, R. (2021). Women's rural cooperatives in Morocco: Challenges and collapses. *International Journal of Interdisciplinary Gender Studies*, 85-103.

Wakhungu, M. J. (2019). An Ethnography of Policy: Water Reuse Policy in Kenya. *Water Policy*, *21*(2), 436–448. DOI: 10.2166/wp.2019.160

Walker, C. (2003). Piety in the sky? Gender policy and land reform in South Africa. *Journal of Agrarian Change*, *3*(1–2), 113–148. DOI: 10.1111/1471-0366.00052

Wambui, N., Kariuki, P., & Ngugi, J. (2019). Integrated legal approaches to water resource management in Kenya. *Journal of Environmental Law*, *31*(2), 123–140. DOI: 10.1093/jel/eqz011

Wampler, B. (2012). Participatory Budgeting in Latin America: A New Challenge for Sustainable Development. *Journal of Latin American Studies*, *44*(1), 71–97.

Wampler, B., McNulty, S., McNulty, S. L., & Touchton, M. (2021). *Participatory budgeting in global perspective*. Oxford University Press. DOI: 10.1093/oso/9780192897756.001.0001

Wang, X., & Zhang, Y. (2024). AI in Environmental Monitoring: Applications and Challenges. *Journal of Environmental Management*, *90*(1), 89–102.

Wang, X., & Zhang, Y. (2024). AI in Environmental Monitoring: Applications and Challenges. Journal of Environmental Management, 90(1), 89–102. *Waste Management & Research*, *41*, 936–947.

Warschauer, M. (2021). *Technology and social inclusion: Rethinking the digital divide*. MIT Press.

WASREB. (2006). *Drinking Water Quality and Effluent Monitoring Guidelines*. Water Service Regulatory Board.

Wauters, B., & Lambrecht, J. (2008). The role of immigrant entrepreneurs in the local economy: The case of Flanders. *Entrepreneurship and Regional Development, 20*(4), 331–355. DOI: 10.1080/08985620802002590

Wekwete, K. (2014). Local Government and Local Economic Development in Southern Africa, Commonwealth Local Government Forum.

Westley, F., McGowan, K., & Tjörnbo, O. (2017). *The evolution of social innovation: Building resilience through transitions*. Edward Elgar Publishing., DOI: 10.4337/9781786431158

White Paper on Local Government. (1998). South African Government Publications.

Whitehead, A., & Tsikata, D. (2003). Policy discourses on women's land rights in sub-Saharan Africa: The implications of the return to the customary. *Journal of Agrarian Change, 3*(1–2), 67–112. DOI: 10.1111/1471-0366.00051

WHO. (2008). Guidelines for Drinking-Water Quality, 3rd edition: Volume 1 - Recommendations incorporating the first and second addenda.

WHO. (2015). Effects of Climate Change on the Social & Environmental Determinants of Health in Africa: What can communities do to strengthen their climate resilience? COP 21/CMP 11 - Paris, France Technical Paper for WHO/UNEP Side Event. Pages 1 – 17.

WHO/UNICEF. (2025). Progress on Household Drinking Water, Sanitation and Hygiene 2000–2024: Special Focus on Inequalities

Whorf, B. L. (1956). *Language, Thought, and Reality: Selected Writings of Benjamin Lee Whorf*. MIT Press.

Wildschut, A., & Hulbert, S. (1998). *A seed not a tree: Community perspectives on local governance, land and development*. Community Agency for Social Enquiry (CASE).

Williams, J. J. (2006). Community participation: Lessons from post-apartheid South Africa. *Policy Studies, 27*(3), 197–217. DOI: 10.1080/01442870600885982

Willness, C. R., Boakye-Danquah, J., & Nichols, D. R. (2023). How Arnstein's ladder of citizen participation can enhance community-engaged teaching and learning. *Academy of Management Learning & Education*, *22*(1), 112–131. DOI: 10.5465/amle.2020.0284

Winans, K., Kendall, A., & Deng, H. (2017). The history and current applications of the circular economy concept. *Renewable & Sustainable Energy Reviews*, *68*, 825–833. DOI: 10.1016/j.rser.2016.09.123

Witte, N. (2019). *Regional integration strategies in Belgium: A comparative analysis*. Routledge.

Wöcke, A., & Sing, L. (2013). Inward and Outward FDI Country Profiles. *International Interactions*, *38*(1), 111–139. DOI: 10.1080/03050629.2012.640254

Wolfram, M. (2016). Conceptualizing urban transformative capacity: A framework for research and policy. *Cities (London, England)*, *51*, 121–130. DOI: 10.1016/j.cities.2015.11.011

Wollesen, B., Wildbredt, A., van Schooten, K. S., Lim, M. L., & Delbaere, K. (2020). The effects of cognitive-motor training interventions on executive functions in older people: A systematic review and meta-analysis. *European Review of Aging and Physical Activity : Official Journal of the European Group for Research into Elderly and Physical Activity*, *17*(1), 1–22. DOI: 10.1186/s11556-020-00240-y PMID: 32636957

Women, U. N. (2023). *Gender equality in Central Asia: Regional overview*. https://www.unwomen.org

Women, U. N. (2024). *Women's political participation in Uzbekistan*. https://www.unwomen.org

World Bank. (2003). *Local economic development: A primer—Developing and implementing local economic development strategies and action plans*. World Bank.

World Bank. (2009). *Gender in agriculture sourcebook*. World Bank.

World Bank. (2012): Inclusive Green Growth. The Pathway to Sustainable Development, Washington. Retrieved from https://siteresources.worldbank.org/EXTSDNET/Resources/Inclusive_Green_Growth_May_2012.pdf

World Bank. (2019). *Innovative waste management practices in developing countries*. World Bank Publications.

World Bank. (2019). The changing nature of work. World Bank Group. Retrieved from https://documents1.worldbank.org/curated/en/816281518818814423/pdf/2019-WDR

World Bank. (2020). *World development report 2020: Trading for development in the age of global value chains*. World Bank Group.

World Bank. (2023). *World development indicators: Labour force participation*. https://data.worldbank.org

World Bank. (2024). *Gender wage gap data: Central Asia*. https://data.worldbank.org

World Commission on Environment and Development. (1987). *Our common future*. Oxford University Press.

World Health Organisation. (2016). Health as the pulse of the new urban agenda: United Nations conference on housing and sustainable urban development, Quito, October 2016.

Writer, S. (2025). One of South Africa's biggest employers under siege. Retrieved from https://businesstech.co.za/news/business/845144/one-of-south-africas-biggest-employers-under-siege/

WWF SA. (2020). Plastics: Facts and Futures- Moving Beyond Pollution Management Towards a Circular Plastics Economy in South Africa. Retrieved from https://wwfafrica.awsassets.panda.org/downloads/wwf_plastics_report_final_2nov2020.pdf

Xie, D., & Lowrey, Y. (2019). A Theory of Entrepreneurial Work. *Theoretical Economics Letters*, *9*(5), 1507–1517. DOI: 10.4236/tel.2019.95097

Yadav, S. (2023). Gender Equality as a Tool for Sustainable Development. *International Journal of Teaching, Learning and Education*, 1-3.

Yağar, F., & Dökme, S. (2018). Niteliksel Araştırmaların Planlanması: Araştırma Soruları, Örneklem Seçimi, Geçerlik ve Güvenirlik. *Gazi Sağlık Bilimleri Dergisi*, 1-9.

Yakar, E. E. (2022). Women's political leadership: One question and two divergent fatwas. *The Journal of Law and Religion*, *37*(2), 332–362. DOI: 10.1017/jlr.2022.15

Yıldırım, A., & Şimşek, H. (2016). *Sosyal bilimlerde nitel araştırma yöntemleri*. Seçkin Yayıncılık.

Zeinilova, A. (2023). Gender regime in Kazakhstan: Multi-layered processes and patriarchal values. *Central Asian Survey*, *42*(1), 105–123.

Zhai, J. (2020). BIM-Based Building Circularity Assessment from the Early Design Stages. Eindhoven University of Technology. Retrieved from https://pure.tue.nl/ws/portalfiles/portal/165207093/Zhai_1311514.pdf

Zhao, L., Dai, T., Qiao, Z., Sun, P., Hao, J., & Yang, Y. (2020). Application of artificial intelligence to wastewater treatment: A bibliometric analysis and systematic review of technology, economy, management, and wastewater reuse. *Process Safety and Environmental Protection, 133*, 169–182. DOI: 10.1016/j.psep.2019.11.014

Zhou, S. (2021). The Chinese path of integration and development among all ethnic groups from a comparative perspective between China and the west. *International Journal of Anthropology and Ethnology, 5*(1), 17. DOI: 10.1186/s41257-021-00058-1

Zondo, R. W. D. (2022). Participatory approach and good governance: The alpha and omega of sustainable local development in South Africa. *International Journal of Special Education.*

About the Contributors

Ndwakhulu Tshishonga (PhD) is an Africanist academic and a research fellow within the School of Built Environment & Development Studies at the University of KwaZulu-Natal. He specialises in political economy, Community Development, Afrocentric-decolonized development and developmental state, traditional leadership, local economic development, Land and Land Reform, Cooperatives, local governance and citizenship and democracy, service delivery protests and social movements, sociology of youth and entrepreneurship, Indigenous Knowledge Systems, and African Politics and governance, public administration and Intergovernmental Relations. Over the past two decades, more than 70 scholarly papers and book chapters have been contributed to local and international journals, and books have been edited. Dr Tshishonga has examined MAs and PhDs in various universties and Institutions of Higher Leraning. His academic citizenship includes presenting at national and international conferences and engaging government departments in policy issues relating to governance, democracy, and professionalizing community development in South Africa. Since 2024, Ndwakhulu has been nominated as a Council of Higher Education (CHE) member responsible for the Bachelor of Community Development Standards in South Africa. In addition, he is a member of the UK-based Development Studies Association (M44098). He is also a Lead for Global Citizenship and Children's Rights Network (GLOCCRIN) and a Political Analyst on African and international Political Affairs.

Takalani Hulisani (PhD) is a Lecturer at the University of Venda's Department of Public and Development Administration. Among his areas of specialisation in research and teaching are development management, public administration, community development, international development cooperation, public policy, and local governance. Hulisani has over ten years of experience working in the socio-economic development field in the public, corporate, and non-governmental sectors. He has had several articles published in both local and international journals.

Eve D Mafema is a British-educated academic and qualified journalist. Her educational background is in Sociology, Anthropology and Gender all obtained at Goldsmith College, University of London and Nottingham University. She has experience in teaching at tertiary level at several universities in England and Africa. Her specialisation is on gender, youth and development. She has written more than 20 peer papers and book chapters on gender, youth and local government. She is currently a Senior Researcher and editor for and peer reviewer for several journal publications and publishers.

Mdletshe Lucky holds an MA degree in Cultural and Heritage Studies, currently pursuing PhD at the University of KwaZulu-Natal under the School of Social Sciences. Recently, he has been identified by the 2023 Golden Key International Honor Society as one of the top 15% performers in the College of Humanities. An emerging scholar with research interests based on: sustainable development, human geography, environmental management, coastal zone management, culture and heritage tourism management, entrepreneurship, student movements, and community development. He is also a member of the South African Council for Educators.

***

Merceline Bosibori Angima is currently a PhD student undertaking Limnology at Kisii University. She undertook her Msc in Limnology at Kisii University, between 2018 – 2021 and graduated in the year 2021. In the year 2016 she earned her BSc. in Agricultural Education and Extension from Kisii University, having completed her Diploma in Agricultural Education and Extension in the year 2014. Before earning her Diploma, Merceline worked as Senior Farm Assistant at the University farm (2009-2017). After earning her BSc., she was promoted to a Technologist level in the school of Agriculture and Natural Resources Management where she is currently. Her research interests include: Water Quality, biomonitoring using aquatic macrophytes, Heavy metal analysis, sustainable Agriculture.

Margaret Barasa is an Associate Professor of Applied Linguistics and the Deputy Vice Chancellor for Academics, Research, and Student Affairs at Alupe University. She holds a Master of Arts in English Language and Linguistics and a Bachelor of Education in English Language and Literature. With over 13 years of experience in higher education, Prof. Barasa has served as a Lecturer, Senior Lecturer, and Associate Professor, holding key leadership roles such as Dean of the School of Arts and Social Sciences and Chair of the Department of Languages, Linguistics, and Literature at Kisii University. She has supervised postgraduate students to completion and actively participates in academic conferences across

Kenya, Tanzania, and the United States. Her research focuses on language, culture, society, and discourse analysis, integrating theoretical linguistics into applied linguistics. She has also explored leadership, gender issues, environmental studies, and indigenous knowledge documentation. A professional member of ELTRCS and KESSA, she has published extensively in books, book chapters, and refereed journals. Currently, she is leading initiatives in university governance, academic research, and student affairs, while also contributing to language policy, economic development, and innovation. Her dedication to mentorship and institutional growth continues to shape the academic landscape.

Rolda Kafaar is a fourth-year Community Development student at the University of the Western Cape, I am immersed in the complexities of social change and community empowerment. As I am currently doing my Honours in the Community Development program, my desire to uplift and empower communities grows stronger than ever. Throughout my academic journey, I came to understand that true progress comes from within communities. It is not about imposing solutions from outside, but about creating an environment in which individuals within communities can identify their own strengths, resources, and solutions to the problems they face. My studies have provided me with an extensive knowledge of the many factors that influence community dynamics, ranging from socioeconomic disparities to cultural nuances. Armed with this knowledge, I am motivated to collaborate with communities in the future, facilitating processes that allow them to realize their full potential and effect long-term change. I have become increasingly eager to expand my knowledge and improve my skills in community development. With each endeavour, I am reminded of the transformative power of collective action and the enormous potential that every community possesses to shape its destiny.

Phathutshedzo Madumi is a Lecturer in the Department of Military Economics at Stellenbosch University in South Africa. He is an emerging researcher aiming to pursue a PhD in Economics. His professional interests include Economic Development, Political Economy, Economic Growth, Economic Theory, International Economics, Public Economics, Income and Wage Inequality, Human Capital and Training, as well as Labour Economics.

Lindani Maphumulo is a Lecturer at the University of Western Cape, in the Department of Social Work, in the Community Development Programme. I am a coordinator for Level 1 Modules in Community Development and represent the department in various internal Faculty Boards. I have worked in various spaces/ units in higher education, private and public sectors since 2015. I worked for the University of KwaZulu-Natal as a Mentor, Tutor, Lecturer, Library Student Assistant, Residence Assistant, Residence Life Officer, and Academic Development Officer.

My roles included among others coordination of student development programmes, tutorial programmes, supervision of Tutors, Residence Assistants, and management of student accommodations. I served in the Department of Correctional Service since 2017 as an Offender Rehabilitation Path Facilitator as well as Victim Offender Mediation and Dialogue Facilitator until November 2022. I have applied my Community Development skills and Social Work expertise in assisting different disadvantaged groups in diverse communities. I have worked and served in many community-based organizations as a board member and volunteer. My approach to community development is that development can take place in any given environment regardless of the circumstances. I have experienced this by adopting the Strength Perceptive/Approach and Asset-Based Community Development. Every community has something positive to work on to build a better society and sustainable local industries. My attitude is that strength can be found in most worst cases, difficult condition produces resilient communities and individuals. Through solid community partnerships and common goals, development is possible.

David Monda teaches Political Science, International Relations and American Government classes at the City University of New York. His doctoral training is situated at the intersection of Comparative Politics and International Relations with an emphasis on foreign policy and international migration. He recently completed a research fellowship at the Vera Institute's Ending Detention Initiative, in Brooklyn New York, studying the perverse incentives of state and local governments in the mass detention of undocumented African immigrants in the United States. His research interests center on foreign policies of the global south and securitization of narratives around migration. This research has included fieldwork in Belize, South Africa, Brazil, Kenya and Argentina. He is also passionate about public facing scholarship with a particular emphasis on citizen journalism. His desire is to apply his academic and research skills to advance civic education, influence social justice, and impact public policy making.

Humbulani Ndou is a postgraduate student at Stellenbosch University in the Faculty of Military Science and an aspiring researcher.

Mehmet Öçal completed his doctorate education at Labor Economics andIndustrial Relations, Pamukkale University, in 2022. He has been working as anAssistant Professor in the social work department of Burdur Mehmet Akif ErsoyUniversity. In 2022, he was deemed worthy of the Outstanding Achievement Award from Türkiye Council of Higher Education. He also received honorary awards from two separate union confederations in 2023 and 2024.

George Mokua Ogendi is a Senior Lecturer and former Chairman, Department of Environment, Natural Resources Management and Aquatic Sciences in the School of Agriculture and Natural Resources Management, Kisii University, Kenya. He obtained a Doctorate in Environmental Sciences from Kisii University (2017), MSc. Environmental Science from Arkansas State University(2009), BSc. Agricultural Education and Extension (2006) and Diploma in Agricultural Education and Extension from Egerton (2003). Dr. Ogendi is an ISO certified auditor of Quality Management Systems and a Lead expert in Environmental Impact Assessment in Kenya. He has authored several articles in peer reviewed journals and related online platforms. He is seasoned writer on environmental reports. Dr. Ogendi has done consultancies in community service learning. His research interests include Environmental Impact assessment, water quality, biomonitoring, global climate change, Wetland ecology, Agroforestry, Climate smart agriculture as well as education for sustainable development. E-mail: jmokua73@kisiiuniversity.ac.ke

Job Omweno is the Sub County Fisheries Officer at the County Government of Kisii and a part-time lecturer at Kisii University's Department of Environment, Natural Resources, and Aquatic Sciences. He holds an MSc in Fisheries, funded by the African Development Bank, and a BSc in Applied Aquatic Science from Egerton University. With experience as a research intern at the Kenya Marine and Fisheries Research Institute and as a project technician on internationally funded projects, Job's work focuses on sustainable waste management in aquaculture, including organic waste utilization, microalgae and aquatic plant applications, and resource recovery for environmental sustainability. Apart from these accomplishments, since January 2025, he is also a fellow at the African Fish Welfare (AFIWEL) program conducted by One Health and Development Initiative (OHDI), where he is exploring best practices in African fish farming for improved aquaculture production and sustainability.

Isaac Orina Nyakirario was born on 10th October 1972. He is an accomplished educationist with a strong background in English and Literature, as well as expertise in curriculum development and instruction. He began his academic journey at Egerton University, Kenya, where he pursued and successfully completed a Bachelor of Education (Arts) degree, specializing in English and Literature, graduating in 1988. Driven by a passion for teaching and learning, he returned to Egerton University and earned a Master of Education in Curriculum and Instruction in 2016. Continuing his academic and professional advancement, Isaac embarked on doctoral studies in 2017. He is currently pursuing a PhD in Curriculum and Instruction at Egerton University, further deepening his expertise in the field of education. Throughout his academic journey, Isaac Orina Nyakirario has demonstrated unwavering dedication to educational excellence and lifelong learning, with all his academic programs completed at Egerton University, Kenya. Isaac Orina Nyakirario's:ORCID iD: 0009-0007-5716-9957

Murat Sengöz holds a Bachelor's degree in Engineering and postgraduate degrees in Management and Finance, as well as a doctorate in Business Administration. He is the author of several academic and non-academic monographs and research papers. His researches focus on critical and reflective philosophical studies in organizational behavior, strategic management, management philosophy, and national security.

Galen Sibanda is an Assistant Professor at Michigan State University where he also Coordinates the African Languages Program. He previously taught at Stanford University, University of California (Berkeley) and the University of Zimbabwe. His research interests are in African linguistics especially the phonology, morphology and syntax/semantics of Bantu languages. He also has interests in language pedagogy. Galen received his PhD in Linguistics from the University of California (Berkeley) and a Graduate Certificate in Education from the University of Zimbabwe where he also did his undergraduate studies.

Fikile Vilakazi is the director of the Gender Equity Unit at the University of the Western Cape. Former Lecturer for Political Science at the University of KwaZulu Natal. Former Director of the Coalition of African Lesbians. Board President of Ikhwelo Healers Collective. President of Southern Medical University of China Alumni's of 2023. Gender, Sexuality, Feminist and Socio-economic and political activist and analyst.

Balungile Zondi is a highly regarded academic and practitioner, known for her extensive expertise in anthropology, public policy and development studies. She holds a PhD in Anthropology from the University of KwaZulu-Natal (UKZN), where she currently teaches and supervises research at the PhD, Master's and Honours levels. Her academic role is complemented by her active participation in various internal committees and boards at the university, where she contributes to shaping research agendas and enhancing the university's academic environment. Before joining UKZN, Dr Zondi dedicated 11 years 11 years to the Department of Social Development, where she made significant contributions at both the Zululand Cluster and the Provincial Office. Her roles included Development practitioner, Assistant Director for Research, Advocacy and Information and Monitoring and Evaluation Specialist. During her tenure, she focused on key areas such as HIV/AIDS, women' programs, and international initiatives in partnership with the United Nations Population Fund (UNFPA). Dr Zondi shares pivotal expertise in the design, implementation, and evaluation of development programs, playing an integral role in

Index

L

M

N

P

R

S

U

W

www.ingramcontent.com/pod-product-compliance
Lightning Source LLC
LaVergne TN
LVHW080910300926
849162LV00003B/631